The Grains

or

PASSAGES IN THE LIFE OF RUTH ROVER, WITH OCCASIONAL PICTURES OF OREGON, NATURAL AND MORAL

by Margaret Jewett Bailey

Edited by Evelyn Leasher and Robert J. Frank
With Foreword by Professor Emeritus Edwin R. Bingham

OREGON STATE UNIVERSITY PRESS
CORVALLIS, OREGON

MT

The paper in this book meets the guidelines for permanence and durability of the Committee on Production Guidelines for Book Longevity of the Council on Library Resources.

Library of Congress Cataloging in Publication Data

Bailey, Margaret Jewett, 1812?-1882.
    The Grains, or, Passages in the life of Ruth Rover, with occasional pictures of Oregon, natural and moral.

    Reconstructed reprint from two incomplete and damaged copies of the author's original novel, part autobiography, published in Oregon in 1854.

    Bibliography: p.
    1. Oregon—History—Fiction. I. Leasher, Evelyn M. II. Frank, Robert J. (Robert Joseph), 1939-   . III. Title. IV. Title: Passages in the life of Ruth Rover, with occasional pictures of Oregon, natural and moral.
PS1059.B14G7   1985   813'.3   85-13749
ISBN 0-87071-346-9

5/8/86

The Grains

Foreword

Margaret Jewett Bailey's *The Grains or Passages in the Life of Ruth Rover* is an unusual cultural document and one not easy to classify. Part autobiography, part religious testimonial, part history and travelogue, it is self-indulgent, unconsciously self-revealing, at times self-abnegatory, at other times assertive and vindictive. The narrative is broken by fragments of sentimental and conventional poetry or by the inclusion of letters and journal entries or by an occasional nature vignette of effective and appealing simplicity. Filaments of paranoia and hysteria wind through the rambling story but the whole is informed by a spirit of independence and a determination not to be cowed in a male-dominated frontier community.

By stretching the definition, *The Grains* may be called a novel, the first novel written and published on the Pacific coast. That it was written by a woman is not surprising for across the nation women were writing poetry, essays, short stories, and book-length fiction to the extent that cultural historians have labeled the decade "the feminine fifties." In 1852, just two years before Bailey wrote *The Grains,* another New England woman of firm religious convictions, Harriet Beecher Stowe, electrified the North and infuriated the South with her anti-slavery novel *Uncle Tom's Cabin.* Other best-selling writers of the 1850s were women, notably Mrs. E.D.E.N. Southworth (*The Curse of Clifton,* 1852, and *The Hidden Hand,* 1859), Susan Bogert Warner (*The Wide, Wide World,* 1850), and Maria Susanna Cummins (*The Lamplighter,* 1854). Most of these writers were responding to a market of educated women who devoured fiction that spoke directly to them, revealing their problems and helping them cope. Margaret Bailey was clearly in the company of these writers who dealt with the joys and sorrows of domestic life but her work has a bite that most contemporary American women writers lacked.

Margaret Jewett Bailey was not alone on the Oregon Country's literary frontier. She was joined by William Lysander Adams, an Ohio Whig who came overland to the Willamette Valley in 1848. Adams, in his day very likely the best-read person in the Pacific Northwest, wrote a sophisticated play called *Treason, Strategems, and Spoils, A Melodrame in Five Acts by Breakspear,* published first in the *Oregonian* in installments and then in pamphlet form in 1852. The drama attacks the Democrats by depicting them as drunkards and spoilsmen conniving to detach the Oregon Territory from the United States and form a Pacific Empire under the rule of Brigham Young. At about the same time, farther to the north, James Swan, another educated eccentric, was writing a perceptive and very readable account of life among the Indians on

Puget Sound, published in 1856 as *The Northwest Coast, or, Three Years'
Residence in Washington Territory,* and still in print in a paperback edition.

These three writers—Adams, Bailey, and Swan—gave this far corner of
the country a literary foundation of which it need not be ashamed. Moreover,
the feminist note sounded boldly by Margaret Bailey was carried on and
strengthened by Abigail Scott Duniway and her *New Northwest,* a periodical
that combined romantic fiction and verse with the dominant theme of
women's suffrage. Add to this the fact that the finest historian of the Pacific
Northwest in the late nineteenth century was Frances Fuller Victor who wrote
the volumes dealing with Oregon and the Northwest coast in Hubert Howe
Bancroft's monumental western history series, and the prominence of women
in the region's cultural development is evident.

Margaret Jewett Bailey herself, despite her essential candidness, remains
something of an enigma. Early in *The Grains* her alter ego, Ruth Rover,
emerges as a young woman both attractive and attracted to men. She denies
that "affections can be engaged but once in a lifetime." However, her
conversion moves her to put piety and religious commitment above all else
and renunciation of carnal love is a persistent theme. Yet the imagery of her
ardent descriptions of religious experience is often sensual, if not sexual. Thus
she "pants after my God" and "offers herself" to the Lord. There is no
question but that her desire to save Indian souls is genuine but she is unable to
withstand Wiley's (Willson's) importunities, though of course when she learns
of his prior commitment to another she breaks the engagement even though
they have been domiciled together. Wiley exploits that situation and Ruth
Rover is maneuvered into confessing the sin of adultery while simultaneously
denying her guilt. Indignant at her treatment by her Christian brethren, she
turns outside the mission to marry Dr. William Binney (Bailey) and her tale of
woe takes on a new dimension.

The rest of the novel deals with the Baileys' stormy marriage. Here the
religious tone is muted, giving way to a fierce feminist recital of the trials of
unholy wedlock. There are, of course, intervals of reconciliation over the
years of marriage but it turns out that Margaret's efforts to reform her
husband are as futile as her attempts to Christianize the Willamette Valley
Indians. Ruth Rover's subsequent unhappy career suggests that her cup of
sorrow was not fully drained until her death.

Aside from the feminist and human interest aspects of *The Grains,* Mrs.
Bailey's novel sheds light on Oregon's beginnings on the bend of the
Willamette. Her shrewd assessment of Jason Lee, her exposure of quarrels
and shortcomings within the mission community, her recognition of her own
and the mission's failure to convert the Indians, and her descriptions of farm
life on the Oregon Country's frontier, all lend historical value to her
autobiographical novel. Moreover, although *The Grains* is uneven in style and
cumbersome in structure, the fact is the reader is inclined to keep reading
right through to the end and that is a sign of uncommon narrative skill and
clarity of statement.

❦

   Margaret Jewett Bailey and her novel do not deserve oblivion. *The Grains* should be acknowledged for what it is—a landmark on Oregon's cultural landscape. Robert Frank and Evelyn Leasher have edited the rare edition with skill and care. Their Introduction provides appropriate historical context and they have ferreted out substantial detail on Bailey's life and career to the effect that at last she may receive a measure of recognition and acceptance denied her all her days.

Edwin R. Bingham
Professor Emeritus of History,
University of Oregon
Mysore, India, February, 1985

CONTENTS

Introduction

Oregon History

The Oregon mission of the Methodist Episcopal Church was one of the best-known missions in the United States between the years 1833 and 1850. Margaret Bailey, née Smith, was a member of that mission sponsored by the Methodist Episcopal Church.

An evangelical religious movement that started within the Anglican Church, Methodism had its origins in John and Charles Wesley's prominent role in a "Holy Club" at Oxford; because of their rigorous devotional and ascetic practices they were called Methodists. In 1738 both brothers experienced religious conversions that transformed their lives and shaped Methodism to the point that it eventually took steps to gain a status independent of the Anglican Church. John Wesley, a powerful field preacher, established a system of itinerant preachers, carrying the gospel wherever souls were to be saved (Ahlstrom 1972:324-329).[1] He had come to America in 1735 without much success, but the ministry of the Wesleys' works and followers eventually established a powerful church in America. The circuit rider system worked especially well as the frontier expanded and was broadened to include the Indians as well as the settlers. By 1844 the Methodists had become one of the most powerful Protestant churches in America, with 1,068,525 members (Ahlstrom 1972:436-439).

The Methodist Church supported several missions to Indians east of the Mississippi. The stimulus for the Oregon mission, which was far removed from the church's other Indian missions, came in a letter which appeared March 11, 1833, in the *Christian Advocate* and was later reprinted in many other Christian publications. The letter

> stated in substance that a delegation of "red men" from the Flathead tribe in the interior of Oregon, sent as delegates by a council of their chiefs to inquire concerning the word of the Great Spirit and to bring back to their people the white man's Book of Heaven, had appeared in St. Louis: that in the prosecution of their great object they had travelled two thousand miles over rugged mountains and barren plains, enduring cold and heat, hunger and thirst, and perils from their enemies; that they had made known the object of their coming to General William Clark who had given them such help as he considered wise; that two of them, not being permitted to carry back the "glad tidings," had died in St. Louis, but that two had returned with the message of life to their people (Barclay 1950, 2:203-204).

In response to the publication of the letter several churches began immediate preparations to go to these Indians in Oregon. Jason Lee accepted the call of the Methodists to go as leader of their mission. He asked his nephew, Daniel Lee, a minister, and Cyrus Shepard, a teacher, to accompany him. Courtney Walker and Philip Edwards were added to the missionary group as lay workers, and the five men traveled overland with Nathaniel Wyeth to Oregon, arriving at Fort Vancouver on September 15, 1833. Headquarters of the Hudson's Bay Company in the Northwest region, Fort Vancouver at the time was the only business establishment in the Oregon country. The London value of a year's fur from the Fort ranged from $500,000 to $1,000,000. Dr. John McLoughlin, a physician-turned-fur-trader, ran this outpost of the Company that was so influential in the region. Many of the overlanders reached the fort with the help of Company traders, and many who came by sea made at least part of the trip on a Company ship. McLoughlin greeted the Methodist travelers with comfortable accommodations, sold them supplies, and offered the advice and protection of the Company.

Jason Lee established his mission along the Willamette River near the only settlement in the area, a group of former employees of the Hudson's Bay Company who had decided to settle in the Oregon country. These first farmers settled in the Willamette Valley about 1829 in the area which has become known as French Prairie. They were joined there by a few mountain men and wanderers who had come to Oregon. Although it was Company policy that all ex-employees must be returned to the place where they were hired, many did not wish to return to Canada when their term of employment ended; they had Indian wives and children and knew their families would not be welcome or happy in the towns of Canada. McLoughlin allowed them to stay by keeping them on the rolls as employees and staking them to the supplies and tools they needed to begin farming. He also bought their surplus crops. There were about twenty such families when the mission was established.

Lee seems to have taken as his missionary philosophy and program that of William Fisk, president of Wesleyan University, who in a letter to the *Christian Advocate* urged missionaries to Indians to "learn their language— preach Christ to them—and, as the way opens, introduce schools, agriculture, and the arts of civilized life" (quoted in Barclay 1950, 2:212).

However, great efforts were required if the missionaries were to establish effective contact with the Indians. When Lewis and Clark wintered in Oregon in 1805, they estimated the Indian population in the Willamette Valley to be about 10,000. The number was much smaller in the 1830s because an epidemic, starting in 1829 and recurring each summer for several years, swept through the area. The disease, called the "cold sick" by the Indians, is now believed to have been malaria (Cook 1955). It spread rapidly, almost destroying the Indians of the Willamette Valley as a social group. The survivors, many of whom left their villages to wander in destitution, offered only slight resistance to the white settlers who came and took their territory.

A bewildering array of languages among the surviving Indians posed another major problem for the missionaries, since the Indians in the Oregon Territory were of several groups and language families. In the Willamette Valley near the Methodist Episcopal Mission lived mainly the Calapooia, but even among the Calapooia there was a variety of groups and languages. Because of this diversity of languages in a small geographic area, a Chinook jargon became widely used up and down the Pacific Northwest Coast and into the Inland Empire:

> In the strip of territory from the mouth of the Willamette to the ocean, several different languages were spoken, the Calapooya [sic], Cowlitz, Clatsop, Multnomah, and other tribes using among themselves only their own tribal language; but in voyages along the rivers or in hunting parties in the mountains, the Wasco Indian who happened to meet the Clatsop, one from the mouth of the Columbia and the other from Central Oregon, made himself perfectly understood in this accommodating jargon…(Gill 1933:4).

In 1836 when Samuel Parker, on an exploring trip for the American Board of Foreign Missions, visited Jason Lee's site, he found a working mission and school:

> Their principal object of labor, for the present, is by means of schools. They had at the time of my visit fourteen Indian children in their school supported in their family, and the prospect of obtaining others as fast as they can accommodate them. Their facilities for providing for their school are good, having an opportunity to cultivate as much excellent land as they wish, and to raise their necessaries of life in great abundance with little more labor than what the scholars can perform for their support (Parker 1840:165).

Jason Lee soon decided he needed more help to carry on the day to day work if the missionaries' ambitions to Christianize and civilize the Indians were to succeed. In 1837 two reinforcing groups arrived. One contingent sailed from Boston Harbor on July 28, 1836, and arrived in Oregon in May, 1837. This party was comprised of Dr. Elijah White, his wife Sarepita, and their two children; Alanson Beers, blacksmith, his wife Rachel, and their children; Miss Anna Maria Pittman, Miss Susan Downing, and Miss Elvira Johnson, teachers; William Willson, carpenter; and Joseph Whitcomb, farmer. In his request for workers Jason Lee had specifically asked for women to come to the mission:

> He believed they were needed to work with the Indian women as well as to set an example for them….The Board had no policy against sending women as foreign missionaries but it had not been deemed advisable to send men with wives and families to distant Oregon. As the missionaries found themselves encumbered with domestic duties, however, they came to feel the presence of Christian women was needed (Decker 1961:64).

The three single women of this reinforcement did not long remain unmarried. On July 16, 1837, Anna Maria Pittman married Jason Lee, and Susan Downing married Cyrus Shepard. The second reinforcement, which arrived in September, 1837, included Rev. David Leslie, his wife Mary, and their children; Rev. H. K. W. Perkins; and Margaret Smith (Ruth Rover), teacher. In November, 1837, Perkins and Elvira Johnson were married, leaving Margaret the only unmarried white woman in Oregon. With the arrival of these added forces a second mission station was established at The Dalles, staffed by Daniel Lee and H. K. W. and Elvira Perkins.

The American Board of Foreign Missions, a joint venture of the Congregational and Presbyterian Churches, also had sent a mission to the Indians of the West. Marcus and Narcissa Whitman, Henry and Eliza Spalding, and William Gray traveled overland to Oregon in 1836. They established missions among the Cayuse and Nez Percé Indians in what is now Idaho (Drury 1963-1966, 1:73-127; 186-205). The Methodists and the American Board Missionaries did not consider themselves rivals and treated each other as fellow workers in the Indian mission fields.

Both mission parties, however, regarded as rivals the Catholic missionaries, Francis Norbert Blanchet and Modeste Demers, who came to Oregon in November, 1838, at the request of the French Canadian settlers, many of whom were Catholics and wanted priests to meet their spiritual needs. Blanchet and Demers had some success with the Indians as well, resulting in a bitter rivalry with the Protestant missionaries (Lyons 1974).

Seeing a great future in the Oregon country, Jason Lee returned to the United States in 1838 to ask the Mission Board for yet more personnel. He spoke to many church groups to raise money for the mission, stirring an interest in Oregon and giving much valuable information to potential settlers. The Mission Board agreed with his assessment of the needs and potential of the Oregon territory and supplied him with a large reinforcement for the mission. Jason Lee and the "Great Reinforcement," a group of fifty-one people, returned to Oregon in 1840 on the ship *Lausanne*.

Missionaries from this group were sent to various locations to establish new missions to the Indians (Willamette Falls, now Oregon City; Clatsop, near Astoria; Nisqually, now Tacoma, Washington; and Umpqua in Southern Oregon), while other workers came to establish enterprises such as a flour mill and a lumber mill, which were to support the work of the mission.

But the mission which had started out with such high hopes did not succeed in converting or helping the Indians. In March, 1840, Leslie reported the number of members at the Willamette Station (the original and central station) at thirty-four: "Whites [including the missionaries at the station] 26, mixed blood 3, Indians 4, Hawaiian 1" (Barclay 1949-1950, II:232, parentheses his).

Nor did the new reinforcements make the work of the mission any easier or any better. Almost immediately after Lee's return, Dr. Elijah White challenged his leadership. White was tried and dismissed from the mission. He returned to the States to lay his complaints before the Mission Board, but they refused to support his charges against Lee. Others of the new reinforcement also were unwilling to work in Oregon under trying conditions; some left the territory and some left the mission but stayed in Oregon. One of the most devastating defections for Jason Lee was the eventual departure of his nephew, Daniel Lee, who left the mission for the States in 1843 because of his wife's ill health.

In fact, most of the workers and missionaries seem to have complained to the Mission Board at one time or another (Gatke 1935). By 1844 Jason Lee decided to go to New York to explain his actions and get new directions. He was on his way when he received word that a new head of the mission, Rev. George Gary, had been appointed and was on his way to Oregon. Lee proceeded to New York anyway and vindicated his actions before the Board, but they did not retain him as head. He planned to return to Oregon but became ill and died in March, 1845.

Rev. Gary, who had directions from the Mission Board to trim the size of the mission, dismantled the mission to the Indians. Workers who were no longer needed were given either their passage to the States or the equivalent in mission property. The support of the remaining ministers was left to the white settlers who were fast coming into the area. In 1843 the white male population in the Willamette Valley was approximately sixty French Canadians, and one hundred American and British citizens (Lamar 1977:880). That fall about 900 persons arrived in the Willamette Valley in the first large migration to Oregon; the following year 1,200 more arrived. There was a large immigration of new settlers each year thereafter, and the population of Oregon grew rapidly.

These settlers played a role in the dismantling of the Whitman mission at Waitatpu, which was a stopover for many of the wagon trains. The Indians had become anxious about the great influx of white people and the Whitmans' increasing attention to the settlers. In addition the settlers had brought with them in 1847 measles which killed many of the Indians, who were helpless before this disease since they had not developed any previous immunity to it. Resentment and fear built up and Whitman's medicine was seen as ineffective. On November 29, 1847, the Indians attacked the mission, killing Marcus and Narcissa Whitman and twelve others in their household (Drury 1963-1966, 1:161-170). After this attack all the Protestant missions were abandoned and attention of the remaining missionaries turned to the settlers.

The settlers came to Oregon for many reasons. Some hoped to escape the divisive controversy over slave holding in their move to the West. Some were looking for a healthier location than the one they left. Many were looking for free land and economic independence for themselves and their families. Some came out of patriotism, hoping to insure the Oregon country would become a part of the United States rather than Great Britain (Bowen 1978:17-20).

The Oregon territory was part of the area covered by a joint occupancy treaty between Great Britain and the United States in 1818. A provisional government had been established by the settlers in 1843 in anticipation of the territory's becoming part of the States. When Polk became President, following the practice of his predecessors, he proposed the 49th parallel as the boundary between the two countries. In view of Oregon's rapid settlement by Americans and their willingness to fight over this line, Great Britain agreed, and Oregon was granted Territorial status in 1848.

In 1848 the big news in Oregon, as elsewhere, was the discovery of gold in California. Oregonians swarmed to the gold fields, leaving Oregon almost deserted for a time. Eyewitnesses report lawyers, physicians, ministers, and merchants leaving Oregon in a state of high excitement (Goodykoontz 1971:276). The government had to be suspended because there were not enough legislators to conduct business. The gold rush provided more than temporary excitement for Oregon; it provided economic opportunity as well. Suddenly there was a ready-made market for goods and supplies in the people of California, who did not want to do anything but look for gold. Oregon's farmers, merchants, and manufacturers saw the potential for export and the economic expansion of Oregon was launched (Dodds 1977:71-74).

With Oregon firmly in the control of the United States, the settlers, who felt their presence had helped decide the matter, wanted clear claim to land. The Donation Land Law, passed by Congress in 1850, granted an unmarried citizen of the United States who had resided upon and cultivated the land four consecutive years 320 acres of land; a married man or one who married within one year, received 640 acres, one half of which was to be held by the wife (Clark 1927, 1:406).

By 1850, when the first federal census was taken, the number of inhabitants had reached 13,294 (Corning, 1956:50). By 1854, the publication date of *The Grains,* there was white population sufficient to support schools, churches, towns, government, and women authors.

Margaret Jewett Bailey

In *The Grains* the heroine is called Ruth Rover, but there seems to have been no doubt in anyone's mind at the time of its publication that this book was a thinly disguised autobiography of Margaret Jewett (Smith) Bailey. Drawing on letters written to and by her, her diary and journal entries, and providing connective narrative description, Margaret Bailey reveals her life to a surprising degree. We learn, for example, about her decision to become a missionary, her quarrels with her fellow missionaries, and her work with the Indian women and children. There are also details about the living conditions at the mission and, after her marriage, about her life as a white woman settler in Oregon.

Margaret Jewett Smith was converted to the Methodist religion at a camp meeting when she was seventeen years old. It appears from her journal entries, reproduced in *The Grains,* that she experienced the transformations in her life expected of such a conversion: 1) an embrace of standards and values exemplified in a new Lord and Master, 2) a redirection of one's life, 3) cultivation of new habits, 4) a new appreciation of the dignity and value of every human being regardless of race, or station, or culture, 5) a new sense of community with other Christians, 6) concern for people who turn away from God and who thus miss the primary reason for being, and, above all, 7) experience of the power of a new and life-giving relationship with God (*Encyclopedia of World Methodism* 1974:577). In addition to these changes, she reached the conclusion that she was not meant to marry but to ''bear some nobler part in life than the mere rounds of domestic duty'' (*The Grains* 46). After much prayer and soul-searching she seemed convinced that missionary work was her calling.

To pursue this goal called for a robust faith and an iron will. Her father objected because he wanted her help for himself in his old age; he refused to give her money for the education she needed to qualify as a mission teacher and threatened to disown her if she pursued that course. Her oldest brother wrote her a letter calling missionaries ''overzealous, enthusiastic fanatics'' and urged her not to join their ranks (*The Grains* 52). She resisted their opposition and resolved to dedicate her life to the Indians in the Oregon mission.

Margaret's efforts at the mission included teaching the girls, sewing for the adult women, visiting the Indians in their homes, and praying with the dying. The work was dispiriting. The children who came to the mission to be educated were often in poor health and many died. The adults did not stay in the area long enough to receive much help. Margaret eventually questioned the motives of the other missionaries and became increasingly unhappy when her efforts to help the Indians led to no lasting accomplishments.

She was even more unhappy when her reputation as a virtuous woman was tarnished by her mission family. Under great pressure to take a husband, she finally agreed to marry William H. Willson (Wiley in *The Grains*). They became engaged, but not before he had written to the States asking another woman to come to Oregon to become his wife. Armed with this knowledge, Margaret refused to marry Willson until it was known if the woman was coming to Oregon. He agreed to this condition but became impatient with the long delay and begged her to confess with him to the other members of the mission that they had fornicated and should be allowed to marry immediately. When she refused, he told everyone they had sinned together; and nothing she could say could clear her name. It was a bitter blow made even worse by the double sexual standard which forgave the man and condemned the woman. There was no way to prove her innocence and she soon left the mission.

Volume Two of *The Grains* is about her marriage to Dr. William J. Bailey (Dr. Binney) and the reasons she felt compelled to divorce him after fifteen years. In 1837 Dr. Elijah White invited Dr. Bailey to renew his medical practice since the people in the Mission area needed medical care. Bailey and Margaret Smith were married shortly after he joined the Methodist church in 1839. She looked forward to a Christian marriage but was soon disillusioned; Bailey did not behave like a Christian and they were childless.

However, she felt she had done her duty to her husband in all respects. To enhance his fortune Margaret worked with the farm animals and in the fields, as well as in the house and garden. "Indeed, the evidence suggests that the transplanted 'pioneer' wife, forced to toil when feminine toil was equated with degradation, often had the worst of two worlds" (Douglas 1977:55). For her, as for many pioneer women and wives, life on the frontier obscured the sharp division between the roles of husband and wife, which contemporaries called the doctrine of two spheres, or separate spheres. Women tried to maintain their traditional domestic roles—as homemakers, rearers of children, bearers of cultural and moral standards—and took up as well many traditional masculine tasks (Degler 1980:46-52). She did her best as she saw it; for this her reward, as she recorded it, was not praise but criticism and abuse.

Even in the best of circumstances their differing personalities would have led to problems. Just before her wedding Margaret was warned by someone at the mission: "Not one of this mission family approves of your union with Dr. Binney...they say that you'll not live together long—they know his character and temper, and think that *you* are too independent to bear with him...they think your dispositions are so different that you can't agree" (*The Grains* 185). Members of the mission had reason to distrust Bailey's character and temper. He first appeared in the Willamette Valley in 1835, having been badly disfigured in a skirmish with Rogue Indians. In 1837 Philip Edwards, the Methodist mission representative on Ewing Young's cattle drive from California, reported Bailey's part in the unprovoked killing of two defenseless Indians and the consequent retaliatory attack (Edwards 1932:42-43). Another of the problems with the marriage was Dr. Bailey's abuse of Margaret when he drank. How often and how much he drank is open to debate as are the reasons for his drinking, but her accounts of his actions when drinking and when sober indicate there was a change in his character and temper.

In spite of these problems Margaret felt she had given everything she could to the marriage. She had forgiven his abuse many times and concluded: "My conscience asserts most positively and approvingly, that, in all my dreadful trials, I have endeavored to perform my duty, faithfully and perseveringly, to my God, my husband, my neighbor, and myself" (*The Grains* 27). She finally decided that she should not have to suffer any more in her marriage or as a consequence of her marriage. She and Bailey were divorced in 1854.

It is impossible at this distance to know the full facts of her marriage and of all that went on at the mission, but judging from what we can know about her reporting Margaret was accurate in her facts.[2] Comparing her accounts of her quarrels with Willson (Wiley), Leslie (Leland), and Shepard with other reports, hers generally seem fair. Her bitterness, for example, at not receiving a teaching appointment at the mission, as promised, was justified, since contemporary reports mention her going to the mission as a teacher (Carey 1922a:309). But Margaret was not always unbiased in her interpretation of events. For example, she accounted for all the disasters that happened to Leslie as divine retribution for his bad treatment of herself: ''But what have been the indications of providence toward Mr. Leland?...they have been that of disapprobation. The *burning* of his *house* and *property*—the *loss* of his *wife*—*three* children carried over into the chasm of the falls—*another daughter* dying at Oahu—his *barn burnt*—*another child buried*—and *sickness* and *infirmity* at every hand...'' (*The Grains* 159). On the other hand, even though she reported on a series of quarrels with Cyrus Shepard, when he died she gave a fair account of his good work with the Indian children. In conclusion, then, although Margaret Bailey's telling of her dealings with the missionaries can be read as an attempt to attack her antagonizers, self-justification was not her only motive. She wrote to deal with a pioneer woman's loneliness and her ostracism from the mission community. And she wrote out of frustration with the failure of the mission system. In his account of the Oregon Methodist Mission, Barclay generally saw little effort by the missionaries to preach to Indians or to establish schools (Barclay 1949-1950, 2:238-252), seeming to support Bailey's charge that personal aggrandizement and colonizing not missionizing were the major motivations behind the missionaries' activities (*The Grains* 137-139; 141-146; 170-174). Of the plans to civilize the Indians she derisively says: ''So, then, to benefit the Indians we must exterminate them. They must no longer be Indians! Who would think that because a wild animal is tamed he must take the name of the person who tamed him?'' (*The Grains* 174).

After her divorce from Bailey, Margaret had the problem of supporting herself, since the settlement gave her only her clothing, personal effects, piano, and one hundred dollars. In addition she had real estate in Butteville which Bailey had signed over to her, and at least one thousand dollars on interest in the United States. She had skills as a seamstress, a teacher, and a nurse, to which she added literary ambitions.

Margaret had had some literary success before the publication of *The Grains* in 1854. Her letters home while with the mission had appeared in the Christian newspapers of Boston and New York. In Oregon, in the very first issue of the *Oregon Spectator,* February 5, 1846, one of her poems had been published, making her the first local poet to be published west of the Rockies. The poem, titled ''Love,'' reflects her unhappy marriage with Bailey and the sense of isolation felt by many pioneer women:

❦

> My heart it is burdened and sad,
> What can I perform for relief?
> Conversation where can it be had?
> And comfort for internal grief?
> The birds they are joyous in air,
> The beasts in the field find delight;
> All insects in liveliness share,
> And flowers are smiling and bright.
>
> But me—ah! my heart is the seat
> Of sorrow intense and forlorn;
> Love's saplings lie dead at my feet!
> Her tendrils are parted and torn!
> Blest Gardener! in mercy draw near;
> Ingraft me anew into Thee,
> Lest, blasted too soon I appear,
> Nor fruit to perfection can see.

She signed her poems MJB and over these initials published her poetry and prose in the *Spectator* for several years.

After her divorce she edited for the *Spectator* a newspaper column called the "Ladies Department." The series was to be her sole responsibility and to run for three columns per paper. In the first "Ladies Department" she echoed many women writers in announcing her literary ambitions:

> In appearing before the public as a writer and editress, it was our favorite wish to have conducted a paper independently of any other, and expressly devoted to the interests of the *Ladies of Oregon;* but the great expense of printing and the uncertainty of obtaining a sufficient number of subscribers to defray the expenses of such a paper, has induced us to accept Mr. G.'s generous offer of appropriating, for the present, a portion of the columns of the "Spectator," for the purpose of gratifying a yearning desire, felt for many years, to indulge in literary pursuits, and to endeavor to render ourselfs serviceable to the female sex, in presenting before them such reading as would be calculated to elevate the standard of piety, morality, usefulness and refinement among them. . . .
>
> Should our efforts be appreciated, and sufficient encouragement be manifested, we may hereafter commence the publication of a journal, which shall be strictly the *Woman's Own Paper* (12 May 1854).

She and many other women in Western settlements, "continued to try to reinstate a culture of domesticity" (Faragher and Stansell 1975:162) and to establish "a community of sensibility with other women where no real community yet existed" (Schlissel 1977:94). Her plans to publish a journal for women was an ambitious project since even the very few newspapers being published in the West at the time were in financial trouble. However, she mirrored literary developments throughout the United States. Between 1784 and 1860 over one hundred magazines were founded, many focusing on women's interests (Douglas 1977:84). The *Statesman* encouraged her plans:

❦

> Mrs. M. J. Bailey edits three columns of the Spectator, under the head of
> "Ladies Department." Mrs. B. is a chaste and elegant writer. We hope her
> desire to establish, ultimately, a lady's periodical in Oregon, may succeed
> (6 June 1854).

The "Ladies Department" ran for six weekly issues, from May 12 through
June 16, 1854, before it was suspended. Each week there was a riddle for
children, fashion news, poetry and fiction, and items of local interest. She also
gave advice on such subjects as keeping the Sabbath and going to dances. In
three numbers she ran a short story by Ruth Rover called "Horace Penley."
In her final column she offered her views on women's rights, thanked Mr.
Goodrich, the editor, and made no further comment about why she was
ending the column. But the differences between them did not remain long
hidden or politely expressed. Mr. Goodrich had violated his agreement with
her and inserted items of his own selection into her space; he also had limited
her space and apparently found constant fault with her selections. He made
some derogatory remarks about her in the paper, and she retaliated with a
three column advertisement in the *Oregon Weekly Times,* answering his charges.

At the same time Margaret also taught school to earn her living. A notice
in the *Spectator* of May 26, 1854, stated:

> We doubt not the young ladies and gentlemen in town would do well to
> attend Mrs. Bailey's class of instruction in grammar and rhetoric, which is
> held on Tuesday, Thursday and Saturday evenings of each week, in the
> Baptist college.

She had some difficulty teaching, however, because she was a divorced
woman. "But 'tis in vain," she wrote, " I attempt any innocent employment,
whether it be intended for recreation or to obtain a livelihood. The young of
my classes are withdrawn, when a slander reaches them, for fear of
contamination" (*The Grains* 27).

Partly, then, to quiet these rumors and slanders, and partly to to earn a
living as a writer, she published *The Grains.* Margaret's turn to writing as a
means of making a living was not an uncommon choice at the time. Whether
we read *The Grains* as thinly disguised autobiography or as a fiction that draws
on autobiography and biography, Margaret Bailey's work had much in
common with the literary developments in the nineteenth century. Some 1,150
novels by American authors alone were published in the U.S. between 1830
and 1850, and a large number of the authors and readers were women (Degler
1980:377), moving Hawthorne to complain about an America "wholly given
over to a damned mob of scribbling women" (quoted in Ticknor 1969:141).
The preoccupations of many of the works written by and for women appear in
The Grains as well: innocence falsely accused, males demanding unquestioning
obedience, the need for self-justification, rivalry between a minister and
heroine, unjust suffering, and consolation visualized as a comfortable afterlife
(Douglas 1977:46-48; 71-73; 103-109; 201-227).

A combative advertisement for *The Grains,* her last known literary effort, appeared in 1854:

> A new work will be published, about the 1st of August, the first number of *The Grains, Or, Passages in the Life of Ruth Rover with Occasional Pictures of Oregon, Natural and Moral,* by Margaret Jewett Bailey.
>> Thou Monster Evil—stand forth!
>> And in whatever garb thou mayst appear
>> Whether harlot,—villain, Priest or Pope,
>> I challenge thee to single combat.
>
> (To be published in monthly numbers till completed.) All orders for the above work will be promptly attended on addressing ('Margaret J. Bailey, care of the publishers of the Times, Portland, Oregon') (*Oregonian,* 8 July 1854).

In publishing *The Grains* she wanted to tell her side of the story and then get on with living, disposing of the unfair reputation she had acquired at the mission and as a divorced woman. Instead, she appears to have stirred up another storm.

The Oregonian, in its first book review, employed the anonymous Squills to review this first book by a woman author in Oregon. He was not pleased with the first volume and thrashed it in what was known for a time as the Oregon style:

> This work does great credit to the printers Messrs. Carter and Austin, the typography being very neat and immaculate in tint. We seldom read books of feminine production, believing *their* (the females) province to be darning stockings, pap and gruel, children, cookstoves, and the sundry little affairs that make life comparatively comfortable and makes them, what Providence designed them "Helpmates."
>
> But afflictions will come upon us, even here in Oregon; where we are castigated with so many already. It is bad enough to have unjust laws—poor lawyers and worse judges—taxes, and no money, with the combined evils *they* saddle on us, without this last visitation of Providence—"an authoress." In the words of Homer (or his translator) we say "and may this first invasion be the last."
>
> Of the style we say nothing—that is as usual apologized for in the preface, and moreover the writer is a "school marm." We have read the book entire—one cover and ninety-six pages, double column. In the second chapter, Ruth has three lovers—now this is unfair, and contrary to rule: modern romances usually devote 2 vols. octavo, to one love. "Young America" is fast however, we quote from the chapter mentioned of the last of the three:
>
>> "I can only think of him as a grave with a poison flag growing above it and contaminating the air with its noxious breath."
>
> We hope she had not the *Standard* in her "mind's eye," when she wrote of the "Poison Flag."

There is considerable piety throughout the book, which is well enough in its way; also, any quantity of epistles, several scraps from journals about camp meetings, the vanity of the wicked world, &c., &c., &c. They are generally of the Brother Knapp and Burchard order and like those gentlemen, she appears to have been on exceedingly familiar terms with the Lord. Our space being limited, we can give no more quotations from the book, so must leave the reader to peruse it for himself. To call it trash, would be impolite, for the writer is an "authoress." Pages 86 and 87 [pages 151-154 in this edition] contain some pretty morceaux from Ruth's diary. We think, however, that private Biographies are an infliction hardly tolerable. . . When a Napoleon, a Byron or any other like lion makes his exit, it is well enough to know
"How that animal eats, how he snores,
    how he drinks,"
But who the dickens cares, about the existence of a fly, or in whose pan of molasses the insect disappeared (5 August 1854).

In the same paper and on the same day another anonymous reviewer—Quintus—had his say:

I have observed in the *Standard,* a notice of the "The Grains, or passages in the life of Ruth Rover," which is non-committal, altogether, with the exception of "that appears to be a compilation of letters, after the *Walpolean* school." May-be after reading it attentively, he will conclude that it is more of *Grub-poling.* [3]

Margaret remembered these reviews and made a rebuttal on the final page of the second volume of *The Grains.* The rebuttal did not go unnoticed when a review of the second volume was written for the *Oregonian,* again by 'Squills':

The Second number of this questionable publication has made its appearance as neatly printed as formerly. The authoress without contenting herself with the past—its equivocal associations, and violent animosities—after defying common sense, common decency, and everything common, and uncommon, takes a leap to the present, and breathes moral defiance to our humble selves. Now we can't afford to make a personal matter of this affair as
"This is no world
To play with mammets and to tilt with lips."

As Hotspur hath it, it is hardly gallant to meet a lady, "at duello" with any other weapons. As to scurrility, we don't deal in it, and deny the *soft* impeachment. An authoress is public property, and when publicity commences, privacy and the lady cease to exist as far as the grasp of criticism extends. Especially in a case like the present does it so, where the exposure of private affairs, and the tone of its morals are not warranted by any importance attached to the life of the heroine. The immorality, not to say indecency of the work, is far too much in advance even for the fast ideas and morals of young Oregon.

We regret that we should be singly challenged to "tell the truth and shame the devil" but *"anei soit il. "* We have a law in Oregon regulating the morals of publications to be uttered in the territory and at the end of this article we shall quote it, leaving it to common judgment whether the "Grains" comes under the statute or not.

General report places it in the rank of a supplement to a certain literary production issued years since in New York, but suppressed long ago both by law and gospel, and only sold secretly in the purlieus of that city, to gratify the curious in that sort of literature, and to be carefully concealed after perusal. It only lacks the illustrations to be twin to it.

We shall say but few words of the present number of the book as we prefer waiting its completion. Our first impression remains unchanged, saving that we think the "what's his name" increases as the religious "pow wow" decreases. As to the truth of the narrative, we never cast a doubt on it. Truth, however, is not to be "told at all times." We only say *"qui bono, "* and quote viz:

Sec. 10, page 200—"If any person shall import, print, or publish, sell, or distribute any *book,* or any *pamphlet,* printed paper, or other thing, containing obscene language or other things tending to the corruption of youth, or shall introduce into the family, school, or other place of education," &c., &c., "shall on conviction be pinished [sic] by imprisonment in the county jail, or be fined," &c., &c.

We refer for a fuller quotation to the pages designated (9 September 1854).

Other newspapers also noticed the book, although their comments tended to be shorter and better tempered. Mr. Waterman of the *Oregon Weekly Times* on September 2, 1854, wrote:

The Second number of *"Ruth Rover"* by Margaret Jewett Bailey was laid upon our table yesterday afternoon. From half an hour's hasty glance at the work, we would not be warranted in reviewing it—though from its general tone and tenor, we should incline to the belief that "Ruth Rover," the heroine of the tale, had received some harsh usage in Oregon and is probably a "victim of misplaced confidence." A portion of the work delineating the history of the early settlers in Oregon—their privations and troubles in missionary times—will be read with interest. More anon.

No more was written in this paper despite the promise of a fuller review. *The Spectator* was short and bitter in its review of the book. Mr. Goodrich, her former employer and editor, concluded his brief review:

It appears that our contemporaries, and the people generally, refuse to praise the production; we beg, therefore, the privilege of offering our sentiments, in this instance, in common with public opinion (26 August 1854).

Margaret Bailey bought space in the *Oregon Weekly Times* to answer her critics:

As far as the press refuse to praise our work we will say it shows their discrimination, for which we are grateful. The 'Grains' was not intended to merit literary honors; it is a business affair merely, and no attempt has been made by the author to render it possessed of literary worth—and besides if we could not avail ourself [sic] of the advantage of having a reviser for fear of placing him in an 'unhappy position with others,' the book would not receive *public praise* for the same reason. It is very gratifying to find that while our book has not been *praised,* it has neither been deprecated, and shows that the press in Oregon is not altogether in unprincipled hands (9 September 1854).

This was the last of the notices of the book in the local newspapers. Mr. Goodrich continued to make personal criticisms of Margaret Bailey in the *Spectator* but the paper soon died, thus ending their public quarrel.

The next newspaper notice about Margaret was the announcement of her marriage to Francis Waddle: "At Salem, on the 4th inst, by Rev. O. S. Dickinson, Mr —— WADDELL, of Polk County, and Mrs. MARGARET JEWETT BAILEY, (her literary *nom de plume* is Ruth Rover) of Salem" (*Oregon Statesman,* September, 1855). Francis Waddle, born in Ohio in 1821, married Sophia Burrell of Indiana in 1840. Francis, Sophia, and their three children came to Oregon in 1852 and settled on a land claim in the Eola Hills near Salem in Polk County. Sophia died June 10, 1855 (Genealogical Forum 1:1114, 5:1114). Francis Waddle and Margaret were married three months later.

Their marriage does not appear to have been a happy one and did not last long. In 1857 Margaret tried to obtain a quiet divorce through the Oregon legislature; she did not succeed, the legislature turning down her petition by one vote. Both she and Waddle then filed for a divorce in the courts. It was not a friendly parting. Waddle three times put notices in the Salem paper about his side of the case. In an effort to defend himself and to deny rumors about himself and his daughter, he published the first notice in February, 1857:

Notice to the Public, to correct *a false report which is in circulation about myself and daughter.* The slander has been started by Mrs. J. Waddle, (Ruth Rover,) the woman that I married something over a year ago. The report is false and black as the heart of the circulator of it, without the least shadow of a foundation.

I have hitherto said nothing about her, but now I am at liberty to defend myself. For the last year myself and the family have lived, as it were, in hell, on account of bad treatment we received from her. I married her for the sake of a mother for my children, but instead of a mother I found a defamer—a woman that has the heart to stab him who has taken care of her. She was unkind to my children. Last fall, when I was at California, she starved my children until they were sick, and she kept it up until I could stand it no longer, and I determined to take them away from her; and now to make it appear that she was innocent, and clear of all blame, and to raise a sympathy in her own behalf, she comes out on my character with a base slander.

—When she thought I was out of hearing, she put in circulation the black slander that is now afloat, which report is false in every respect, and I shall prove it so to the satisfaction of every one, at the proper time. And I shall hold every man accountable who talks after her. I hope that this will answer for the present (*Oregon Statesman* 17 February 1857:3).

The base slander to which he refers was about his incestuous relationship with his sixteen-year-old daughter and the resulting pregnancy. There is no record of Margaret answering his charges against her in the newspapers, but both Waddle and his daughter Mary again inserted sworn statements for two weeks running in the newspapers. Mary Waddle's notice read in part as follows:

> ...that the reports invented and circulated by Margaret J. Waddle, (alias Ruth Rover) in relation to the conduct and treatment of myself by my father, are entirely false, malicious, and without foundation. The said Margaret J., has often resorted to threats, abuse, and persuasion to induce this dependent to admit that her father and herself had been guilty of a most heinous crime, but this dependent never did any such thing, and hereby pronounces all such charges and insinuations utterly false (*Oregon Statesman,* 14, 21 April, 1857).

Francis Waddle's sworn statement repeated

> ...that the reports invented and circulated by Margaret J. Waddle in relation to my having seduced my daughter, are entirely false and without foundation. The said Margaret J., in all her conduct has evinced a devilish and malignant spirit, often threatening to destroy, not only my character and reputation, but also that of my motherless children (*Oregon Statesman,* 14, 21 April, 1857).

The divorce petition presents both sides of the case with sworn statements from both Margaret and Francis Waddle. He restated his position that she had mistreated and starved his children while he was away on business. Margaret responded by stating he was the provider and she had made do with what he had left for them, and that it was perfectly adequate. She also stated that he had told her he was responsible for his daughter's pregnancy and that she had not spread rumors but had asked the advice of her clergyman and her husband's business partner. She had taken $1,000 into the marriage with the agreement that it was hers alone and not joint property. Waddle, however, had been using it to set up a business in Salem and she wanted to be sure she got it back. She further stated

> Defendant believes that plaintiff's object in endeavoring to cast upon her the guilt of fabrication was *solely to save himself;* and possibly in revenge for her requiring the payment of said sum of money.... (Bailey Mss 126)

The judge granted the divorce on September 6, 1859, each party retaining the property brought into the marriage.

There is little known about Margaret's life after her divorce from Waddle; bits of information do provide hints about her activities and whereabouts until her death. While married to Waddle, Margaret bought property in 1856 in Salem from Chloe Willson on what had formerly been the Methodist mission land claim. She paid $50 for property on the north half of Lot 3 in Block 49, located on Commercial Street near Reed's Opera House. It appears from census and land records that she must have lived at least some of the time for the next several years at this location. In 1856 Margaret sold a small strip of her lot to William Watkinds, a harness maker; in 1867 she again sold him a small piece of the land. She bought and sold a lot in Gervais in February, 1871, and another lot in Hubbard in November, 1871 (Marion County Deed Books 1:407; 8:4; 9:32, 228; 13:59; 14:399).

The 1870 census of Salem provides this information: "Waddle, M. J., aged 45, female, from Massachusetts, occupation—keeping house, value of real estate $2,000." Although the age given for M. J. Waddle is wrong—at this time Margaret would have been 58 years old—the rest of the information seems to apply to her. The census taker may have guessed her age instead of asking. At this time two girls were living with her: Martha Hyatt, a twenty-year-old student born in Indiana, and Nelly Wilson, a five-year-old girl born in Oregon of a foreign born mother.

There were two items in the Salem *Statesman* in 1869 and 1872 which may refer to Margaret even though they are about Mrs. Bailey, the name, it seems, that she preferred for all except official purposes. On September 17, 1869, the newspaper has this small notice: "More Stores. Mrs. Bailey has moved back the wooden building on her lot, north of Starkey's block, and will immediately proceed to erect brick stores on the same site." In the same paper, on February 6, 1872, appeared the following: "Piano for Sale. A second-hand piano belonging to Mrs. Bailey, will be offered for sale by Mr. Friedman, tomorrow morning at 10 o'clock, at the residence of Rev. J. Bowersox. A good chance for a bargain."

In 1872 she sold her property in Salem for $200 to the Trustees of the Zion Church of the Evangelical Association of North America, of which Rev. Bowersox was pastor. In the deed she specified that the money they received for the property was to be used to pay off the debts of the church, with any money left over to go to the Missionary Society of the Church. In 1875 the Trustees sold the property for $1,500 (Marion County Deed Books 15:116; 18:154).

This is the last item found about Margaret for a period of ten years. The next mention of her appears in May, 1882. Dr. Tolmie, now retired from the Hudson's Bay Company and living in Victoria, B. C. (he had taken Margaret horseback riding on her first day in Oregon) sent a letter to his friend John Minto, asking: "Did you know in days of yore a Dr. Bailey of Shampoeg? His wife of 13 years ("Ruth Rover") originally a Miss Smith of the *original* Methodist mission called on me the other day. She has been twice unhappily married since leaving Bailey, and now aged 70 lives at Seattle in destitute circumstances—she half thinks that Bailey is still in the land of the living that is to say on this earth—can you inform me on that point as I am under promise to her to make inquiry'' (Tolmie Mss 752). Since she was inquiring for Dr. Bailey, it seems likely she had not been living in Oregon since 1876, the year when he died.

In another letter to Minto, dated August 6, 1882, Tolmie mentions that ''Ex Mrs. Bailey (Ruth Rover) died of a lung fever a few days after her return to Seattle'' (Tolmie Mss 752). Her obituary appeared in the *Puget Sound Weekly Courier* on May 19, 1882: ''Mrs. Margaret J. Crane, author of Ruth Rover, a novel that created a great sensation in Oregon in early days, died in Seattle, Tuesday night of pneumonia and was buried from Brown Church, Rev. J. F. Damon, officiating.'' Nothing is known about Margaret's third husband, Mr. Crane.

What of Dr. Bailey after the divorce from Margaret Bailey? On November 2, 1855, he married Julia Nagel Shiel, the widow of Dr. James Shiel, who had practiced medicine in the French Prairie area until his death. They lived on a farm in the same area, and Dr. Bailey continued his medical practice. One of the leaders of the pioneer government, Bailey was chairman of a committee that conferred in 1841 with Commodore Wilkes and Dr. McLoughlin to form a constitution and code of laws for the Willamette Valley community. In 1844 he was one of an Executive Committee of three to head the Provisional Government, and in 1848 he was elected to the Territorial legislature. He twice stood unsuccessfully as the Democratic gubernatorial candidate, in 1844 and in 1855 (Frost 1959). He died February 5, 1876, and is buried in the Catholic cemetery at St. Paul, Oregon. He had converted to Catholicism in 1870.

It is interesting to note that both Dr. Tolmie and the obituary refer to Ruth Rover as a way of identifying Margaret. ''Squills'' had asked in his book review: ''who the dickens cares, about the existence of a fly, or in whose pan of molasses the insect disappeared.'' He might have been surprised to discover that the fly was of interest so long after the book was written which told of her life.

Nina Baym concludes that woman's fiction of the early and midnineteenth century told a story of women beset by trials which they overcame by drawing on their resources of intelligence and will (Baym 1978:16-17). Margaret Bailey's life is part of that story. In Oregon she was among the first white women settlers, the first person to publish poetry locally, and the first woman to have a newspaper column and to publish a book, leaving a record of what life was like for one woman in the early days of Oregon. She undoubtedly felt an affinity with the Biblical Ruth who labored in the fields of the wealthy Boaz for years; unlike the Moabite Ruth, however, her wanderings and difficult labors persisted.

Bailey intended to issue *Ruth Rover* in monthly numbers. Only two are known to have been published by Carter & Austin in Portland, in 1854, in double columns, each volume 7 x 10½ inches, selling for $1.50. Volume I contained Chapters I through XIII and concluded with two poems and the "Sally Soule" story; Volume II contained Chapters XIV through XXII and concluded with two poems and Bailey's response to reviews of Volume I. It is not known how many copies of the two volumes were published, "and all but two copies of *The Grains* had been destroyed by outraged citizens of the Willamette Valley" (Duncan 1973:240). For many years it was assumed that no copies of the two volume book had survived. Alfred Powers, for example, in his 1935 *History of Oregon Literature* mentions *Ruth Rover* but assumes there are no extant copies. However, in 1944 Professor Herbert B. Nelson of Oregon State University called the public's attention to two copies of Volume II: one in the Oregon State Library, which it had acquired in 1922 (the copy has the name of J. Quinn Thornton, an Oregon pioneer, on the front cover) and the other copy in the Beinecke collection of the Yale University Library. Nelson mentioned, too, the single known extant copy of Volume I, also in the Beinecke collection.

On the title page of this copy of Volume I appears a handwritten statement:

> This volume was sold to me by Frederic W. S[hift or kiff] of Portland Oregon in 1922. He purchased it from Geo. H Hymes of the Oregon Historical Society, and at my request had Mr. Hymes make out a receipt and certificate of ownership. The book was his own personal property and had been loaned to the Oregon Hist. Scty, where it was on deposit. Mr. Hymes was the Curator and Secty of the Society.
>
> Edw. Eberstadt.

For this re-issue of *The Grains* we rely on the extant copies in the Oregon State Library and the Beinecke collection. The two copies of Volume II are complete; the one copy of Volume I is incomplete, missing some pages at the conclusion. Fortunately, the concluding pages are a separate story, titled "Sally Soule," which had been published by the American Tract Society and in a different version in Z. A. Mudge's *The Missionary Teacher*. We use Mudge's version of the story; it begins on page 165 of this edition with the sentence: "Thus appeared Sally Soule, the loved Indian girl of ten years. . ." Bailey used the same "Preface" in both volumes of *The Grains,* and we give it only once in this edition that combines the two volumes.

In editing the two volumes and the "Sally Soule" story, we have followed the extant copies exactly, including dialects and typographical and spelling errors. Asterisks and blanks after names and places are also Bailey's. So as not to clutter the text, we have not used *sic* to note errors or Bailey's efforts to recreate dialects. We hope, of course, that we have not introduced any errors of our own. The unnumbered footnotes at the bottom of the text are Bailey's; numbered endnotes are ours. Ruth Rover, Dr. W. J. Binney, Mr. and Mrs. Leland, Wiley, and Robert Newhall are pseudonyms and are identified in the introduction and endnotes. All the other names mentioned in *The Grains* appear to be the names of actual people who were involved with Margaret Bailey. In some cases the spelling of the name does not appear to be correct, but in those cases it seems to be a matter of not knowing the correct spelling or of spelling phonetically. In other instances Bailey notes people and places with an initial, usually followed by dashes. This appears to be the correct first initial and was apparently done to disguise the person and place.

The brackets and numbers 1 through 9 near the end of Chapter XXI, pp. 289-296, are part of Bailey's text. She notes: ''Those parts marked with figures, and denied by Dr. Binney, were afterwards proven in court by the testimony of witnesses; and those parts which are in brackets are untrue, but no testimony was sought to prove so...'' (288-289).

The sources of the poetry in *The Grains* are not always clear. At times Bailey gives the author, for example, Byron, Dryden, or a ''pious poet''; at others she is clearly the author. But there are quotations, usually from religious verse, that are not identified and the sources of which are not known.

For their encouragement and financial support of this publication, we wish to thank Dean Wilkins of the College of Liberal Arts, the Oregon State University Foundation, and the Oregon State University Research Office. Research was done at the libraries of the following: Oregon Historical Society, Oregon State Library, the University of Portland, Seattle Public Library, University of Washington, Portland Public Library, Willamette University, and Oregon State University. Special thanks to Patricia Brandt of the Oregon State University library for her help with aspects of Oregon history and her encouragement of this project.

E.L.
R.F.

The map opposite is a copy of part of a map of the Oregon Territory drawn in 1841 by Charles Wilkes, a member of the United States Exploring Expedition. Wilkes visited Margaret Jewett Bailey in the same year (see note 3, page 322 of this volume).

The original map is in the Map Library of the Kerr Library of Oregon State University; the editors and publishers gratefully acknowledge the cooperation of members of the Kerr Library. This copy retains the terminology and spelling of the original map, including the names and locations of Indian tribes.

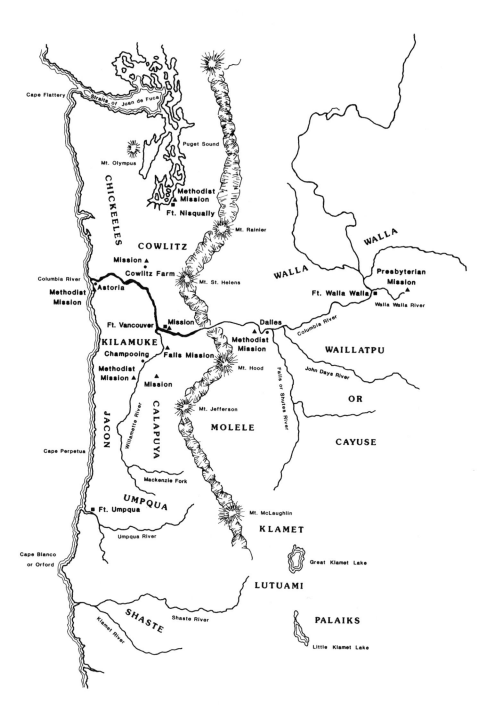

THE GRAINS

PREFACE

All the reasons which have induced the compiler to publish this work, at the present time, cannot now be given. The reader will perceive many as he advances, and they will be better understood at its close.

The undertaking is considered by her to be bold and hazardous—in consideration of her inexperience as a writer.

Unwilling to place any one in an unhappy attitude with others, she has not consented to submit the work to a revisor, whose better judgment would prevent many inaccuracies and oversights in the style, and nature of the subjects introduced, from becoming so apparent as they inevitably will, in consequence of relying altogether upon her own knowledge and understanding.

The RELIGIOUS parts of journals and letters, have been much abridged, because not interesting to the general reader, and only so much retained as is thought sufficient to present the story in its true light.

Scenes, and language of a revolting character, must sometimes be presented; and the indulgence of the public is most earnestly entreated, while the compiler shall endeavor to do this with as little shock as possible to the finer sensibilities of the heart.

For the most part, the manuscripts are presented in their original form; the compiler considering that the involuntary expressions of the mind will better denote its nature, than those highly cultivated passages, which loose all their native beauty by the labor with which they are brought forth—and herself being solely responsible for what may here appear, she allows this the more readily. "Silver and gold I have none; but such as I have I give unto thee."

CHAPTER I

PARENTAGE, CHILDHOOD, &c., &c.

❧

On the subject of this publication, Miss Rover, in a note to a friend, dated June 13th, '54, after referring to some insults and opposition to which she had lately been subjected, and had given the names of the authors, &c., &c., all of which will be considered in their proper place, says:

> "It appears very evident that the work of which I once spoke to you, should be published in Oregon. * * * My conscience asserts most positively and approvingly, that, in all my dreadful trials, I have endeavored to perform my duty, faithfully and perseveringly, to my God, my husband, my neighbor, and myself—burying within my own bosom the injustice and injuries which have been done me; and there the remembrance of them would have remained had my enemies been content to have suffered me to pursue my course in peace. But 'tis in vain that I attempt any innocent employment, whether it be intended for recreation or to obtain a livelihood. The young of my classes are withdrawn, when a slander reaches them, for fear of contamination; I am avoided, and shunned, and slighted, and regarded with suspicions in every place, till my life is more burdensome than death would be. I have, therefore, in this conclusion, been impelled by a sense of justice due to myself and a wish that my future life should not be overshadowed by the gloom of the present."

Ruth's parents, when they commenced life together in 1794, were poor and unpretending. Unlike each other in mental capacities and inclination, they nevertheless endured the marriage yoke together for a term of fifty years, when it was dissolved by the hand of death. The father, an industrious, upright citizen, inherited the respect of all who knew him.[1] Not highly educated himself, he thought a common school system of education sufficient for his children, and anything beyond this, rank extravagance. Good trades, good habits, and good homes for his boys, was all he asked to make them respectable in life; while the daughters were submitted solely to the management of the mother, with, however, the caution often presented for her not to indulge their wish for finery. The mother was, in appearance, when a girl, one of those old-fashioned bonny lasses from the State of Maine—buxom, blithe and worthy. She spun and wove all her own household linen before her marriage—knit thirteen pairs of stockings during the evenings her lover passed with her. She instructed her daughters in the same useful arts, as well as how to prepare a good meal for the family or friends, to set and keep the house in order, and to attire themselves in such apparel as was becoming, neat, suitable to their station, and could be afforded by their parents, or obtained by their own industry.

Ruth was the youngest of these genuine country girls. Of her childhood we cannot speak much. She undoubtedly did many "cunning tricks" in learning to live—as all children are supposed to do until a younger one supplants them in the place of pet, when *their* very witty capers are forgotten in the zeal to proclaim those of the new comer. It has, however been told me of Ruth that she was excessively fond of her books—that when she commenced the reading of a story it was in vain to expect her to cease until she had finished it—that the kind of punishment inflicted by her mother, for errors, was to keep her from school, and to promise her some additional privileges of that kind for rewards of good behavior.

She says: "My childhood was not vicious, nor particularly religious. My mother, however, was a pious woman, and early instilled into my mind the fear and love of God. She taught me to pray and early explained to me good books, particularly the bible. It was on an occasion like this that I acquired through her a confidence in God which has been the leading star of my existence. Having read and explained to me the nature of the passage which says 'enter into thy closet and when thou has shut the door, pray, to thy Father who is in secret, and thy Father who seeth in secret, himself shall reward thee openly,' I retired to a dark closet which I had never before dared to enter alone and having closed the door, I besought God to hear and bless me. My fears of darkness vanished—I believed He had heard my requests, and I found myself joyful in the thought that in my life I should always be protected by the great God who had shown himself so ready to listen to my simple prayers.

"In subsequent times of danger from hurricanes, to which the place was subject, I always retired to my closet and with much confidence asked my Heavenly Father to quell the tempest and preserve us from harm. And I have many times since been ashamed of a lack of faith in trying circumstances, on remembering the delightful emotions excited within my mind by this early exercise of faith and hope.

"My first attempt at poetry was made at three years of age, before I knew the meaning of words. But selecting words which sounded alike I placed them at the ends of lines, and getting an elder schoolmate to write for me, I concluded that I should at last have seat in the Temple of Fame for this great production. So much was I ridiculed by my brothers and sisters for this, that I resolved that whatever else I might attempt, I would never again try to make rhyme; and I had adhered to this resolution most strictly till one day, in after years, I found I had addressed a letter in my imagination to a beloved sister, in rhyme, which I found as difficult to reduce to prose as to cultivate into poetry, and I suffered it to go with all its errors."

Another anecdote of childhood of Ruth will be given, inasmuch as she, with her characteristic superstition, always regarded it as prophetic.

Mr. Rover had had a new bowling alley erected at the hotel where they resided, and when completed it was decided by the workmen that Ruth, being the pet of the family, should roll the first ball. She was carried out and placed at the head of the alley, and the ball laid upon her arms. At the given signal she let it drop upon the floor, when it rolled its slow course along towards the pins, and entering among them threw some down, and they falling on others threw them also down till every one had fallen and the ball remained in their midst, when the company loudly cheered the unpretending child and told her she had accomplished what no other person of the number could have done.

CHAPTER II

OMENS

Ruth Rover evidently possessed a belief in the manifestation of the Providence of God, as well in the trifling as the most important affairs of human life—hence she frequently derived much comfort as well as instruction from the appropriateness of many texts of scripture to her peculiar situations, as also from scraps of reading from other sources; and although she sometimes feared she was merely superstitious, yet she had the example of many others, one of which will be given:

"The leaf of a folio bible, burned on the four edges, was last night conveyed from a fire in Brighton street to the chamber of a physician who keeps a private hospital in Howard street, Boston. The leaf was carried by the wind a distance of a half a mile and taken into a chamber window which was open. On it was found written:

"Honor a physician with the honor due unto him—for the uses which ye may have of him; for the Lord hath created him.

"For of the Most High cometh healing, and he shall receive honor of the king.

"The skill of the physician shall lift up his head, and in the sight of great men he shall be in admiration."

Another coincidence is found in the fact that the day before the funeral of a stranger, who died in the house, took place. The 16th and 17th verses of the same chapter read as follows:

"My son, let tears fall down over the dead and begin to lament as if thou hadst suffered great harm thyself; and then cover his body according to the custom, and neglect not his burial.

"Weep bitterly and make great moan, and use lamentation as he is worthy, and that a day or two, lest thou be evil spoken; and then comfort thyself in thy heaviness."

We have no superstitious inferences to draw from this event. The circumstances as we have detailed them, are all facts. It is one of those remarkable coincidences which sometimes occur in the particular providence of God, which according to the doctrine of chance could not be calculated upon in one of many millions of cases. It is more remarkable, even, than the incident which occurred at the great fire in New York, some years since, respecting the Methodist book establishment and the leaf containing the verse, "Our holy and beautiful house is burned," etc., which was conveyed to Long Island." —*Zion's Herald*.

As it is premised that Miss Rover's mind might have received some inharmonious tone from the remembrance of disappointed love, to which she was early subjected, we will allude to the subject here.

Some may affirm that the affections can be engaged but once in a life-time, but we aver to the contrary. None was ever more ardent, more pure, or more woman-like than that which occupied the heart of Ruth at three different times before she took up her residence in Oregon, and from which she resolutely called off her thoughts when she had discovered they were ill placed. She had arrived at her seventeenth year before she had met any person who had awakened in her mind any stronger sentiments of regard than her school-mates, till she met in company a young student, son of a physician in ——, Mass. They each became attached to the other at first sight—the acquaintance was continued and marriage was proposed—when Ruth learned that a friend of hers, a very excellent young lady, was devotedly attached to him, and, moreover, that he had sworn to marry no other but her, and whom he had ceased to visit on account of some slight misunderstanding. Ruth visited her and found these facts confirmed, and assuring her that she should forever decline his addresses thereafter, left the town.

'Tis useless to attempt to portray the sorrows of mind which ensued. With that one loved image before her mind by night and day—worthy, yet offered in sacrifice—she passed dreary months of grief uncomplainingly, sustained by the consciousness that she was doing right—even as she "would be done by"—till she made a new acquaintance with a teacher in W. Academy.

This gentleman was a candidate for ministry in the M.E.[1] church. His attentions were rendered the more agreeable to Ruth from the circumstance of the disappointment she had lately endured—and which also caused her to be wary in arriving hastily to any conclusions in relation to a union. In her own words we will cite the event:

"In a few weeks I discovered that there were in the academy others who entertained towards Mr. ——— attachments corresponding with my own, and that he was equally studious, on his part, to encourage them. This was a death blow to me. I at once detested his deceit and avoided his society. He suspected the cause, and instead of coming to an explanation, as a man of honor would have done, he pursued his course with increased ardor, as he perceived it to give me pain. My situation by some may be imagined, but can never be described. As a proof that my mind was painfully affected, I need only to add that my days and nights were mostly spent in excessively weeping, and in extreme agony of mind.

"During this state of feeling, I was obliged to attend to my studies—keep up good appearances—be regular in my attendance at school—and wear a smile on my countenance when my heart was wrung with grief. Yet, notwithstanding all my endeavors to conceal my anguish, I was suspected, though the cause was unknown. Some attributed my sadness to a melancholy turn of mind; some to sullenness; and others to a carelessness of obligation toward those who had placed me at school free of expense. I did not cherish his memory with pleasure—and I can think of him now only as of a grave with a poison flag growing above it and contaminating the air with its noxious breath."

She continues: "I loved again, and with all the ardor of the first love, a gentleman of Boston, of exemplary and ardent piety, and glowing and pure affections. I resigned him, to become a missionary, believing that whatever appeared in opposition to duty should be sacrificed, though dear as a right hand, or the apple of an eye."

As time bears us onward toward the grave, how is its gloom lightened by the belief that we shall meet such kindred spirits again, where duty can demand no sacrifice, but, where love—holy and eternal as the source from whence it came—will exist, free from all the admixtures of evil, which despoil its beauty here.

These references, so early given, will explain many passages which will occur hereafter.

CHAPTER III

CONVERSION

❦

Nor is the objection to a person's keeping a daily record of God's dealings with his own soul, after the manner of Lady Maxwell[1] and others, founded on the fact that his religious experience is not as rich and diversified as theirs, of any serious weight, since, in most cases it is not desirable that such memoranda should be published during the person's life-time; and the opinion of those who survive him may be very different from his on this, as well as many other points. Nor do we think that a person's proper character, as it will appear in the day of judgment, is to be determined by the feelings of the present moment, or the transient experience of some gracious visitation of divine mercy, or the heart-cheering hopes of future good, which he may at times indulge; for though we are unquestionably pleasing or displeasing to God every moment, yet the general character is not to be determined by the conduct of the moment. The present is a state of warfare, in which the christian is the subject of "fightings without and fears within," of occasional victories and incidental defeats. He is the subject of storms as well as calms, of temptations from Satan, as well as of divine succors from the Father of mercies. We consider therefore that a man is not to be judged so much by the temper, words, and action of any given moment, as by the steady purpose of the soul, the undeviating course of conduct amid all the varieties of life.

FROM AN OLD JOURNAL

"The fourth day of August, in the year 1829, I humbly trust the Lord forgave my sins, while at a camp-meeting in Eastham, Cape Cod. I had felt the need of religion for some years, and many times had the prayers of the people of God been offered in my behalf. But foolishly believing that I could do nothing toward my own conversion, I there rested, supposing that God in his own good time would convert my soul without any of my exertions. But in this idea I found I was mistaken, and that if I would enter into the straight gate I must 'strive.' With this conviction I resolved that there should, no longer, be anything wanting on my part. With these feelings I left my employment and went to camp-meeting, and the result proved that the Lord had been always ready, and the delay had been occasioned by myself."

"Twenty-one years have elapsed since that event and I can never forget the kindness and assistance I received from my friends in Saugus.[2] Their instructions and prayers removed my fears and strengthened my hopes, and so enlightened my mind with regard to my duty that but for them, I often consider, I might never have known the advantages and delights of being a child of God."

"The first night we were on the campground, at the prayer meeting, the Lord appeared and blessed me. I felt the burden of sin removed, but not till the next morning did I feel a bright evidence that they had indeed been forgiven. O! what joy did I find pervade my breast when, on awaking, I heard the saints—some singing, some praying—while all the wood echoed with the songs of the redeemed! I was at first surprised at my new feelings. How it was that everything seemed so delightful, I could not tell. No unholy thoughts—no disquietude, sorrow, or uneasiness—but peace, love and joy at the sound of God's worship, which I never knew before, while all within me was calm and serene as heaven. But when I remembered the evening before I had supposed I had been converted, an ecstacy of joy filled my heart. I thought the evidence I enjoyed that this was genuine was as good as I could desire, and the reflection that now I could be remembered with the people of God and with them go to Heaven, inspired me with great happiness."

"I cannot help mentioning here the indebtedness I felt and continue to feel to that holy man of God, Rev. A. D. Merrill. I surely may consider him my spiritual father. He seeing my tears in the afternoon, conversed with me, and learning the state of my mind, invited me to rise for prayers, telling me, on witnessing my emotions, that I was "not far from the kingdom," and during his prayer the Lord blessed me. Elder Hyde, long since gone to Heaven, preached in the tent that afternoon, it being rainy, from the words,

"Sanctify yourselves to day, for to-morrow the Lord will do wonders among you." God did not wait for the morrow, but even then He was in our midst."

"The 20th of September I was baptised by immersion and joined the Methodist Episcopal church in Saugus, then under the pastoral care of Rev. E. K. Avery. I soon lost the bright evidence I at first received, by seeing others, when first meeting a change of heart, in a far more rapturous frame of mind than I had been, and indulging the suggestion that I could not have been converted or I should have been exercised like them. By giving place to this doubt I lost my happiness and did not for a year regain it.

"Burdened and sick and faint, to thee, O! God, I come. To whom else shall I go, for thou alone hast the words of eternal life. Weary almost of life—tired of sin—cast down with sorrows, and buffeted by satan—oh! what a suppliant! Can I expect mercy at thy hand? Can a God so supremely glorious for a moment regard me? Can I come to Jesus all guilty as I am and cast my burden on him? Will he receive me? Did he ever—or was it all delusion? Was I tempted to believe I had found him when indeed I had not? My soul is struggling to know—I cannot rest short of a brighter evidence! Oh! God, suffer me not to be deceived. Oh! never let me rest in carnal security, fancying I am on the road to Heaven, when, in fact, I am in the broad road to hell.

"'Tis a point I long to know—
Oft it causes anxious thoughts—
Do I love the Lord or no.
Am I his or am I not?"

"Oh! thou most holy God who now seest me, I beseech thee show me the depths of my depravity—let me see myself in thy light. How do I appear in thy sight? Thou knowest my heart, how much of sin is there, and how much I am tempted by the enemy of my soul. Suffer him not to destroy me or tempt me above what I am able to bear.

"This day I find a revival in my heart and the necessity of living more in accordance with God's most holy will. I have seen a peculiar beauty this morning in reading Paul's Second Epistle to the Corinthians—of dying to the world daily that we may grow in grace. "For the light of affliction which is but for a moment, worketh for us a far more and exceeding and eternal weight of glory." The rich reward we shall have if we are faithful in the discharge of every duty is worth more to the immortal soul than any sacrifice we can make for here.

"How soon, my soul, must I lament your stupidity. When shall I feel the worth of immortal souls to lie near my heart? Every day I see some new instances of mortality. The bell that now tolls, reminds me that we are mortal. Yesterday the awful news of a young man but nineteen years of age, condemned to die upon the gallows, reached my ears; and shall satan and sin abound, and christians not use every effort to convince sinners of the errors of their ways?

"To the believer, Christ is precious, and to me he would be were I not so unbelieving. Faith is required of the sinner, but my faith is weak and wavering. Do I not see enough of the Lord's goodness every day and hour to swell my heart with gratitude and love? Has not my Saviour suffered enough of want and calumny for guilty me? Has he not, from my earliest childhood, been trying to win my affections to himself, and if I have in any measure given him my heart, has it not been with dreadful reluctance to give him my whole heart? O! my dear Jesus, come and possess my whole regards, and let me be altogether thine own.

"Another week is gone, and what new scenes have I passed through? I have witnessed a new instance of mortality: a man in the full bloom of health and strength cut down like the flower of the field. I saw him at night when fell disease had seized his vitals, restless throw his limbs from side to side—again at morn I heard the death-like groan—I saw his sunken countenance—I heard his dying gasp and saw his eyes closed forever. And all this without an interest in Christ! He had always been a great opposer to religion—he doubtless thought (like many) that old age or a dying day would be time enough to think of these things—but of these privileges he was deprived. Dying as he did at the early age of thirty-three, and without his senses during his illness, gave no time or ability to attend to the concerns of his soul, and thus, without hope of a saving change, he was launched into a boundless eternity. Have I learned, by this dispensation of God's providence, to seek the Lord in my youthful days, before the evil days come, and the danger of procrastinating the day of repentance? Surely I have seen this many die without hope, and shall I not learn from this never to despise the religion of Jesus or be ashamed of his cause?

"O! thou vain world, where are thy boasted charms that millions sacrifice their all, their everything, all to enjoy? What has thou so attracting? What are thy riches?—what thy honors? Riches but take to themselves wings and fly away—honor is but a bubble, and friendship but a name—"a shade that follows wealth and fame"—and love is still an emptier sound. How friendly will your gay votaries be to the rich, while the humble poor, though possessed of heavenly riches, yet, if they have not what you esteem—wealth—from them you will turn away in disdain. With the pious poet, I exclaim:

"O! tell me no more of this world's vain store!"

"By my own foolishness, this morning I am deprived of going to church, and O! my wicked heart, how much must I suffer from you? How long, because your carnal nature is not subdued, must I be led captive at satan's will? How long shall I feel the corruptions of human nature springing up within you? When shall I be renewed in the spirit of mind, so that every desire of my soul will be drawn out after the Lord. I have of late more than ever felt an awful influence from my foes within. My pride has led me to be vain—to speak vain words and to think vain thoughts, which should be placed on God alone. The fear of man has kept me from doing my duty—and unbelief has kept me from the throne of grace. O! cursed roots of inbred sin, how long will ye torment me?

"This day I have been favored with hearing an instructive discourse on the words, "Grow in Grace." I would now ask myself: Have I the evidence that a growth in grace has been carried on in my heart?—have I grown in humility—in love to the church of Christ?—and is my conscience tender, so that I cannot sin without reproach? Is it my desire to be given entirely up to God? Do I hate the world, or still cling to its vanities? These are important questions and yet I lack in many points.

> "Thou on the Lord rely,
>   So safe shalt thou go on—
> Fix on His work thy steadfast eye,
>   So shall thy work be done.
> No profit canst thou gain,
>   By self-consuming care,
> To Him commend thy cause; His ear
>   Attends the softest prayer."

"Sabbath had an excellent meeting—partook of the sacrament—get greatly blessed, and go home encouraged.

"Devoted to God; resolved to serve Him as well as I can, and make every necessary sacrifice for Him.

"Earnestly desire to be freed from *all* sin and sanctified to the Lord, soul, body and spirit. Addressed a letter to my father, entreating him to seek religion.

"More than ever desirous to be entirely the Lord's, and to have every affection of my heart placed on Him; cannot rest without a clean heart.

"Find my affections placed on that which I think is not for me. 'Tis dangerous to love anything more than God; would have him possess my whole heart.

"Mixed in worldly company and talked too much.

"Where will this wicked heart lead me? It seems that everything unholy is centered here. 'Tis good to live for heaven, and I desire never to rest till my carnal nature is subdued and I am prepared for heaven.

"At the Lord's table thought much of the words, "This do in remembrance of me." How strangely have I even forgotten their import, and how ought I to blush and be ashamed of my luke-warmness. I should never go to the Lord's table without remembering Him in the garden in agony, and pour out my soul in grief that I have ever sinned against Him. I should remember Him on the cross, extended between the heavens and earth. The sun hides her face and refuses to view the sight. The earth trembles, and even flinty rocks break at a scene so awful. I should remember Him in His resurrection, when He burst the bars of death and conquered the grave. I should remember Him in all his goodness to me—in the tokens of His love—His adopting me into His family, and making me an heir of salvation; in bearing with me in all my sinfulness; in healing my backslidings, and in His long continued forbearance and tender mercy towards me. O! that I might never again forget my Lord and what He has done for me, but in all my ways remember His life and death and cross!''

About this time Ruth received a proposal of marriage from a pious man in ——— , Mass. and, thinking fit to decline the offer, wrote him thus:

''DEAR BROTHER IN CHRIST:—* * *I am sensible that there are relations in life which are tender and endearing, and when ordered by God and enjoying His smile must be increasingly so. I can conceive of no greater happiness, in earthly relations, than for two to be united whose hopes and joys and aims are one, and they both united to Christ the Living Head. I could ask no greater joy, in the married state, than to be united to a man who was consecrated to God, and whose greatest object was to promote His glory. I should think myself greatly blessed in having a friend like this to lead me on in the way of heaven; but, my brother, I have learned to cease to look for bliss to the transitory joys of time. I have seen the frailty of earthly hopes; and in a great degree my affections are weaned from earth, and I can with composure look up to my Heavenly Father and say:

> ''Though waves and storms go o'er my head—
> Though strength and health and friends be gone,
> Though joys be withered all, and dead—
> Though every comfort be withdrawn,
> On this my steadfast soul relies:
> Father! Thy mercy never dies!''

''I think that a married state entered into without suitable attachment and a proper sense of duty, would prove miserable, and should be discountenanced by every professor of religion. I have, therefore, resolved to wait the approbation of heaven, before I take a step which involves my well-being through life.

R.R.''

It appears that while the writer of these extracts was closing, resolutely, her ears to every enticement of an earthly nature, she was not left without the cheering influences of the spirit of the Most High—for we find in her journals and diaries many passages like the following:

"The Lord is precious to my soul—blessed be His holy name. After church meeting I retired by myself for prayer, and the Lord was with me. I don't know that I ever before had such access to God. It seemed as though He unfolded anew His glories for me, and I saw such a fulness of love and such a willingness to bestow, that at once was silenced all my objections to the doctrine of full sanctification."

These relations are unimportant only as denoting the operations of the spirit of grace upon the mind of Ruth previous to her resigning all her worldly hopes for the cause of Christ in a foreign land. Notes of her "every day walk" for a year, is nearly all omitted; and many religious letters omitted at this time. In all these are discovered the same strugglings to overcome sin, and be conformed entirely to the will of God, as is felt by every christian, especially when he first commences the divine life.

"Much troubled in consequence of worldly disappointments, I have for some time held an idol in my heart; though in God no sin perhaps, yet it has much interrupted my happiness in God. Endeavored to order my mind aright. Find imperfection mixed with all my ways. Am truly wretched and undone without Christ. I am willing to resign all my hopes of happiness in the world for the pure religion of Jesus Christ. It is my prayer that God will divest me of everything that hinders my growing in grace, and make me a humble christian.

"This evening has been glorious. After a day of great trial, a few sisters met for prayer, and the Saviour came also, according to his promise. I was able to rejoice with joy unspeakable and full of glory. My faith was great—I could fully believe that Jesus was my friend. After walking a short distance and conversing about religion; it seemed as if the heavens were opened and my soul drank deep into the love of God. O what mercy and goodness thus to favor me by dispelling my doubts and fears! Can I cease to love and bless the Lord?

"The sanctuary of the Lord is my delight. Under the preaching of the word I obtain sweet peace of mind, and every thing around me is peaceful and happy.

"Blest at the table of the Lord. How sweet is peace with God! "I would rather be a door-keeper in the house of God, than to dwell in the tents of wickedness."

"January 24, 1832:

> "Thus far the Lord hath led me on,
> Thus far his power prolongs my days."

"Another year has rolled round and I am still spared. The Lord Jehovah is yet my friend and I am numbered with his people, and while my hands have been diligently employed the Lord has been with me blessing and encouraging my heart. Many have been my trials and temptations, and many my wanderings—but the God whom I love and worship is the same yesterday, to-day, and forever. Bless His holy name! I have not so far wandered from Him but He deigns to have mercy on me and bless me with His love.

"Returned from a visit to my sister's. Am glad to be again where I can frequent the house of God, as I have there been deprived of the privilege. I have found the Lord is not confined to the meeting-house, though He there blesses, but in all places He can meet with His children and fill their hearts with His love. O! how many times, while there in my walks and secret retirements, have I shouted glory to God and joyed in His divine favor. Bless the Lord! O! my soul! O! how exultingly do I love the Lord, my maker! I will glory in His presence, and praise Him for His love.

"Since my return to Boston I have been favored with much of the joys of the christian. Last Sabbath was a precious season, and I have been since panting for my God and desiring to be like Him in holiness and love. Dear Saviour, make me all thine own.

"I commence again to record my trials for surely they are great and numerous. I sometimes believe I shall sink under them, and I find my mind so excited that I fear reason will leave me; I too keenly perceive the errors of others, viz: those of ministers and church members, and the glaring wickedness of the world around me, and my own constant failings and imperfections wound me and destroy my peace. My wandering affections—coldness in duty—want of confidence—unbelief and ignorance—and want of courage, and the fear of man, all tend to harrow up my feelings and make me exclaim—ah! me!—''From the crown of my head to the soles of my feet I am full of wounds and bruises and putrefying sores." And yet, in all this, I forget that Jesus' blood can heal my wounds, and that thro' Him I am saved. Oh! what a mercy that I am spared still.

"God is my refuge in distress, a present help in time of trouble." Never did I so fully realize the truth of these words as I have of late. For a short time I have been in —— and I find not that height of holiness in the church I could wish to see. Many of the professed followers of the Lord have become lovers of pleasure more than God—saints are sleeping—sinners are dying all around us. A plague is spreading through the land and hurrying millions to eternity without time for repentance. O! I could weep that Zion has no more friends—that my God has no more worshippers—that his former children are becoming indifferent to his service. Some of my dearest friends, whom I fancied almost unchangeable in their devotion to the Lord's cause, have become reversed. But why do I mourn? God is my refuge, and what a blessed nearness do I feel towards Him. When every other source of comfort fails, there seems but little distance between Him and my soul, so sweetly does he cheer my heart and bid me look forward to my happy home in heaven. O! my god! my *Father!*—by what nearer title can I address thee? Thou art my friend and deliverer—I give my all to thee and I beseech thee to keep me from every evil.

"This is a period when every child of God should be alive to the performance of their duty. That dreadful disease, the cholera,[3] has, within the last year, swept many unprepared beings into eternity, and is fast approaching us. Already has it commenced its work of death on our continent, and who can tell who shall be its next victim? I have been asking myself if I were resigned to die, and have been able to say—I am. Never was I so completely weaned from earth as now—I have not one tie to bind me here—all are severed. All earthly hopes are fading and transitory. "There's nothing here deserves my joys—there's nothing like my God. No—how gladly would I leave earth to be refreshed with heavenly bliss. 'Tis He that makes my paradise, and where He is 'tis heaven.''

CHAPTER IV

JOURNAL CONTINUED

✿

"When thy father and mother forsake thee,
then the Lord will take thee up."

"Much disturbed in mind of late from various causes. This world is not
my home—I am more than ever weaned from it. For these ten years I have
looked to it for happiness, but all in vain. It has ever happened that those
objects on which I have placed my fondest hopes have been taken from me,
and those plans which I have laid out for myself and thought unalterable, have
worked in a way contrary to my desires; but I will not murmur—'tis undoubtedly all for the best. "God moves in a mysterious way, His wonders to
perform." I find so great a sense of my weakness resting upon me that I can
only ask mercy at the hand of God, for I deserve no favors. I would rather die
and leave the world than to live for nothing but myself.

"I have at last resolved to attempt to prepare myself for a teacher to the
heathen, by working diligently for two years, that I may be able to defray the
expense of going to school to review my studies for this purpose. My father is
able to do this for me, but being opposed to my plan, he will not. He said to
me, not long since, "My daughter, I have raised nine children; they have all
left me and settled elsewhere but you and Isaac. I have worked hard for many
years to provide for them, and I think out of them all I have a right to claim
one, at least, to live with me as long as I live, and *you,* being the last, and at
present free to choose, I have determined to claim your services during my old

age, and when I am dead you will be released and can take any course which will best suit you." I replied, "Father, I could not do anything more gratifying to my feelings—'tis just what I wish to do—to live with you as long as you live." He seemed greatly pleased and satisfied, and has many times reminded me of this duty which I had promised—and when I have asked for money to go to school, that I might be qualified for a missionary teacher, he has been so utterly opposed to the idea that he has never consented to furnish me a cent. My mind has become much interested in the heathen and I have been able to find peace only in resolving to go and teach them, should an opportunity present itself. But I am not qualified without better learning, and I must make some endeavor to obtain it. My father never felt the importance, as some, of giving his children a good education, and many times has my mother taken me from school for punishment of errors I have committed—it being the greatest punishment she could inflict on me, and, when threatened, was always sufficient to ensure to her any amount of obedience she might require. Hence, if I would succeed in my favorite plan, I must work and obtain means of my own to enable me to do so, that my life may be spent in some useful way, and that I may be the instrument of doing some good in the cause of Christ. I would like to obey my father, but if a higher authority calls me elsewhere, I must regard it with the greatest preference. I was led to shed tears of joy this evening on reading my portion of "Daily Food"[1] for this day. It was so encouraging that I will set it down at length. "They that sow in tears shall reap in joy."

> "Let those that sow in sadness wait
> Till the fair harvest come—
> They shall confess their sheaves are great,
> And shout the blessings home."

"He that goeth forth and weepeth, bearing precious seed, shall doubtless come again rejoicing, bringing his sheaves with him."

"O! will this be the case with me? Shall I even be the means of winning *one* soul to Christ? If so, then what are all my sufferings here compared with that blest moment when the Lord shall say, "Well done good and faithful servant, enter into the joys of thy Lord."

"Heard today of the death of Dr. Albert Orne. He was a young man of uncommon promise who for some years had labored assiduously, alternately teaching and studying, to obtain a collegiate education. He had injured his health, and now his life has paid the forfeit. He died at one of the West India Islands, alone, unattended and unconsoled by friends. Yet he died in hope to rise again in the resurrection of the just.

"For two weeks my mind has been troubled in view of my unfaithfulness and weakness, but the Lord did appear for me today. As I was going to prayer He removed the burden of unbelief I have for so long felt, and I would now rejoice in God. I love the Lord, and I realize much pleasure when I remember that I have given myself up to Him while I live. I thank God that He ever called after me while in sin and caused me to love His word. It gives me unspeakable happiness to believe He is my father and friend, and I am His child and servant.

"I have been at home eight weeks and enjoyed the blessings of life and the society of friends, yet for the most time my mind has been oppressed and ill at ease. To-morrow, if the Lord will, I intend going to B——— to work for means to enable me to go to school. 'Tis hard for me to disappoint my father, but I hope he will live yet many years and I may have the privilege of being with him at the last.

"Let all that is within me praise and bless the name of the Lord. Since I came to this place I have enjoyed an unusual sense of the favor of God. All things have been caused to work together for good. What reason have I to rejoice that I was ever drawn to seek and serve the Lord and to give myself entirely to him. I have felt that all my concerns were known to God, and, as Mrs. Fletcher says, ''In all my ways Thy hand I own, Thy ruling Providence I see.''[2] Yes, my God, Thou knowest all things—Thou knowest that my being in this place is intended for Thy glory, and if it be not agreeable to Thy will why should I have Thy presence? Why should I rest with so much confidence on Thee? Why should I enjoy such peace of mind? Why should I now, while I write, shout glory to Thy name?—and why should I, in the toil of the day, when I reflect that I work for Thee, feel all pain removed and pursue my task with pleasure? Thou hast been with me since I came, and directed events for my good. O! continue Thy goodness, indulgent parent, and fill my heart with gratitude and my mouth with praise.

"My soul, break out in praise and never cease thy grateful song. The Lord is mine and I am His! Should a voice from heaven speak this sentence I could not believe it more fully than I now do. Every day confirms me in this faith and gives me increasing cause for gratitude. I have the presence of God within me and I feel His love. I rely on Him, and all things are ordered aright. I trust in Him, and he does all things for me that is best. I love Thee, O! Lord, and I trust with all my heart. If anything on earth has more of my love than Thee, O! take it from me, and *thyself* possess the whole of my affections. I give all to Thee—my life—my time—my property—my soul and body, I give to Thee. Use them for Thy glory and the good of Thy cause.

"Last week was a week of favors from the Lord. I enjoyed his presence by night and by day. I thought I could never again indulge in doubt of my acceptance. This week my faith has been put to the test; my mind being beclouded I have not found the same freedom in prayer, yet my faith has not failed. I have been enabled to trust in the Lord though the appearance of his immediate presence has vanished. 'Tis blessed thus to feel in every time of cloud as well as sunshine.

"I will now record the goodness of the Lord. Formerly I have written much of my trials and little enjoyment, but now I will speak of rejoicing and faith. From all indications I can discover, 'tis right for me to continue to work, and by-and-by the door will be opened for usefulness. Yesterday and to-day I have felt a full confidence in God, believing that I am owned and taken care of by Him. In all ways His arm has been underneath me, and, though invisible, He has been and is doing all for me I need, and clearing the way before me."

During a few weeks Ruth Rover devoted herself enthusiastically to the object she had resolved to accomplish, viz: to educate herself for a missionary teacher; but a fit of sickness made it necessary for her to return to her friends. We find, by her journal of this time, that her mind became much depressed in consequence. She says:

"I know not whether to attribute this to unbelief, or to having taken a wrong course; I verily thought I did right, and was many times greatly blessed in the reflection that I labored for God, and sometimes He seemed so near me that I had only to whisper my wishes to Him and they were gratified. But now it seems that all communications with Him are cut off and I hardly dare to pray, and I often come from the throne of grace unblest. What can the hindrance be?"

When her health returned she consented to take a school and remain with her sister in G———, but still fearing she had done wrong, she says:

"Since writing the last time I have had many trials and dark moments; but now I perceive the Lord has led me by a way I knew not; He has made the darkness to give light, and the path of sorrow steps to glory; His right hand has upheld me amid thousands of snares, and when I fancied myself alone and exposed to the devices of satan, He was with me and kept me from harm. I bless Thee, thou God who hast made me, for Thy mercies fail not. I love Thee and will praise Thee while I live, when I die, and through eternity.

"A few days since I was brought to have a very humbling view of myself; my weaknesses and sins seemed all arrayed before me—and then came the question, can you *thus,* with all your vileness, cast yourself on Jesus? It seemed a wicked thought at first to suppose He would receive me, but at an evening meeting I beheld such a fulness in Him that I was able to cast myself upon His mercy, all sinful as I was, and believe He received me.

"I was also, when in that low state of mind, asked by some spiritual enquirer, 'you have always been willing to be something—are you now willing to be nothing?' I had placed such strong hopes on being a missionary, and had anticipated so much pleasure therein, that the idea of resigning this hope was very painful; but considering the poor state of my health—my inability to perform any good work—my poverty and ignorance, I was induced to conclude that I must be willing to be *nothing*. I however felt that if it were God's will it should be so, I should be happy in submitting to His chastisement. I have a strong desire that, whether living or dying, sick or well, I may be entirely the Lord's.

"How singular are the events of my life! I verily feel as though I stand on holy ground. I know not which way to move for fear of moving in the wrong way. I know not what God has in store for me—whether joy or grief; my mind has been *exceedingly* disturbed. I have covenanted to life for God, and have many times said I was determined to live not for myself but for the cause of God alone. At present I see no way to live more devoted than in the common duties of life, and these do not content me. My disposition seeks to bear some nobler part in life than the mere rounds of domestic duty; I may glorify God in these I know, but with all their pleasures they do not appear so inviting to me as a cross-bearing and self-denying life.

"While in G——, I consented to receive the addresses of Mr. D. O., a member of the Baptist church in that place. Considering that there was no longer any probability of my going to the heathen, I did this the more willingly. I never engaged to marry him. And now I find I must part with him. As he is a man differing in many points of doctrine from myself, I think we should not live in perfect harmony together and be of one heart, as married persons should be; and I feel the importance of this the more as I have often resolved to devote my life to the Lord, and I have therefore no desire nor intention to marry until by so doing I may aid the cause of religion more than by remaining single.

"My mind is still cast down. I pray—I agonize—but still something rests upon it which I cannot describe. My spirit groaneth within me as I go about my work; my mind is restless and I do not find peace. It really appears to me that God is preparing some event for me which now I do not understand. I have met so many disappointments as to cause me to be weaned from earth. I think I can never enjoy a *married* life, except it be where holiness and devotedness to the cause of Christ are united. Perhaps I am wrong and take erroneous views, but I have prayed that if I am deceived the Lord will undeceive me. I want very much to know the will of God concerning me, and I think I can never rest contented till I do. My case is, I think, singular. I know of no christian that ever felt as I do. I am sensible that some unseen hand is leading and directing the events of my life, and shall I not be grateful that I am so much regarded as to be led on, even through affliction, for some wise purpose? I will be thankful and bless God that he afflicts me and deigns even to notice me.

"I have this day parted with my dear friend D. O., and to me, at least, it was a *painful* parting. I am sensible that I loved him, and were I content to settle here I think I should give my hand to him. We have *parted* and I hardly realize it. Have I so willingly given up a friend I love? and am I again in this drear world alone, without the reflection that there is one who will interest himself for me? Yes, so it is, and I almost fear to form new acquaintances for fear of new sorrows. And am I right thus to disappoint a man who had placed his hopes on me and given me many assurances of his love? I cannot tell, for at present my mind is dark concerning a knowledge of the will of God. But I have resolved that if an opportunity presents itself for me to go to the heathen I shall go. "Thy will be done"—this comprehends all. I dread nothing more than for God to change his purposes concerning me, to gratify my wish. I know if He rules over me and directs the concerns of my life, I need not fear. Let me but be sensible it is He and I am blessed in every event—if *scourged,* let me but see my Father's hand and I bear it with pleasure.

"'God moves in a mysterious way, His wonders to perform,' I am often led to exclaim. Surely I am the Lord's in a peculiar sense—or not His at all. If some divine power has not influenced me for three years past never was mortal more deceived. I find that it is in vain that I devise plans for my own gratification and enjoyment, they are often thwarted and I left to acquiesce in the command, 'Be still and know that I am God.' There is a prospect of my going to Africa as a teacher. If such be God's will, I trust the duty will become yet more evident. Should I be called upon, I shall leave all and go.

"A noble resolution has been passed by the members of the conference in favor of the missionary cause—perhaps a better could not have been suggested. A society has been organized, to be called the 'Missionary Education Society of the M. E. Church,' for the purpose of educating teachers of both sexes, who are unqualified, yet are willing to devote themselves to the work of missions. I believe there are in the churches many young females who are desirous to sacrifice every earthly object to become teachers in heathen lands, but for a want of suitable learning and friends to assist them, are kept back. This society is a remedy.

"Last Thursday I offered myself to brother Lindsay, one of the executive committee of the missionary education society, as a missionary teacher. He said he considered me a suitable person to be devoted to this work, and as soon as he could see the agent he would make my case known. I rejoice that the prospect is brightening. My greatest desire is, and has been for years, to become a missionary. I care not where I am sent, let me but go where God would have me. The ties of nature and affection encircle around my heart at the thought of separation arises; but for *this* cause I can break through them all. I know not of one person or interest in all the earth that I would relinquish the life of the missionary to enjoy. O! my God accept me—may the missionary society accept me—and may I be a missionary and win souls to Christ.''

Ruth having received sufficient encouragement from Mr. Lindsay, of the missionary society, to lead her to presume she would be a recipient of its bounty, visited her father to acquaint him with her resolution.

He, as usual, disapproved of it, and told her that by the time she had been to school a year she would have given up the idea. Next morning being New Year's day, the younger members of the family got their bibles and opening them, said they were going to see what was coming to pass in the future, for 'twas said that whatever was opened to on New Year's morning always was fulfilled. Ruth did not feel much interested in their fortunes, but was somewhat surprised at what seemed to be indicated for her, as she, in compliance with their request, opened the bible. Her eyes rested upon the first chapter of Jeremiah, and she read it aloud.

Her thoughts were particularly interested in these words:

''Then said I, ah! Lord God, behold I cannot speak, for I am but a child.

''But the Lord said unto me, say not 'I am a child,' for thou shalt go to all that I shall send thee, and whatsoever I command thee thou shalt speak.

''Be not afraid of their faces, for I am with thee to deliver thee, saith the Lord.

''Thou, therefore, gird up thy loins, and arise and speak unto them all that I command thee; be not dismayed at their faces, lest I confound thee before them. And they shall fight against thee; but they shall not prevail against thee; for I am with thee, saith the Lord, to deliver thee.''

She was much inclined to think 'twas all a whim and that she had done wrong in so far yielding to a wish to comprehend the future, when she considered the verse which said:

''And they shall fight against thee, '' &c.

She thought that at any rate this could never be fulfilled on missionary ground, where brethren dwell together in such unity, the service of God being the paramount business of their lives. How true that she was *then* only a child in knowledge. Her mind became overcast with fear, which was, however, somewhat lessened when considering that which was added in the same verse, ''but they shall not prevail against thee, for I am with thee to deliver thee, saith the Lord,'' and she concluded that if the first applied to her, the last might also be claimed as applicable to herself.

On recurring with her father, she perceived he was very sad, and from this time his manner towards her was changed.

She endeavored to draw him into conversation on the subject, but he was not inclined to converse and would only say:

"If you persist in this ridiculous resolution, I shall disinherit you. By hard work I have saved a little to leave to my children, and they'll soon obtain it; but, Ruth, if I should die to-morrow, and you be gone from me, I shall give you nothing only what the law allows, which is one dollar, and, furthermore, if you go out of the country on this missionary business, you need never write to me, for I'll not answer you a syllable."

Ruth could only weep and tell him she hoped he would live many years, and that if she joined the missionary society she should engage herself only for a term of six years, and then she would return and devote her entire self to him for the remainder of his days.

"And they'll be short," he added, "long before the six years are ended I shall be sleeping in the ground."

There is a zeal which is not according to knowledge, and Ruth Rover appeared to have imbibed some of it. 'Tis said, in the good book, "Thou shalt love the Lord thy God with all thy heart," and in the same book is also written, "Children obey your parents in the Lord."

One duty never conflicts with another; but Ruth, in her lack of experience, considered herself justified in disobeying her father in this instance, by the words which say, "He that loveth father or mother more than me is not worthy of me." She loved her father, but believed she loved her God more, and for the sacrifice she was making she comforted herself by reading:

"There is no man that hath left house, or brethren, or sisters, or father, or mother, or wife, or children, or lands, for my sake and the gospel's, but he shall receive an hundred-fold now, in this time, houses and brethren, and sisters, and mothers, and children, and lands, with persecutions; and in the world to come eternal life."

Mrs. Rover regarded this subject in a very different light from her husband. She felt that she belonged to the *world,* and that *this* life, with all its flickerings and vanities, was but the prelude to one that was eternal, and whether spent in sorrow or joy it was soon past; and hence she thought that the best way to spend it was in a preparation for that which was to come, and consequently told her daughter to decide on this subject as was most in accordance with her own conscience, and the obedience which she considered due to Him who had the best claims to her services.

We find a few items more in the journal on this subject, and again refer to it:

"Some time after the above date I called again on brother Lindsay to learn the result of his interview with the agent of the Methodist Episcopal Society in my behalf. He informed me that the "committee" could not be assembled on business till the day which had been appointed for their regular meeting, but he said he was so well acquainted with me, with my family and standing in the church, he was willing to receive me as a recipient of the benefits of the education society, on his own responsibility, and he believed the "committee" would approve his choice. He accordingly gave me a letter of introduction to the Principal of Wilbraham Academy,[3] stating to him that I was to enter that academy on the foundation of the Missionary Education Society of the Methodist Episcopal Church in Boston. I have, accordingly, this day come to Wilbraham with a view to being educated as a teacher to the heathen.

"Two years ago I went to B——— with a view to obtain means to educate myself, but the Lord saw fit to frustrate that design *and now, in the same time that I expected to come here at my own expense, the Lord has sent me and inclined his people to furnish me with the means.* This is like our God. His wisdom exceeds our own and His truth and faithfulness never fail. It is my intention to be diligent and make all the improvement I can, and studiously to strive to have my deportment such that my friends of the education society may never regret having made me a recipient of their bounty.

"Still in Wilbraham, and if I have not made great proficiency in natural science, I have made some in moral; and what I have learned of my own heart has nearly discouraged me. I find my mind weak and easily affected, and I have suffered extremely with temptation and disappointment. But hitherto the Lord has helped me, and I discover much wisdom in the arraignment of providence, and only regret that I have not been more submissive and relied with more confidence on God. This summer I was absent from school nearly three months. I labored during that time all that was possible to obtain means to replenish my wardrobe and supply myself with books,—but with the greatest economy in dress I was not able to obtain books. I made my case known to two of the executive committee and they kindly interested themselves for me and presented me with eight dollars and twenty cents, obtained by a collection taken up for that purpose, at a prayer meeting in Boston. I was also favored with a short interview with brother ———, who said he would esteem it a privilege to correspond with me and occasionally to assist me with money. Thus could I see the hand of a benevolent, heavenly parent, supplying all my wants and delivering me from all my perplexities. When at home my father treated me with a coldness bordering on severity, and neither assisted me to any favor or made me welcome to my board; although my mother refused any compensation, I could not but think that my absence would be more acceptable. My sisters were kind, but they so much disapproved of the course I had taken that I did not well enjoy their society. I have left my home feeling much as though I had none and my friends as though they were enemies. This, in a measure, depresses my spirits, but I have an evidence within that God, the mighty God, is my friend, and is and has been doing for my comfort and happiness all that is necessary. He has raised up for me many valuable friends in the Methodist Church for which I am grateful.''

About this time Ruth Rover received the following letter from her brother:

"—— Ill., Oct. 8, '35.

''DEAR SISTER RUTH: Although we have been separated nearly seventeen years, I have not, I believe, held the least intercourse or correspondence by letter with you during the whole period. You must not for a moment presume that a lack of brotherly affection for you has been the cause of my not writing to you particularly, as well as to some of my other sisters, but believe me when I tell you I am incapable of expressing the regard and interest I feel for your prosperity and happiness, and that my negligence was owing altogether to other causes.

''I hope, dear sister, since I have concluded to write, that provided I should differ from you a little in some matters, and say some things rather cross-grained before I close, you will have the goodness to impute it rather to my ignorance of the matter than to a wish to cause you any unpleasant feelings.

''About ten days ago I received a letter from sister Vonsar replete with tenderness and affection. After sympathising and condoling with me for the loss of my wife and child, she informs me of the warm reception and kind offices I may expect from my friends in Massachusetts when I return, and then concludes by saying: ''Our dear sister Ruth has gone to Wilbraham to prepare herself to go as a teacher among the Indians.'' Now this is very grievous—news that I was by no means prepared to hear. My dear sister, if the above is a fact, I beg of you in the name of all you hold dear, be prevailed upon to relinquish the desperate resolution; a resolution which if persisted in will, I fear, bring more sighing and sorrowing upon your relations than if they had followed you to the silent tomb. For my own part, my grief is audible! I lament bitterly to think you possess no more common sense than to be led astray like silly women, to be butchered and tomahawked by the relentless and savage Indians. You very well know, my dear sister, that ever since I have lived in this country there has been a continual and unceasing supplication for me to return, and now, to gratify you all, after an absence of so many years, I will inform you that I have sold my houses, my lots, my almost everything, for the sole purpose of returning and spending my remaining days with you. If your resolution to go is so firmly fixed that you cannot be deterred from it, I insist upon it that you postpone your departure until my return. I must confess that my knowledge of these missions to the Indians is somewhat limited, but from what I *do* know, I am irresistibly led to the conclusion that they are altogether uncalled for, and are senseless squandering and waste of life and treasure; and further, I believe that none but over zealous, enthusiastic fanatics engage in them. You must not blame me for talking plainly—the occasion is one of importance and demands it. Do, I pray you, revolve these things in your mind and reflect well before it is too late to retrace your steps, and write me immediately your determination on the subject. I shall not rest till I hear from you. My dear little Mary and Harriet burst into a flood of tears when I read their aunt's letter to them, and would scarcely believe you had not already gone.

"Mary writes that father is in a very bad state of health and probably will not live long. I do hope and pray that I may see him again in this world; it would be extremely painful to return and find him laid in the dust, and you in a situation more to be deplored.

*   *   *   *   *   *   *   *   *   *

"Let me repeat that I shall expect to hear from you by Christmas or New Year at the farthest, and in the meantime I shall fervently pray that your thoughts on this mission to the Indians will be entirely changed. *   *   *   *

"I remain, as ever, your most loving, affectionate, and anxious brother.

S. ROVER

"P. S. Write me how it happened you got such a wild notion in your head. Convince me you are doing God a service, and I will take back all I have said and ask pardon a thousand times.

S. R."[4]

CHAPTER V

❦

> ———"though the heart
> Be consecrated to the holiest work
> Vouchsafed to mortal efforts, there will be
> Ties of earth around it: and through all
> Its perilous devotion, it must keep
> Its own humanity..."

At Wilbraham Academy Ruth Rover made many agreeable acquaintances and formed some lasting friendships, as letters to be hereafter introduced will show; yet the pleasures to be derived from the pursuits of literature and the advantages of so agreeable a situation were greatly lessened by the unhappy state of feeling which existed between her and one of the teachers to which reference has been made.

"The one great purpose of her heart, however, from which it seems nothing could cause her desires to swerve, is made very apparent in the following first piece of composition she offered the grammar class for correction. We believe it is her first attempt at blank verse, and is introduced not because it is supposed to possess intrinsic merit, but to denote the object which was uppermost in her thoughts. The student will readily perceive the inaccuracies in the measure and the arrangement of the words; and we prefer to present it to the reader in its original form than to attempt to improve it:

"THE MISSIONARY.

"Say not he is not moved—his heart is cold,
No tender feelings vibrate there. What means
That throbbing breast, those stifled sighs? Go see
Him when he prays and wrestles with his God, till he
Is half bedewed with tears, and tell me if
He leaves his home and friends unmoved. Does not
An aged father's hoary hairs announce to him
You'll see my face no more? Does not
A mother's wrinkled brow bespeak to him,
No more, my son, will these fond arms embrace
You round; no more you'll lean upon this breast
And on your cheek receive sweet pledges of
My love; I soon must sleep in death? Do not
The falling tears of brothers, sisters, friends,
Proclaim to him, We may not think to meet
Again but in the world of spirits? And
Is he not affected? Can he pass through
These scenes and never burst a sigh? let fall
A tear? send forth a prayer for needful and
Sustaining grace? Ah! no; his heart's o'ercharged
With pain which he may not express. The grove,
The closet, every place, go with him where
Thou wilt, is witness to the griefs he feels within.

"And would he rather, then, give up
The work assigned him—barter endless bliss
For earthly toys?—for some alluring scenes
Lay down a starry crown—a treasure more
Than earth can boast? e'en life eternal? No!
He that is moved by sympathy can feel
For woe—he hopes to live again, and with
That hope will pass through life's dark pilgrimage
And bear all trial patiently. What means
This flutter in my breast? these tears why drop
They down so fast and quite disfigure what
I write? Shall I who have espoused God's cause
And entered in the field, look back? I
Cannot, do not, will not. No, my throbbing
Heart be still—my eyes keep back your briny
Drops. Cheer up, my soul, obtain the prize, for
Thou shalt live again. This life is but the
Embryo of thy existence. Soon—soon
The morn will break on thy enraptured sight
And souls shall glitter on the heavenly plains,
By thy endeavors in heavenly light
Enshrouded. Will yet not cease, but wound me
Still? Then flow my eyes, and burst my feeling
Soul—but I my Master's work must do."

Among the many acquaintances and friendships which Ruth formed at this school, to which the many cards, notes and keepsakes in her possession bear ample testimony, none was more endearing than that with Miss C. B. Moody, a young lady of great worth and most affectionate disposition.

"During the time passed together by Ruth and Miss Moody their affections became entwined together like those of David and Jonathan, and delightful, refreshing and restoring was the effect produced upon the mind of the former by this sacred friendship; and the regards of the latter may be best denoted by the following note addressed to Ruth on her leaving the school:

"TO MISS RUTH ROVER, *Wilbraham:*

My Dear Sister—It is with no small degree of emotion that I address you on this occasion. I cannot let you go to your home without again expressing my regards for you and asking a continuance of your friendship. By the order of providence we have met and formed an acquaintance and have passed a few fleeting hours together, and now you are called to leave me. Must it be so? Can I now give you the parting hand? I had anticipated spending much more time in your society but now I am compelled to say *farewell.* Would that it could be otherwise! Already does the big tear struggle for release from my eye, in anticipation of the unwelcome scene which I must witness. I have many times been called to part with friends near and dear, but I think I have never felt more keen regret on any former occasion. The pure feelings of friendship I entertain for you, and the prospect you have before you, together with the probability that we part to meet no more, are sufficient to render our parting truly painful. But I would not enhance your unpleasant feelings. I believe your heart is already surcharged with sorrow. I know that you feel much, and feel *deeply,* therefore I would endeavor to lighten your burden and soothe your sorrows. Yes, my dear Ruth, you have *one* friend who feels for you, and, though you leave me, I trust we shall often think of each other, and that with no small degree of emotion.

"Who can know what changes a few short years can make? *You* are probably destined to some far, far distant land, and I, *where?* Alas! me—perhaps while *you* are employing all your talents in teaching the unenlightened savage, your friend C. will be sleeping beneath the clods of yonder valley. These are solemn yet pleasing considerations. How exulting the thought that we shall ere long have done with all the things of earth and ended all our trials here.

"Go, my friend, to yonder distant land—teach the savage the name of the Saviour—teach him to look beyond this world for happiness—teach him that there are substantial joys in religion— teach him there is a God in heaven who careth for him and has paid a ransom for his salvation. And may heaven strengthen you in the arduous undertaking. May you be successful, and finally, should we meet no more on earth, may we meet in that better land where parting will be no more. May heaven make me worthy to meet you there.

"Though you'll be far from me, yet, when I supplicate the throne of grace, I shall ever remember you in your trying situation; and that the grace of God will be sufficient for you till the end of life, is the sincere wish of your friend,

CATHERINE B. MOODY.

> "Farewell, if ever ardent prayer
> For other's weal availed on high,
> Mine shall not all be lost on air
> But waft thy name beyond the sky.''

After spending something more than a year at Wilbraham Academy, Ruth Rover was much pleased when she was informed by the principal that it was Mr. Lindsay's opinion she could leave the school, and though there was not then a prospect of an immediate call being made for a teacher in any foreign mission under their control, yet, by holding herself in readiness, she should be considered the first on the list, and meantime she was at liberty to pursue her own calling, and recommended to take a school if it were possible, thereby the better to progress in the improvement of her own mind.

Mr. Lindsay had visited the academy and conversed with Ruth, and learnt that she was being subjected to severe trials. He instructed and consoled her like a true servant of God, and moreover, as a man who could appreciate her feelings as she thus sacrificed all earthly considerations and prospects for that course in the service of her Maker to which she gave the greatest preference. On bidding her adieu he prayed most earnestly for God's blessing to rest upon her, and putting his hands to her eyes told her to "keep back the tears," and to "look forward to a better land."

Among the names of those persons with whom Ruth became acquainted at Wilbraham and whom she speaks of with christian love and gratitude, is that of Rev. Mr. Raymond, a teacher in the school.[1] Not only (according to her notes) did he ever conduct himself toward her as a true gentleman, but as a man of humane and sympathetic feelings, acting on every occasion as a friend and brother.

Ruth Rover passed a few months in Boston and then visited among her friends, the better to withdraw her hopes from every earthly prospect of happiness, which was likely to increase the regrets she felt on leaving her native land. On this subject she speaks thus in her journal:

"I have thought it better to part with brother ——— now than at a future period, after having given him encouragement by continuing to receive his addresses. If I know what manner of spirit I am of, I know I love God to that degree that I freely give up all for Him who died for me. Father and mother are dear, but they can be surrendered to God. Friends—oh! here's the trial, as in that word is included one whom I esteem the dearest among all earthly friends—but if the word comes *"Go!"* I resign him also, well knowing the time will come, if both are faithful, when we shall meet again."

Some time after this we find Ruth keeping school at Nahant, Lynn. She remained for one term, but so great was her impatience to be away to some mission station that she could not force herself to remain any longer. The school was very interesting, the schoolhouse pleasant and possessed of the advantage of having a fine large library of free access to the teacher and scholars. She had board in an excellent christian family, and she made some acquaintances with persons of intelligence and worth, but her "mind was not at rest." She ever felt that she was wasting time to be employed thus, and her greatest anxiety was to be engaged among the heathen. With these feelings, she felt compelled to inform the committee, at the close of the term, that she must forgo the pleasure of teaching the school any longer, and having bidden farewell to her scholars and friends she returned to the society of her sister in Malden.

CHAPTER VI

VOYAGING

❦

Ruth had passed but two days with her sister, when the Rev. Messrs. Pierce[1] and Leland[2] called and informed her that an opportunity then presented itself for her to become a teacher to the heathen, if such were her desire. She had been a member of the church under Mr. Pierce's pastoral care, and he was aware that she had been for some time most anxiously awaiting an appointment to some missionary station. In her own words we can best present the prospect before her:

"Mr. Leland previously to his embarking for this mission, in view of the ill health of his wife and the number of his family, made known to the board his resolution to not proceed to the mission field without they would provide means for him to take into his family a female domestic. They consented to provide for her maintenance by sufficiently increasing his salary for that purpose, and paying her passage to Oregon. He was not able to obtain such a domestic during the season in which he was making preparations for his departure until the time previous to that in which the vessel was to sail, had expired within ten days.

"It was known that *I* had been for some time waiting for a situation as teacher in some mission, and was recommended to him as a suitable person to be so employed, provided it were agreeable to me thus to go. I was interrogated on the subject and objected. It was then proposed that, as there was not time to obtain an appointment for me from the board at New York, I should accompany Mr. Leland without one; depending on him for my support until the board should be apprised of the measure and send me an appointment. To this I did not particularly object, but my friends urged the propriety of a pledge being given by these ministers, under whose auspices I left home, that I should be employed *as a teacher* in Oregon, when I should have reached that country, which was given me. Mr. Leland said, in presence of several gentlemen, that he did not wish or expect me to serve him or his family, but he wished my company merely for the pleasure of his wife, as she was not well, and might sometimes very much desire a female associate. Mr. Leland also promised, before these gentlemen, that he would be to me in every sense a *father,* and would provide for me as he would for one of his own daughters, which promise he several times repeated to my brother![3]

"PLEDGE"

"Lynn, January 16, '37

"To Miss Ruth Rover:

   "Dear Sister—We, whose names are undersigned, do hereby pledge ourselves that you shall be employed and sustained *as a teacher* in the Oregon mission, when you shall, by the providence of God, arrive in that station. If the board at New York do not do this, we pledge ourselves to do it.

TIMOTHY MERRITT,

THOMAS C. PIERCE,

N. S. SPALDING,

J. HORTON,

R. SPALDING,

D. S. KING,

D. LESLIE,

H. K. W. PERKINS,[4]

A. STEVENS."

The time being very short which could be employed in making preparations for the voyage, her friends in Saugus, with great kindness and alacrity, exerted themselves to assist her, and assembling in the parsonage, most industriously prepared for her comfort and convenience every article their kindly feelings could suggest, to render her comfortable at sea and for a length of time after she should have arrived at her place of destination. Presents were sent in by the people of the town till there was scarcely room for more.

This had been the place of her birth and childhood, and where she had for about ten years attended school, hence they felt, as some expressed themselves, as if they were "preparing a child to leave them" and the attachment of mother, sister, and brother could not exceed that which was manifested by the good people of Saugus on this occasion.

Her own sister, the Rev. Mrs. B. of Malden, though greatly opposed to the step she had taken, yet made every possible exertion for her comfort and convenience. As also another sister, Mrs. H. of Saugus. Her brother, S. Rover, who had written her from Illinois, when she was at school at Wilbraham, and who had ever been so utterly unreconciled to her becoming a missionary to the Indians, now devoted himself entirely to her interest—procuring and preparing for her every article which others named, or which his own generous thought could devise, to render her happy.

Every preparation being now made and the time nearly arrived for the reinforcement to sail, Ruth endeavored to nerve her mind to bid farewell to her father, by appropriating to herself every text of scripture which she could consider applicable, till she considered she was well approved by heaven; and this thought was sufficient to encourage and strengthen her. Weak child! how erroneous your judgment! how fatal your decision!

Right, although it might have been, for Ruth to devote herself to the work of the missions, yet we verily believe she was wrong in point of time. Had she been content to have waited a better offering for her to go, she could have devoted herself to her father's service while he lived—obtained the legacy of his blessing to have cheered her own heart till she should have descended to the tomb, and found *but one short year taken* from those which she wished to have devoted exclusively to the missionary work in a foreign field. And who can tell how different the course and events of her life would have been? What trials might have been averted and what blessings bestowed, had she, after performing her duty to her earthly parent, been resigned to the disposition which her heavenly Father should have made of her.

She reached her father's house about midnight, accompanied by her sister and brother-in-law. The old gentleman received them affectionately, complained of ill health and seemed depressed in spirit. He conversed with tolerable freedom till he had been informed by the brother-in-law that Ruth had come home to bid him farewell, for she was to sail in a few days for Oregon. He said no more to his daughter, but told Mr. B. that if she persisted, he was fully determined to disinherit her and no more recognize her as his child.

In the morning, when ready to leave Ruth had taken the parting hand with all the family, her mother included, and approached her father. She earnestly begged his forgiveness—expressed her determination to return home after six years and serve him faithfully—entreated him to answer her letters—imprinted many kisses upon his cheek, and left him in tears. During all this he spoke not, but his feelings were betrayed by his tears which fell profusely.

Men seldom weep, and 'twere wisdom if women would weep less. Tears afford relief to the o'ercharged heart—but it were better to think lightly of sorrows, as they are so soon past, than to weaken the nerves by pondering over them, while we cannot in this way make the number less.

Mr. Rover loved his daughter, and the keen disappointment he felt on her leaving the States, together with the conviction which he seemed to carry about with him that he should not live to see her return, caused this weakness.

It was the expressed wish of Messrs. Pierce and Leland that Miss Rover should not attend the farewell missionary meeting in Boston, with the mission family, but, while *they* should attend there, she, according to their request, should attend a farewell meeting of a similar kind, held in Saugus. The reason of this arrangement was, as one said, that Mr. Leland's family might realize the advantages of the most interesting occasion without the interest being divided.

When Ruth joined them in Boston she received: From the hand of Rev. N. S. Spalding, $50.00; the Saugus collection by the same, $26.00; and by Rev. J. C. Pierce, $24.00. The whole one hundred dollars being considered her outfit for the Oregon mission.

The members of the reinforcement were now considered as *one family,* and many presents were sent to the vessel in which they were to sail, directed to *"The Mission Family."*

Her favorite sister, Mrs. B., left in her hand an affectionate letter, in which she gave her some good advice. She says:

"Your friends have done much for you—O! remember 'tis all of God and be determined to devote your all to Him. This is now a time of prosperity with you. Don't let the enemy creep in here. Don't forget your dependence on Divine grace. If you knew, like me, the danger of relying on human strength, you would rely on that arm alone which can save you.

"I have been much dejected to-day in view of the trials and exposures to which you will undoubtedly be subjected on your passage at sea, and when you shall arrive at a foreign shore and be situated among strangers. Nothing but the grace of life can sustain you in going, and us in surrendering you for this purpose.

"Go, sister, go, but with thee bear
A sister's wish, a sister's prayer."

The members of this reinforcement were Rev. Mr. Leland, his wife and three daughters; Rev. Mr. Perkins, and Ruth Rover. They sailed from Boston on the 23rd of Jan. '37, in the brig Peru, Capt. Kilham, of Boston.

They had also in company, two or three gentleman passengers destined to the Sandwich Islands.

We cannot find any record of this voyage, and presume if any were kept it is with the friends of Ruth in Massachusetts.[5] We have, however, a few letters before us, written at different periods while at sea, and from which we will make some extracts. The first date is:

"Brig Peru, Jan. 25, '37.

"BELOVED SISTER: The most keen and painful feelings I have felt at parting were realized when I took the last look at Boston, when the vessel left the wharf. I had left a large circle of true friends, to whom I was much indebted, and whose kindness I expect to be never able to repay. The word farewell, as it involuntarily fell from my lips, was accompanied with indescribable emotions. My prayers for your happiness were never more urgent than at that moment, and I the more earnestly besought *God* to bless you, as I was satisfied *I* could never return the kind acts of your love.

"I wish I was near enough to you this fine morning to converse without having to wait for my pen to commit my words to paper, and then some months, perhaps, before I shall receive your replies. In a ball of yarn I found, to-day, a scrap of paper concealed by you, on which you had written many assurances of your love to me and regrets at my leaving, &c. I was much gratified. What so consoling, in a trying moment as the voice of friendship? What so cheering in this lower world as the evidence of affection in our acquaintance?

"I have, notwithstanding the disagreeableness of the weather, attended considerably to reading, writing and working, and anticipate much more pleasure therein, after the weather shall have become settled. I have reviewed my journals and manuscripts with much satisfaction, as I see the hand of God in ordering the events of my life; and I cannot repine that I was disappointed in a union with those I loved; as to that disappointment I am indebted for the agreeable situation in which I am now placed."

"I take much pleasure in working for those on board who cannot use the needle. I have made for the steward, cook, and waiter, each a cloth cap; have made a new coat and mended old ones—and have made aprons for the steward, &c., &c. The rest of the time I employ in working for myself, reading, writing, painting, drawing, studying, star-gazing, and exercising on deck and in the cabin. So you see I need not be idle. Sometimes I have a pleasant discussion with one or more of the passengers, on different subjects, which prevents the wheels of time from always passing heavily. I have other exercises, too, which are still more pleasant—I have seasons of devotion, when I am peculiarly favored with the Spirit's influence, and find my mind greatly invigorated by meditation on divine subjects.

"This morning there were several sails in sight, and I hoped to have been able to send my letters, but they have all passed without speaking us. They were not very social, because, perhaps, they thought we might be too much that way inclined. The shore of Brazil is so near that we can readily distinguish the trees. Two fishermen on a raft passed directly by us this morning. It was very reviving to see a new human countenance, after being so long shut up in this small place. A curious fish, which is called the nautilus, or man-of-war, is sometimes seen on the surface of the water. It carries a fibrous sail, which it unfurls when its suits its convenience.

"A tremendous shower last night kept the officers and men up all night. Poor fellows! how hard they have to toil who get their living on the seas. We have frequently sudden tempests which continue about ten minutes, and threaten to overwhelm us in the deep; but hitherto we have been preserved; and are blessed with good health, good spirits, and unnumbered blessings.

"Not yet any religious exercises on the Sabbath. The seamen and passengers complain bitterly and say, "If these preachers cannot preach or pray here, they are not fit men to be missionaries." O! dear, 'tis hard to be an occasion of reproach to the ungodly.

"We have all things in order on board, I assure you. Charley and steward tend the table, which is set in style. The knives ever shining like polished silver, and the spoons and castors glowing with brilliancy. Our food is well prepared, and relished with smiles and compliments from the officers and passengers. I often say, where now are all the kind friends I left at home? and the good will and kind heartedness, and benign affections, and peace, and pleasure of all together?—where are they?—far, far away! The big tear will start—the heart will feel, and groan, and suffer; nor would I have it otherwise. You have won my *best affections,* dear brother and sister. You have been to me of all earthly friends *the best,* and you have ('tis all I have to give) my unfailing friendship and my constant prayers for your prosperity and happiness.

"*March* 6th. Yesterday we had religious services for the first time since we have been out. Mr. Leland spoke from the words, "What is truth?" The gentlemen spread an awning over the deck to screen us from the sun, and we found it very pleasant to sit thus quietly in a fine day, on the smooth ocean, and listen to the words of divine truth. Let me tell you, I have delightful religious exercises. I find a sweet submission of my own will to the will of God. In prayer, ''Thy will be done,'' is the sweetest language I can employ to express my feelings. So judiciously has my heavenly Father ordered the events of my life, and so agreeably to my best wishes have they thus far terminated, that I cannot but submit all my interests to his direction—and O! how I mourn that I was so repining and unbelieving in those times when thick darkness covered my path.

''We are within a few miles of St. Catherine's. The view of the coast is very fine indeed, and if it were not the Sabbath day I would give you a sketch of it. You cannot imagine how pleasantly we pass our time. Occasional accidents and exposure to dangers, cause us, when free from them, to rejoice in the many mercies and favors which we receive.

''The anxieties and cares which devolve upon our captain are very great, and I never knew a *christian* conduct himself in seasons of trial with more prudence, or sustain himself amidst difficulties with greater composure and fortitude than does Capt. Kilham.

''Our sympathies ought to be awakened for the seamen. We should consider how great are their deprivations, and exposures, and sufferings, when we are comfortably situated in our happy dwellings, secure from storms and the dangers of the deep.

''A squall of wind has helped us into the harbor of St. Catherine's, and we have just dropped anchor. I really wish I could describe to you this beautiful coast. On the mountain tops rest the clouds—their sides and the valleys are admirably covered with green shrubbery and grass—and occasionally appears, near the water's edge, or on the mountain side, a neat white cottage.

''Capt. Cathcart, said to be from Nantucket, who resides on the Brazilian coast—having married a Portuguese lady—earnestly requested us of the mission family to take up our residence at his house, while the brig proceeds to the island to make repairs. We were most happy to accept his invitation, and are now enjoying the hospitalities of this very hospitable people. Mrs. Cathcart does not speak English, but renders herself very agreeable by her attentions and acts of kindness to us. She will have her slaves wait upon us, taking all our wardrobe to the springs in the mountains for washing, and returning them beautifully fresh and clean, and refusing any compensation. Every day I wander about the plantations, seeking and finding ever new delights in this enchanting place. Beauty is seen everywhere and in everything. The air is filled with birds of every variety of colored plumage, and with insects of rich and varied lustre. Wild flowers, which no art or cultivation can improve in splendor—tropical fruits in a richness and variety luxury could never wish excelled—insects astonishing you with the order and occupations of their lives—and, in short, every delight in scenery and production, which is necessary to make the place a paradise, is here. Here are found oranges, lemons and limes in great abundance—the ground literally covered with those which have ripened and fallen from the trees, while *on* the trees are seen those of all sizes, many nearly ripe, and the contrast of these with the young oranges, which are always as green as the leaf, is very beautiful. The blossoms, too, follow the fall of the ripe fruit almost immediately, and hence, on the orange trees may be seen at all times flowers and fruit of different degrees of perfection, from the smallest to the perfectly ripe. This tree knows no change of seasons. The coffee and cotton plants are also novelties to me; and the pine apple I have never seen growing before, and here are large fields of them, growing each upon a single stalk and the apple not more than a foot from the ground. The prickly pear is also a curiosity. That frightful looking plant which you cultivate with so much care in your parlor window, grows here a large tree, the bulk of the size of a person's waist, and is as ugly looking as anything you could wish to see in nature. The fruit, however, is delicious. It grows about the size of the common apple—looks as forbidding and disagreeable as the tree itself, but on examining it you find it perfectly white, interspersed with fine seeds, very sweet, soft, and rich. 'Tis very hard to obtain, as it grows high upon the guarded stalk, and woe be to him, who with unqualified hands, shall attempt to gain it. With much difficulty a Portuguese gentleman who, with his wife, was taking me to view the shore on another part of the coast, obtained one for me, and as I ate and admired its delicacy and richness, I could not help expressing my astonishment at the contrast between its internal excellence and outward appearance.

"I often observe, in my rambles, processions of emmets, one following another, and each with a bit of orange leaf in his mouth, for a distance of a quarter of a mile or more, and to which I never find the end. Spiders, too, would frighten you from the size. I have seen them three or four inches in length. Butterflies are numerous and of a splendor I never before saw equalled. This gentleman, to-day, caught one in his hat which would measure, I believe, five inches between the tips of its wings, and was of a rich blue color, speckled with gold.

You may conceive of the beauty of the smaller insects from the fact that the native women collect their wings for the manufacture of wreaths to adorn their persons.

"From the feathers of birds, in hues which nature has given them, are made those fine feather flowers, of which you have seen some specimens; and from *sea shells,* without any artificial decorations, are also formed elegant boquets, one of which I send you. You will perceive that the roses, buds, and other flowers, are in the natural form and color of the shells, and the green leaves are fashioned from sea weed. Nature here performs her own adorning and provides her own material.

"To Capt. Cathcart and family we shall ever be indebted. I did not even *attempt* to cancel my obligations, for all I could do was to offer a few presents to the slaves. We left this enchanting spot with regret, although wishing to proceed on our voyage."

When approaching Valparaiso, Ruth writes to the same sister:

"How much I wish I could see you, and to you confide all my troubles. I am unpleasantly situated in some respects. The many little petty annoyances which one unavoidably meets on a long voyage, cannot in a small vessel be shook off by an occasional visit to a friend, or a walk, or a ride, but we must bear them, hoping for the time when we shall be again on terra firma and free as birds. Among other disagreeables which I have to encounter, is the infidel conversation of Mr. Perkins. He ever seems to think he can convince me that our faith is erroneous—that he has discovered a new and a better way, and urges me to read the books which have fallen into his hands. Sometimes I consent to read some passages, but this indulgence is ever followed with darkness and condemnation of mind; and he is so confident of his own ability to rightly appreciate the divine word, that 'tis useless for me to reason with him. He says I am not "*Logically qualified* enough to contend with those who have received collegiate educations!"—and I know I am not *conceitedly qualified* enough to argue with one so superior in point of intellectual acquirements and capacities. He calls himself a Utilitarian.[6]

"Our captain has been during the voyage very anxious about the event of passing Cape Horn—even saying that if he were only safely past it he would be happy. We did safely pass that point, and attempt to run up along the coast of Patagonia. The captain was in high spirits—came below and offered the passengers extra refreshments and delicacies, but while partaking them a head wind

met us and blew us far south, where we had to remain for three weeks
and endure the cold, the rain, and gales, &c., &c., so common in
these latitudes, until we thought that the next time, at least, we would
remember our dependence till we were out of danger. Besides the
stormy days, the nights were rendered unpleasant and sleepless by
violent winds and the rolling of the vessel. With all my efforts to
retain my self-possession, I have sometimes become disconcerted. I
had flattered myself considerably in my adroitness in preparing for
the violent motions of the vessel, so as to preserve myself from
accident, but I must resign the palm to others, for I have many times
had my work-basket upset and all its varied contents thrown about
the cabins—have found myself, when dressing, thrown immediately
before the open door, in view of the gentlemen—have spilled my
plate of soup time and time again, and been thrown from the table,
food in hand, against the side of the cabin, and had the vexation to
perceive, on recovering myself, that the captain was laughing at me,
&c., &c., till I have made up my mind that I, too, must be submissive
to old Neptune, and think lightly of his wayward habits.''

CHAPTER VII

VOYAGING CONTINUED.

❧

"Valparaiso is very singular in appearance, viewed from the harbor. Built upon the side of a mountain the houses appear to be contiguous, and you obtain the idea that a heavy shower of rain would wash them all into the sea. They are built mostly of adobes and never of more than one story, on account of frequency of earthquakes which happen in this region. A few of these are boarded in front and painted white. We took lodgings to day with Mrs. W———. Mrs. Capt. Scott has just called and invited us to her house to tea. There are but three American ladies resident here. Gentlemen, however, from almost all parts of the world throng the place on matters of business, and soldiers numbering about seventeen hundred, from the sloops-of-war lying in the bay, added to a population of several thousand, caused no small degree of bustle about the mountains. The Chilians are also making preparations for war with Peru, and I can find no time for walking but early in the morning. The scenery here is grand, but there is little of that luxury in the productions of nature which is so manifest at St. Catherine's. The mountains are almost barren of vegetation, but in a few nooks and crannies of the valleys I have seen very good plants. The native women, however, cultivate flowers to a great extent, in their small door-yards, and many of these are of a most enchanting beauty. The different species of geranium, of some tender slips of which you are so proud, grow here to bushes as large as the hazel bush in Massachusetts. Indeed it is a splendid plant, and seems to grow on scanty soil as well as any,

❦

and I verily believe depends more on the atmosphere for its healthy and beautiful appearance than on the ground.

"The natives are Spanish and Portuguese, and a more hospitable and agreeable people I don't believe inhabit any part of the earth. I cannot pass these little, unpretending houses, without being saluted by the ladies, invited in to rest and to see the flowers, and literally burdened with boquets when I leave. And when I walk on the mountains, if I meet a milk-maid who has been to milk her cows, I must take a drink of milk from the pitcher. Nor is *money* the object, for 'tis always refused when proferred. If hospitable and kindly feelings render people so agreeable, let me possess and cherish them as long as I live."

At Callao, Ruth did not go on shore, but of the natural productions she says:

"The gentlemen bring and send fruits and flowers in abundance to the vessel, perhaps in consequence of the deprivation I suffer in not going on shore. The flowers, I think, must have come from the garden of Eden, if I am to judge from their splendor and richness. The fruits are new to us and very delicious. Among them are the pomegranate, cherrymoi,[1] and the fruit of the passion flower. The pomegranate is the least agreeable to the taste of any other."

[From Zion's Herald]

LETTER FROM ONE OF THE MISSIONARIES

The friends of Miss Ruth Rover, one of the missionaries who sailed from this port in January, 1837, for the Oregon mission, have furnished us with one of her letters recently received. The first date in the letter is made at Callao Harbor, Peru, June 4th, and the last at the Sandwich Islands, Aug. 9th.

We make some extracts from it, not because it contains any missionary news, strictly speaking, but for the purpose of letting our readers into the heart of a devoted missionary, while on her passage to the scene of her future labors. Here they may see how grace will sustain that heart, in absence from friends most dear, in fears that depress, in loneliness which dejects, and in the despondency of the heart, when the sweet remembrances of home press upon the heart with irresistible power:

"BELOVED BROTHER AND SISTER: I am again so situated that my thoughts are irresistibly led to the society of loved ones in New England, and especially to that of yours. Our vessel anchored in this harbor last Friday evening, (June 2d). All our passengers have gone ashore, and the captain and first mate. Brother Leland and family have gone on board the sloop Enterprise, where he is to conduct divine worship. My disposition for solitude, led me to prefer spending the time by myself.

"Since I have been on board, I have again commenced the reading of the New Testament in course, and it never before was attended with so much pleasure to my mind. I never before so viewed the Saviour in divine character. I never so loved, so adored the Son of God. Insensible and undeserving as I am, and notwithstanding I have so often lost divine influences by my carelessness, I am often, when reading the words of Christ, nearly overpowered by a sense of the excellency and glory of his character. With the bible for my treasure, I find the yoke of Christ is easy, and his burden is light. My whole soul is alive to the sentiment when I repeat:

"I thank thee, uncreated Sun,
  That the bright beams on me have shined;
I thank thee who hast overthrown
  My foes, and healed my wounded mind.
I thank thee, whose enlivening voice
  Bids my free heart in thee rejoice."

"I am glad to find myself on the passage to the Sandwich Islands, for which we left Callao last evening. While at that place we were requested to visit the sloop-of-war North Carolina, and were much pleased with the appearance of a school on board of her. There are two able teachers for the instruction of sixty boys, and twenty midshipmen.

"My time at Callao passed pleasantly, except for the pain I received by witnessing the profligacy of some on board our vessel. One of our officers lost his office by being on shore in a state of intoxication, and without leave for more than forty-eight hours. Coming to bid me farewell, and confessing his fault, I exhorted him to turn from his bad habits and be a better and a happy man, when he, with tears of penitence and sorrow, said to me: "Why have you not conversed with me on this subject during the voyage? You might have saved me." Reproof coming from such a wicked man, I assure you, was not very grateful to the feelings of a missionary.*

"We crossed the equator last night. We have the finest weather imaginable, and are making our way rapidly and pleasantly. Our

---

*This person, some months afterwards, at a religious meeting in Saugus, Mass., said he had lately abandoned a profligate course of life and was endeavoring to live like a christian, and he had been brought to make this resolution by conversing with one *Ruth Rover* a missionary teacher—not knowing he was among her friends.

star-light and moon-light nights induced me, a short time since, to
leave my berth and take a ramble on deck about midnight. All was as
quiet and beautiful as nature could be. I enjoyed the season the
better, as I was conscious no eye but the Invisible was upon me, for
even the watch appeared to be asleep.

"I had a very comforting season this morning, in praying God
to enable me to spend every moment of my future life, entirely to the
good of his cause. I wish to be useful in private conversation. I have
already seen some good effects arising from pointed conversations
with individuals on the conversion of their souls, and I take much
pleasure in this duty. I desire in future at every opportunity, to
recommend a life of purity and consecration to God.

"This day has been exceedingly pleasant. Just clouds enough
have floated in the atmosphere to prevent the rays of the sun being
too warm and bright; and a good breeze has filled our sails while the
ocean's wide and beautiful expanse, with its surface alternately
variegated with black fish, whales and flying fish, and the scenery
above us rendered beautiful by the appearance of tropical birds have
produced in my heart grateful adorations to Him who made them all.

July 4th. "This is not a very cheerful day to me, though our
friends seem to possess the joyful feelings so prevalent among our
countrymen on the day of independence. My mind has been made
solemn by excessive weeping yesterday, occasioned by reminiscences
of the past. After my feelings had become excited, they would not
leave the sweet remembrances of home, but completely triumphed
over me, and while my tears fell in streams, seemed to rejoice at the
desolation of my heart. To-day I feel a loneliness and a solemnity of
spirit which I cannot describe. But, after all, I would not exchange
my situation with many others who are much flattered and caressed.

July 29th. "Arrived at the Sandwich Islands this morning, and
in two hours found the presbyterian missionaries on board to
welcome us to their homes. I will write you the particulars in another
letter."

"Honolulu, August 2, 1837.

"MY DEAR BROTHER: We are finally settled for a short time at
the Island of Oahu, after having been on our passage to this
place one hundred and eighty-seven days. It has been to me an
unusually interesting space of time. Throughout our voyage I have
admired the wonders of the mighty ocean, as well as the beauties of
the firmament above; I have adored that providence which has

protected and blessed me; and I have constantly rejoiced at the step I have taken. Our captain, one of the most agreeable of men, has exceeded, in his kindness and attentions to us, our most sanguine expectations, and has endeared himself to our memory in a manner that can never be forgotten.

"Notwithstanding there has been so great a reformation among the native population of these islands, yet the *foreigners* are in a situation truly deplorable, and very great hostility is indulged among them against all missionary operations, and indeed against every exertion which individuals are making for moralizing and christianizing the human family.

"This day I have been to the top of Punch Bowl Hill, which is very steep and of difficult ascent. Long before I reached the top I found it quite necessary to climb with my hands as well as feet. On the top are placed several cannon for the defence of the island.

"Accompanied by Mr. Hall,[2] I took a ride the other day, on horseback, to what is called the Pari. It is truly a delightful and romantic spot, on the opposite side of the island. I could by no means learn the height of the lofty peaks, and can only say they are immensely high and were doubtless formed by volcanic action, as the rocks in the vicinity have a good deal the appearance of blacksmith's cinders. The summits of these mountains are very fertile, being indeed about the only part of the island watered by the rain of heaven. The soil of the low land is also very rich, but owing to the lack of rain vegetation is generally very backward. A few of the residents have succeeded very well in the cultivation of plants, but they are obliged to water them daily.

"I am not pleased with the scenery of Oahu, about the town. The mountains are very rugged in appearance, probably thrown up by volcanic action; there is but little shrubbery apparent—a few cocoa nut trees with their scarcity of foliage but render the barreness of the place the more apparent. You may walk along the dusty streets and scarcely see the indications of a resident's house, the high mud walls so completely screening them from view.

"The advantages of missionary effort among these natives is, I think, most apparent in the manner of their spending the Sabbath. Their immense large thatched church is ever well filled with attentive hearers, mostly sitting upon mats on the ground, and after church they are not seen strolling about the streets or heard engaged in any boisterous conversation. They evidently consider the Lord's day is not *their* day, and appear to use it as property they feared to injure.

"The missionaries and many of the residents have excelled, in their efforts to benefit us, beyond our conceptions, and we *cannot* soon forget them."

"Barque Sumatra,
"Columbia River,
"Waiting for a Breeze.

"DEAR BROTHER: Again on the water, but not as pleasantly situated as when on board the Peru. I fancy one will hardly ever again find so fine a vessel, officers, and accommodations, as we found, who were six months thus highly favored on our passage from Boston to the Sandwich Islands. We are now on board the Sumatra, Capt. Duncan, in the service of the Hudson Bay Company, but we are not at home. The vessel is good, but not new; the sailors are brave and faithful, but they are so different from Americans; the captain is very kind and attentive to our wants, but he is not Capt. Kilham; my stateroom is commodious, and my bed gives me repose, but it is not the after-cabin of the Peru, neither is my bed as comfortable as the hard mattress I reposed on there.

"There are with us about twenty Howaiins, destined to Oregon in the service of the Hudson Bay Company. These, when we have a calm, are delighted with pranks in the water; jumping from the decks and yards into it, disappearing for some time, then rising with a shout. The females, also, are quite as fearless in this element as the men.

"Messrs. Leland and Perkins have gone to Vancouver, and Mrs. Leland, the daughters and myself remain on board till the vessel shall arrive there. The canoe which took them up has just returned. Brother Shepherd sends me a note of congratulation on my safe arrival, and remarks that the harvest is truly great, but the laborers are few.[3] Indeed, I had learned that before I had proceeded thus far up the river. The degradation of the females, to say nothing of the others, is sufficient to call forth the deep sympathies of the sympathetic, and fire their bosoms with ardor to exert every faculty in the labor of convincing them of the errors of their course.

Sept. 12th. "A week last night in the river, and only half way to Fort Vancouver! I assure you I am very lonely. The scenery around us is grand, yet I cannot enjoy it alone. The evenings, particularly, are exceedingly lovely, the banks of the river are clothed quite to the water's edge with tall spruce and hemlock trees, and while we are lying at anchor with the moon beaming her resplendence upon us, and the water around smooth and glittering in the moonbeams, it is then I wish, as I sit alone upon the deck, that my dear brother was with me, to behold and enjoy these works of nature, and expatiate on the grand works of creation.

"We have just passed an Indian burying ground. I beheld in it, not those stately monuments to mark the place where the dead repose, which are generally the pride of Europeans, but a number of canoes nearly decayed, with the bodies enshrouded in the garments, and surrounded by the property of the deceased. This is the most common way of disposing of the dead among the Indians. Some, however, burn the body, and gather the ashes, with the chattels of the dead, which is seldom much more than a blanket, put them in his canoe, and place it upon an elevated part of the land or the rocks, and leave it for the slow hand of time to mingle with its kindred earth. I found two dead bodies at Fort George, (formerly Astoria) one upon the high land in a canoe, the other in a coarse box raised upon stakes, with a rude image of death in its front. I had the audacity to take away some ornaments from it and the canoe, which I will send you by and by. We receive frequent visits from the Indians as we slowly pass up the river. They appear perfectly friendly, often bringing us deer's and bear's meat, salmon, berries, &c., for which, if they receive a glass of spirits, they appear to consider themselves well paid.

"I observed, at Fort George, the burying place of an European, neatly enclosed with a white fence, and overgrown with tall shrubbery, through which I observed a white marble monument with the following inscription: "In memory of D. McTavish, Esq., aged 42, drowned in crossing this river, May 22, 1814.''[4]

"The two voyages I have taken since I left home have been very different from each other; the latter was like going to sea with sailors, the former like spending a winter evening in a circle of agreeable and accomplished friends. There are, indeed, with us, some who make low bows, and observe the ordinary forms of etiquette; but the refinement of the mind is wanting, and this deficiency renders these external accomplishments more odious.

Sept. 14th. "Anchored, last evening, a mile from Fort Vancouver, and proceeded to the fort this morning in a canoe. Dr. McLaughlin entertains us while we stay.[5]

Sept. 16th. "I was, this morning, sighing for a ride on horseback, that I might, by the exercise, overcome some of the stupid feelings which for so long a time attended me, depriving me of the enjoyment attendant on a life of activity. I had not long waited for the horses to be in readiness, when Bro. Shepherd requested my assistance in opening the clothing for the mission, which had lately been sent them. By half past one I had them all spread in the sun; in the extensive field of Dr. McLaughlin, and such a display! Such a variety, tissue, texture in such a land, for such a purpose! I really gazed upon them with admiration, and involuntarily exclaimed, "The desert blossoms as a rose." They appeared like so many monuments rising without design to give glory to God and credit to the benevolent in New England. I was particularly pleased with the evidences of sound judgment displayed in the choice of articles. Here were colored shirts, common factory gowns, crash pants,[6] &c., coarse, strong, and cheap, precisely the right kind to meet the wants of these natives. By five o'clock I had these folded again, and myself in readiness for a ride, accompanied by Dr. Tolmy, the resident physician at the fort.[7] I had a very pleasant ride through the prairies and over the high lands, and to-night feel completely tired for the first time during seven months.

Sept. 18th. "Bade farewell to kind ones at Vancouver, this morning at 11 o'clock, and embarked on board a canoe, for the mission house, in company with Mr. L——— and family, and Bro. D. Lee;[8] also had with us two Indians to paddle, and a plenty of baggage to annoy us; kept upon the water, in the rain, mist and dampness, until our vessel struck a stump in the centre of the river, and tore away her head, when we put on shore for the night, made a fire, and sought repose under the trees, while the rain was descending upon us as fast as we could desire. I placed myself beneath a projecting old tree, with my head on the roots and my body on the mud, with no other shelter but the limbs and a blanket. I mistake: Bro. Lee spread an umbrella over my head when I was nearly asleep, which perhaps did much towards preventing the bad consequences of such exposure.

"I proceeded in the morning, and remained until one o'clock without any nourishment, although the day before I had taken but one slice of bread beside my breakfast, all in consequence of ——— mismanagement and inattention to me. Took some tea and bread this afternoon at Bro. Shepherd's tent, at the falls, (where he stops to take charge of goods belonging to the mission, as they proceed up the river.) and received many assurances of friendship from him and Bro. Lee, which tended greatly to raise my spirits and console my troubled mind. After this refreshment I strayed away to the falls, and finding myself too weak to walk much, I reclined on a log, and indulged in long and melancholy, yet gratifying reflections. I there reclined my head on my dear Redeemer's breast, and received many assurances of love and consolation from heaven, saying, ''Fear not for I am with you.''

Sept. 20th. ''Half an hour before sunset, left the water finally, but had fifteen miles to ride on horseback. After travelling, partly in darkness and partly by moonlight, over and through almost every variety of rough and level country, joined our friends at half past twelve on the mission ground in the Oregon Territory. I partook of the supper kindly provided for us; and not caring much to converse, I amused myself by observing the pleasure others enjoyed in reading their letters, and hearing their expressions of joy at the good news they received.

*   *   *   *   *   *   *   *   *   *   *   *

''Our mission is on the Willamette river, the Multnomah of geographers, a branch of the Columbia. The Indians are exceedingly kind, bringing us mats, rushes, &c. While I am now writing, there is an Indian woman before me on her knees, gazing most intently at my movements, thinking, probably, that what I am doing is a great wonder. There are also six young Indians in the room, nearly naked, some with a piece of flannel around them tied on one shoulder, and others with a piece of deerskin about them, and a deep fringe around their loins, with their long hair dangling about their shoulders. Poor things! I wish I had enough clothes to cover them. I have disposed of nearly every article of my own clothes that is possible to spare; I wish I had more to distribute gratuitously. The Mr. Lees do not *give away* clothes only to those in their care. Most of the above articles are for the natives, and if you find any good friend disposed to contribute anything I have named, or anything else, for me to give the Indians, who are not receiving benefit from the mission, I should be extremely thankful. I am happy in my labors, though not engaged in school-keeping. I visit the natives, talk with them, as well as I can, sing and pray with them, hoping the Spirit of God may impart to their minds serious impressions.''

CHAPTER VIII

"Face thine enemies—accusers;
Scorn the prison, rack or rod!
And, if thou hast truth to utter
Speak and leave the rest to God."

Ruth Rover is now on mission ground—that *holy* place where she had so long desired to be, and among those devoted servants of God with whom she had most ardently wished to associate—that people who had *left all* to *follow Christ*—among whom she had expected to find "fathers, mothers, sisters, and brothers." But, alas! she is still on earth—in the kingdom of this world. Men may have changed the place, but they have kept their nature. They find the same hearts with them on mission ground, as they had to mourn over in their native land.

We have accompanied Ruth through her preparatory course and over the seas to the field of her future labors, through which we shall also attend her; but we shall not always find sunny skies and perennial flowers—smooth seas and golden twilights—invigorating and perfumed gales—hospitable and loving hearts; but clouds and storms, and blight-raging billows, and threatening skies—sickening miasmas, and fiend-like hatred; converting this glorious earth into the abode of demons, and appropriating these sublime intelligences which we feel within the heart, and which well might lead us to fellowship with the holy and eternal Omnipotent of the skies, appropriating them to the base purposes of hatred, detraction, and revenge!—employments fit only to occupy the attentions of the spirits of Tartarus.

As a compiler, we should much prefer to omit this part of the work, but consider it our duty to proceed, inasmuch as these occurrences had so great an influence on the life of the subject of these memoirs.

The relation which Ruth held to Mr. Leland's family has been explained, and it may be rendered somewhat more clear by making a few quotations from a letter addressed to her on the subject, during the voyage to the Islands, by the Rev. Mr. Perkins. He says:

"Brother Leland is obliged to consider you *one of his family. Why,* I will explain. In consenting to come on this mission, he took it for granted that another family would accompany him. On my coming to Boston *single,* he was disappointed, and refused to carry out his wife, unaccompanied by another female; but to remedy what would otherwise have prevented the present expedition, he proposed to the people of Boston to take *into his family* a single female, *on his own responsibility, and in case the board of missions did not take her off his hands,* which was uncertain, to provide thereafter for her maintenance. The proposal was accepted. You were recommended, and by him received, and *I suppose* were made acquainted with the circumstances. If, therefore, you conclude to take yourself from under his guardianship, as I am informed, it should be done with a fair understanding and due consideration of the consequences; and, let me add, not without reasons publicly known, otherwise you would wrong him and yourself very much.

"You may say that you do not consider yourself one of his family and under his guardianship, but let me assure you that *your friends at home do,* and until you choose another guardian it would be imprudent in you to disclaim the connection.

"You will soon mingle with strangers. Bro. Leland will consider himself *bound* to furnish you with a house and things comfortable, unless you order otherwise; if you disclaim connection his *obligations* will of course cease, and whatever he may do then will be a matter only of courtesy."

When the proposition was first made to Ruth to accompany Mr. Leland's family, without an appointment, as there was not time to obtain one, *she,* in the fullness of her confidence, would have decided to go, and would have considered any pledge of proper treatment, on the part of her mission friends, unnecessary; but her relations and friends of the church, and particularly some preachers who had been connected with the mission in Africa, decided differently. They knew more of the world and of the hearts of men than she did, and said to her plainly: "If you go out to Oregon without an appointment from the board, it is possible, yea probable, that you will be required to serve *in the kitchen,* and *that* you will not consider to be the work for which you sacrifice so much to do.''

From the diary of Ruth we also copy the following on this subject:

''The executive committee of the education society also objected to this course, but as the time was limited to a week for the sailing of the vessel, in which time they could not obtain an appointment from the board, they consented, provided I were willing, to send me as a member of Mr. Leland's family and have me remain so till such time as I could be regularly appointed by the board as a teacher. They, and many acquaintances, felt great solicitude for me on account of my leaving them *single* and without acquaintance to befriend me in those seasons of exposure and danger through which I must necessarily pass during a long voyage and in foreign ports, and in every possible instance gained from Mr. Leland assurances of the kindest attentions, which he promised to bestow upon me and to treat me as one of his own children, being in every possible respect father to me.''

Therefore, the *''pledge''* was given her, signifying that Ruth Rover should be sustained *as a teacher,* and in case the board should not do this, those persons whose names were signed were obligated to do it.

Her time during the voyages was said to be entirely at her own disposal.

Preliminaries now being arranged as was thought to be satisfactory, the missionaries prepared to bid their friends farewell, when Miss Rover was requested to *not* attend the farewell meeting in Boston, and was informed that it would ''probably be a hundred dollars in her pocket if she should go, instead, to the farewell meeting in Saugus.'' She was greatly disappointed at this announcement, for she had many warm friends in Boston.

At the boarding house in Boston, when waiting for the brig to be in readiness, Ruth was requested to eat at the second table, and wait upon Mr. Leland's children. She *did* wait for the second table but we believe she did not pay much attention to the children.

On the commencement of the voyage she suffered some from sea sickness, as also did Mrs. Leland and the family, and was asked by Rev. Mr. Perkins why she did not wait upon Mrs. Leland and the children, in taking care of their clothing, &c. She was much in want of a few articles which she had been informed were on board the vessel, directed to the ''mission family,'' and that she could use whatever she pleased of them. On enquiring of Mr. Leland, he told her she had ''no more right to any thing he had than any other stranger.''

At Valparaiso, Mr. Leland returned from shore and requested his wife to ''hurry'' and go on shore with him, for he had a place provided, &c. Ruth was informed by Mrs. Leland that she had better request Mr. Perkins to provide her a boarding house. This she declined as she knew she had no right so to do, and besides it would be indecorous for her thus to go among strangers. Mr. Leland told her there was no room where they were going, only for his own family. She nevertheless felt compelled to leave the vessel with them, hoping that there would be some place found for her. She rested the first night in the dining parlor on a sofa, without covering, and afterwards received a very acceptable request from Capt. and Mrs. Scott to remain at their house while she should be in Valparaiso.

At Callao, in consequence of finding herself so unpleasantly situated at Valparaiso, Ruth resolved that she would not go on shore at all, and remained on board the brig, under the protection of Mr. Sheldon, an elderly gentleman from Boston, and Capt. Kilham of the brig.

The Rev. Mr. Leland, during the voyage, very seldom attempted to conduct divine worship on the Sabbath, or to hold family prayers, and when he did, was generally very irregular in regard to time; and on those occasions Ruth sometimes happened to be on the deck, and whenever she heard the voice of prayer, she would pay attention at the sky-light till it was concluded.

Before arriving at the Sandwich Islands, she had discovered that she must rely on some other source for assistance and care when on shore, than on Mr. Leland, as he had a family to look after which occupied much of his attention and had the first claim on his regards.

At Oahu it was necessary to change vessels, and proceed to the Columbia River in a barque belonging to the Hudson Bay Company. Mr. E. O. Hall of Oahu, offered every attention to Ruth Rover, while at the islands, and she requested him to see to the removal of her trunks to the other vessel and that they were placed as they had been in the Peru, so as to enable her to have access to them when at sea. Mr. Leland desired that he might be entrusted with this business, said it was quite unnecessary to trouble Mr. Hall, that he knew how they should be arranged, &c., &c. Mr. Leland was accordingly trusted.

This seems a trivial and simple affair to record here, but 'tis introduced merely because of the results which it produced.

After leaving the islands 'twas found that all of Ruth's trunks and chests had been put under the hatches and could not be obtained during the voyage, and that Mr. Leland had not attended to their disposal at all. Hence Ruth was compelled to submit to the inconvenience of suffering for warm apparel, and of doing without her work and books for twenty-five or thirty days. The weather was becoming quite cold and she had only some light clothing which she had taken on shore at Oahu as suitable for that climate. She did not submit to this deprivation with a very good grace, especially as she perceived that the cabins and closets were very much encumbered with chattels belonging to Mr. Leland and family.

Had this been a solitary instance of neglect we don't know but Ruth might have borne it without speaking, but as many such had preceded it, and her mind was unreconciled to the thought that there was any necessity for this neglect, she found herself saying to Mr. Leland:

"I do not wonder there is no more union in our midst, while so much feeling of selfishness is apparent."

"If you mean *I* am selfish," said Mr. Leland, "you must show that I am."

"I think you have been selfish, not only in this affair but in other things since we left Boston."

"Well, we shall soon see our brethren in Oregon, and then we'll have it decided whether I am or am not selfish."

"Very well, then, it shall be decided there if you say so."

"I *do* say so, and other things, too, I guess will have to be settled before we come to the communion table together."

Mrs. Leland then exclaimed, in haste, "My dear! my dear! what are you saying—do be careful what you say."

"I know very well what I am saying," he replied, "and I don't wish to be interrupted when I'm talking!"

"Well, Mr. Leland," said Ruth, "you say this shall be decided by our brethren in Oregon, whether you are selfish or not, and also other things must be decided which you have against me. What are those other things?"

Mr. Leland, after a pause, replied, "Did you not say that in other things, as well as this, you thought I had been selfish?"

"Yes, sir."

"Well, that is what I meant. These other things in which you said I had been selfish, must be settled before we come to the communion table together."

Ruth readily discovered that this was changing ground, and considered there was more involved, when coming from a preacher of the gospel, than the trifling offense of looking more after his own property than another's, which any person might have done. We all are selfish, to a greater or less degree, and this is criminal only when involving a breach of some known duty, or the commission of some wrong.

No more was said on the subject at this time, but the next day Mr. Leland handed Ruth the following letter, which led to others being written, and for the consideration of justice to the authors they are presented entire. On the subject about which they are written we have only to say, it is, in many cases, easier to speak or preach than to practice:

❦

"*Barque Sumatra,*
August '37.

"SISTER ROVER: I shall offer no more justification for obtruding
myself upon your attention at this time, than what presents itself upon
the very face of this communication.

"I have desired an opportunity to converse with you, in a
christian manner, on the subjects which I shall here introduce.
Subjects which I conceive involve moral principles, and affect the
vital interests of christianity, and merit the most prompt and candid
attention. I speak in reference to whatever may exist in your mind or
my own, which interrupts the cordial reciprocity of christian
fellowship and sympathy. Of the existence of feelings and tempers
which are incompatible with the spirit and precepts of the gospel, we
have painful demonstration in the humiliating fact which cannot be
disguised, but which stands forth as a monument of reproach and
disgrace, (must I say to the christian cause? God forbid,) but to those
through whose guilt and folly it has been occasioned, and on them let
the confusion fall till tears of penitence shall wash it away. My
language may be thought severe, but my feelings are not unkind. My
heart bleeds, my spirit weeps, and shame mantles my cheek, whilst I
record the fact that a missionary family—honored with the
confidence of the church—sustained by the prayers and beneficies of
the christian community—sent forth to inculcate the holy principles,
practices and influences of the gospel of peace among infidels and
pagans; that they should so far lose sight of their high and holy work
and of their awful responsibilities—that they should so far betray
their trust and abuse the confidence of the church, by cherishing
unholy tempers and dispositions which gender disunion and
harshness, and which causes the milk of brotherly kindness to
degenerate into gall!

"And are not these facts in reference to ourselves—to our own
missionary family? And what tends much to aggravate the case, it is
well known to those with whom we sailed from our own country and
to those with whom we now sail, that a state of feeling exists among
us which will not suffer us to unite in our devotions! And have we not
exhibited, to our own lasting disgrace, the revolting spectacle of a
house divided against itself, in that while some of our numbers were
engaged in reading the scriptures and invoking the throne of grace,
others of our own company have absented themselves from the scene
of devotion, and have manifested the appearance of disapprobation

or contempt by reading histories or novels, or walking on deck in company with those who profess no fellowship or sympathy for christianity or its disciples.

"I repeat it. My heart bleeds! my spirit weeps!! and shame mantles my cheek!! that I am connected with a scene so revolting—so derogatory to the christian name.

"You must needs perceive, my sister, that there is something wrong—radically wrong—and that this wrong must be righted. I am not disposed to exculpate myself and cast the blame on you or any other person—but there is blame somewhere. It may rest wholly on me—if so, the greater the work of repentance before me; may God grant me grace to perform it.

"I wish to assure you, sister Rover, my object is not to cause you unnecessary pain, though I use plainness of speech. I am still your friend and harbor no other than the best of feelings towards you, however you may view the subject. I wish, however, to be understood as decided in my feelings that this state of things referred to must be put away, and to this I'm sure you will not object. And why, then, should we not avail ourselves of the facility which the gospel provides—the blessed privilege of confessing and forsaking our sins, that we may obtain mercy—and exercise the christian graces of forgiveness and forbearance that we may dwell together in love.

"I think that I can bear to be told my faults. Try me in this case, my sister—tell me plainly in what particulars I have offended, and what are those delinquencies of mine which have thrown a stumbling block in your way, by which I have forfeited your christian fellowship, and by which your confidence in my christian character is so shaken that you cannot be present when I attempt to conduct divine worship, nor hear a poor offending brother pray.

"This I ask, not as favor, but as my right to be told my faults, and trust, by the grace of God, I shall be disposed to make reasonable satisfaction.

"You will here allow me to present to you some things which have been a source of pain and grief to me during some parts of the voyage, and which, I think, require some explanation on your part.

"The things referred to are the following, viz:

1st. "Your reading histories or novels on this voyage, and in some instances in time of prayer.

2d. "Your *charging* Mrs. Leland and myself with selfishness.

3d. "Your absenting yourself during the time of reading the scriptures and morning and evening prayer, and thus treating the institutions of God with the appearance of disrespect, on board the Peru.

"These things may appear to you unworthy of notice, or you may have reasons which in your estimation are sufficient to justify your conduct and reconcile it with the claims of our holy religion, but in my view some explanation is required.

"I have thus undertaken the unpleasant duty of presenting this subject to your consideration. I have undertaken to discharge this duty with christian frankness and fidelity, and also with christian tenderness; and I trust that you will find me ready at any time to confess my faults—to make reasonable satisfaction, and render a reason for my conduct.

"And now, sister Ruth, we have no time to lose—if the providence of God favor us we shall soon join our brethren on missionary ground. Let us then be prepared to enter on our work in the unity of the spirit and the bonds of peace. But with what feelings would our brethren regard our arrival among them, should we introduce into their peaceful borders a spirit of strife and contention. Would they desire our arrival? Would they not rather wish we had tarried at home?

"The above is respectfully submitted with assurances of respect, &c.

D. LELAND."

Following was a supplement, in which Mr. Leland says:

"DEAR SISTER: I would first invite your attention to the within enclosed sheet, and to what follows here as a supplement to the foregoing communication. I know that I have already written at length, but my heart is burdened—my mind is oppressed, and my spirit groans within me for utterance, and I feel it incumbent on me to present a few considerations as additional inducements for a speedy reconciliation.

"And, first, we are members of the same christian community. By our high and holy profession and baptismal vows we are incorporated with the mystical body of Christ, and members one of another. Is Christ our head? Are we his members? Do we possess the mind that was in him? and have we no forgiving spirit—no spirit of forbearance to exercise? Have we forgotten those golden precepts of our divine master? Have we lost sight of those blessed injunctions which teach us to put away all wrath, and bitterness, and malice, and

hatred, and every evil work—and to walk in love, to dwell together in
the unity of spirit and the bonds of affection? No, say you, I have not
forgotten those blessed rules! but how can they be practiced while
things remain as they are? Things must not remain as they are—they
are not right; but they may easily be set right if we will take gospel
measures, and apply the gospel rule provided by our blessed Saviour
for the healing of those wounds which disgrace ourselves and
dishonor the christian name.

"And what are these rules which furnish a sovereign antidote,
and what are the duties which they enjoin?

"I answer—rather the word of God answers—

1st. "That we forsake not the assembling of ourselves together
for religious conversation and prayer.

2d. "That we confess our faults one to another, and pray one for
another that we may be healed. But, say you, I have particular trials,
&c., and that I cannot join with you in devotions. Well, admit that
you have trials, and that those trials are occasioned by the faults or
failings of your brother. What then?

3d. "If thy brother trespass against thee tell him of his fault, and
if he repent thou hast gained thy brother." Thy brother can bear to
be told of his faults.

4th. "Our Lord's instructions are, "when thou bringest thy gift
to the altar, and there rememberest that thy brother has aught
against thee, leave there thy gift, go first be *reconciled* to thy brother,
and then come and offer thy gift."

"Thus it appears that our blessed Lord has provided for the
removal of every root of bitterness, that there need nothing remain to
hurt or destroy in all God's holy mountain.

"I had thought of urging other reasons for a speedy adjustment
of this affair, but I forbear. I am sure that if what I have written is
received in the spirit in which it is indited, there will be no difficulty
in restoring a proper state of feeling, which if cultivated will lead to a
proper course of conduct—but, whatever may be the result, I feel
that I have done my duty, and I wish here to record my solemn
appeal to the Judge of all hearts that *I hold myself in readiness to do all
that is in my power, consistent with the nature of the case, to effect an immediate
and happy reconciliation throughout our missionary family.* Have I faults to
confess?—I am ready to confess them. Have I restitution to
make?—I am ready to make it. If I am required to extend the mantle
of charity over the failings of others, I am ready to do it.

"With a tender regard for the cause of Christ, and many prayers for your present and future peace, I subscribe myself

Yours, &c., D. LELAND."

To these letters Ruth Rover briefly responded thus:

"Barque Sumatra

"THE REV. MR. LELAND:

"*Sir*—I conclude the long communication you have handed me this afternoon is worthy of at least *some* reply.

"In regard to the explanation of my conduct which you think is required, I will only say now that I have read histories during the voyage and thought it no harm; if it ever happened during the time of prayer, 'twas accidental. I also have read the last volume of the "Children of the Abbey,"[1] and thought this no harm, either, as you allowed your daughters to read those volumes. Whatever other books I have read were of their selection. I have had no others.

"Of the selfishness of Mrs. Leland and yourself, I have been caused to think so by your having, in every instance, appropriated entirely to yourselves every article which has been sent on board the vessel directed to the *'Mission Family.'*

"With regard to my joining you in devotion, I approve your desires, but can never do it while the stumbling block, you have placed in my way to the sacramental table, is not removed.

"I have been unjustly accused and my feelings seriously wounded, and I will never suffer this affair to be smoothed over till it may be done with honor to the cause of Christ, and with justice to myself.

Respectfully,

RUTH ROVER."

"P.S. I await your determination of laying this before the brethren in Oregon for a settlement.   R.R."

Mr. Leland appeared very anxious that this misunderstanding should be rectified before they should arrive in Oregon, and with this view he addressed Ruth again in the following words:

"SISTER ROVER: I have no assurance that I shall live to see the Oregon, and I do not wish to appear before my Judge with my sins unrepented of and unforgiven. I therefore consider that there is no time for *me* to delay the work of humiliation and repentance.

"In your note of yesterday you mention the "stumbling block" I have placed in your way to the sacramental table. I am left to guess your meaning. If you refer to what you call my *threat,* I beg leave to explain my meaning. I intended no threat, nor did I mean to express an intention to refer the adjustment of any matters to the discussion of our brethren in Oregon. I will state the case as I understand it: You blamed me because your chests were put under the hatches, and charged me with being selfish in that and in other things which you said you had discovered. I replied to you that it would not answer—there must be an explanation—that as we were shortly to join our brethren on shore, these things must be settled before we could consistently come to the communion table together. I meant to be understood to speak with reference to an immediate settlement. I meant no threat. I am sorry that I spoke as I did, seeing it has given you offense. As far as you feel yourself injured in this case I hope you will forgive me.

"Having already stated to you my feelings in reference to other matters, I wish only to add, that, as far as I am able to judge, I have endeavored to remove all the obstructions which I have cast in your way, or my own, to the sacramental table. I have nothing to refer to our brethren in Oregon. I shall not appear there as your accuser; and I will only add, that, as far as I am concerned, *I am perfectly willing that this whole affair and all my conduct should undergo the investigation of my brethren in Oregon, if it is your desire.*

D. LELAND.''

Ruth Rover having *once* made up her mind—which she thought was sufficient on any subject—resolved not to waver, and simply told Mr. Leland that she had already informed him of what she thought was the proper course for her to pursue, and that it was useless to insist on any change. As he was willing the subject should be talked over by his brethren, it was the best way, and would be the most satisfactory, in the end, for both parties.

She was influenced to this decision, not so much for the injury she thought she had received, for she considered Mr. Leland had fully atoned for it, and even humbled himself much more than she could have desired—but she considered there was a *principle* involved, inasmuch as Mr. Leland was a preacher of the gospel and she believed he had been guilty of falsehood, and not only in the instance referred to, but at other times during their acquaintance. She wished merely an expression of the opinion of some other person on the subject, and she knew of none who would treat the case more properly than her brethren of the mission in Oregon.

This determination was perhaps well intended, but it did not result in good. Better would it have been for her had she forgiven Mr. Leland his trifling neglect and have left the rest with him and his Maker; and, if he had faults, to have suffered others to have found them out.

At several times during the remainder of the voyage Mrs. Leland, with her characteristic *christian* spirit, urged Miss Rover, with her arms around her neck and tears on her cheeks, to suffer the affair to drop, that they might join their brethren in love and peace with each other. But, no! Ruth Rover was firm as adamant, and tears and entreaties were in vain.

Energy and firmness of character are admirable in some circumstances, but when youth and inexperience resolve that they will accomplish certain ends, without knowing what will be the consequences, and in spite of all the admonitions of experience and the suggestions of wisdom, 'tis very lamentable. It seemed to be a component part of Ruth's character to resolve that, whatever she *should* accomplish, that she also *would* accomplish; and obstacles might rise in vain—they only nerved her to greater effort—and we verily believe that had she, at different periods of her life, become persuaded that it was proper for her *to change the course of a river,* she would have attempted it. But such confidence in one's self, or in a superior power, implies limited knowledge. Experience, 'tis said, is the best schoolmaster, and well would it be if his instructions came before it was too late to profit by them. Had Ruth Rover consented that the difficulties which had existed between Mr. Leland and herself should have been settled before they met their brethren in Oregon, the whole tenure of her life would have undoubtedly been changed; but she persisted unflinchingly in what *she* thought was the only honorable and just course—*and well did she atone for it.*

We just now find a paragraph in Ruth's hand writing, penned probably many years ago, which, as it does great credit to the amiable and lamented Mrs. Leland, we will transfer it here. She says:

"Occasionally, during the remainder of the voyage, Mrs. Leland introduced the subject of our disunion, deeply regretting that there was discord among us and entreating me most affectionately to be reconciled to them, and urging the propriety of living together in christian fellowship and love. And in doing this she exhibited a degree of meekness and love which I never witnessed in any female before. She truly was *christian-like,* while *I* was unyielding to the last degree. In one of those instances, in referring to Mr. Leland's conversation about joining the brethren in Oregon, she said, 'I'm sure I never heard him speak so before—I don't know what he meant—I'm very sorry.'"

When at the Sandwich Islands Mr. Leland informed the Rev. Mr. Bingham that Ruth Rover was to remain in his family as a teacher or governess to his children.[2] When they arrived in the Columbia river, the report reached the mission, at the Willamette, before the missionaries, *that Ruth Rover had come out as a servant in Mr. Leland's family.* If there was not existing somewhere an expectation or hope that such would ultimately be Ruth's destination, it would be interesting to know from what source came these reports. But 'tis said that "bird's of the air carry the news," and them, at any rate, we will hold responsible for the present.

The singular modes of living which Ruth discovered as she passed along among the people of different nations, occurred to her as outrageous and insupportable. Hence, we find her, when first at sea, astonished that the Hawaiian boy Charley could bear such a deprivation as sleeping in bed quilts without sheets, and gave herself no rest till she had made a pair for him out of cloth belonging to herself. She wondered how the seamen could handle the ropes, when off Cape Horn, without mittens—and how the steward could run about deck without a cap—and how he and Charley could bear to wear shoes without socks—and employed much of her time in providing these articles for them.

And when the company arrived at Champoeg, at the house of De Porte McKoy,[3] and were served with supper—tea made in a tin kettle and drank from two cups, which had to answer for the party—meat set upon the table in a tin pan, vegetables mixed with it, and bread laid upon the bare table—she thought it most astonishing that they would consent so to live, and when informed by Mr. McKoy that conveniences for the table could not be obtained in the country, she told him that she would bear his needs in mind, and if she could obtain any things for him, at the mission, for the use of his table, she would send them to him. The gratitude she felt for his hospitality induced her to make this offer, as he had provided every possible comfort for the party and had refused any compensation.

Ruth Rover's introduction to the mission we will give in her own words, making no improvements in the style, considering the *original* as the best:

"The Rev. Mr. Lee enquiring of Mr. Leland the destination of the different members of the reinforcement, asked him what *I* had come to do. Mr. Leland replied that I had "come without an appointment from the board, and he did *not know what I intended to do!*"

"Believing that Mr. Leland intended, if possible, to hold me in his family to teach his children, I asked Mr. Lee what situation in the mission he would be able to give me—if I could have a school, &c. Mr. Lee replied that he had 'no particular business to assign me—he already had more females in the family than could be well employed,[4] and he did not understand why the people at home were sending teachers to him—he had sent for none, &c., and concluded by telling me that he had just decided on an arrangement in relation to the employment of the females in the family, and that every

department was taken but the one with Mrs. Lee—that *she* had to cook and
wash dishes, and I might take a situation in that department if I chose.' I told
him that I had come without an appointment 'twas true, and gave him the
reason which had caused me to do so, but told him I had received a ''pledge''
from certain preachers that I should be employed as a teacher till the board at
New York should signify what they wished me to do. He said he 'no other
situation to offer me than that he had named.' I told him that if he would give
me liberty, I thought I could obtain a school of Indian girls. He said he
'already had more Indians dependent on them than they could feed.' I asked
him if he were willing that I should return to Mr. Burnie's family, at Fort
George, for I could obtain a school there.[5] He replied that he 'could give me
no other business than that he had named, viz: to assist Mrs. Lee in the kitchen.'
I told him again that I was unwilling to accept that situation—not that I was
above such work—but because my feelings had already been injured on that
subject. He then replied that 'if I would not accept such employment as he
offered me, he should not recognize me as a member of the mission family,
and I had no right to expect it of him.' I retired with feelings too disconsolate
for utterance, after asking permission to remain till I had in some measure
recruited my strength, put my wardrobe in order, &c. In a few days I
obtained leave to tarry with Dr. White and work for my board.[6] I made it
known to the mission that I was willing to do any kind of work, while there,
for the good of the mission or members of the family, accordingly Messrs. D.
Lee, Wilson,[7] and Edwards,[8] sent me their clothes to wash and mend; also,
Mr. J. Lee sent me some sewing to do for himself, some work for the Indians'
cook, and some bags to make for wheat.''

In another journal we find the following:

''Was introduced to the Rev. J. Lee, the superintendent of the M.
Mission, by the Rev. Mr. Leland, as a person who had 'come without an
appointment, and he did not know what it was my intention to do.' Mr. Lee
also told his wife that he 'supposed I had come out to get a husband, and he
did not want any such persons around him.' Mr. Shepherd, also, one of the
missionaries who had accompanied us from Vancouver, had said that he 'knew
I was a *maniac* from what he saw of me when at McKoy's, at Champoeg, in
thanking him for the dinner he had served, and telling him I would send him
dishes,' &c. Mr. Leland did not try to remove this impression, but encouraged it by saying I had come out '*on my own footing,*' which led Mr. Lee to
suppose that I was some over-zealous, weak-minded enthusiast, and he did
not respect me in travelling so far from home on such an errand, without
authority, and he did not wish to give me any encouragement. My feelings
cannot be described.''

To conclude the controversy with Mr. Leland—Ruth says:

"I found an opportunity to tell Mr. Lee, that there were difficulties existing between Mr. Leland and myself, which until they were settled, must prevent us from meeting at the Lord's table together, and would be glad if I could have an expression of his, or some other's opinion as to the one in fault. He said he should listen to nothing, for he had found himself involved in great difficulty when the other reinforcement came, by listening to stories, and he should never listen to any more.'⁹ I then asked him to tell me what was my proper course of conduct if I believed a preacher had been guilty of uttering falsehoods; if it were necessary for me to speak of it, or if I should say nothing about it; and told him that I had made mention of it to no one, and only to himself in a private manner by way of obtaining advice. He replied that "speaking untruths, in a preacher was a criminal offence; and that if I knew it of any one I should not conceal it, but first I must take the scripture course, viz: 'tell him his fault between him and thee,' &c., and if I could not be persuaded by this but that he were guilty, I should tell it to the church.'"

The result is embodied in the following note:

"REV. J. LEE:

Respected Sir: I have had an interview with Mr. Leland, and I think proper to inform you of the conclusion of our conversation. He declares he knows no reason why I should not be received into the mission family and into the church here, and enjoy the privileges of the same as I have been accustomed to enjoy them. He was able in some instances to lead me to suppose I might have been mistaken on the subject of his speaking untruths, but in *two* instances, at least, my impressions remain as they were. I however told him that I now had done what I considered my duty and I should trouble him no farther—the matter now rested with him and his God. As you refuse to hear the particulars of the case, there is no more that I can do.

Very respectfully,

RUTH ROVER."

Rev. Mr. Leland, soon after this, called on Dr. White and told him he was very happy to be able to say there was no longer any difficulty existing between himself and Ruth Rover, but all their troubles were amicably settled.

Ruth Rover also called on Mrs. Leland and asked her forgiveness for occasioning unhappiness to her for so long a time, and expressed hope that it would now be all forgotten. Meeting Mr. Leland, as she left the house, she said to him that she supposed the difficulty was all past and there was probably nothing more to be spoken about. He replied: "No, only the certificate." Not comprehending his meaning, Ruth passed on to her employment. She had by this been received into the mission family and was teaching the Indian school.

Rev. Mr. Lee was about this time holding meetings on business with the male members of the family, on subjects connected with the mission. One morning Ruth found written on a slip of paper, lying on the floor of the mission house, the following *resolution,* by Mr. Leland. Ruth says:

"I found this on the floor of the mission house the next morning after Mr. Leland's house had been burnt, and which had, I suppose, been lost in the hurry. I showed it to one of the brethren, and he acknowledged that it had been read at one of their meetings. I laid it, as I supposed, in a secure place till I should go to my room, but when I returned it was among the missing!

"Resolved, That we consider the remarks made by Ruth Rover, in relation to the character of Rev. D. Leland, are worthy of no consideration."

In a few mornings after I found in the desk of the school room a certificate for Mr. Leland, of which the following is a copy:

"TO WHOM IT MAY CONCERN.

"We the undersigned members of the Oregon mission, in view of the statements and representations made by Ruth Rover, viz: that she believed Mr. Leland guilty of selfishness and falsehood, do hereby certify that it is our opinion that those and any other statements by her made, tending to injure his character, are groundless.

JASON LEE
DANIEL LEE
H.K.W. PERKINS
ALANSON BEERS
JOSEPH WHITCOMB[10]

"Given in the Mission Hall,
December 13th, 1837."

Sometime before this Ruth had learned that Mr. Leland wished some such certificate from the brethren, and had told Mr. Lee that there could be no justice in such a one being given, as he had refused to listen to any explanation of the source of her impressions against Mr. Leland; and he informed her that Mr. Leland had utterly refused to have the subject investigated there, saying he "did not come to Oregon to be judged by his brethren—he should appeal to the conference at home."

Mr. Lee, it appears, had reported to the mission family what Ruth Rover had suggested to him in private, and Mr. Leland, in consequence, found himself much embarrassed. To this proceeding Ruth objected immediately, in the following note:

"REV. MR. LEE:

"*Sir:* I have become acquainted with the proceedings of the brethren last eve, in relation to Mr. Leland and myself. You have known my objections to such a course, it being in my opinion wrong. There now remain but two things to be attended to, previous to the settlement of this affair, one of which must be attended to immediately. The certificate must be withdrawn and my name removed from it; or, if given at all, bearing my name, it must be done in such a manner as not to convey the impression that *I* am guilty of falsehood;—or, if neither of these will be consented to, as I can labor with no pleasure or advantage in this place, while suffering the ill opinion of my brethren, *I shall leave the mission.*

"I am unprepared to continue my labors in the school till one of these particulars be attended to.

With respect,   RUTH ROVER."

In the journal we find this item:

"I had attempted to relate the particulars of the case to Mr. Lee, and he told me he had 'resolved to listen to no more complaints from individuals in the mission.' As, therefore, none of the members of the mission family knew aught of the particulars connected with my suspicions in regard to Mr. Leland, I fully believed they were not qualified to present such a testimony of their favorable opinion of him as the certificate contained, as it was an opinion founded on no knowledge whatever. Mr. Lee contended that he had a right to his *opinion,* and a right to do as he pleased in giving or not giving such a certificate. I allowed that *he had a right* to do by a person as he pleased, and as that person should consent to, but he had *no* right to injure *me* for the benefit of another.

"Mr. Lee also added that it was not *his* place to call for an investigation, and Mr. Leland had said he would never submit to be judged by his brethren in Oregon—hence, Mr. Leland perceiving he could not safely retain the certificate without a previous investigation, resolved to cause me to meet him *'face to face'* as his *accuser.*

"Mr. Lee accordingly forwarded the following note to me:

"MISSION HOUSE,

"December 15th, 1837."

"*To Miss Rover:*

"MY DEAR SISTER—I have this hour received a letter from brother D. Leland, of which the following is a copy:

"*To the Rev. J. Lee, in Charge of the Oregon Mission:*

"DEAR SIR—Finding myself under report of being guilty of crimes of selfishness and falsehood—and inasmuch as these reports originated with Ruth Rover, who is a member of the M.E. church within your charge, I do hereby respectfully desire you to take speedy measures to effect an adjustment of this matter, as provided for in our Discipline, section eight, question first.

Yours with respect,

(Signed,) D. LELAND."

"The above, being addressed to me in my official capacity, I deem it necessary for me—however painful the duty—to take measures for the investigation of the matter referred to. I do, therefore, appoint that Monday, the eighteenth of December, half past ten o'clock, P.M., to be the time *when,* and the apartment of Mr. Beers' house, fitted for a school room, the place *where* you are required to meet Mr. Leland, *'face to face,'* and give the grounds for the above reports, before the regular constituted authorities, according to the discipline of our church.

"There is no objection to any member of the mission family being present at the investigation, if they desire to attend, or any one should desire them to do so.

"If the time does not suit your convenience, please let me know.

Yours, respectfully,

(Signed,) JASON LEE."

On this occurrence Ruth says:

"I perceived at once that notwithstanding I had wished an explanation of the opinion of some of the brethren on the matter of differences between Mr. Leland and myself, that in complying with this requirement of Messrs. Lee and Leland, I must appear as the *accuser* of the latter—the which I never was, nor wished to be—and also if I *had* thus appeared, I could produce no proof, of which they were well aware, as the occurrences happened at sea and were observed by none but ourselves; and furthermore the Discipline required that a minister should be tried by *three ministers,* and there were none in Oregon but the three who had already signed their names to the certificate saying, in their opinion, Mr. Leland was *not guilty*. Hence there was little chance of my obtaining an impartial judgement.''

Ruth, therefore, sent to Mr. Lee, the following answer:

''*To Mr. Lee:*

''SIR—I find myself unable to comply with your requirements, and meet Mr. Leland, 'face to face,' 'and give the grounds for the reports against him, before the regular constituted authorities, according to the Discipline of our church,' unless I *can* so comply *according to the regular constituted authorities.*

''Mr. Leland says: 'Inasmuch as these reports '*originated*' with Ruth Rover.' I find not in our Discipline, section 8th, any instructions given in regard to the treatment of the *originator* of a *report.* If any person has reported that Mr. Leland is guilty of the crimes of selfishness and falsehood, that person is not myself. Farther, the Discipline requires that the '*accused* and the *accuser*' be brought 'face to face.' I am not Mr. Leland's accuser, nor he the accused, therefore it belongs not to me thus to meet him.

''I therefore decline meeting Mr. Leland on Monday, as you appoint.

With respect,

RUTH ROVER.''

The following was soon after received by her:

''MY DEAR SISTER—Your remarks in reference to the originator of the report I consider mere cavilling.

''If I understand the true sense of the matter it is this: The person with whom an idea originates, if it be known to a second person, must necessarily be the reporter of it—for if it remain with the originator it is but an idea still, and not a report; but, if it be known to another, it is then a report, and a report implies a reporter, and this can be no other than the originator. And, if the report contains a charge or accusation, the reporter is of course the accuser. I think, therefore, you are bound to meet Mr. Leland, 'face to face,' as appointed, or amicably adjust the matter with him in some other way.

''Mr. Leland informs me that the certificate to which you refer, is not, and never has been in his possession—and he does not desire it should be if this matter can be fairly settled. You are aware that I earnestly desire that this matter should be settled by yourselves—but feeling myself *obliged,* by his letter, I took the course the Discipline directs, to have it investigated. Mr. Leland will consent to no investigation but what is according to Discipline, and if you utterly refuse to have such an one, there can, of course, be none.

"I have not much reason to think that you will put much confidence in what I am about to say, yet I feel it to be my duty to say to you that I entertain no other than *friendly* feelings towards you, and that I should be happy to do anything to remove your embarrassments, and make you comfortable and happy, that I can do in justice.

"With earnest prayers to Almighty God to direct us all in this matter, by His unerring counsel, I am,

Yours truly,

JASON LEE.''

This produced the following reply:

"REV. MR. LEE:

"SIR—On reading your letter of this morning, I find *myself* compelled to take farther trouble for the adjustment of this foolish affair, as well as to trouble *you,* and which, if you are as tired as *I* am, it must be unpleasant to read, as well as to write.

"Of your remark in regard to 'cavilling,' I think I need not take much notice, as I cannot perceive that it affects the conclusion at all, for, if I am the *reporter,* I am only the reporter of saying I *believe* Mr. Leland is guilty, not of saying he *is* guilty.

"Farther, admit that I reported my belief to you, *you* must have reported it to others or it would never have done any harm.

"With reference to the Discipline, it is the *accuser* not the *reporter,* who is required to meet the accused, for, in my opinion notwithstanding what you say to the contrary, the reporter of a suspicion is not the accuser of a crime.

"Mr. Leland's not having the certificate in his possession does not alter the case at all, for you remarked to me that 'it was as much Mr. Leland's as if he had it, and you had no right to add anything to it without his consent.'

"I thank you for your expressions of *friendly* feelings towards me, but from my limited acquaintance with you, I am not able to judge whether you are or are not thus friendly, only by your treatment of me. If you are sincere in these expressions, I must conclude that for want of penetration you did not discover the fallacy of the certificate you lately authorized to be written without my knowledge, which I believe any person would think was synonymous to saying: We consider her a person who talks at random, and therefore it is our opinion that her statements are entitled to no credit.

"The present difficulty, Mr. Lee, if I understand it, is between the persons whose names are on that certificate and Mr. Leland—or, perhaps, with them and me—and *not* with Mr. Leland and myself.

"If I have done wrong in any particular of this affair, let it be shown. You say 'I should not express an opinion unless I can sustain it.' I suppose you mean, unless I can *prove* to *be* true what I *think* to be true. If a friend cannot to a friend unburthen his or her burthened heart, farewell forever to social intercourse. The turning point now seems to be the *certificate*. Shall it be given as it is, or as I said it must be if bearing my name? If you decide it shall be given as it *is,* I shall, as I have informed you, leave the mission. I think that to decide thus would be to treat me unjustly, and I am willing to abide the consequences; and if you are uncertain about its propriety, I think to retract would be no more than honorable.

"If there is likely to be much time consumed before the final conclusion, I object not to again commence the school if it be desirable.

Yours, with respect, and
Much weariness,
RUTH ROVER."

We now present another item from the journal:

"Mr. Leland being unwilling to be without the certificate, called on me frequently, in company with Mr. Lee, and once appointed a committee of three to wait on me to see if I could not be persuaded to consent. I told them I could not discover at all why Mr. Leland should expect such an article from the brethren, as the case did not affect them, and that I thought I was the person of whom he should ask a certificate, and if he desired one of me I would give him one, and such an one as he would not show very often. I related to this committee some of the reasons I had for my suspicions of Mr. Leland, and asked them their opinions; and they said they thought I had very good grounds for believing Mr. Leland guilty of selfishness and falsehood.

"Finally, after many altercations between us, Mr. Leland said he did not intend to show the writing to any body unless he should learn that I had spoken of this to others, and was willing to promise in writing that he never would show it only for this reason; and Mr. Lee also said he was willing to give me in writing their conviction that they did not suspect *me* of speaking untruths in this affair, and having informed Mr. Lee that, as my principle objection to an investigation had arisen from the fact that Mr. Leland must be tried, if at all, by the three ministers present, viz: Messrs. J. Lee, D. Lee, and H. K. W. Perkins, all of whom had expressed an opinion, yet, if at any future time there should arrive ministers in Oregon who were disinterested, I would consent to the trial. It was decided that Mr. Leland should retain the certificate as at first written.

"Just at this moment the dinner bell rung, and as there was not then time for the interchange of papers, it was agreed that immediately after dinner they would come over for that purpose. But they did not come and I heard nothing farther on the subject."

Ruth Rover having informed Mr. Lee that she would give Mr. Leland an opportunity for a fair trial, if one should ever present itself, informed him, on the 6th of July, 1840,[11] of her willingness to this, in the following note:

"To Rev. Mr. Leland:

"Sir—In addressing to you this note my object is not to revive unpleasant sensations which some time since existed between us, but to remind you that it is now your privilege to improve the present advantage in the decision of the case about which our minds were exercised in the winter of '37.

"If, therefore, you desire it, the same may be acted upon by any member or number of members of the late reinforcement of missionaries, at any time you shall choose for that purpose.

"Perhaps I should have addressed this note to Mr. Lee rather than yourself, but, as I suppose you will acquaint him with its import, it is probably unimportant.

Respectfully,

RUTH ROVER."

We again refer to the journal:

"Mr. Leland did not reply to me, and I did not see him again till the December following, when I asked if he received my note. He said he did, and he had not informed Mr. Lee that I had written it to him, and he concluded it was not best to disturb the minds of the brethren with it; but he did not know but Mr. Lee might yet wish the case investigated."

The inquiry here suggests itself: What was Mr. Leland's object in endeavoring to obtain that certificate? Was it merely for the security of his own reputation? If so, why did he not take it when it was surrendered to him? On the other hand, does there not appear reason to suppose he wished it more for the purpose of obtaining disgrace to Ruth Rover, in the fact that when the object was to be counteracted by his restrictions to show the certificate to no one, and by one to be given to Ruth by Mr. Lee, certifying that her character for veracity was not injured in his estimation, then, he was not all anxious to obtain it?

From this time Rev. Mr. Leland was to Ruth Rover a confirmed enemy. And although at times he wore the garb of a friend, yet *revenge* was in the heart, and only waiting an opportunity to appear in its own hideous colors.

CHAPTER IX

JOURNAL AND LETTERS

❧

Sept., 1837. "A few days since was received into the mission family and have since been treated kindly and affectionately by my brethren, which has greatly relieved my mind of unpleasant forebodings and given rise to my former anxiety for the good of these Indians.[1] I find them in a suffering and benighted condition, with the exception of thirty children who are at school at the mission house. These natives, as far as I can discover, are without instruction. The members of our family who have been in this place three years have made a few attempts to teach them the knowledge of God, but find it a very difficult task to convey to their minds a correct idea of his existence or nature, or of their accountability. Their language is by no means copious, and presents no words capable of conveying an understanding of these things. The missionaries of our reinforcement, with those here before us, consider it to be of great importance that an effort be immediately made to moralize the adult portion of the Indians—but we may labor, and labor in vain, if we make not God our dependence.

"Visited some Indian huts this afternoon; saw several small and beautifully intelligent looking children—a babe but a few months old, healthy, pretty and happy; several women, and one extremely old female, wrinkled, tottering, dirty, and, I should think, wretched. Their houses are made of boards resting upon the ground and against each other at the top, or with a blanket, or skin, or pieces of bark thrown upon bushes. In these poor shades these comfortless beings will spend their lives, exposed to all the changes of weather, and depending upon anything but their own endeavors for a livelihood. 'Tis no wonder that many of the tribes are extinct, so great is their degradation and misery.

"After divine service this forenoon, at the mission house, visited the Indians, and talked, and sang, and prayed with them. I did not expect to be understood by them, but hoped they might be led to ponder upon their condition. I am led to reflect much on the present and future state of the heathen. On christians now sleeping in their graves will fall the guilt, I believe, of there being one unenlightened mind now on the globe, and if their souls are lost their blood will be required at their hands.

"Eighteen hundred years ago the commandment 'Go into all the world and preach the gospel to every creature,' was as plainly laid before christians as that which says, 'Thou shalt love thy God,' and I believe that had they commenced and continued to exert themselves, as it was the design of their master they should do, there would not now be a soul on earth unacquainted with the way of salvation.

"Visited the Indians again. Although 'tis the Sabbath, found one aged woman making a mat—others laughing and hallooing most indecently, and some sick lying upon the ground with only a straw mat beneath them and a deerskin over their naked bodies—no pillows, no sheets or quilts, or beds, or clothing, or nourishment—no sympathy, no friends, no heavenly consolations, and these are the heathen I hope to benefit in some measure, at least. I wish to improve every moment of leisure learning the language—imparting what instructions are possible, and gaining their good will and confidence.[2] The Indian children are generally very rugged in appearance; the babes I have seen are extremely fleshy. Have been much pleased with one Indian girl—call her *my* girl, and have named her Olive Davis, for one of my dear sisters. May she become as worthy a woman.

"Isabella Derton died on Sabbath morning. She was an Indian woman aged fifteen years, and was married when but twelve years of age. A pulmonary consumption terminated her existence. During her illness she gave remarkable evidence of patience and submission, and had evidently met with a change of heart. On the night of her death, being asked if she were happy, if she loved God, &c., she made great exertions to answer yes, and to answer with emphasis, as if greatly desirous that we should know that she was happy and willing to exchange worlds. When she breathed her last, I had the unspeakable satisfaction, yet solemn privilege, of holding her in my arms, and directing her to give herself into the hands of God; and when praying that He would receive her spirit, was myself greatly favored with divine influences. It seemed almost as if heaven were opened to us both, and I could hardly resign her to go alone, so great was my desire to dwell also with the blest. O! how pleasant is the work of God! how delightful the employment of guiding the departing soul in the way of heaven.

Monday. "Isabella was buried to-day. The corpse was attended to the grave by the members of the mission family, our French neighbors, some wild Indians, and the children of the school—the procession numbering seventy or eighty persons.

"Called at chief Caleb's huts. Found four Indians sick and lying upon the ground without clothing or beds—others sitting idly in the ashes and smoke, with the entrails and hoofs of a horse lying about, they having eaten the body. Find myself very happy in the mission field, although not particularly engaged except for the temporal wants of the missionaries. My school will afford me opportunity to become better acquainted with the native language, and by giving me such free access to the children, will multiply the probabilities of my benefitting this race. Great is the goodness of my heavenly Father in reviving me in the spirit of my mind—in strengthening my faith—in sustaining and comforting my broken spirit, and in granting me that strength of mind which my severest afflictions have not been able to overcome—that fortitude, resolution and patient endurance I have found so requisite to my support—and that trust in Him which all my enemies, the infirmities of the flesh, and the artifices of satan, have not been able to destroy.

"To-day had painful evidence of the strength of sin over the mind which has never been under the improving influence of christian tuition, in that of the stubbornness of one of the Indian boys. By no persuasion or threat could I induce him to yield the point about which he contended. I felt the keenest sorrow for having to resort to severity, and could not refrain from weeping before God in interest for him. The child is an orphan—his only sister died in my arms, and is doubtless praising God in heaven, and perhaps hovers over her brother with deep interest. I never felt more anxious for any one's conversion than I do for this dear child's.

"The dispositions of these children are materially different from children in the United States, or elsewhere, that have been subjected to rigorous discipline from their earliest childhood. The slightest provocation—even the request to pronounce a word the second time, which was not distinctly heard, will excite their anger beyond control—the child often retaliating with blows and most abusive language, if his teacher resorts to chastisement. Much discretion is necessary in a teacher, and the best way I have discovered in teaching is to be mild and lenient, and, without stooping below a requisite dignity, endeavor to convince them of the advantages of well-doing, as opposed to stubborness and misconduct.

"Visited an aged sick woman—wife of one of our French neighbors. She is very low in consumption, and three members of her family have lately died of the same disease. Although a member of the Catholic church, where baptism is considered to produce a saving change, she is quite unreconciled to death, and anticipates no happiness in leaving this world. The Indian girl whom I named Olive Davis, has offered herself to Mrs. B———, to live with her, and her sister, E. Davis, whom I had taken to raise, I have given to the mission.

Sabbath. "Went to the lodges, early this morning, and invited the Indians to come to church when the bell should ring. Several came in their best attire, and gave very patient and respectful attention to the services—kneeling in prayer, and standing with the congregation when singing. Although it is not supposed that they understand what is said, yet they have some idea of the difference between the Sabbath and other days, and also that it is the Great Spirit above us whom we address and talk about.

"Some time last week an Indian chief murdered an Indian. The mission brethren expostulated with him, and the reasons which he gave were that he was his slave and had attempted to take his own life. Had an interesting conversation with Mr. R———, a French neighbor, on the subject of religion. He is a Catholic, but says he likes any religion which will learn him to do right. There are a few families of French near us who are decidedly kind, and too *polite,* apparently, to do a mean act.

"Rev. Mr. Leslie has been appointed by Mr. Lee missionary to the Calapooyas. He said, a few days since, he could never allow them to live in such wretched houses, and went out, axe in hand, to build them better, but he has cut his foot and got discouraged.

"Invited the Indians again, this morning, to attend church. They came in larger numbers—the women with their best dresses and their hair in its best braids—evidently thinking they were honoring and being honored by the circumstance. Visited them in their huts, much to their and my own gratification. They tell me if I will learn to talk with them, they will give me plenty of *wah-wah*[3] for nothing—probably more than I could stow away.

"The Indians came to church to-day and took seats very orderly, when Mr. Leslie told them to sit outside on the steps, and make room for the French. They left altogether, and probably will come back no more."

The journals of Ruth Rover, at this period, are copious, but as they related to subjects which are not interesting here, we make but few extracts. The same of her letters. We shall copy only such parts as will denote her employments, wishes, and prospects, relating to missionary operations. To her parents she says:

"This is probably thanksgiving day in Massachusetts, and how delightful is now the recollection of the last I spent at home with you and my sisters and brothers. When I recall *them* to mind 'tis with pleasure, and with almost an assurance that I shall see them again—but when my thoughts revert to yourselves, the big tears will start and threaten tremblingly to fall and mar the impress of my pen—but let them start and fall till their fountain is empty, and they cannot denote all the love I entertain for my dear parents. How differently I am situated to-day from what I was one year ago, in my father's house; *then* surrounded with friends, and burdened with the sight of luxuries and dainties—*now* lonely, and in the strictest sense destitute of indulgences to temper the appetite—*then* I could feast on good things to surfeit—*now* can see before me only *stewed peas, fried bread, and pea coffee*—*then* could see my mother pleasantly and assiduously laboring to have every little service performed to render her guests happy, and my father, also, making every effort to be agreeable, anon kissing the babies, stirring the fires, regretting that he could not do more, and expressing his own satisfaction in having us at home on such an occasion; but *now* I look around and stretch my eyes far and wide without their meeting one kindred spirit, and listen to every sound that vibrates on the ear and hear no salutations—no anxious enquiries about health, or happiness—and no regrets for want of more to gratify the appetite. O! dear! I sometimes like the Israelites, almost sigh for the dainties of Egypt, yet I am not sorry that this thanksgiving day finds me in Oregon.

"Dear parents, *do* continue to please, and cherish, and support, and sustain each other amid the infirmities of old age, as shall enable the thread of life to be lengthened out for the six years for which I am engaged here, that I may be blessed on my return with a sight of yourselves in health and happiness. And you, my little brother, let me request you *particularly* to provide for the comforts of the old gentleman, my father, that he may live till my return to make me unspeakably blest.

"Please tell brother S———, who inquires what he shall send me, tell him everything but *finery* is needed here. You could gain some idea of the wants of this people if you should go away into the woods and make a fire of a few sticks—divest yourself of clothing—attempt to live without food, or prepare that of some putrid animal without any conveniences for doing so but a stick and the fire, and realize that you have no society but that of wolves, panthers, bears, snakes, &c., &c. If you can obtain any idea of the destitution of this people will you not have charity for them and endeavor to encourage it in others? There have been many boxes of clothing sent here for Indians, but the superintendent will part with them only to the Indian children in the mission family. There are many adult Indians in the huts near, especially females, who are very destitute—indeed I can scarcely bear to go among them in consequence of their nudity. Of the articles I brought for two years use, nearly all are disposed of. I have given away of my own apparel till I am almost comfortless, and I can do but little more. But I will trust in God and to the sympathies of the good people of New England. As often as I have leisure I assemble a circle of Indian women around me to learn them to sew and knit for themselves. The employment, how delightful!—the spectacle, how revolting!—for they are mostly unclothed, *Do* give me old garments, or anything to cover them—and give them to *me, not* to the superintendent—that I may, when I clothe myself, do so with pleasure, and not with pain that others must be destitute.''

''BELOVED BROTHER:—You wish me to write *particularly,* and give you such a description of the state of things as will enable you to understand our situation, prospects, wants, success, &c. I wish I might write something interesting, but I presume but little connected with our mission will be gratifying.

''I hardly know *what* to write, there is so little of novelty connected with a mission to the Indians. In respect to them, I will, however, say, that we find them the most inoffensive, as well as indolent and degraded people imaginable. Indeed, we go about the prairies and forest with as much careless indifference as if we were surrounded with insects only. With entire confidence we leave our door and windows unfastened, and admit numbers of them into our houses, with muskets, tomahawks, and knives in their hands. The Kallapooya tribes are considered the most inactive upon the coast. Even other tribes if reproached with being lazy, will reply that they are not Kallapoyas. They appear willing to work, however, when they want to eat and have no food, and are pleased with acquiring any new art. The coming summer, Mr. Leslie intends to superintend them in the agricultural department, having improved land for that purpose. The produce of their labor is to be their own. They seem pleased with the project, but will, it is likely, fancy that they must be highly rewarded for their pains. The native language of these Indians, has not yet been learned by one of the missionaries, consequently our labors are confined mostly to the children in the mission family, who are learning English. There is, however, a kind of jargon spoken and learned for purposes of trade, which is familiar to several tribes, and easily acquired, by which some knowledge of their lost condition may be communicated to the adults.

"There are in the Mission family and Mission house, twenty-five boys and ten girls, who are provided for by Mr. and Mrs. Shepherd, Mr. Whitcomb, and myself. To conduct them properly is not a small task. Mr. Whitcomb has the superintendence of the farm, Mr. Shepherd the first oversight of the boys and the school, while I endeavor to supply the place of Mrs. Lee in the Mission family, and am to have the care of the girls.

"The Mission house, built of logs, is situated near the banks of the Willamette. We expect, by two winters more, it will, notwithstanding its great firmness (for the logs are oak, and were strongly laid up by Mr. Jason Lee himself,) be drifted down the stream, and away from our sight. Dr. White has a fine block-house, situated upon a pleasant and extensive prairie, with a delightful evergreen grove of fir trees upon one side, and the agreeable variety of valley, hill, ponds of clear water, bushes, brakes and groves of fir, oak, maple and cotton wood, and deer, wolves, snakes, &c., upon the background. Mr. Leslie lives in a one story square-logged house, formerly owned by one of our French neighbors, and inhabited by half-breed people and Indians. The number of rooms has been increased to three. Mr. Beers' house is of logs from the delightful fir grove in front of the mission, laid together without squaring, barking or straightening, and the openings filled with moss and mud. He has the finest situation in the potato field.

"Our provisions are good enough for us, who have tasted the luxuries of another land and were never thankful for them. We have fine salmon in plenty, about two-thirds of the year, and bread, potatoes, and milk, perhaps the same length of time. Some of us have the remains of sweetmeats which we brought with us, and which we occasionally taste, yet sparingly, for fear of tasting the last. This brings a train of reflections, melancholy and pleasing, which we indulge a little, and then chide, hide the remembrance, and proceed about our duties."

TO THE MEMBERS OF THE
M. E. CHURCH, SAUGUS

"OREGON MISSION,
Willamette, Nov. 30, '38.

"AFFECTIONATE BRETHREN AND FRIENDS: The long, pleasing and profitable
acquaintance I have had with you—the proofs I have received of your
sympathy for the distressed, and the liberal encouragement you gave
and rendered to one who was lately membered with you in church
privileges and social intercourse, has begotten within my breast a
wish to acquaint you with some of the wants of the suffering in this
portion of the world.

"A large share of the bounties of providence to you has been
cheerfully bestowed to promote the spread of the gospel in heathen
lands; and here are numbers who are daily made happy by your
generosity, while your humble petitioner has hourly reason to be
reminded of your kindness, and to find increased within her breast
the great affection she has for you.

"With others of your acquaintance, I am laboring to raise the
condition of the heathen; and in our field of labor we find men of
intelligent minds—women of endearing natural qualities, and
children possessing promising talent, in the lowest condition that
ignorance and poverty can place them.

"To benefit them is the employment of this missionary band.
And while thirty-two beneath this roof are depending upon our labors
and the benevolence of christians in this wide world, others are
thronging our path, wandering about almost uncovered—surviving
upon wild roots, flower seeds and carrion—needing, suffering, yet
insensible and contented.

"For these, our hearts bleed. For these, my beloved
acquaintance, I have, with the fullest expectation of success, resolved
to invite you to make yet another effort to befriend them. *Will* you
assist in so clothing them that they may, with propriety, come into
our presence for the purposes of instruction, &c.?

"I ask no more. For their tuition there will doubtless be
abundant means provided. For their sustenance our brethren *hope* to
be able to induce them to labor—but for their *garments* where shall we
look?

"The clothing already sent to the mission (which, thanks to the
benevolent, has been ample for the purposes to which it has been

appropriated.) has hitherto been restricted to the wants of the Indian children belonging to the family, except when some Indian hunter, having had good success, has been able to pawn a deer's skin, or beaver, or some wild meats, to purchase enough to cover his naked and perhaps dying woman or children.

"The sisters of our mission have resolved to form themselves into a society, to be called the Oregon Female Benevolent Society, for the purpose of clothing the Indian females in this section of the country. Their intention is to improve one afternoon in a week in making dresses for this purpose, and they intend to continue so to do while they shall find in their possession the necessary materials. Being one of the number, I have promised and resolved to supply them, even if my salary must be devoted to the object.

"My dear friends, will you assist me? And will my female acquaintances join our society, and if they do not make clothing, give us cloth that we may be employed? I believe you will; the evidences I have before me of your liberality warrant me in indulging such a faith. I am sure I need not *urge* you, (nor would there be long delay in attempting so charitable a design, were you told by this people, as I have been on every occasion, when inviting them to attend our meetings, *"we have no coats, and we would be very shamed to go without any!"*) for I flatter myself, that while we, a feeble band, shall be busily employed on Monday afternoon of every week, my sisters and female friends in Saugus will be engaged to carry into effect the same design of improving the condition and appearance of (in the great family of mankind) our sisters and travellers to eternity.

"With dearest regards to and prayers for you all,

I subscribe myself,
Your unworthy,
Yet grateful friend,

RUTH ROVER.''

Ruth Rover, feeling very sensibly the need of seeing the Indian women clothed, and finding but little prospect of this being done by the mission, for Mr. Lee did not approve of the Indians receiving much gratuitously, as he thought it encouraged them in idleness, but whatever they would *work* for he was pleased to have them receive, and *they,* being so accustomed to habits of idleness and deprivation, would not make an effort to obtain that of which they did not know the advantages and had never realized the comforts. Hence, Ruth conceived the plan of *giving,* in the first place, dresses to the native women, and believed that after they had worn them and been accustomed to their benefits, they would afterwards *make an effort* to obtain them, rather than to again be destitute. In this she was not mistaken.

Having called upon and conversed with the ladies of the mission, and gained their promise of co-operation, she drafted the following form of organization of the

"OREGON SAUWASH BENEVOLENT SOCIETY.

Article 1. "The *principal* objects of this society shall be to clothe the destitute Indian females within the circle of its operations, and instruct them in the art of needle-work.

Art. 2. "The *minor* objects of this society shall be to provide for the sick of both sexes, to the extent of its power, such articles of medicine, food and raiment as shall render their situation comfortable, and be calculated to awaken within their breasts grateful emotions to the Supreme Being, who is well pleased to behold his children following the example of their Lord, who "went about doing good."

Art. 3. "The officers of this society shall be a president, (male,) vice president, six managers, (females,) and six male assistants.

Art. 4. "The duty of the president shall be to attend the public meetings, report the general aspect of the society, the state of its funds, the apparent wants of the natives, and endeavor, on all occasions, to promote the objects of the society by soliciting contributions and members and reporting to the vice president such cases of the suffering Indians as may happen under his observation.

Art. 5. "The duty of the vice president shall be to attend all the meetings of the managers, to close, or provide some person to close, said meetings by prayer, keep the treasury, dispose of garments, keep a regular diary of the proceedings of the officers, report such proceedings to the president, and render to the managers such assistance as they, from time to time, may require.

Art. 6. "The duty of the managers shall be to cut and make the garments, instruct the native females in needlework, choose officers, give supplies to the assistants, and report their doings to the vice president.

Art. 7. "The duty of the assistants shall be to acquaint themselves with the necessities of the sick among the native males, as far as shall be practicable, report accordingly to the managers, furnish them with given supplies, and give a stimulus to the public meetings by their presence or address, or both."

This plan operated well. Although all the objects embodied in the form of organization were not carried out, in consequence of Ruth's leaving the mission, yet she had the satisfaction, two or three years afterwards, of having Indians come to her and offer any price she pleased for dresses for their women and girls, saying they could not now, after having worn dresses, be willing to go without as they used to do.

Some gentlemen who visited the mission contributed handsomely to its support, and Ruth Rover found great pleasure, in the former part of the day, in going to the lodges and telling the women the time had again come for their meeting, and in seeing them, sometimes to the number of twenty or twenty-five, sitting around the room, learning to make clothes for themselves.

Ruth received, about this time, many letters from her friends at home, which greatly comforted her mind. Some extracts will be made, merely to denote their kindly feeling for and affection towards her. They say:

"Notwithstanding this is the holy Sabbath, I cannot let it pass without devoting a few moments to you. I cannot, should I attempt it, describe the pleasure I received on the receipt of your letters from St. Catherine's and Sandwich Islands, and in learning you were well and was so well contented with your situation. You are probably now in Oregon, and removed from all your relatives, you will, I am sure suffer many moments in loneliness. Be assured, you have become doubly dear to me from this consideration. Could I pass over the mountains, occasionally, and spend a few hours with you to relieve this sadness, and to cheer, also, my heart with your presence—but, alas! 'tis useless to think of it. I can only *write* to you, and I would I were better qualified for *this* duty—but knowing as I do the goodness of your heart, I know you will excuse my *poor* attempts and believe in my ardent affection for you, if I cannot, by many flowers of speech, express it.

"You will doubtless perceive extracts from some of your letters published in the papers. Were it possible for you to conceive the interest a large portion of christians take in the Oregon mission, and the eagerness and avidity with which everything relating to that country is received, you would, I'm sure, pardon us for suffering the extracts to be made. In this I hope you will find some apology. In a conversation with Mr. Brown of "Zion's Herald," he remarked: "The friends of missions give their money for their support, and they have a right to know what becomes of it, hence the public expect to receive some information from the missionaries themselves, and," he added, ''nothing would please editors of public journals better than to have letters addressed to them personally, on these subjects.''

''I was at home yesterday, and hoped that father had in some measure relented in his feelings towards you, but he said, ''I would not write to her, were twenty vessels to sail from here to-morrow.''

''You may find you have neglected to provide yourself with many indispensable articles which you cannot obtain in Oregon. If such should be the case you must not fail to inform us immediately of your wants, that they may be supplied—for, rest assured that whatever you shall find yourself in need of, by making it known to your friends here, shall be forthcoming as soon as may be.

''Dear sister, could I but see you, if but for an hour, how it would gratify me. It is not possible to describe the interest I feel for you in the step you have taken. O! live for God, and God alone. Be an example of good works. I know you will, and may the Lord bless you abundantly.

''We send you some articles you may need. Do take care of your health, and inform us of whatever you want and we will take great pleasure in forwarding them.

''I cannot tell you how much I wish to see you—much more than ever, since receiving your letters.

''What can it be that distresses you? I thought 'twould make you happy to do something for your fellow beings, for you always aimed at this. But you still find troubles, it seems. O! remember this world is not to be our abiding place forever. Look to the Lord—He is able to save. Do not expect happiness in this life—look beyond this vale of tears. Think of your reward, if you can be the means of saving any of the perishing heathen; if you can be instrumental in saving *one* soul 'twill reward you for all you suffer here. Labor and pray, and take courage from the thought that heaven will be your great reward.

''We want you to write something to the Sabbath school children in Saugus, I know they would be much pleased. If you are in need of any articles you cannot procure, let us know, and they will be forthcoming.

''By-the-bye, let me tell you that your friend D. O—— is married, and has named his daughter Ruth Rover. Mary Ann has been a short time on a visit to her grand-pa's. She says she could not prevail on him to put as much as one cent in her missionary box, for he said he had given his youngest daughter, which he thought was more than any of us had done. I guess he had forgotten he did not *give* you.

"Last Sabbath we had a collection taken up for the purpose of buying sacramental vessels for Oregon. Forty-two dollars were raised almost without effort, and there were but few members present. It gives me very sad feelings every Sabbath morning to hear the bells ringing for church, knowing that you are so remote and so far deprived of the privileges that we enjoy. It also pains me to think of the heathen who never heard the glad tidings of salvation. O! sister, be not weary in well-doing, for in due time you shall reap if you faint not. "Hope on, hope forever," and

> 'Let us think of Him who wore the thorn
>   without the rose,
> And bear, as patiently He bore, our fewer,
>   lighter woes.'

"Let me assure you, my dear Ruth, that we were all exceedingly happy to hear of your safe arrival in Oregon, and that you were so well pleased with your voyage, and received so many kind attentions from those with whom you sailed, as also from those with whom you sojourned in strange lands. We feel ourselves to be under obligations to them, and wish it were in our power to cancel them.

"You will receive by the Fama, besides the letters, a box of articles we thought you might need. Be assured they come from warm and loving hearts; and let me tell you now, that whatever you want from here, if you will but furnish a memorandum, we will take great pleasure in forwarding them to you. In the selection of the articles we have sent, we were of course guided by our own judgment, fearing at the same time there might have been other things which you would greatly prefer, but, such as they are, we beg you to accept them as tokens of our regard."

One of Ruth Rover's sisters it had been impracticable for her to see, to bid her a last adieu, on her leaving for the Oregon. She writes thus:

"MY DEAR SISTER: Although so far separated from each other, and in so unexpected a manner, yet I still remember you, and never can I forget the heart-achings and anxious hours I have spent on account of your going away without bidding me a last farewell.

"I did not receive intelligence of your leaving till the last evening before you were to sail, and then my babe was quite sick which prevented me from travelling to Boston next day to see you, although it was supposed I could not reach there before the vessel would have sailed. Be assured I love you sincerely, and would walk many miles even at this late hour of the night if I could but have the pleasure of an interview with you; but when I think of the distance between us I wonder if we shall ever meet again in this world.

"O! Ruth, can it be that we shall see each other again here? Little did I think of it the last time I saw you at home. But I hear you are happy, and why should I not be resigned?

"Brother S—— brought down all your letters, and I sat up nearly all night reading them. Sometimes I laughed at your nonsense and then wept because of your sorrows, but on the whole I found the letters very interesting.

"Your friends here all send love. E. G—— is going to school in Ipswich. She always inquires about you in her letters—says she thinks you must be very sad and lonely in that far off land, among strangers and heathen.

"We are all engaged to spend next thanksgiving with Bro. S——. If you could but be there with us—but no, we must be deprived of your dear company.

"Let me entreat of you not to think of spending your days in that far off land. If you could not be happy without going, and felt it to be your indispensable duty to go, now do feel it to be your duty to return, and we will not blame you in the least.

"'Tis late and I must retire, after commending my family and my dear sister Ruth to the care of that Good Being who orders all things right. Good night, 'May angels guard thee with distinguished care.'"

These few extracts will show that Ruth, in the midst of her trials and deprivations, was favored occasionally with evidences of the affectionate remembrance of her friends—her oldest brother, particularly, was never tiring in his kind services in obtaining letters for her, and rendering her every possible service.

He had experienced great affliction in his family relations. In Illinois he had buried the wife of his youth and several children. He had been skeptical on the subject of religion, till his second marriage.

These extracts, on account of referring to his conversion, and affording a pleasing picture of domestic felicity, are admitted here:

     *   *   *   "Let us help you now, dear sister, to a small dish of matrimonial matters. You will remember our last conversation on the subject, and your advice to me.

"Well, after waiting for some time, I called on Miss ——— for a definite answer. Her reply was that my 'hopes were vain,' which you may well suppose threw the business all aback in that quarter.

"Shortly after, I am happy to inform you, I was introduced to Mrs. T———,[4] the lady you have heard me speak of—waited on her to church—'popped the question,' and was married on Sabbath morning following, by Mr. M———.

"Now, although I do abominably detest to hear a man praise his wife, I will venture this time to give you a little of my opinion of my better half. It is a God's truth that no man living ever was more supremely blest in a companion than myself. I have thus far found T——— possessed of the most amiable disposition of any person with whom it has been my fortune to meet. She is kind, loving and affectionate, not only to myself, but to all around her. In her domestic affairs, prudent, frugal and economical, and unceasing and untiring in her endeavors to please. To sum up all, she is everything a reasonable man could wish—much better far than I deserve. I have been wonderfully blest, indeed, and my friends I believe, without an exception, consider I have been remarkably fortunate.

"It no doubt will rejoice you much, my dear Ruth, to learn that my views in relation to things of a divine nature have very materially changed since I last wrote you, and when you are assured that this change was effected through the instrumentality of my dear wife, it will, I'm sure, cause you to love her till your latest breath.

"Yes, sister, it was her prayer in class-meeting which first lit up the spark of grace in my heart which had so long laid dormant—it was *her* intercession which awakened me from the dangerous slumber in which I had so long been resting, and brought me to see my error; and I must praise God anew and forever that he has saved me from the impending ruin to which I was so fast hastening. * * *

"I can only say, in conclusion, that I enjoy excellent health, and that no man since Adam, was ever more pleasantly situated, or enjoyed more of this world's benefits than

> Your humble servant
> And brother,
>
> S. ROVER."

We perceive that Ruth did not soon recover from the effects of the disturbance which had been occasioned by her contentions with Mr. Leland, and we find her writing thus:

December 21, '37. "In consequence of the late serious difficulties with Mr. Leland, I find myself, in a great measure, unqualified for the duties of the school. My mind is depressed, and my bodily health is feeble. During this season of trial I have felt the influence of the Spirit of Grace in a very consoling manner, and I was satisfied of sharing the approbation of heaven, until I so submissively suffered the affair to rest.

"I am still satisfied of the truth of my suppositions of that individual, and could they in any way be removed I should be most happy. Our late troubles and conversations with him have had the effect to impress them more fully upon my mind. O! that the way of duty were plainly before me, how gladly would I walk it!

"Have been greatly afflicted in mind. Meditating on my situation at this great distance from my home and friends, who have known me from my youth, and were thereby enabled to judge favorably of my disposition—the treatment I have received from the mission family, (whether it were good or bad doubtless had better be decided by others,) and the dark prospect before me, and the fact that the board at New York have not sent me an appointment, as I was led to expect, I became so far discouraged that I felt compelled to inform Mr. Shepherd that I must resign the school for a time, for I had 'that to trouble which my nature would not bear and leave me qualified for the undertaking.' Mr. Lee visited me, and wished me to engage to keep the school till his return from the United States, which will be probably in about two years. I told him I would keep the school till he should leave, but I could not engage to keep it till his return, for I did not know what change might take place before that time, but for a little while I would go to Vancouver, and after that I would decide my course.

March, '38. "Went to Vancouver intending to remain there till circumstances connected with my stay in Willamette shall appear more favorable and agreeable to my wishes.

April 4th. "Messrs. Lee and Edwards left Vancouver for the United States.

"Been at Vancouver for a week and find my mind in a more tranquil frame. My kind friends here, of Dr. McLaughlin's and Mr. Douglass' families, are attentive and kind to me, which has relieved my mind of many unpleasant forebodings.[5] Visited, this afternoon, six families of the laboring people, and conversed with them as well as I was able in jargon. It has been customary, it appears, for these servants of the Hudson Bay Company, who are mostly Frenchmen, on settling here, to buy wives of the Indians, and for whom they pay a blanket, a musket, a horse, or more or less, accordingly as she is prized by her relatives, and with them they live in apparent tranquillity without the ceremony of marriage having been performed—indeed there has been no priest in the country who could perform the ceremony till quite recently. These wives and mothers appear to be attached to their husbands and children, and I have known some parents who have raised children to maturity before an opportunity presented for them to be married. These people appear to consider the private contract they have made is equally binding as if it had been sanctioned by a ceremony of law.

"In one house was an exceedingly old woman wrapped in skins and making moccasins. She was so decrepit with age that she could hardly direct the awl and thread. After some little conversation with her, I asked her if she considered that life could not be continued to her much longer. She said 'yes' and she 'must make haste and get the shoes done,' which excited a laugh in the children and herself. I asked her if her heart was good, and she replied, 'truly it is,' which is the answer ever ready with this people.

"Another woman almost dead with consumption was fancifully trimming a dress with different colored ribbons! Stepping into the grave, yet playing with children's toys. She acknowledged that this world, where people are sick and dying, is not good, and appeared pleased to hear that there is a place where sickness never comes, but said she never prays. Poor woman! she knows not what it is to pray.

"Mrs. R———[6] and her mother were weeping to-day for the absence of her father, who has gone to England to be gone two years:—and I not only am separated from father, mother, sister and brother, but am many thousand miles from them and far from the expectation of seeing them at present—also reproached, slandered and neglected by my relations in the church—dependent upon strangers for protection—harassed by reflections on the past and fears for the future—and without constant living faith in God, and a firm trust in Him for the time to come;—and yet I do not always weep—indeed, I weep but little compared to what I have done, for, verily, I have formerly not only 'watered my couch with tears,' but in school I have been unable to keep my cheeks and eyes dry, much to the astonishment of the children and my own mortification. Am I not now sensitive, or am I becoming hardened to sorrow so that I find it of no use to always grieve about these things?

"Rev. Mr. Leland arrived here from Willamette. He is very desirous for me to return—says I can have board in his family, and promises to do all he can to make me comfortable—which certainly is very kind. He says also, if I choose, I can have accommodations in Mr. Shepherd's family, who have commenced keeping house by themselves.

"Last night I was enabled to pray with unusual earnestness for the blessings of God's grace to be manifested to me. In my sleep I dreamed much of my early friend Harriet T———, an intimate friend of my earlier years, but who about two years since departed into the joy of her Lord. It is not unfrequently the case, when I go to rest with my thoughts depressed, that her spirit seems to be hovering around me, and I awake in the morning in a tranquil and happy frame of mind.

> "Happy soul, her days are ended—
> All her mourning days below."

"She possessed a remarkably amiable disposition—was the joy of her widowed mother's heart—the agreeable and affectionate companion of her husband, and the faithful and loving disciple of her Lord. She has gone to that better land before me, and may I have grace to follow in her steps.

Evening. "Mr. Leland has returned to Willamette, and I am undecided whether or not it were better for me to return. I think I am not likely to be more unhappily situated here—but I shall be without the certain means of support, unless I can be able to obtain a school which will be sufficient to defray my expenses. And the most important of all is, I shall be dependent here, as well as there, on God for success, to attend my labors. If *He* bless me not, I shall find the labor of a life in vain, in point of benefit to any individual.

"How vascillating is the life of man!—'tis first a smile, then a tear. This morning Mrs. R. was rejoicing in prospect of her husband's speedy return, and joy has been beaming from her countenance all day—to-night she is in tears. I could not but ask myself why I should mourn at all the ill fortune of my life, because I have not in possession an equal share of the blessings of friendship and society with others, and felt to take shame to myself that I ever grieved for those things, and in prayer again found my mind refreshed and strengthened to endure still these deprivations. On kneeling, the sweet reflection of the privilege I enjoy in being permitted to go to a Throne of Grace, and ask Him who sitteth thereon for needed blessings, almost for a time overwhelmed me. Can I tell my wants to a being who is omnipotent in power to perform, and whose willingness to bestow exceeds our most enlarged conceptions? —and shall I talk of deprivations? What is there that He is willing to bestow, which I may not receive? The difficulty lies here: I have a will of my own, and do not at all times cheerfully say, '*Thy* will be done.'

"This morning called on Mr. Douglass to enquire if it would be agreeable to him for me to attempt to instruct the Indian children about the fort. He said it would be pleasing to him, as well as a worthy undertaking to instruct them, but there was no place in the fort which could be improved for that purpose, as the only school-room was occupied by the boys. He said, however, if it would be agreeable to me, he would give me a class of ladies to instruct, in which was included his wife and Mrs. R——. I regret that I cannot be benefitting the Indians, yet I may thus find employment sufficient to defray the expense of my board. For this I would be thankful. I learned from him that

Mr. Lee, in speaking about me to him, said he 'had offered me permanent employment at the mission and that I did not see fit to accept it, and that he did not know whether or not I intended to leave the mission—if I did he knew not the reason for it.' This very much astonished me, though it is true he wished me to make an engagement to remain a teacher in the mission until his return from the States, which I objected to do as I did not know what change might take place before that time—but that he knows the reasons for my dissatisfaction in the mission, and of my leaving it, if I should, I am well aware.

"Yesterday a company of Chenooks arrived to visit their friends here, and to-night they are all singing in their native wild airs and beating an accompaniment on boards and kettles. I very much admire to hear their native airs in the open grove. There is, indeed, sublimity in the sound. They generally sing on two, and sometimes three different octaves, and I have never been able to detect any accompaniment of words. Mrs. McLaughlin has told me they have a song which they sing when dancing, which in purport is: 'I am acquainted with all the hills and mountains and streams, and every place birds even see there have I been.' I think unless they improve they'll not soon gain the 'laurel.'

"Commenced my school at Vancouver, with Mrs. Douglass and Mrs. R—— and the little girls belonging to the fort. I instructed the same also on the Sabbath, before and after service, at church. For want of question books, could exercise the scholars only in singing, reading, and reciting hymns and portions of scripture. In the evenings show the girls how to arrange the patchwork. These children are between the ages of seven and fourteen years, and for want of mothers and sisters really appear as sheep without a shepherd. They are daughters of gentlemen who are residing mostly at remote stations of the company, and are here for the purpose of security and to obtain instruction.

"After school this afternoon the kind Mrs. McLaughlin, ever ready to be cheerful and to render others so, invited the ladies of the house, and the girls, to a walk to the old fort, and a cup of tea on the grass. The day has been unusually fine and our party, amounting to seventeen persons and five dogs, were in unusually high spirits. After tea and a short session of work, the ladies amused themselves by throwing and catching the stick and sign, in which I had to join, though a new play to me—but as they engaged to learn me, I concluded the fault would be theirs in case I made any blunders, and was presently as wild as any of them. But I was soon cured of this frivolity, for becoming tired I reclined upon the grass, and resting my head upon a log and catching a glimpse of heavens above me and the tops of the tall green firs, as they contrasted with the blue sky and white clouds, I became forcibly impressed with the beauty of the scene—the stillness, purity, grandeur and glory of the works of God, and especially when contrasted with the works of man—and preferred much to leave the party to their sports, while I had found what yielded more satisfaction, in meditation on the works of God. Messrs. Rae and M'Cloud's boat being seen descending the river increased the hilarity of the moment and hastened us to the fort. Gathered some beautiful wild flowers, and found ourselves very much refreshed.

"To-day and last night enjoyed an unusual sense of the blessings of the good spirit of God upon my heart. Destitute of the society of relations, and indeed almost of every one with whom social intercourse is interesting, I yet mourn not much, for I am comforted with the thought that I shall, when done with earth, live again in the blessed enjoyment of the company of saints in heaven. Latterly, the name of the Redeemer spoken by any one has seemed to touch a chord which has vibrated through my whole soul, so much am I comforted with His presence.

"Last Sabbath the Rev. Mr. Beaver of the Episcopalian church, contrary to what he has before done since his residence in the place, deferred the morning service until eleven o'clock, and previously in the morning assembled the girls in his house for the reading of the scriptures.[7] This was, without doubt, done to prevent their meeting with me, after service, for Sabbath school. Agreeably to Mr. Douglass' wish, I have several times sang hymns with them that they might improve in singing, and have met them in the evening for that purpose. When Mr. Beaver became acquainted with this, he requested the girls to come to his house to read the scriptures in the evenings. This he also did, I have been told, when Mrs. Spalding and Mrs. Whitman were once here; and forbade the schoolmaster to copy a hymn the ladies sung and which the children wished to learn, and sent a letter to these ladies requesting them to have nothing to do with the children.[8] Mr. Beaver, I suppose, considers the fort his parish, which is undoubtedly right—yet, he manifests a spirit of disunion not becoming a servant of the Most High.

"My mind is exceedingly troubled in consequence of being unable to benefit the Indians. When I consider that for eight years the predominant desire of my heart has been to devote my life for the good of the heathen, and the kindness of many christian friends in favoring me in the plan, and the money which has been expended for me to gain a sufficiently thorough education and to assist me to come among them, and that now, apparently, I must relinquish the hope—for I see them every day thronging my path in the most degraded and abject state imaginable, while I am unable to benefit them at all. I suffer continually an intense pain and disquietude of soul which deprives me of all satisfaction in every pursuit I can devise to improve my time.

Sabbath. "Walking out to-day I observed three Indians working in their gardens. They promised to desist, when I told them of the impropriety of working on this day.

"Been to ride with Dr. Tolmie to see the Indians' gardens in the lower plains. These are the first attempts they have made at agriculture. In doing this, this season, they have been assisted and instructed by this gentleman, who may, with propriety, be styled the Indians' friend. The small plantations were neatly fenced and planted with potatoes and peas. One old man had prepared a large piece of ground for the reception of seed, but had none to plant in it. Dr. Tolmie offered him and another Indian potatoes if they would come to the fort for them.

"To-day was invited to see the Indian school, it being the Sabbath, but was unable to enter for the crowd of Indians about the door. I heard this gentleman teaching them the Lord's Prayer. After that they sang a hymn. How melodious is the sound of any one's voice when employed in soothing the afflicted, or in instructing the ignorant!"

About this time Ruth received many letters from home, and friends in different places, but before we refer to them we will close this chapter by saying that Messrs. Leland and Shepherd went to Vancouver from Willamette to endeavor to persuade her to return to that station, saying the board had appointed her as a "teacher in the Oregon mission," and she, with revived spirits, accompanied them.

CHAPTER X

LETTERS

❦

We find some letters written by Ruth to her parents and sisters when at Vancouver, from which we make a few extracts. To one who had experienced great family bereavements she says:

"I was greatly afflicted to receive intelligence of the death of your lovely daughters—not so much for them as for yourself. Knowing as much of the trials and sins of the world as I do, I am more inclined to rejoice than sorrow, when one of its inhabitants escapes to bliss. Your babes were lovely and blooming, and a very great addition to your domestic pleasures—they are now in heaven, (such is our faith,) spotless before the throne of God, and you, my dear sister, though greatly distressed at their loss, may be comforted that their home is the family of angels, and so fully supplied is our father's store-house with blessings that they can never want. Rejoice, my dear Olive, that our best Parent has so timely and well provided for your tender offspring, and be thankful. I rejoice that you find religion so great a support, and thank you for the encouragement you have given me to be 'dauntless.' Take the same encouragement yourself, and let us go forward."

To another sister she says:

"After the regret I felt at not seeing you and Fitz and leaving my father better reconciled to the step I had taken, had subsided, I had a

pleasant voyage to the Sandwich Islands. The visit we made at St.
Catherine's Island was very pleasant. You must think it so when you
consider the confinement on board a vessel for so many days was
quite novel to me, and we had just passed through the most intense
heat in the torrid zone, after having so shortly before that been
hugging my cloak about me to screen me from the fierceness of the
wintry blast. The shades of the orange and lemon trees and the cool
breezes from the mountains were delightfully agreeable. The fruits,
including the pine apple, berries, &c., were very refreshing after so
many days confinement to salt provisions, and the interesting society
of the Portuguese peasants was very pleasant.

"At Callao I did not go on shore, but from Mr. Leland's
description of the place, and of Lima, the capital of Peru, I presume I
should have been much gratified. The people there, as well as at
Valparaiso, and indeed nearly every town in South America, are
strictly Roman Catholics. No other religion is tolerated. At
Valparaiso Mrs. Scott told me that the few foreigners there who are
protestants, were obliged to hold their religious services privately or
be dealt with according to law.

"In all these places the poor are wretched, and the rich glutting
in luxury and ease. The middle class alone appear happy.

"I think I have spoken of Valparaiso in another letter, but to the
Sandwich Islands I may again revert. I can never be weary of
thinking and speaking of our dear friends there. We found their
society remarkably agreeable, and received from the missionaries
and residents every possible necessary and refined attention.

"After a detention of fourteen days in this agreeable place and
society, which passed like an hour in a summer's eve, we took
passage for Columbia river, where we arrived after a passage of
twenty-three days.

"I was pleased with Bro. S———'s choice of a wife, as far as I
am acquainted with it, and hope she may daily appear to him more
exemplary as a christian and endearing as a wife.

"You speak of E———'s disappointment, and I am only
surprised that her excellent qualities had not irresistibly bound
Henry to her forever. I long since learned that an aspiring young
man would not be governed in his choice of wife by considerations to
her or her friends.

"I thank you, dear sister, for the affection you express—I am, as
you know, unworthy of it, (would I were worthy,)—but do not
already urge my return home—I have not yet, as I understand it,

commenced my labors in the mission field. There are four years more which I have to remain, and before they'll be past you'll be tired of your endeavors.

"In different letters I learn much that is discouraging concerning our father's health, and I fear the next letters from home will apprise me of his death. I am pained deeply in the remembrance of the last view I had of him—how he hung his head—how the tears stole in silence between the long seen furrows—how sad and strange his countenance when he refused to look at or speak to me—but he is my father, and I mourn over him with all the affection and fond remembrance with which I was ever possessed."

"NAPOOPOO,

"Sandwich Islands.

"To Miss Ruth Rover:

"DEAR SISTER IN CHRIST—I congratulate you much on your arrival at Honolulu, which brings you so near the scene of your future labors, and though separate from you, I unite with you in returning thanks to our Heavenly Father for His Divine protection in the midst of all dangers to which you may have been exposed, either by sea or land, since you left your paternal roof and the fond embrace of all your dear acquaintances.

"As a missionary I feel a deep and general interest in all who are commissioned on the same errand, but in your case I feel particular interest, for I have but little doubt we were schoolmates at the Wesleyan Seminary, North Wilbraham, in 1835. If so, you will recognize me by the name of O. H———, though a new name has since been transferred to me. I feel quite solicitous to know whether it is really so, and should be beyond expression happy to see you if in the providence of God you may be permitted to come here.

"I hope you will write me, and if you recognize me, give information the latest you have from Wilbraham, from the perceptress, &c.; and will you also favor me with some items from your preparation and voyage journals, both in relation to your religious exercises and your temporal trials or prosperity.

"I have sometimes been disheartened in my labors, but am again encouraged when I think of the words of our precious Saviour, 'Be of good cheer, I have overcome the world.' I hope yours will be a light path—your course cheerful—your life useful—your death happy and triumphant—and your eternity be spent with many who through your instrumentality will be converted to God.

"The field to which you are destined to go, is one in which I feel interested. I shall be happy to have a correspondent there, and shall ever afterwards feel that I am acquainted with you, whether it proves that I have ever seen you or not. I shall look for a letter from you by the next ship.

"Remember me to your associates, and do not forget me at the Throne of Grace.

Yours affectionately,

O. H. VANDUZRE

From the same:

"MY DEAR SISTER ROVER—How sincerely I thank you for your kind letter, which came to hand December 11th. I think you must have thought mine to you was in some respects quite foreign to the good work in which we are engaged. I only intended it for a little note, and did not think it would be so long in finding its way to you, or travel so many miles ere it reached you—but as it has faithfully sought out an old friend, and procured for me a new correspondent in the dark but dewy vales of Oregon, I will be thankful, and no longer think of its deformities.

"When we were in Wilbraham together, did you think of coming to these ends of the earth? I did not think of coming to these Islands, though my mind was on a foreign mission for sometime in the future. It was little more than six months after I left school that I decided to come here, and perhaps my memory can never revert to a more dreary season in the whole course of my life. My temporal circumstances were of a nature and tendency to greatly depress my spirits, which brought with it also leaness of soul and only gave me 'tears for meat continually.' But at length light sprang up out of obscurity and my feet were set in a large place, the Lord having hearkened unto me. O! how blessed is Christ's deliverance! If we hold our confidence in Him it brings us great reward. He is ever nearer us than we sometimes imagine.

"My family cares have increased so much the past year that I cannot now do anything in school—but I do not think it possible for the wife of a missionary to reside in the midst of a heathen population and guide her house in the fear of the Lord, without exerting a good influence upon the people, especially upon the mothers, to whom it is given to mould the characters of the succeeding generation. We have doubtless both of us learned enough of missionary life to find that we did not leave all our spiritual enemies in our native land, and that their strength is not a whit diminished from the fact that we are missionaries. It appears to me that till since I have been here I did not know how much of the corrupt nature my heart contained, nor do I now know, but can most emphatically exclaim: ''Who shall deliver me from this body of sin and death?''

''How do you enjoy your health in Oregon? How large a school do you teach? and how do you proceed in discipline? Is the language difficult to acquire? Are the people kind to you? Do their habits and course of life manifest as much ignorance, degradation and misery as you expected? Have the mission, at this early period, comfortable accommodations to make it seem like home? How is the surrounding scenery? Is the soil productive of the same kinds of fruits, flowers, &c., as in our loved States? What are the tastes of the Indians for cultivation? What their habits of labor? What their personal appearance? How many hopeful converts as fruits of the mission's enterprise? How do they wear? Can you not in your next, give me some anecdotes illustrative of these questions?

''Will you not write soon, fully and frankly, your feelings, your joys and sorrows and trials, consequent upon a missionary life, &c.,—for anything which will be of importance to you will be of interest to me. Pray for the peace of Zion here.

Most truly and
Affectionately yours,

O. H. VANDUZRE.''

''TOLLAND,
''Connecticut,

''MY DEAR SISTER ROVER: I think I need make no apology for writing to you, as I have a good opportunity to send. It may serve to support and strengthen you in the midst of your arduous duties, in a far distant land, to know there are some in our own favored States that sympathize with you and remember you in their supplications before our Father in Heaven.

''With pleasure memory often points to my mind the pleasant interviews we enjoyed together at Wilbraham in the fall of '35. Together we ascended the rugged hill of science, and in hours of relaxation from study we used to converse on the things of God and the interest we felt in the great work in which you are now engaged. But sweeter far were the seasons of social prayer we enjoyed when with united hearts and voices we poured out our supplications and praises to Him who hears and answers prayer.

"Yes, dear sister, those are seasons on which I love to reflect, though mingled with sorrow at the thought that probably they will be renewed no more on earth. But there is a brighter, better world where I trust we shall again unite our voices in unceasing praise to Him who hath washed us from our sins in his own blood.

"I was happy to learn that Oregon was to be the field of your labor, as you had expressed to me a desire that you might be sent there. And I have since then rejoiced to hear that you have been supported and strengthened by God's grace in the great work. Without doubt you have found many difficulties and trials in the way, of which you could form no adequate idea till you commenced your labors. But while you lean on the arm of Omnipotence you shall not, you need not fear, you will be sustained.

"I have been attending camp-meeting the past week at Bolton. It was a season of profit—some were sanctified and some converted. Of this privilege I suppose you are deprived, but the time may come when in the grove with the sons of the forest you may worship God. O! how I should like to see and converse with you concerning your joys and sorrows. But this may not be on earth—but it will be but a little while before we shall close all our labors here and enter upon those joys that are abiding. It matters but little where our lot is cast on earth, if we can glorify God and make our election sure.

"Perhaps, dear sister, you may see little fruit of your labor—you may meet with unkindness and ingratitude from those for whom you have forsaken all that is dear to you on earth. But remember your record is on high—your reward is in heaven. It was not for worldly honor that you engaged in the work, but to labor for God and the salvation of souls, therefore if God approves you can rejoice. Sometimes you may be ready to faint in the midst of the discouraging scenes that surround you—prejudices against the gospel and the white man may have grown with their growth and strengthened with their strength, until it seems to be an almost insurmountable barrier in the way of the spread of the gospel. But Jehovah has promised that his word shall not return to Him void—that the whole earth shall be filled with His glory, and He will accomplish it in His time.

''I still love the missionary cause—I am willing to go to the ends of the earth if God calls. I am waiting the direction of His providence. Wherever I can be most useful I desire to be. I would like to know the portion of work assigned me and be about it.

''I trust my soul is becoming more and more deeply acquainted with the mysteries of godliness. In Christ I possess all things—He is my all. O! the blessedness of that gospel that brings full salvation to the soul. What a privilege that worms of the dust may become heirs of God—heirs to an incorruptible crown. Is not this worth suffering for? and may we not rejoice that we are accounted worthy to suffer with Christ? for if we do, we shall reign with Him. Heaven will abundantly recompense our labor. Here we toil for a moment, but our rest will be eternal.

''You have, I suppose, a few kind friends with whom you can hold sweet converse. These you must prize highly. But the best of all is, God is ever near. The blessed Jesus sympathizes with his followers—having suffered in the flesh he knows our infirmities, and His grace will be sufficient.

''Let this, my dear sister, cheer and comfort your heart in the midst of your sufferings. Be not discouraged at the difficulties in the way. You are not alone—underneath you are laid the everlasting arms. Labor and suffer on a few more days or years, and then thy warfare will be ended, 'the toilsome strife will be o'er,' and thou shalt hear the welcome sound: 'It is enough, come up higher.' I too will strive to meet you in that better land.

''Many of our dear friends with whom we associated at Wilbraham have gone to rest. I know not where I shall spend my days on earth. But, whether it be in our own favored New England, the islands of the sea, or the wild forests of Oregon, with Christ in my soul I can be happy.

''Accept, my dear sister, these lines, written in haste, from one who loves you and who will continue to remember you before the Throne of Mercy. Farewell, till we meet in heaven.

> Yours in the bonds of
> Christian love,
>
> L. HOWARD.''

"WILBRAHAM————.

"MY DEAR SISTER RUTH—It is with a heart overflowing with emotion that I have taken my pen to address you.

"The thought that you, with whom I have formed a pleasing and endearing acquaintance, and who was with me but yesterday, as it were, are now so far from me, and that I may not indulge the hope of seeing you again, almost overwhelms me.

"Yes, sister, the very lines which I here pen for your perusal cannot reach you for many months, and probably not until after many more changes shall have occurred.

"I often think of you and imagine that I can see you engaged in the arduous labor incident to the missionary life, and sometimes say to myself, O! that I were with Ruth, engaged in teaching the poor degraded Indian. We occasionally hear from you by way of your letters addressed to your friends and which have been published, and I assure you it is with eagerness that I have perused them. The name of Ruth is dear to me, and every line, however small, penned by your hand, deeply interests me. The intelligence of your illness has been a source of affliction to us, but we hope that ere this, you have been restored to perfect health.

"You have the consolation of knowing that you are spending your strength for the advancement of the Redeemer's cause and that He who called you is able to carry you through the last conflict.

"We are this day to give the parting hand to some very dear friends whom we meet no more on earth. It will cost us a struggle, but we will be reconciled to the will of God, hoping that though we see them no more here, we shall meet them at the right hand of God. O! consoling thought! Does not this cheer you, my dear Ruth? The consideration that these trials are but for a moment, and that you are (if faithful to the grace given) to enjoy the society of your friends in your Father's kingdom, does it not cast the light of sunshine over your darkest trials?

"My mother and sisters often think and speak of you with much affection. While we enjoy all the privileges which you have sacrificed for the good of the heathen, think not that we are unmindful of you.

"That the Lord may sustain you and make you abundantly useful in your capacity, and that you may be prepared for a triumphant entrance into the kingdom of rest, is the prayer of

Your sincere friend,

C. B. MOODY."

❦

"HONOLULU————.''

"DEAR MISS ROVER: "I was glad to hear from you, but sorry to know that you were suffering from sickness.

"We are often led by a path we know not, but generally find in the end it was just the discipline we needed. When we possess that meek and humble spirit which will lead us, without anxious solicitude, to commit our way unto the Lord, and trust also in Him that He may bring to pass the desires of our hearts, it matters little to us whether it be by labor or suffering that we are called to serve Him.

"I wanted to know a little more particularly how you live, what comforts you are deprived of, how your time is employed, how you succeed in the language, what you can do to benefit the natives with your present knowledge of it, &c. Suppose you give me the history of a week, in short, with its duties, its trials, perplexities, labors, discouragements, &c.

"Cast *all* your care upon God, and it is doubtless true that when you have done this you will go from the throne of grace with a light heart. You will not carry away the burden you brought there. Are you growing in all the graces of the spirit? Do you find it as easy as you expected to live like a follower of Jesus on missionary ground? Have all that ardor of feeling and warmth of love which you anticipated? Do you feel as deeply and constantly for the perishing multitudes about you as you thought you should?

"You spoke of trials, but did not tell me of what nature they are, so that I cannot either sympathize with you or tender a word of council or admonition. I know that when here you was laboring with some spiritual trials, and that on other points you were not quite happy. I can only say to you, trust in the Lord, wait patiently for Him and He will bring you out of affliction, if it be what he visits upon you, with increased light and love.

"My own course has been marked with some trials, though probably had I exercised, as I ought, the meek and quiet graces of the gospel of Christ, they might have spared me. I ought, then, to learn a lesson of wisdom and forbearance towards those who are similarly tempted.

"Write again soon,
Yours truly,

M. SMITH."[1]

❦

"WIEHTPOO,————.²

"Miss Rover:

"DEAR CHRISTIAN FRIEND—Mrs. Whitman has kindly invited me to answer the letter she was happy to receive from you a short time since, as she is unable at this time to answer it herself, owing to her little daughter's illness and other duties which demand her time. This must answer as an apology, if one is needed, for missionary sisters unacquainted to write to each other.

"I have often heard Mr. and Mrs. Whitman speak with interest of the brethren and sisters of your station. Your names have already become very familiar to me, and I almost forget that we are strangers. But if strangers to each other in person, I trust we are not in heart. Our united prayers for each other have doubtless often ascended to the mercy seat. O! may they continue to rise as one unbroken cloud of incense, and ere long blessings will descend upon us. Prayer is a link that will bind christian hearts together. 'Tis also a proof of christian love.

"We, dear friends, have each of us left our home and country for the purpose of lending our feeble aid to advance the cause of Christ in this dark portion of the world. O! let us consider the responsibility resting on us, and endeavor to be faithful to our Master's cause. Ours is a privilege that angels might envy, could envy enter heaven.

"As yet I have learned but little of the language of this people—hope, however, to be able to converse with them soon. Have made some attempts at teaching the children English, but have almost done with it, as there are few here now. It is thought best to teach the native language as soon as possible. We feel that it must take much time and immense labor to teach them the English, although that would be desirable, as it would introduce them into a wide field of useful knowledge. If duty seems to demand it we shall teach them the English hereafter. As yet we can see nothing to discourage us in our work. I think our expectations have been realized. We find this an interesting people, anxious to receive instruction, and, as far as we can see, their prejudices are in favor of religion.

"There seems to be wanting but faith and prayer, together with the means appointed, to secure blessing. We believe that God has designs of mercy towards these Indian tribes, and that ere long they will become his peculiar people. O! my friend, will not the joy of introducing to the heavenly world some of these benighted tribes more than reward us for all our toil and suffering? Let us then engage in our work with ardor, knowing that the time is short. Let us labor—forgetting ourselves—not seeking our own enjoyment—knowing our reward is in heaven.

"Should our lives be spared, we may have the happiness of meeting each other and conversing and sympathizing together. Till then I shall be happy of the privilege of corresponding with you, if agreeable to you—at least, will you not favor me with an answer to this?

"Please present my best regards to the other sisters of your station—should be happy to receive letters from them.

"Lest I should weary you I will close this by subscribing myself

Yours in the cause of a
World's salvation,

S. G. SMITH."[3]

Lest we tire our readers with a sameness of subject we will defer remaining letters of this description for another place and refer to those which produced in Ruth Rover's mind feelings of a very painful kind.

The death of her father took place in one year and two days after she left home. It is thus referred to:

"DEAR SISTER RUTH—It gives me pleasure to have another opportunity to write, although a part of what I shall communicate will be of the most distressing character.

"I allude to the death of our dear father, who departed this life January 29th, 1838, after being confined to his bed but three weeks, although he has been quite poorly for some months. He was quite resigned latterly, and very patient under his sufferings. The Rev. Mr. W—— visited him daily for some time and prayed with him, and he took much pleasure in having christian people call on him and converse on things of a divine and heavenly nature . From prayers he seemed to derive great consolation, and those best qualified to judge are of an opinion that he met with a change of heart and died happy. His disease, on post mortem examination, was found to be cancer in the stomach and ulcerated liver."

A sister says:

"DEAR RUTH: It becomes my painful duty to inform you of the death of our father. * * * * * *

"I was not with him in his last moments, but he died without a
struggle. When I saw him last I went to his bedside and gave him a
parting kiss. He returned it and said, 'we must part—you must do the
best you can—I shall live but a short time, I do not wish to—I have
given all to God—to God I have given all.' Gladly would I have
stayed with him till he breathed his last, but I thought of the dying
groan which I had so recently witnessed in my own house, and felt it
would be too much to hear.

"Mother bears her trouble with great fortitude.

"I wished to speak to father of you, but feared it would too much
disturb his feelings to refer to your absence, therefore I said nothing.

"I suppose S——— has told you how he made his will, if so you
will perceive he has kept his word about disinheriting you. But I
cannot think it was from any hardness towards you, but in
consequence of his disappointment and from having passed his word
to you to that effect, and also because you are so far away he thought
you would never be benefited if he willed you anything.

"But, sister, you have much to comfort you. The bible says,
'when thy father and mother forsake thee, then the Lord will take thee
up.' You have, I trust, a rich treasure laid up in heaven. Christ says,
'no man that has forsaken father, mother, houses, lands, &c., &c, but
shall receive in the world to come eternal life.'"

We perceive here that Ruth's sister omitted a part of the promise, viz:
that which refers to possessions in this life. Did her faith fail her because Ruth
received nothing from her father? and did she think that God consequently
would be only half as good as His word?

Another sister says of this event:

"We have lost our poor old father. O! could you have been here
and waited on him in his last moments 'twould have been such a
consolation to him. We all feared to speak of you to him, and he only
once during his illness spoke of you to anyone. When I bade him
farewell the last time, hoping to see him again before he should die,
he said no! he should not live to see me again, and bursting into tears
said it was hard that all his children must leave him, and exclaimed
with much feeling, 'Now is the time that I want Ruth!' O! sister,
could it have been ordered that you had not gone till after this event,
what a satisfaction to us all, and especially to him, and I believe also
to you, since it proves that he is called away so much earlier than you
expected. But try to be resigned.

"I believe *you* will suffer more than us all by this dispensation. *We* are in the midst of the pleasures of home, friends, and social advantages; but you—oh! it chills me to think of what may be your deprivations. Do not—do not think of remaining there:

"Come home! thy earthly friends with sorrow see
The vacant chair that waits so long for thee;
Wand'rer return—return no more to roam—
Come back to thy native land! Come home! Come home!''

By Mr. Rover's will, the widow was to receive her third of all property. Ruth and two brothers, in consequence of their having left home without their father's consent— they to the western country, and she to a foreign mission— were to receive each *one dollar,* the law making it necessary each child should receive this sum. The youngest son was to receive fifty dollars, having been undutiful; and the balance, three thousand eight hundred dollars, to be equally divided among the remaining four children.

Ruth's brother added:

"The grave stones have been lately placed at the grave, which is the least we can do for our departed parent. We send his portrait to *you,* thinking you will prize it much as well as ourselves, for, taking all things into consideration, we concluded we could not do otherwise.''

We will here add, as still further indications of Ruth's feelings on her error in leaving her father contrary to his will, and her regret for his death, the following, written in August, 1841:

"LAMENTATION FOR MY FATHER

"Thou art laid in the grave, my affectionate father,
    And low lies thy head on its pillow of death;
Worms sport on thy body, and the mandate of heaven
    Is being fulfilled—thou art mingled with earth.
O! could I recall those once favored moments,
    When thou wert in life, and I by thy side—
My ambition contented, I never would leave thee
    While reason held empire, or till death did divide.
Dark—dark was that moment when in youthful persistence
    I left thee, not heeding thy sorrow of mind;
Or, if I regarded, 'twas to blame its existence,
    And think, (how mistaken!) that thou wert unkind.
Never since that sad moment, howe'er I have wandered,
    Have I found such a friend as thou wert to me;

Nor shall find again, while life bears its standard,
　　Another who can be likened to thee.
Many and deep are the cups of true sorrow
　　Which to me have been given since thy threshold I passed,
With no change for to-day, nor hope for tomorrow—
　　Each draught I have taken, nor found it the last.
In these moments of anguish if my eyes meet thy picture
　　Which hangs by my bedside, my tears flow apace,
And grief rends my soul as I trace every feature,
　　Which told me with smiles in thy heart I'd a place.
And oft I've exclaimed in passionate fondness,
　　O! if he were here, how my foes he'd subdue,
And break their oppression—but alas! oh! the coldness
　　That seizes my spirit when I remember it true
That I am alone, and thou hast departed
　　Afar, and thy smile I shall never meet more,
Nor thy hand see in friendship extended
　　To me, who my loss I in sorrow weep o'er.
Thou sleepest, my father—oh! the peace of thy slumbers,
　　As low 'neath the sod, with close curtains around,
Thou takest repose, nor heedest the numbers
　　Of storms that rave o'er thee, nor even the sound
Of thy daughter's devotion. Oh! had I been by thee
　　When thou to thy kindred dust bid a good night,
From my soul had exuded such drops to embalm thee
　　That thou hadst there waked, not as now, but in light.
Should heaven, indulgent, permit me, a sinner,
　　To return to my home and its strength'ning power lend,
The grave-yard I'll visit and thy tomb stone shall witness
　　The depth of my love, my father, my friend.
When my work's all accomplished, my pilgrimage ended,
　　And to give my account God calls me to die—
When my body's deceased—with its native dust blended,
　　May my spirit with thine be united on high."

CHAPTER XI

❦

"I've heard it said you're quarrelsome:
Of this I've not a doubt!"
And so is fire—when water's thrown
On it—to put it out.

When Ruth Rover arrived at the mission in Willamette, she enquired for her "appointment," and learned that no one had received any intimation of one having been made for her, only by what had been gathered from the missionary report of the Oregon Mission, viz: that "Miss Ruth Rover, a pious young lady, had been sent by the board as a teacher to the Oregon Mission."

There did always appear something strange about this, especially as her brother had written to this effect:

"The Rev. Mr. Pierce seemed to regret that you did not send your compliments more particularly to him than you did. He says his efforts and exertions to procure you a good situation, and to render you as comfortable as possible, were as unremitting as any persons could well be, and that since you left he has been continually engaged in your behalf, and did not relax his exertions until he succeeded in *procuring for you the appointment* you have so long sought *as a teacher,* and that it was chiefly, if not altogether, through his instrumentality that you received it at all. Considering these circumstances he was in hopes you had not so soon forgotten him."[1]

What became of that appointment, if the board ever sent it to Ruth? She never received it!

Perhaps there never was a mission organised and established which excited so deep and general an interest in the christian world as the Oregon Mission; and perhaps none other ever received such large and voluntary contributions for its support, as this; and perhaps none other ever received such large and ready acquisitions of missionaries; and perhaps no man ever bore the responsibility of conducting such a plan in whom there was so general and unbounded confidence placed as in the Rev. Jason Lee; and perhaps, too, no mission ever existed which so fully disappointed the hopes of the church as the Oregon Methodist Mission.[2]

Of the interest felt in the United States for this mission, there need be no proof produced. Every one who was there between the years 1830 and 1840 must have become acquainted with the fact. This interest arose, in a great measure perhaps, from the conviction that the aborigines of our country had been wronged by the white man, and that in the remote and extensive country of Oregon there was a vast opportunity presented for this injury to be repaired. And the hope to repair this injury was encouraged by the consideration that the Oregon tribes, being so remotely situated from the communities of white men, there was little probability that avarice would lead them, for many years, to endeavor to supplant the Indians and obtain their lands, thus making it necessary for them to retire beyond the influence of missionary operations.

To carry out this idea and obtain this object large, *very large,* contributions were offered. Societies were formed in almost every town and village to obtain more funds—while almost every little girl and boy had a missionary box, into which the small sums given by parents and friends for toys and sugar plums were dropped for the purpose of helping support the Oregon Mission. Many a widow contributed her mite, which she herself needed more to replenish her winter fire or to clothe herself more comfortably—and many a servant girl gave of her hard earnings for this purpose. The seamstress resolved to take another hour or two from those already too few for the proper restoration of nature, in order to drop a dollar into the contribution box—and washerwomen, and nurses, and draymen, and wood-sawyers, all partook of the general enthusiasm which was felt for this cause. And those who could not give all they wished, in ready money, formed themselves into "Dorcas Societies," to make up and furnish clothing for the destitute Indians of Oregon—contributing cloth, bed-linen, quilts, comforters, ready-made clothes of every description, hose, shoes, yarn, thread, books, provisions, &c., &c., till the store-houses in Oregon were filled to overflowing with these evidences of generosity and good will in the people of the United States.

In addition to this, when Rev. J. Lee was in the United States in 1839, he received funds and contributions to the amount of about forty thousand dollars, (as informed by J. Peck, Lynn,) which he brought here with him. There also came with him at that time a reinforcement of thirty-two persons, whose passages around Cape Horn and outfits were paid by the people of the States; and there had, before this, been added to the mission about nineteen persons, whose expenses there had been borne, as well as those of the first company—the Rev. Messrs. Lees, Shepherd, &c.,—by the people of the United States.

So great was the interest in favor of this mission, and *"so sure the support"* offered the missionaries, as one expressed himself in our hearing, that little delay was occasioned by waiting for volunteers to secure its interests. An advertisement that men and women were wanted for Oregon was readily responded to, and as the qualifications required were not difficult to find, as thus: "Those who apply will recollect that they must be recommended by the preacher in charge, for their piety and standing as members of the church, and by at least three others for their competency in that particular branch of mechanical labor in which they propose to engage, signifying also their willingness to devote themselves exclusively to the service of the missionary society for at least ten years, unless sooner released by death or by the superintendent of the mission," many were almost immediately on the spot. These qualifications may be easily found in persons who are, nevertheless, totally unqualified for missionaries.

The Rev. Jason Lee was a *good* man, and possessed the true missionary spirit. He was devotedly pious, ardent and dauntless, but deficient in judgment; easily influenced by those whom he considered his superiors, but obstinate and unyielding to his inferiors. His great *forte* was in talking. He could keep the whole body of the people around him, listening to his conversation and waiting for his nod, but he could not set them to work or decide on any work for himself which gave him satisfaction. Hence, affairs at the mission were generally in the condition he once said ‘they were, and for which he could apply no remedy, "When there was nobody here but Daniel and brother Shepherd and myself there was some work done—when the first reinforcement came the work began to cease, but when the *last* came everything came to a dead stand."

The fact was, he could not with a glance see what should be done, and resolve upon it. He had located the mission in a wrong place and was unable to determine how to get out of it, and being too easily influenced by others his mind was ever vascillating and fluctuating. The wish to fulfill the intentions of the board, and to perform his duty as a missionary, rendered him tardy in complying with the wishes of the mission family—one of whom wanted a farm, another an orchard, another a band of cattle, &c., &c.; another could not go to a remote station for he wanted his children schooled—another could not teach school, for he must attend to his family—another could not build houses, for he had a new plan in his head, he was going to study physic—and another could not accept this or that appointment, for he had no wife—and another could not leave his wife to do this or that, for he had no laundress! —and thus the insufficient intellect of that good intentioned superintendent was not found adequate to those pressing emergencies, and he resolved to go to the board in New York for advice, and probably for more of the same stamp.

This tardiness of operation, arose, too, perhaps, in consequence of his entertaining so great a conscientiousness on the subject of *time,* for while one said he must have cattle broken in, and a farm and orchard in process of operation for the support of his increasing family, Mr. Lee declared that he did not consider *"the time in which he wrote his letters home to be his own,"* and therefore *time* was unimproved because belonging to no one.

Another error was apparent in the fact that while he was so scrupulous in expending the mission funds that he would not give a carpenter one dollar per day to build or improve houses for the accommodation of the families who needed them, the mission carpenter was wasting his time in trying to devise some plan which would justify him in wearing a black coat, instead of a carpenter's apron.

Mismanagement and waste both operated to the ruin of the enterprise. There was very little done because there were so few to labor—nobody labored because the work belonged to no one.

Other causes there were which produced a more apparent effect. The wrong locality of the mission operated eventually to its disbandment.

We have seen two reasons in print that were given by Mr. Lee which induced him to commence his first operations in the heart of a Roman Catholic settlement. One was that "having few agricultural implements, he felt dependent on obtaining loans of others!" and he stated that they had "selected the valley of the Willamette as the seat of their missionary operations on account of its central relation to other eligible parts of the Territory and peculiar advantages for agriculture. They moreover found it occupied by small settlements of traders who had taken Indian wives and had families growing up around them. Their moral habits were such as to corrupt the Indians, and he concluded that their influence must be corrected before any hope could be entertained of the conversion of the natives around them. This was one of the principal motives for establishing the mission in their vicinity."

We consider that *these* motives should not have influenced him, for, in the first place, with such a generous sentiment in his favor as affected the people of the States, he could have obtained agricultural implements without *borrowing,* and there being abundant lands in the vast Territory of Oregon, fit for agricultural purposes, besides this, and tribes of Indians remote from all pernicious influence from white men, he should not have located his mission in the midst of Romanists, whom he might have known would exert what influence they possessed in favor of their own religion tenets; and he might have known that wherever there were *catholics* there would also be *priests,* and consequently the religion of *heart* would, by Indians, be readily rejected for that of the *head*—consisting in outward form, tinsel and ceremony.

It is a lamentable fact that not one of the Indians, half-breeds, or whites, who joined the mission church during the great revival of religion (to which we shall refer again) in 1839, or previously to that time, are now members of the methodist church. *Every* half-breed or Indian child who was then under the influence of that church, is now a Roman catholic! We believe there is *one* exception. *Angelica* is not a catholic, neither does she profess to enjoy religion.[3]

After this digression, which may be regarded as *one shade* of the "Pictures of Oregon," we will return to her who is more particularly the subject of these pages.

On her return to the mission it was arranged that Ruth Rover should board with Mrs. S—— and take charge of the Indian girls. This she did for a week, when Mrs. Jason Lee died.[4] The ladies of the family being in poor health, Ruth at once gave her whole attention to perform whatever appeared necessary to be done. The evening before Mrs. Lee's death, she prepared for burial her little son, and next day, with some assistance, prepared also the person of Mrs. Lee for the grave; then labored energetically to prepare the house for the funeral, and after this restored to perfect order Mrs. Lee's wardrobe; and then devoted herself to the care of the Indian girls, in which employment she was very happy.

It was intended that the fourteen girls in her charge should be entirely subject to her will, with the exception that they attended to Mr. S——'s school. She wished to learn them much, and arranged her plan to have *one* of them every week do the house work with her, in order to learn the art, and the others to attend to sewing, knitting, &c. She had them wash their own clothes, always waiting till Wednesday that Mrs. S—— and the boys of the mission had each had a day for these purposes. After school she allowed them to exercise in the open air, in walking, playing, or in gathering berries; and in the evening she took her seat among them and instructed them in dressing their dolls, in making patchwork, or in explaining pictures in their books, or conversing or singing as they might be disposed.

In the leisure she could obtain on the Sabbath, after service in the church and sabbath school, she spent some time with the Indians in their lodges, in conversation, singing and prayer, and teaching them what she could.

She also commenced to learn the Calapooyah language, and succeeded well till she was interrupted by her labors being so increased at the mission as to leave her little time, and by being told by Mr. Leslie that *he* had been appointed missionary to the Calapooyahs, which she thought was hint enough to deter her from proceeding.

But these were employments and favors too great for Ruth to be allowed to enjoy uninterruptedly. She soon discovered there was a spirit of disaffection at work. Mr. S—— wished the control of every affair connected with the mission to be subjected entirely to him. Hence, if he wanted any extra help on any occasion he would direct whichever girl he pleased to perform it, without regard to any arrangement Ruth had made, and this soon produced such disaffection among them that when she wished any service performed, either for her good or their instructions, she would be denied by them and be told that Mr. S—— wanted them.

This soon was carried so far that she could gain no service from them without insolent language, and finally she informed the superintendent that she declined having any care of the girls of the mission unless she could exercise authority over them. Mr. L. enquired into the case, and gave as his decision that Ruth Rover had not done wrong in any particular, but that Mr. S—— had, and he should be subjected to censure.

It was again arranged that Ruth should take charge of the girls, and it was thought there would be no occasion for Mr. S.—— to interfere at all, as he had been permitted to choose from among them any two additional servants he chose for Mrs. S——'s service, and he had already the control of the whole number of boys. But this resulted in no better success, for they had learned what was most agreeable to Mr. S—— and for him they had a particular regard, as he had sought them out among the natives and brought them there, and hence to do as they pleased and as would please him, was their principal object. And on one occasion, when Ruth was trying to enforce obedience, he interfered, and attempting to take the child from her hands in some way caused an injury to her person, which led her to lay another complaint before the superintendent, which resulted in the decision of the members of the mission that "Mr. S—— had been found guilty of abuse of the character (by abusing her before strangers) and person of Ruth Rover, and shall be subjected to reproof from the superintendent of this mission."

At the same time, it was thought by some that Ruth had not yielded the child to Mr. S—— as readily as she might or should have done, and requested that she should receive some reproof also—probably somewhat to mollify his feelings—and she was waited on accordingly, when she said she acknowledged it was foolish for her to attempt to resist Mr. S———, as he was so much stronger than herself, but all she regretted was that she was not able to take him over her knee and give him a good whipping, as he deserved.

Whatever faults were attributable to Ruth Rover, and she undoubtedly had faults, we believe she had not that of deceit. She abhorred it in others, and endeavored to avoid its practice by herself. The same unshrinking fortitude which led her to attempt to perform whatever she supposed to be her duty, however great the barriers, also led her to face error fearlessly and endeavor to have it removed. She could see no need of its existence. Why should not every one do right and then there would be no trouble? she frequently asked—but her knowledge and experience were limited. Different circumstances and appearances produce different impressions of what is right or wrong, hence in the midst of such an immense variety of character, tastes, habits, circumstances, influences and aspirations, none can be too cautious in forming an opinion of the motives and dispositions of others.

In the ''business world'' 'tis said to be good policy to practice deceit, but we do not believe it. If it is *good policy,* 'tis bad principal—and abominable practice, to use it for purposes of trade, and when once discovered must lead the upright mind to abhor and avoid the deceiver forever after. But when employed to please those whom we think above us in point of wealth or honor—passing over all their errors, even though they are so outrageous that the very dogs bark at them, is a degree of degrading sycophancy that disgraces this lower world, black as it is with crime.

Whatever Ruth Rover dared to think that she also dared to say, and this disposition obtained her many enemies when she might, by closing her eyes to error, using flattering speech, telling a few lies occasionally, and suffering evil to exist however hideous its shape, have had more friends—but for this kind of friendship she was not anxious—she preferred a quiet conscience and peace with God, to the false glare of *numbers* of friends, whose integrity of character could not be relied upon.

During her residence of nearly two years at the Oregon mission she saw much which was wrong. Supported as that mission was by the church, she believed the missionaries should have acted in compliance with the wishes of that church; property which had been given for the benefit and elevation of Indians should have been appropriated to that purpose; articles which had been given to enable them to carry on their operations successfully should have been preserved and used with as much care as if belonging to individuals; and the *time* of the missionaries, for which they were receiving salaries, should have been appropriated, at least in the main, to the benefit of the mission.

With these impressions Ruth believed it wrong for the goods and clothing intended for gratuitous distribution among the tribes of Indians to be *sold* to them, and at high prices, taking their beaver and deer skins from them at not one twentieth per cent of their value, while those who were unable to buy were obliged to go without—lying sick and destitute—uncovered and unfed, within view of the mission door, till death closed the scene, and then be tied up in the rags on which death relieved them, and be carried to a hole, swung across the back of a husband or friend.

She believed, too, that it was wrong for fanning mills to be left in the open air during all weathers, and till at last burned by accident; and to say nothing of harnesses, farming utensils, &c., &c., that were uncared for till they were destroyed, or stolen, or burned; or of barrels of salt left in the rain till they were liquefied. She believed it was wrong for those who were paid for these very services to waste their time together in lounging, reading, riding or visiting, or in any other way than in doing their duty in these respects.

And in relation more particularly to herself, she felt it was wrong to circulate the story that she was a maniac, because she presumed to think she could render a neighbor more comfortable in his table fixings, and because she pinned a handkerchief over the back of her bonnet when she was working in the sun, saying one to another, behind her back, *there* is a sign she is a maniac! what is that handkerchief pinned on her bonnet for? and for several days observing every movement to obtain a confirmation of these suspicions. And she felt it wrong, when she had fallen from her horse and was ill in consequence, to so far neglect her as to suffer her to live for three weeks on roasted potatoes, brought her mostly by an Indian girl, with only one exception to this kind of food for that length of time—the considerate Mrs. Leland once sent her an apple pie and some preserves. She felt this was wrong and cruel, inasmuch as in the same house Mrs. S—— was living with every luxury the mission afforded. And to interrupt her in every plan she undertook to benefit the Indians, because it was doing more than themselves—and to abuse her before strangers because she cut a piece of soap for the girls' washing without asking Mr. Shepherd, and offered a bowl of milk to a visitor, and clean plates to his daughters when at Mrs. Shepherd's table, without "her orders," being told by Mr. Shepherd that his wife was the mistress of the house, and no one would be allowed to sit at her table and take such liberties—and because she took a wash tub from Mrs. Shepherd's servant for the girls' washing, on the day assigned them for this work—and because she used an old tin pan to remove the ashes from the fire place, thereby making it much sweeter, being told by Mr. Shepherd that Mr. Lee had left all those things in his care and he had to see that they were taken care of, notwithstanding Ruth told him she would not suffer it to be injured for she was aware it should be used very carefully, for her mother had *two* once, and when she was a good girl she used to allow her to sit and hold them! and that she believed she was old enough to have some idea how articles of that and different value should be used—and to hide the molasses cup because Ruth had put some molasses over some blackberries she was eating —and to put some small pumpkins under lock and key for fear Ruth would use them—and to put about half a barrel of rocks on top of salted meat that she might not use it, being about fifty pounds more than was needed or used generally to press it under pickle—and to refuse for her table, flour, and tea, and coffee, and sugar, and butter, when people from abroad were coming to the mission house to eat, at the time of the protracted meeting, saying there was none to spare when, their own table was loaded with every luxury—and to use altogether themselves, excepting what little the superintendent could obtain by much difficulty and contention, and almost using deceit, all the stores sent by the board, or raised on the farm, or purchased at Vancouver —and to endeavor to annoy her by having the milk set in her closet, when there was one built purposely in their own part of the house, frequently leaving slops of cream and milk upon the floor for her to remove—and by placing every Saturday twenty or twenty-five pumpkin pies, baked for the Indian children, on the library floor, where they had to remain till Sunday evening, (although there was plenty of room elsewhere,) much to the satisfaction of cats and dogs and the discomfort of certain feet clothed in moccasins—and by insisting that the door between her room and the Indian children's should be open at meal times, keeping a watch by its side for the purpose of opening it again when Ruth would shut it—and by insisting that the boys' clothing should be kept in that room, notwithstanding all her desires to have it kept in order, it being the principal room of the mission house, where were held all meetings except on the Sabbath, and was the only place where company could be received—and by insisting that the Indian boys should, at another time, in carrying their pails of milk to the cellar, take it through the front door, when the back door was nearer, by which means they frequently spilled it upon the floor, and seemed to take a pleasure in doing so, and if any word was spoken to induce them to be more careful, they were sure to throw it out of the pails purposely and give some insolent language besides—and by ordering Indians to throw mud out of a tub which Ruth had mixed for her to mend the mud fire place and chimney in the mission room, before Dr. Binney, just at the time she was engaged in the work, and which would have prevented her from accomplishing it—and by bringing an old shelf which had been suspended in this same room, and bore upon its delicate shoulders an old broken pitcher of salve, two tubeless lamps, one half a pair of scissors, an indefinite number of old lamp tubes, rags for scrofula purposes, two old knives for spreading with salve, torn books, a broken crane hook, half burnt ironing holders, one or two necks of broken bottles with the corks in them, &c., &c., and junks of mud, quantities of cobwebs, dead flies, rat signs and broken nails without measure, so repeatedly to its former place, and burdening it again with most of its usual treasures, that its disposition to return could not be conquered until she had sawed down the pins which supported it, and this at a time when Ruth was lining the room with mats at her own expense and nailing them up herself alone, Mr. Shepherd telling her she had no business to make any changes or improvements in the place.

She believed it wrong, too, when, after she had washed and put in order Mrs. Lee's whole wardrobe, in addition to many other heavy services by which she had injured her health and was obliged to use restoratives, for her to be obliged to sleep in an open log house at Mr. Beer's, thereby taking colds, and teeth-ache, and agues, till she was almost unable to perform any labor, and when told by the superintendent to occupy Mrs. Lee's room till another could be prepared, to find herself twice locked out and her things thrown upon the floor—and when she had slept there the third time and was in the act of making the bed in the morning, to have the bed taken away, Mr. Shepherd saying, "This is sister Lee's bed—you have no business on sister Lee's bed"—the bed quilt, though her own, torn out of her hand, and herself violently thrust out of the room.

And she believed it wrong, too, when any members of the mission wanted any article which was for sale in the mission, (and which was originally intended to be *given,* if anything may be understood by the directions on packages, which were generally of this nature: "To the mission sisters." "To the members of the mission family," "For the children of the missionaries of the Oregon Mission," &c.,) for prices to be set upon them far exceeding their first cost in the United States.

These are some of the things which Ruth Rover considered wrong about the transactions of that mission, and about which she dared to say so. Reader wasn't she quarrelsome?

A few items from the journal will show how, while these things were going on *in* the house, Ruth was endeavoring to be useful *out* of it:

"Having had leisure to-day, after service at church, went to the lodges, where were six adults—some sick and lying upon the ground, others stupid and indolently idling away the Sabbath. One young man repeated with me the Lord's prayer. I asked them if it would please them to have me come among them when I could teach them, they replied yes, 'twould be very good for me to do so.

"Visited the Indians again today and found eleven adults. Sickness, filth, indolence and extreme stupidity are glaringly prominent to the visitor on entering these lodges. Only one woman would repeat a prayer after me. *Squipick's* wife will apparently soon be relieved from her miseries; endeavored to converse with her on the subject of death, but she appears entirely senseless. Been for a week or more engaged in the study of the Calapooyah language; find it pleasant and very regular in its syntax.

"*Squipick's* wife this morning left this world, of which she knew so little, and departed to one of which she knew still less. A loud wailing we heard assured us of this fact, and on my going to the lodge I found *Squipick* tying her in a piece of dirty blanket, in the same position in which she had died—coiled nearly double, and in dirt and filth. The chief and some others came to assist him in burying the corpse, which he carried away upon his back, the supporting rope resting upon his forehead.

"These tribes bury their dead under the ground, with their property, if it be but an old pail, or knife, or blanket, hanging or resting about it, and although they have as great a propensity to steal as to breath, yet no one is ever found to rob the graves of their dead.

"Visited the Indians; eleven present. Nearly all responded prayer with me, and three attempted to sing. When going to their lodge felt very sensible of my weaknesses and want of the graces of the spirit, but was interested and blessed while with them, especially when in praying for their conversion, and that I might be enabled to be useful to them.

"Nine Indians present, and a greater interest manifested by them than I have before discovered. All responded with me and tried to sing. One woman interrupted me by saying, ''tis very good for you to come every Sabbath and talk with us.' May the Holy Spirit accompany my endeavors and teach them the way of salvation.

"Very disconsolate! The great trials to which I have been subjected, during my residence in this far off land, most perpetually prey upon my spirits, and I suffer extremely. Since last Sabbath have been extremely blessed and comforted by my Heavenly Father, and last evening enjoyed a most refreshing season in praying for my dear christian friends in the United States.

"This afternoon visited three Indian lodges, about one mile and a half from here. Witnessed sickness, misery and pollution. On going to my people (if such I may call them) only four adults were present, the rest having been called away by Mr. Whitcomb to account for stealing squashes. They said it was good for them to speak with me.

"Conversed to-day with a young Indian from Walla Walla, who can speak English tolerably well, having been for some time under the instruction of Dr. Whitman. He has, since his stay among us, manifested a disposition to absent himself from the lodges of his people and spending the time in our houses, seeking instruction in reading, &c. He has been singing me some of the hymns he has learned, and telling me what he knows about the bible. He says that Jesus Christ came here, and wicked men made holes in his hands, and feet, and sides, and he died and was put in the ground—came up again and went to heaven—and that by-and-bye he will come here again, blow a trumpet and all the people will come to him—to the good he will say, 'come, come'—but to the bad he will say, 'go away.' Also, if good people wish to speak to him he will turn his ear and listen, but if bad people speak to him he will stop his ears. Repeating the names of the apostles he said Judas was bad and put something around his neck and he died. He also spoke of the Holy Spirit, and of angels, but I could not comprehend what he wished to convey concerning them.

"I was much gratified in witnessing *this* proof of the capacity of these Indians to learn, so dark and degraded do they appear to be in their minds. Some of our mission family have attempted to learn the languages of this people—have written about one hundred words and given up the task as hopeless. Some have tried to instruct them in needlework, housework, mechanism, agriculture, &c., and have each failed of accomplishing the good anticipated.

"*I* have made endeavors too, and probably many are saying I shall soon also give up the task and I do almost every day find my spirits lagging, so great are the number of difficulties to be accomplished, and many of them appear so nearly insurmountable—and in what way my anxieties will terminate I am unable to determine. Here are classes numbering perhaps fifty or a hundred Indians, each of which speak a different language, and are continually wandering from one tract of country to another. *They* have no books and we no interpreters; and if by earnest attention we obtain the names of a few nouns, we have no method of obtaining the intervening words to connect them into sentences—and by this time, perhaps, those of this dialect will have gone and another taken their place. So that one obstacle after another rises before us and we decline in our work.

"Not like this our presbyterian brethren in the interior, as the case of the young chief will show—and to my regret I will add that I have not, since I have been in Oregon, seen an instance of an adult Indian who has been as much benefited by the labors of our mission family, as this chief by the labors of our brethren in the interior.

"Six adults in my congregation to-day, besides several children.

"Ten present to day, besides children. This morning prevailed on six of them to come to church, where they had an opportunity of seeing the members partake of the Lord's supper. In endeavoring to explain to them the reason of our doing so, they gave a general and deep attention to what I said and seemed to understand me.

"One of the women, when I went to the lodge, was using her enchantments over a sick man in order to restore him to health. The facility of these prescriptions I do not understand, but suppose they have confidence in them as they are frequently resorted to.

"For some months have been suffering from ill health caused in the first place by very hard labor in the mission subsequently to Mrs. Lee's death, and by laboring before recovering my health after the injury received by falling from my horse. For this reason, and the shortness of the days, it is not best, perhaps, to continue my visits to the lodges on the Sabbath.

"Our sewing society promises well, but the people are so unstable in all their ways we dare not flatter ourselves with great success.

February, 1839. "Being somewhat in improved health the superintendent proposes that I receive the boarders again, and that Mr. Whitcomb, the farmer, eat again at my table. Mr. Whitcomb says he will consent to leave Mr. Shepherd's on condition that I promise to pay him the respect which is his due as master of the house, and also promise to obey him. Mr. Whitcomb is a man of very inferior mental capacity, and although I can readily engage to render him all the respect which is his due, yet I cannot bind myself to *obey* him. His disposition is of a very meddlesome and officious character, and he has formerly been the cause of much trouble in the family by going to Mr. and Mrs. Shepherd with every small kind of gossip he could make up; and rather than again be subjected to the same round of troubles, I have begged the superintendent to give me any other situation and employment in the mission rather than this—consequently he has proposed that I live in Mr. Shepherd's part of the house, taking charge of the Indian girls as usual, while Mr. Shepherd lives in the mission proper and boards the laborers,'' &c.

CHAPTER XII

❦

"God knows I'm not the thing I should be,
Nor am I even the thing I could be
But twenty times I rather would be
    An atheist clean
Than under gospel colors hid be
    Just for a screen."

It cannot be supposed, considering the scarcity of females in Oregon in the days of its early settlement, that Ruth Rover, even with as few fascinations as she possessed, could be long in the country without receiving an offer of marriage—whether it were dictated by love or as a matter of convenience—consequently, she had been but a few days in the Willamette settlement when a very officious gentleman said to her, "Well, sister Ruth, I suppose you will have no objections to marry? it is pretty generally understood that the young ladies come out ostensibly on that errand, although they *profess* to be teachers."

Ruth, offended at the start, remarked: "'Tis a great error to suppose that was *my* object in coming. I have no idea of marrying!"

"Not of marrying? Why how could you perform your duty to God and to others and not marry? Why 'tis the best thing you can do, to take a husband and raise a family, and show these degraded women and mothers how to keep house and govern their children, &c. Why 'tis the best missionary work you could engage in."

Ruth begged he would excuse her from taking part in such conversation, as 'twas entirely foreign to her feelings, wish, or calculations.

He begged her to explain how she could possess such views, when she must know there were men all around who wanted wives—and *three* in the mission of whom he knew she could have her choice![1]

She told him frankly she was engaged to serve in the mission for the space of six years, when she proposed to go home and remain with her aged father during his life; that this was her firm resolution and nothing could cause her to swerve from it.

He professed great astonishment that she should have come to Oregon on such a *singular* errand, and told her she would get over it, for one of those *very* pious young men she could have at any moment—though Mr. Wiley was the one *he* should prefer that she would marry, as he was a great friend of his; and if at any moment she felt disposed to signify such a wish, he would be most happy to act as her advocate, and meantime she must believe him her friend, and he hoped before he saw her again she would be deeply in love with Mr. Wiley!

At every opportunity this subject was urged, with no better success, till one morning this gentleman requested her to walk with him, and being a short distance from the house, commenced his favorite theme. Ruth told him, plainly, if that was his object in asking her to talk—to urge her to marry *Wiley*—it was useless to go, and she preferred to return to the house; for she had no intention at all to form a matrimonial alliance in Oregon, and if she should ever come to that conclusion, Mr. Wiley would not be her choice at all!

The gentleman, greatly offended, told her to bear in mind that he would *never* name the subject to her again, for he had tried his best to benefit her by offering her a good opportunity to secure a husband—and if she would be guided by him she might be well situated in a home of her own—be her own mistress, instead of being at the beck and command of every one—and be more respectable when a married woman than while a girl—and that, by-the-bye, if she persisted in this plan she would be an old maid, and then *nobody* would have her.

Ruth told him that she hoped he would not make himself uneasy for she thought she could take care of herself, and she was pleased to learn that he would not name the subject to her again, for she was tired of hearing it.

Under date of September, 1837, we find this item in Ruth's journal:

"Since my arrival at this station Mr. Wiley has made his addresses to me and solicited my hand in marriage. My engagements with the M. Education Society, and desire to labor unshackled and unencumbered in this mission, has induced me to decline bestowing it. This I have done with satisfaction—finding my mind relieved of a burden which before oppressed it. May my

Heavenly Father preserve me from imprudent acts while I remain single, and render me abundantly useful in this heathen land.''

Again under date of March 28th, '38:

''Have to-day come to Vancouver for a little relaxation and rest from trouble—and also to be relieved from the importunities of Mr. Wiley. Though I respect him, and believe he would make a *kind* husband, yet he is not possessed of that strength of intellect and sedateness of mind which I should wish to find in a man with whom I was destined to be engaged in missionary labors. And, besides, the duty I owe to my parents and to the education society would, perhaps, make it necessary for me to decline his offers.''

Again, June, 1838:

''A little more than a week since, in view of my lonely situation, and the little prospect I had of being of any service to the heathen, as I am afraid almost to be seen speaking to an Indian on account of being single, I concluded to accept the hand of Mr. Wiley, which has, until I came to Vancouver, been almost unremittingly proferred to me. I have to-day received a letter from him expressive of great regret for the obligations he was under to a young lady of Boston whom he had concluded to address, supposing that by my continued rejection of his offer I must be disgusted with him.''

Ruth soon returned to the mission, and in a few days Mrs. Lee's death occurred. The brethren concluded that as Mr. Lee could not have proceeded farther than Walla Walla it was best to send an express to him and acquaint him with his misfortune. This being resolved upon, Mr. Wiley proposed to Ruth that he should send for the letter he had addressed to Miss J———, of Boston, making proposals of marriage to her—it being in the care of Rev. Jason Lee—in order that himself and Ruth might be united, *she* being his preference to any other.

She objected to this plan, as she said it might occasion the loss of the letter, and consequently to him the loss of Miss J———, whom he might perhaps obtain if the letter should reach its destination, but for herself she could never marry him unless it were returned.

He urged that there was no danger—the company could be overtaken in a month at the farthest, and the note returned within two months—and if she would obligate herself to wait until September, he would run the risk and recall it.

She again replied that he was making a venture which might result to his disadvantage, but if he were resolved upon it, and was willing to make that sacrifice for her, she certainly would bind herself to him for the period he named.

The express was forwarded, and September came, and all the months till January, 1839, and the letter not returned. Meantime Mr. Wiley and Ruth Rover had been considered as engaged in marriage, and whenever the word should come that the letter addressed to Miss J—— had been withheld, they were to be married.

His attentions to her had been unremitting—in sickness and in health he was her constant associate—and in all her troubles with other members of the mission family he was apparently her only friend. She reposed confidence in him as a brother—told him all her troubles—and on every occasion sought his advice.

An item from the journal may not be uninteresting here:

"This winter we have boarded together alone. The persecutions I have met in the mission family have made me often-times very much depressed in spirit, and I have sought the sympathy of friends wherever I could find it—excepting that I have not, perhaps, looked to God for support as much as I had ought. Of a warm confiding temperament, I am apt when I find a friend, to repose my whole trust in him or her, and it may be to this disposition, which perhaps is erroneous, that I am indebted for the severe disappointments I have three times sustained, in which it has seemed the very fountains of life have been scathed and withered by sorrow. No one, I'm sure, could more sensibly realize the need of a *friend* than myself in this heathen land—so far from those who care for me, and where it is almost impossible for a female to return to her home, if she should desire it, and with nearly every one of the mission family censuring and condemning me.

"These things I name as one, and a great cause, of my putting so much confidence in Mr. Wiley, which has proved the greatest curse (and yet a blessing) which ever attended me in the course of my life."

Mr. Wiley ever expressed great regret for the uncertainty of the prospect before them, and declaring it his settled belief that Mr. Lee had received his note requesting him to withhold his letter from the young lady addressed, endeavored to persuade Ruth to marry him at any rate. He urged in fact that they were as man and wife to each other, having been engaged for some months, and it was only misfortune which kept them separate, and if Miss J—— should happen to come out to him and he were married to another, 'twould be overlooked under such circumstances—especially he urged, *if certain circumstances could be admitted as an excuse.*

From this moment Ruth Rover was in the highest degree censurable for spending any more time in his company. She knew his purpose, but trusting in her own strength to avoid danger, did not at once summon resolution to break from the snares which bound her. At length, finding resolution necessary, she obtained supernatural strength and told him resolutely she would *never become his wife under any circumstances!*

She says in her diary:

"In conclusion about Mr. Wiley. I have reposed all the confidence in him which I could have done had I been married to him. Boarding with him for several months has given me an opportunity to become thoroughly acquainted with him, and many circumstances combined have given me an extreme dislike of him and led me to tell him plainly that I had no intention whatever of ever marrying him.

"He became violently angry, and declared that I was 'engaged to him till Mr. Lee's return—that we had confided in each other for a length of time, and 'twas not right that either one should marry another—and that if I refused him and received the addresses of any other man he would expose to every one every particular I had ever confided to him, and would *give me a cup of sorrow I would have to drink to the dregs!*'"

He went out in anger and haste, and finding Mr. Beers told him, crying, that he was in a most unfortunate situation in regard to Miss J—— of Boston, for he had requested her to come out to Oregon to marry him, and then had sent an express to have the letter withheld, being encouraged to expect to marry Miss Rover, and he did not know whether the letter had been received— she might come, and he was in great pain to confess that his intimacy with Miss Rover had been such that it was proper that he should marry her instead of Miss J——, and he wanted the church to befriend him in so doing—that Miss Rover was opposed, but he was sure with their influence she would yield.

This was immediately communicated to Rev. Mr. Leland, pastor of the church, who called on Miss Rover, in company with Mr. Wiley, and said he had come on an unpleasant errand, but if she would take the proper steps it might be soon passed over, and then asked her, as he said, "in the authority of her pastor, if she had committed the crime of adultery or fornication with Mr. Wiley?"

She, astonished, replied quickly, "No!"

He then asked Mr. Wiley if he had "been guilty of committing that crime with Miss Rover?"

He attempted to answer, but his deeply wrought feelings choked his utterance, and he only articulated, "O! dear!—I—I—am in the hands of my brethren—they—they—may do as they ple—ple—ease with me!"

Mr. Leland then told Ruth that "her best course would be to *confess* her fault, and 'twould be all over—'twould not hurt her at all—the brethren would forgive her—he knew of two methodist ministers who were guilty of that error before marriage, but they confessed it and it was all passed over. But he would have her remember that if she refused to confess, it was in his power to suspend her labors in that mission."

Ruth replied that she was not at all disinclined to make confession of any wrong act of which she was guilty—that she fully and freely confessed she had done wrong in keeping company with Mr. Wiley after he had proposed improper intercourse with her, but the *crime of which he spoke she never had committed with him nor with any other.*

Mr. Leland added: "'Twill not do—you must acknowledge it, for the brethren will be satisfied with nothing else!" and having told her he should call again, he went away.

In a few hours he came again with a paper on which was written:

"To the M. E. Church in Oregon:

"DEAR BRETHREN—With deep regret I have to acknowledge to you that I have been guilty of the crime of fornication,—hoping God to forgive me,' &c.

He asked Ruth to sign it. She read it and gave it to him again, saying she was *not guilty.*

He endeavored to induce her to sign it, by entreaties, assuring her it would "do her no harm at all—'twould never go out of the mission—and 'twould be forgotten;" and by threats that she "certainly would be allowed to labor no more there if she refused, and her situation in that case would not be enviable, to have it go abroad that she had been expelled for such a crime as that, when it was so easy to have it all passed over—and it very frequently happened that persons in high standing in the church had to make such confessions." But still she refused, and he went away again.

In the evening he called at her room after she had retired, and told her "the brethren were below and awaiting her acknowledgement of the error in question," using the same sophistry as before, and that he should not ask her again if she refused *then, and she knew what the consequences would be.*

Ruth Rover, in despair—helpless—friendless—and *reckless*—seeing ruin before her on either hand, concluded to take that which would be the longest time in coming—put her signature to the fatal paper!

Mr. Leland at the church meeting informed the members, still holding the paper in his hands, that "Ruth Rover had *confessed* the crime of which she had been accused," without naming any of the facts in relation to her denying the crime, and the flatteries and threats he had used to induce her to confess it. What would he more?—she had *confessed* herself guilty, and that was all he wished.

Mr. Wiley embraced the brethren, put his arms around their necks, and wept, or tried to weep.

The meeting being closed, Mr. Leland called at Ruth's door late in the evening, and told her he was happy to inform her it was *"all ended—the papers were burned—the brethren forgave her, and all was peace again!"*

We offer no remarks. The future part of Ruth Rover's history will be the best commentary on this subject.

By reference to Ruth's journal we find in connection with the former quotation:

"Our situation becoming unpleasant, as we were boarding together, I begged of the superintendent that some means might be devised whereby we might not be subjected thus to meet—and he was requested to remove to Mr. B——'s family. * * * * * * * * *

"I am thus far separated from a man who has nearly proved my ruin, and who had only repaid my trust with abuse the most flagrant.

"A person acquainted with human nature can form some idea of the state of suffering to which I have been subjected since this last severe trial of my life. How desirable has appeared the rest of the grave. In the language of sister Summers, I have 'asked this boon alone—'tis all I crave—to sleep, forgetting every anxious fear, and every wrong which hath this bosom torn—and every secret sorrow I have known—O! then I'm happy, then I'm blest indeed!'"

Poor Ruth! don't give up yet—this is but the *beginning* of sorrows!

This very unpleasant affair occurred just at the time of the revival of religion at the mission, in which several of the settlers and Indian children were hopefully converted. We say *hopefully,* and we mean so. The work was undoubtedly that of the Spirit of God; and it was excited and kept up for a few days with the ardor which ever characterizes similar excitements when the *Spirit* and *men* are *ready.* The blaze went out as suddenly as it ran through the stubble of sin; and what is more lamentable, no living embers remain to show that it ever had been.

Mr. Wiley went from the place of accusation—confession and *crime,* (according to his own report)—and revenge, into the praying circle, and prayed, and groaned, and exhorted, and wept, and shouted, till Mr. Leland said "the reformation is more indebted to brother Wiley for its life than to any other here!" O! yes, indeed, for putting it out—for how could it burn with *such* oil poured on it?

Ruth Rover having received an offer of marriage *out* of the mission, resolved to accept it. And this suspicion having got abroad, and Mr. Wiley finding he had not been urged to marry Ruth, nor she him, tried another way to secure her—and persuaded some of the brethren and Mr. Leland that it was wrong to suffer a member of the church to marry another under such circumstances—that Dr. Binney[2] ought to be informed of what had occurred— and that if he were, he would undoubtedly refuse to marry Miss Rover.

Accordingly, Mr. Leland, Mr. Wiley, and one other waited on Ruth. Mr. Leland informed her that he should never consent for her nor any other member of that mission to marry any person under such circumstances as were connected with herself, without their being first made acquainted with those circumstances—that he understood she was expecting to marry Dr. Binney, and he should not give his consent for her to marry any other than Mr. Wiley.

Ruth replied that she could "never marry a man for whom she entertained not sufficient respect to induce her to render him the service which would be required of her, and that it was entirely useless for him to urge her union with Mr. Wiley—she never would marry him—and if he refused to marry her to Dr. Binney she should decline his offer, for there was no other priest in that part of the country who could perform the ceremony."

He at last said he would not oppose the match if she would consent to have Dr. Binney made acquainted with the late occurrences in relation to herself and Mr. Wiley.

She replied she had no objections whatever, and preferred he should be made acquainted with those occurrences.

Mr. Wiley, thus again defeated, in a few days came into her room without permission, when Ruth, with *as much* good breeding, requested him to leave it—and thus ended, for the time, this interesting affair.

Perhaps the reader would like to have a little description of this individual. We will favor him:

> He said his prayers and learned the creed,
> And went to sea, and knew to read,
> And whiskers wore, cravat and glove,
> And blew the flute, and talked of love,
> And tailored some, then took to teaching,
> And coopered more, then went to preaching;
> But losing favor as a rector,
> He next resolved to be a doctor,
> And studied "Thomas," "Bell" and "Burns,"
> And "Cooper's Surgery" by turns,
> And made some pills, but still was he

       As feeble minds will always be,
       Puny and poor when all was done,
       Like plant in shade which seeks the sun.

As the subsequent history of this person may be told in a few words, we probably had better add it, and then we shall have done with him for some years:

       It being thought a "duty," soon he found a mate,
       He got one vote, *his own,* for "people's delegate"
       And not one more, the feeble minded creature,
       When, void of common sense, he *ran* for Legislator.
       He stamped his name on coin—then on a blazing sign;
       Then turned to selling pins and smaller things, and wine—
       And thought to found a city, to which some debtors went,
       And tried to make *his* choice the seat of government.
       He prayed and sang most loud—then next resolved to try
       His skill in writing slang for the "Vox Populi"—
       And unpraised still, except with "Grub" for name—
       All efforts failing him, he scarcely *strove* for fame.
       Two wishes granted him—none greater do appear;
       He is a father and the ladies' accoucher.

CHAPTER XIII

It has been very distressing to the compiler to find it necessary to present to the public the matter contained in the foregoing chapter, but as it is her purpose to bring the *truth* to light, irrespective of whom it may injure, she has felt compelled to submit it.

It appears that Ruth Rover did not know till the year 1843 that Mr. Leland did not present this matter at the church meeting as he understood it and received it from her, viz: That she acknowledged fully that she had done vastly wrong in remaining in Wiley's company after any improper intimacy had been proposed, but that she denied fully and positively the committal of the crime. Had she known *then* as much as she has since learned of the disposition of many persons on this subject of woman's weakness, she would have perished at the feet of her persecutors before she would have suffered them to possess so good a shaft against her. But, beguiled as she was, by the pretended friendship of Mr. Leland, and the assurances that there was nothing required to bury it forever in oblivion but her acknowledgement of the error, and that the brethren understood the case and were ready, when she had acknowledged it, to be on the same terms of friendship with her as before—and further, discouraged and reckless as she felt, in view of the protracted troubles she had endured, and without a person in the remote wilds of Oregon to assist her, she suffered the accusation to stand as they desired it—and for the consequences of which a whole life cannot atone.

This was the whole object of Mr. Leland. She was *disgraced now,* sufficiently to never do him any more injury, and the satisfaction he felt was expressed in a note to her the next morning, when he congratulated her on "the happy termination of a disagreeable affair," and added, "as long as you manifest so submissive and becoming a spirit, I shall be most happy to be your best friend."

Long years often afford convictions and evidences which cannot be gained in a brief period.

Fourteen years have elapsed since the occurrences we have named. Mr. Wiley has been urged and encouraged by Rev. Mr. Leland to the occupancy of the pulpit and offices in the church, as well as to public offices, for which, however, he was totally inadequate, on every possible occasion, and he may be seen on every Sabbath day, in the methodist church in Salem, sitting in the altar, leaning his head upon the pulpit, with as much complacency as the loved disciple leaned his head upon the bosom of his Lord—or hurrying officiously through the aisles of the church into the pulpit or gallery, with all the apparent consciousness of superior piety and influence.

While on the other hand, Ruth Rover, although her life since that period, as well as before, has been unimpeachable, lately passed *six months in that town, and in their very midst, and not one individual of that mission spoke to her during the time.* *Once* Ruth extended her hand gratuitously, to Mr. Leland, feeling grateful that he had not attempted to injure her cause in court—although, perhaps, had he been interrogated he would have been glad to have done it. Aside from this, the prisoner *"Sellers"* was not treated with more contempt than herself.[1]

But we have much more to say by-and-bye, on this subject, and we will recur again to Ruth. She had relied on Rev. Mr. Leland, in leaving home and sacrificing her father and inheritance, as on a *"father."* She was an orphan in a strange land. Her suspicions against his character for veracity were well supported in the mission, as well as elsewhere* —and if Mr. Leland was not guilty in this would not *Heaven,* who befriends the upright, have protected and befriended this man?

It is written: "It were better for a man that a mill-stone were hung about his neck and he were drowned in the depths of the sea, than that he should offend one of these little ones which *believe in me."* If Ruth Rover could not claim to be one of the "little ones" who served her God in strict purity of life, she could claim to be one who did *"believe"* in Him, and this belief was the guiding star of her life. But for this belief—this super-human existence—no *mortal could* have endured the intense burdens which it has been her lot to bear for a term of sixteen years.

---

*In the year 1843, Ruth remarked to a gentleman with whom she was sailing: "My troubles in the mission were probably all occasioned by my suspecting Mr. Leland guilty of speaking falsehoods." When he added, "and he *will lie*—I *know* he will lie—for I have had dealings enough with him to know."

But what have been the indications of providence toward Mr. Leland? While we feel disposed to "lay our finger upon our lips and distrust our own judgment," we will say, in our humble opinion, they have been that of disapprobation. When we consider the *burning* of his *house* and *property*—the *loss* of his *wife*—*three* children carried over into the chasm of the falls—*another daughter* dying at Oahu—his *barn burnt*—*another child buried*—and *sickness* and *infirmity* on every hand, we cannot, even while we feel disposed to extend sympathy and commiseration for his afflictions, we *cannot* help coming to this conclusion.

A few items more from Ruth's journal will conclude her labors at the mission. Under the date of March 2d, 1839, she says:

"A few days since one of Mr. Shepherd's servants, wishing to go to the chamber above my room, came to the door and finding it fastened, for I was just then dressing, attempted to ascend the stairs on the outside, when Mr. Shepherd told her to go through my room or he would *push* her through, and added, in the presence of the mission Indian boys and Mr. Whitcomb, that "tis abominable of her to act so like the d—l as she does.' Not knowing what he could have against me, I asked Mr. L——— to enquire, and he has been here this evening to tell me the result. He says Mr. Shepherd informs him that he knows nothing against me, nor any reason why I should not enjoy all the privileges of the church which others enjoy—that he spoke improperly, and he regretted that he so indulged this passion. Another unpleasant occurrence thus far settled. From the fact that Mr. Leland and myself have been unhappy together since we came here, and were so when we arrived, the other members seem to have taken strength to oppose me, supposing, and naturally enough, that *I,* and not the older and more influential members of the family, were to blame.

March 3d. "Had the happiness of meeting at the Lord's table. Dr. W. J. Binney, who has lately given evidence of a work of grace upon his heart.

March 4th. "Was this morning, by Rev. Mr. Leslie, married to Dr. Binney and left the mission to proceed to our house, about twelve miles distance."[2]

In our next number we will continue our narrative of Ruth Rover, and endeavor to show how fully she drank the *"cup of sorrow to the dregs!"*

THE CONVERTED INDIAN CHILD.

I was a little Indian, I lived in the wood,
My bed was the wet cold ground, and I stole for my food;
   But now I have bedding,
   Food, shelter and clothing.
This love of my Maker merits praises most loud.

Do you ask who showed favor? My benevolent Saviour
Was a little poor boy without friends, even like me;
   He pitied the suffering;
   He said to the halting
Go tell the degraded their helper I'll be.

I am fed by His bounty—I am taught by His mercy—
I am clothed by His goodness—and praised by His name.
   If I love Him He'll bless me—
   If I trust Him He'll save me,
And will quite from my nature wash each sinful stain.

O! where is my father? O! where is my mother?
O! where are my sisters and brothers so dear?
   I'm sure they are wretched,
   And ought to be pitied—
Good Lord by Thy Spirit to Thyself bring them near.

Farewell, my dear play-mates, friends, teachers
     and school-mates,
I'll now seek my dear kindred to bring them to God.
   I'll tell them of Jesus
   Who died to save us,
And admit us to heaven by the loss of his blood.

SONGS OF THE INDIAN GIRLS.

Pleasant is the evening of each setting day—
Pleasantest the evening of the Sabbath day;
   Then we much love to be taught
   In the work which God has wrought.

All the week we spend, full of childish glee—
Every changing scene brings hilarity—
   But the Sabbath's heavenly joys
   Far surpass these earthly toys.

All the Sabbath bright, seeking God we spend;
Praising him at night, on our knees we bend,
   For such love as we have seen,
   Sinful heathen though we've been.

Then we join and sing, imperfect as we are,
Songs unto our king, that we his favor share;
   While with us our teacher dear
   Swells the chorus high in air.

Thus would we live below, in these sweet ways of love.
'Till we to heaven go, the home of love above;
   There, with friends and teachers, loud
   We'll raise one anthem to our God.

SALLY SOULE.

by Ruth Rover
[Published by the American Tract Society.]

❦

The following quotations from *Zion's Herald* will explain the origin of "Sally Soule's" name. The first is from H. Cummings and the latter from Cyrus Shepherd:

"Duxbury, Nov. 4. 1839.

"BRO. BROWN: You requested me, through the Herald, to send you a copy of the letter which I received from Oregon. It was from brother Shepherd, and of an earlier date than some which you had previously received. It does not contain much that will be interesting to any but intimate friends, and that relation brother Shepherd and myself hold to each other. With the exception of a few lines, I will submit it to you for perusal, and you are at liberty to make what use of it you please. I will just say that Mrs. Cummings' sister, who died in the summer of 1836, near the close of her life requested that all her school books, of which she had many, should be sent to Oregon after her decease, and that a native child might be called by her name, Sally Soule. She felt a particular interest in this mission from its first establishment.

H.C."

"'MISSION HOUSE, WILLAMETTE,
"'NOVEMBER 4th, 1838.

"'DEAR BROTHER AND SISTER CUMMINGS: I received your letter and note, and agreeably to request have named a little girl after your deceased sister, Sally Soule. She is about ten years of age, has a flat head, short neck, and thick set body, which is the general shape of the native females. She is rather shrewd, and quite an adept in mischievous pranks. Sometimes, when the Indians come about, she has come and asked me to let her have some wheat to give to her people. I always ask her how many people she has, and the answer invariably is one. She is an orphan, and it appears knows but one relative, an old woman. When we took her in, which was in the summer of 1837, her only articles of clothing consisted of a wild-cat's skin thrown over her shoulders, and a fringe of dressed deer-skin around her waist. These were her clothing by day, and bedding by night.

C.S.'"

DEAR MARY ANN: I believe in my last letter to you I told you I would comply with your request, and write you some account of the Indian children here, to be published in the Sabbath School Messenger. I then intended to do so, but have since that time considered myself very inadequate to appear as a public writer and therefore have concluded to give the same account to you in a private letter, with however, the permission to publish it if you shall think it possesses sufficient merit.

One thing it is very necessary you should consider when reading memoirs of heathen children, viz: The disadvantages of their early lives. Should I tell you that a little girl in Boston or Malden was very neat, and attended well to her studies and was industrious and pious, you would at once, I presume, think it not strange she should be thus interesting, because you would suppose that she had been favored with examples and instructions of older persons who had tested the advantages of exercising such agreeable qualifications. But should I give you the same relation of an Indian child who had till recently been taught nothing better than to roll in the ashes, or to spend the sunny day in hunting wasps' nests that she might devour the young—and had never been told who made that "big fire without smoke," which daily rises in the east to give us light and heat—or seen a book—you should, I think, conclude that to the instructions of the better learned had been added the grace of God, which had so sanctified them to her good that they seemed to be inherent to her nature, and enabled her to appear in all respects but that of a red skin—to be an educated child from christendom.

"Thus appeared Sally Soule, the loved Indian girl of ten years, who had resided in the mission family three years, I think, previous to her death, which occurred in February, 1839, while the girls were under my care. She was, if I mistake not, of the Yam Hill tribe, from the Yam Hill country, a few miles from the mission, on the opposite side of the river. Her English name was given her in respect for the excellent lady of Bishop Soule. I can relate none of the particulars of her introduction into the mission family, as I was not then in the country, but I soon discovered, on my arrival, that in the circle of the girls being educated by the missionaries, was one who was frequently styled the *old maid.* ' I, of course, felt a little curiosity to learn the cause of this epithet being applied to her, who was the youngest and smallest of the group, and regarded her for a short time with some degree of suspicion. I soon discovered, however, that, if there was among the girls' tasks an article of sewing which required especial care, it was given to Sally Soule; that when the others, in their moments of recreation, were running about for berries, or gathering gum to masticate, she was in the house observing the ladies work, of which she was fond. I also observed that when the other girls soiled or tore their clothes, or were carelessly dressed, she, the 'old maid,' was neatly attired; and when the children around were loudly talking and jesting, this little pattern of excellence would be silent, or simply smiling to show she was not heedless of their enjoyment. Yet she was not a stupid child. She loved to play, but her spirits were less noisy and more useful than those of her mates. On her toy babies was displayed her taste for neatness, and the propriety with which every article of their dress would be arranged, was one cause of her being styled the *old maid.* ' I cannot say that she had received much instruction in this kind of amusement; for, as regards myself, I seldom had occasion to assist her, otherwise than to indulge her very modest request for thread and pieces, for which one of her sweet smiles, which I was sure to receive, amply repaid me. As this little girl was thus lovely in her plays, the reader will suppose, almost without any intimation from me, that she made a right use of her books. She certainly did. She studied and learned her lessons; and when the children in the school had carelessly destroyed their books, Mr. Shepherd would hold up hers before them, and exclaim, 'See here is Sally Soule's book, which she had had so much longer than you have had yours, and it is scarcely injured.'

"Being a great favorite with the children, it was very amusing, when they had permission to play outside the house, to see the anxiety of every one to have her for a mate. No sooner would the word 'yes' be pronounced, than you would hear all the voices at once, crying out, 'I must have Sally.' 'No,' says another, 'she is going with me,' 'She went with you before, and now I'm going to have her.' 'Come go with me, Sally,' says another, 'and I'll give you something.' Thus would they generally contend, until some older person interfered, and appointed her place. She loved them all, and was happy and pleasant with any one, which was, perhaps, the reason why her society was so much desired. In 1839, when several of the children professed to feel that God had given them new hearts, Sally Soule was among the number. She was very young, and as it could not be expected that she had a perfect understanding of what she professed, we thought it possible the effect on her mind was a mere childish sympathy with the feeling of others; however, we knew it was best to encourage her to be good; to approve of her praying, singing, and going to meeting; and whether she had experienced a work of grace on her heart or not, we could not then determine; but her behavior in her last sickness, and her death, furnished us with good evidence that she was a converted child. She was ill, to our knowledge, but ten days before her decease, although her disease, the dropsy of the chest, must have existed for months, and perhaps for years. I had observed, during the winter, that she was more sedate and less playful than formerly, and often, as I unhappily concluded, dull; yet I did not have the least apprehension she was sick. She made no complaint, attended to her work and books, until she was sent to me from the school for medicine. On calling our physician, he pronounced her very sick; but mistaking the nature of her disease, his efforts for her recovery were not well directed, although, had it been otherwise, it is probable a cure could not have been effected. During her illness she appeared peculiarly interesting and lovely. She was, if possible, more gentle, more interesting, and more patient, than she was in health. Every intimation that she would not get well was received with pleasure; and when I talked about her probable decease, and prayed in her hearing that she might be prepared for death, the brightened and intelligent appearance of her countenance told me that it was already done. She even manifested a willingness to die; and once, when I wished to ascertain more certainly if she understood the change from life to death, I asked her which she had rather do, get well, go to school, and play with the girls, or die and go to God, and have her body put in the ground. She replied, she had rather die, and go to God. None of us were prepared for her sudden exit, though pretty well convinced she could not recover. We thought she might possibly live a considerable time. I was even surprised when her physician said she could not live ten days; yet that was the last evening of her life. At the hour of retirement, I again endeavored to lead her thoughts, by conversation, to another world. I prayed with her, and she said the Lord's prayer with me, as was her custom. I observed that her voice faltered, and attributed it to drowsiness. I gave her a kiss, and bade her good night, when she replied with a sweet smile, and so peculiar an emphasis, that I can never forget it, 'Good night, ma'am.' I was at that time peculiarly affected; but as it proved to be her dying breath, it can never escape my memory.

''Not long after I had retired, one of the girls aroused me by saying, 'Miss Smith, Sally is making a very strange noise.' I hastened to her bedside, and found her indeed dying. I several times attempted to arouse her, so she might speak and give some evidence that she understood what we said, but all in vain. Mr. Shepherd desired she might be baptized, and Mr. Leslie was called to perform the ceremony. This done, we could do no more than to pray the Lord to receive her spirit. It was my happy privilege to sit alone by the bedside of that loved heathen child, in her dying moments, waiting to see the last flickering flame of life, and know she was no more. This took place after daylight, but before sunrise. The moon, which, during my stay at the bedside of death, had been shining with a light as feeble as the life which was then waning, was now lost in the sun's effulgence, while upon Sally's spirit had burst forth the resplendence of the Son of righteousness. Mr. Leslie pronounced a funeral discourse, and she was conveyed to the grave-yard, a few rods from her chamber, to sleep with several of her mates who had been called before her. During the service the rain was falling very rapidly, and nothing but an imperative refusal was sufficient to prevent the girls from following her to the grave, so ardent had been their attachment to her. She sleeps, or rather wakes, in heaven, where I desire to meet her, adorned with the spotless robe which alone can entitle us to a seat among the just.''

CHAPTER XIV

"PICTURES OF OREGON"

❦

INDIAN MISSIONS.

"We call them savage—O be just;
Their outraged feelings scan;
A voice comes forth, 'tis from the dust—
The savage was a man!
Think you he loved not? Who stood by,
And in his toils took part?
Woman was there to bless his eye—
The savage had a heart!
Think you he prayed not? When on high
He heard the thunders roll,
What bade him look beyond the sky?
The savage had a soul!''

"Alas! for them—their day is o'er,
Their fires are out from shore to shore;
No more for them the wild deer bounds;
The plow is on their hunting grounds;
The pale man's axe rings through their woods
The pale man's sail skims o'er their floods.
     Their pleasant springs are dry;
Their children—look—by power oppressed,
Beyond the mountains of the west,
     Their children go to die.''

"His heraldry is but a broken bow,
His history but a tale of misery and woe,
His very name must be a blank.''

The mission of the Methodist Episcopal church in Oregon, or the "Oregon Mission" as it has been called, may in all propriety be termed a failure. Its wrong locality, and the erroneous pursuits of the missionaries, both operated to make it such.

The objects of the Oregon Provisional Emigration Society, and its defeat, were so similar that we presume to make a few selections on the subjects, and also express our own ideas of the mistaken calculations therein treated of.[1]

"This Society, formed in August, 1838, has for its object the planting of christian American settlements in Oregon.

"Our purpose in making these settlements will be, first, to spread civilization and christianity among the Indians of that country; and secondly, *to avail ourselves of the advantages of the Territory offers for agriculture, manufactures and commerce.*"

Here is one error made apparent at the commencement, viz: *avarice.*

"For the benefit of the Indians, we propose to establish schools, in which instruction in elementary science will be connected with labor; the males being made acquainted with farming or some useful mechanic art, and the females with household duties and economy.

"The age at which we shall admit the pupils, and the length of time for which they will be retained, will enable us to break up their Indian habits."

Never! You may rear them from infancy, and they are Indians still.

"And to persuade them to turn their attention to the cultivation of the soil, and to the erection of permanent dwellings."

We have seen this attempted. They might be induced to cultivate the soil, but for the houses they care nothing. We have known them to refuse to live in log houses built for their residence—liking those better which are easily transported to a different place.

"Having reached the Territory, we shall seek such points of settlement as will afford the greatest facilities for our intercourse with the tribes; *for agriculture, manufactures and commerce;* and also for defense, in case of hostilities from any quarter.

"Our design to elevate the Indians will make it necessary to be somewhat cautious in the selection of our men, and we shall encourage the migration of none whose character for industry and virtue is not well established.

"Let there, then, be planted in Oregon, at several eligible points, settlements, from which missionaries and teachers shall go out in every direction among the aborigines, and to which they may look for any assistance they need in the prosecution of their labors. Let these settlements be the centres around which shall be gathered, in new organization, the converted and civilized red men, and where, free from oppression and scorn, they shall, for the first time, find themselves on a *level with white men,* and it *will not be long before such privileges* will *win the entire multitude to embrace a new mode of life,* and above all the gospel of Jesus Christ.

"We go to Oregon not as the enemies of its aboriginal inhabitants. We go not to scatter fire and death among them, but to carry the branch of peace and the blessings of religion and civilization to those degraded men. We go as their friends, and shall entwine ourselves in all the generous and noble sentiments of the children of the wilderness, and we shall be safe.

"As a race, they cannot be saved until they are treated like men. The patient and enduring African may look around upon the wreck of all he loves, and even respect the man who plunders him; but from such subserviency the lofty and chivalrous spirit of the Indian recoils, and he could with greater pleasure die amid tortures than receive benefits from one who would degrade him.

"They esteem the whites as a race superior to themselves, and copy them in all things, as far as possible with their limited knowledge and means; nor is there room for a doubt that the arms of civilization and christianity might embrace the entire people in a few years, at most, from the hour when the first *general* effort for their salvation should be made. They are men—men of a high order—they should be treated as such, and they who would save them must not subject them to scorn and disabilities, because they are not white, nor withhold from them those social and civil privileges which they would give to white men of equal intelligence and virtue.

"They who would save them must go among them, and while they do not countenance or encourage the savage and wicked practices they may witness, they must, in a certain sense, put themselves on a level with the Indian himself. Civil society, instituted in their midst for the purpose and having provision made for receiving the red men into the enjoyment of all rights, social and civil, which the whites enjoy, so soon as he should become prepared for it, by renouncing his savage habits and obtaining the qualifications required of a white man, would be a more powerful motive than any which has ever been brought to bear upon the Indian's heart, and would doubtless prove the salvation of the race."

All this looks very well in print—but how chimerical! Where was ever a body of men who, though professedly pious, would remain *entirely* so amidst such inducements to aggrandizement as are, or *were,* presented in Oregon? And where would a community of whites be found who would, for the benefit of Indians, submit to the following "principle" of the above-named society?

"That white men, dwelling with them, should have no interests, rights or privileges, personal, social or civil, separate from those of Indians, who possess the same moral and intellectual qualifications as themselves."

Nowhere, assuredly, among the fallen sons and daughters of Adam.

"That to save and elevate the Indians, the great influences must be those of example and personal instruction, given by residents among them."

This is also a "principle" of the same society. We need only refer to Oregon to find illustrations of the working of this plan. There are many professedly *christian* people in every settlement here, and how much have they benefited the Indians?

For instance, where is a settlement more professedly christian, and that retains a greater number of Indians among them than Oregon City? and what is the situation of the latter there? It is but too apparent!

But what are the purposes of this society in regard to themselves? Let us read:

"It may be inquired, "What is this society? What do you mean to do?"

"The territory west of the Rocky Mountains has long been regarded as one of the most interesting portions of our globe, both as it regards the country and its inhabitants. The works of nature are there wrought upon a large scale, and the sublime scenery is more than equalled by the unrivalled productiveness of the soil and the perfect salubrity of the climate. By its situation on the sea coast it has every advantage for trade with California, Mexico, the Western States of South America, Sandwich Islands, Japan, China, Hindoostan, and other parts of the East Indies, Eastern Africa, Java, the Spice Islands, and all the multitudes of islands in the Pacific and Indian Oceans; while the Atlantic is quite as accessible from Oregon as is China or Calcutta from the United States or England. The whole inland country is connected with the coast by canals which nature herself has sunk—the mighty rivers of the land; and the products of the soil would find an easy conveyance to points where they might be exchanged for the wares of distant nations.

"The fur trade, once the source of many a princely fortune, and even now, in its decline, a very lucrative business; the salmon fishery, for which there are advantages in the rivers of that Territory to be found nowhere else in the world; the cultivation of silk, for which the climate is peculiarly adapted, and which is an article commanding a ready sale the world over; the culture of flax and hemp; the raising of flour, for which a ready market is at hand, together with a thousand other productive employments, would crowd those streams with commerce and the ports with activity and wealth. The oaks and pines of the mighty forests might blend in staunch vessels, which should go forth with the fruits of industry and return with the profits of commerce; and many a trader and many a whaleman would seek the hospitable ports of that country to trade and refit, and thus advance the interests of those who make it their home. Nor is it only for trade the country offers advantages. The farmer and mechanic might there find a home and a competency—the philanthropist a field for the exercise of his charity—and the teacher a school in which he would have opportunity for labor and assurance of success.

"We intend to avail ourselves of these advantages, and yet we do not propose to act for mere personal aggrandizement. We have nobler purposes in view. One of the principal objects of the enterprise is the civilization and conversion of the Indians, and the salvation of a remnant of that noble race from utter extinction."

Again:

"For our own emolument we shall depend principally upon the flour trade; the salmon fishery; the culture of silk, flax and hemp; the lumber trade; and perhaps, a local business of furs. We shall establish a regular commercial communication with the United States, drawing supplies of men and goods from thence; and, ultimately, we shall contemplate the opening of a trade with the various ports of the Pacific. A few years only will be required to fill the plains of Oregon with herds as valuable as those of the Spanish savannas; and various sources of profit will reveal themselves, as the increase of population shall make new resources necessary."

But what about this contradiction on the subject of land?

"We shall wish that no person in connection with us may have a claim upon any tract of land, unless he shall actually settle upon and improve that land; believing as we do, that a *land speculation in that country would be most prejudicial to our best interests, and, above all things, calculated to destroy the last hopes of the Indian race.*

"Such are the objects of our society, which we shall doubtless accomplish, if the government of the United States regards us favorably. We shall of course *be very unwilling to settle in a savage wilderness, without having first obtained a sufficient title to the land* we may occupy, and without being assured that political obstacles will not be thrown in the way of our prosperity."

Another impracticability is apparent in the following:

"Such is the Indian character and mode of life that no general and lasting reform can be effected among them by mere spiritual instruction. In order to do any essential good to this portion of our race, their progress in the arts of life and in civilization must be equal to their advancement in christianity. To save the Indians they must be brought to settle upon and cultivate their lands; to erect permanent habitations; to abandon the chase as a principal means of support, and to engage in the manufacture of whatever may be necessary to the prosecution of their agricultural labors. In a word, they must change entirely their mode of life, and ceasing forever to be wandering hordes of hunters and warriors, they must become a people abiding in their habitations and living upon the produce of the soil.

"We are happy to learn that Mr. Lee cordially agrees with us in the primary opinion that in the elevation of the Indian race we must, if we would succeed, teach them the arts of life as fast as we do the truths of the gospel; that civilization and religion, to benefit these savages, must keep pace with each other; and that if one is pressed on before the other, the labor is lost."

And yet he says:

"Brother Lee, we understand, has come over to consult upon *some new plan* for the elevation of the Indian race."

It appears, then, that he is satisfied that the above plan of operation would produce no lasting benefit.

"Christianity is perfectly incongruous with the habits of migratory hordes, and can never be sustained among them. If it prevails among them it will induce them to locate and cultivate the soil; if they continue wanderers, it must fail of success."

Why so? Can't they carry religion with them?

"It has been deemed of primary importance to tell the Indian the story of Jesus and his dying love, in the hope it would follow him in his savage wanderings and save him. And some, it is true, have been favorably affected."

And why is not the prospect as good for many as for few?
But these are all false premises. The same author says:

"Experience has taught that what by construction, and what by violation, the Indian has little left to depend upon in the white man's promise. He makes them, he changes them, and he breaks them at will.

"We unhesitatingly avow it as our decided opinion that the example and conversation of wicked men is now more than counteracting all the labors of missionaries to the Indians, and this, too, for the simple and natural reason that the number of enlightened christians among the tribes is so small."

The same difficulty appears here as before, that of finding any *large* "number of christians" who will make the elevation of the Indian the business of their lives.

This writer's remarks result at last in the following:

"In the civilized society of the United States there is no attraction for the red man. If he enters it, he must do so as an Indian; he must enjoy no privileges, because he is an Indian; he must be cheated and ridiculed, because he is an Indian; and he must sacrifice his honor, his interest, and his happiness, all because he is an Indian!

"Indian society will never be inviolate. The ruthless hand of white cupidity will always be invading its peace and security. It must cease to be *Indian* society. The tribes, *as such,* must become extinct and a new organization must take their place, in which there shall be found white men and their rights, to an extent sufficient to secure the respect of civilized nations, and thus the safety of their own community."

So, then, to benefit the Indians we must exterminate them. They must no longer *be Indians!* Who would think that because a wild animal is tamed he must take the name of the person who tamed him?

But we have other resources for reference besides these. President Van Buren says:

"That a mixed occupancy of the same territory by the white and red men is incompatible with the safety or happiness of either.

"That the country to which they are removed is one 'much more extensive, and better adapted to their condition than that on which they resided.'

"That the United States 'guaranty to them the possession of this country forever,' so that it will be *'exempt from all intrusion of the white men.'*"

Our own views of this subject are embraced mostly in the following quotations:

"On motion of the Rev. Mr. Remington of Troy, seconded by the Rev. Mr. Stratton of New York:

"Resolved, That as all attempts to save the heathen, by teaching them letters and the arts of civilized life *first,* have failed, therefore, in the opinion of this meeting, the only effectual way to bring them to the knowledge of the truth, is, *first of all,* to carry to them the gospel of Jesus Christ, and that civilization and domestic economy will follow a reformation of heart and life."

We have evidence of the feasibility and success of this plan in the instance of the pious Brainerd, who labored among the Indians about the years 1743-7 inclusive:[2]

"The account which Mr. Brainerd gives in his journal respecting the work of God at those places is replete with interest to the pious heart and argues well for the christian religion. The instances of conversions which he gives are so many—among the very aged, the youth, and those in the meridian of life, among all grades of character, even those addicted to the grossest vices—that we can only glance at them in this article and extract a few paragraphs as specimens of the glorious triumphs of the cross of Christ. In mentioning his first visit at Crossweeksung, he says his hearers increased daily, and the power of God attended his word, and many began to feel a serious concern for their souls and shed many tears. When he left them one of them said, 'she wished God would change her heart' another said 'she wanted to find Christ' and an old man, one of their chiefs, wept bitterly.

"He says again, respecting the Indians of the same place—'O! what a difference between these Indians and those on the Susquehanna! To be with those seemed like being banished from God and his people; to be with these like being admitted into his family and the enjoyment of his presence. How great the change lately made upon these Indians, who, not many months ago, were as thoughtless and as averse to christianity as those on the Susquehanna!' Whenever he preached there seemed to be a melting down among the whole assembly, and scarce a dry eye was to be seen among them. After public service the Indians would continue praying among themselves for two hours together.

"Again he observes with respect to them in the worship of God: 'These poor Indians, who so lately paid no regard to the glorious truths of the gospel of Jesus Christ, now embrace every opportunity to hear it preached. I have often thought that they would cheerfully attend divine worship twenty-four hours together.'

"He commenced his labors April, 1743, among the Indians at Kanuameek, in New York, situated between Stockbridge and Albany. Here was a small tribe which received him very kindly. Mr. Brainerd labored there about one year with all the zeal and diligence his feeble state of health would endure. It was a year of privation and hardship. Yet not a sacrifice too great for such a spirit as that of Brainerd to cheerfully make for Christ and the souls that he had 'purchased with his own blood.'

"In a letter to his brother he mentions his mode of living while with them. 'I live,' said he, 'mostly in a melancholy desert, about eighteen miles from Albany, and board with a poor Scotchman. My lodging is a little heap of straw laid upon some boards in a log room without any floor. My diet consists chiefly of hasty pudding, boiled corn, and bread baked in ashes.' After living with this family a few weeks, he removed and lived with the Indians in one of their wigwams, and subsequently he built a small house and lived entirely alone.

"The whole time Mr. Brainerd labored among the Indians was less than four years, yet how much was wrought through his instrumentality in that short period, among this much abused portion of our degenerate race! It may truly be said of him, he 'counted not his own life dear unto himself'—he was a willing and whole sacrifice to the cause of degraded humanity. He was unwearied in zeal until entirely prostrated in body, and unable to render any further service to the Indians.''

Here is an example which it were well for the credit of missionary societies if more would follow.

But are there any Indians in Oregon who would thus receive the gospel? Let us turn to Rev. Mr. Parker's Exploring Tour.[3]

Of those on the tributaries of the Columbia he says:

''The moral disposition of these Indians is very commendable, certainly as much so as any people that can be named. They are kind to strangers, and remarkably so to one another. While among them I saw no contentions, nor did I hear angry words from one to another. They manifested an uncommon desire to be instructed, that they might obey and fulfill all moral obligations.

''Providentially there came to us this afternoon a good interpreter from Fort Hall, so that to-morrow we can have public worship.

''*Sabbath,* 6th. Early this morning one of the oldest chiefs went about among the people and with a loud voice explained to them the instructions given them last evening; told them it was Sabbath day, and they must prepare for public worship. About eight in the morning some of the chiefs came to me and asked where they should assemble. I asked them if they could not be accommodated in the willows which skirted the stream of water on which they were encamped. They thought not. I then inquired if they could not take the poles of some of their lodges and construct a shade. They thought they could, and without any other directions went and made preparations, and about eleven o'clock came and said they were ready for worship.

''I found them all assembled, men, women and children, between four and five hundred, in what I call a sanctuary of God, constructed with their lodges, nearly one hundred feet long and about twenty feet wide; and all were arranged in rows through the length of the building, upon their knees, with a narrow space in the middle, lengthwise, resembling an aisle. The whole area within was carpeted with their dressed skins, and they were all attired in their best. The chiefs were arranged in a semi-circle at the end which I was to occupy.

''I could not have believed they had the means or could have known how to construct so convenient and so decent a place for worship, and especially as it was the first time they had had public worship. The whole sight, taken together, sensibly affected me and filled me with astonishment; and I felt as though it was the house of God and the gate of heaven.

"They all continued in their kneeling position during the singing and prayer, and when I closed prayer with amen, they all said what was equivalent, in their native language, to amen. And when I commenced sermon they sunk back on their heels. I stated to them the original condition of man as first created; his fall, and the ruined and sinful condition of all mankind; the law of God, and that all are transgressors of this law, and as such are exposed to the wrath of God, both in this life and the life to come; and then told them of the mercy of God in giving His son to die for us; and of the love of the Saviour; and though He desires our salvation, yet He will not save unless we hate sin and put our trust in Him, and love and obey Him with all our heart. I also endeavored to show them the necessity of renovation of heart by the power and grace of the Holy Spirit; told them they must pray to God for forgiveness of their sins and for salvation.

"They gave the utmost attention, and entire stillness prevailed, excepting when some truth arrested their mind forcibly a little humming sound was made through the assembly, occupying two or three seconds. I never spoke to a more interesting assembly, and I would not have exchanged my then audience for any other upon earth; and I felt that it was worth a journey across the Rocky Mountains to enjoy this one opportunity with these heathen, who are so anxious to come to a knowledge of God. I hope that in the last day it will be found that good was done in the name of Jesus.

"If christians could have witnessed this day's service they would have felt and they would have been willing to do something adequate to the conversion of those perishing souls."

Of the Sioux Mr. Parker says:

"On the 30th met in council with the chiefs of this tribe to lay before them the object of our tour, and to know if they would wish to have missionaries sent among them to teach them to read and write, and especially how to worship God. They expressed much satisfaction with the proposal, and said they would do all they could to make their condition comfortable. There can be no doubt that this community of Sioux would be a promising field for laborers. They are inquisitive, and their language is distinct and sonorous.

"Who can read these extracts," says Mr. Parker, "without echoing the enquiry of the writer, 'Where are the young men in the christian churches who will go out to these heathen?' Where are they? Let the churches search them out and send them. Let the young men wake up to the call. Let them ask themselves, ought not I to leave all and go seek those lost sheep in the wilderness? What hinders? Are you not qualified to teach these ignorant savages the way of salvation? Can't you beg the means of traveling to their land? Can't you start off, trusting in providence for protection, even if no christian friends, or churches, or mission boards, will grant you aid? See what thousands of young men are wasting their health and energies, in those regions, in the service of the fur companies, moved by a spirit of enterprise and the hope of a paltry recompense of gold and silver. They are hunting for the wild beasts of the prairie and mountains—you may hunt for the recovery of lost immortal souls.''

In relation to Mr. Parker's account, Hon. Mr. Cushing says:[4]

''His manner of relating his discoveries inspires the reader with confidence, and there is no doubt but that his statements may be accredited. They are corroborated by the reports which have come from the missionaries sent out since he was there.''

We believe, then, most fully, and we consider this belief is supported by the convictions of many persons who have had experience, that to benefit the Indian tribes the work of grace must take *precedence,* and all other efforts for their improvement may then be made with a reasonable expectation of success. Or, in other words, the Indian must first be *caught,* and then he can be instructed. Or in other words still, *gain his affections,* and you have gained your object. You may tell an Indian that 'tis good for him to raise potatoes, and he will believe you as long as he has them to eat; and you may tell him to love and fear God, and he will try to do so during the danger of a thunder storm, unless his *heart* has been affected with *love to God,* and then he can *trust Him* in its greatest severity.

The unsuccessful attempt of the ''Oregon Mission'' has had the effect greatly to discourage the friends to *Indian* missions *particularly.* But this should not be. There are still opportunities to benefit the Indian tribes, and if properly improved may undoubtedly result in great good.

The Presbyterian Mission on the upper Columbia failed, also, from the same errors which operated against the ''Oregon Mission,'' viz: The influence of Romanists and the faults of the missionaries—more particularly that of *avarice.* This latter mission started well and for a time was productive of great good to the natives. They were, to a considerable extent, reformed by the preaching and religious instructions of the missionaries, and they readily gave their attention to agriculture and household economy—as knitting, sewing, weaving, &c.—and learned, to some extent, to read their own language, and were rapidly becoming improved in their habits and way of living—but becoming jealous of the designs of their teachers, by seeing them become possessors of large bands of stock and herds of cattle, and knowing them to receive large supplies of goods from abroad, which, however, they *sold,* and thus obtained and secured their monies, and being excited by white traders who wished to monopolize this trade to themselves; and furthermore being informed by the Roman priests that they were listening to a false religion, it was *not* very strange that the *savage* nature of this people should have become so far excited as to induce them to the committal of the horrid massacre which stains the history of their nation.[5]

Avarice of power and wealth is sure to affect, more or less, the mind of every person who enters a country as rich in resources of competency, and even aggrandizement, as Oregon; and *firm* must that mind be which can resist all their allurements and pursue a course of self-denial and devotion to the true interests of the cause of Christ.

"Ye—can—not—serve—God—and—Mammon!" is a sentence which we wish was *ever* apparent to the vision of the professed followers of the humble Nazarene, and those who cannot endure its meaning and practice its divine intention are *not fit* to elevate the *cross* of the crucified before *any* people.

We believe the principal cause of the unprecedented success which has attended the Presbyterian Mission at the Sandwich Islands, has been the restriction placed upon the missionaries by the "Board," viz: "that *they shall not engage in trade of any kind to enrich themselves.*" This has restrained the natural inclination for wealth—insured the application of their time to the objects of the enterprise, and been an evidence ever apparent to the eyes of the Hawaiians that they came among them for *their* good and not to benefit themselves. Consequently the blessing of heaven has followed their efforts, and all the combined forces of sin, and the intrigues of the church of Rome, have not been able to overthrow or to interrupt their labors.

Therefore, to benefit the Indians, men must not go among them to enrich themselves, but to enlighten them as to a better way of living. They must not draw them into the settlements of the white men, but go into *their* settlements— and the farther they are removed from white men the better.

The writer of the first extracts we made seems to be of this opinion, for, in 1838, he says:

"But neither rum nor oppression have yet affected the tribes of Oregon. They have roved, as yet, in their native wilds, undisturbed and uncorrupted by the white man, and there is a chance to save *them;* it is the only chance left upon the continent. If the work of entire civil and religious redemption begins at all, it must begin there."

To hope that the races of white and red men will ever blend in one is absurd in the highest degree. A white man will *never* degrade himself to an

Indian, in order to benefit the race. He may live among them for this purpose, but they are and must remain as distinct as those of the English and African.

There is also an impediment existing in the minds of the Indians themselves, and this same writer admits it:

"They will not now, though the opportunity were afforded, coalesce with the whites, even though the safety of their race depended on it."

If the truly devoted missionary would enter the forests occupied by none but the red men, and teach them salvation by the way of the cross—trusting for safety on the arm of Omnipotence—being willing to live as did Brainerd, if it were necessary—we believe that the songs of the redeemed world would be heard there; and if these people preferred to depend on the chase rather than the cultivation of the soil, for support, let them do so. Suffer them to remain *Indians,* as they were born, and, with the blessing of God, they will become *good Indians,* and then they are good enough.

CHAPTER XV

DOCTOR BINNEY

A true son of Erin, inherited in his disposition the characteristics of his countrymen—intelligence—generosity—recklessness, and frivolity—these were inherent in his nature. His temperament was sanguineous combined with nervous.

When arrived at manhood we find him *dissipated.* But if this were the effects of early improper training, or occasioned by circumstances which surrounded him when away from the restraining influence of watchful parents, we are unable to say. Probably both had an effect.

In addition to this, we find him, in maturer years, apparently totally devoid of principle, and so easily influenced that the least temptation would lead him to break resolutions which had been the result of deep penitence. *This* was his greatest weakness—*that* his greatest error.

His father was said to have been a very passionate man; but he was a member of a presbyterian church, and we believe was greatly respected. He acquired a very handsome fortune at the wholesale provision trade in Londonderry; educated two of his sons at college in London, England, and indulged his wife's and daughters' extravagant manner of living, till, in connexion with the improper expenditures of his sons, he found his fortune fail him, and at the early age of forty odd years he died, 'tis said mostly of a broken heart. His reply, which 'tis said he always gave when asked concerning his age, viz: "Few and evil have the days of the years of my life been," is probably his best epitaph.

Mrs. Binney was an excessively passionate or quick tempered woman; and this peculiarity of disposition, which is so very apparent in every member of the family, had foundation enough in the mother without attributing the same to the father. To be thought superior to the "common" class was seemingly her greatest object in relation to her children; hence, to give them a *polished* education was her only endeavor, while the solid rudiments of learning were passed over.

In illustration of this we find them, when reduced to labor, after their father's failure, learning embroidery, music and dancing, and buying season tickets for balls, &c., and at the same time one of them directing a letter thus: "To Doctor W. J. Binney, Oregon Territory, Columbia River, United States of America."

Dr. Binney, while at school in England, indulged in every excess of dissipation to which London affords so many facilities. With liberty to draw on his father's banker for sums of money when he pleased, and associating with gay students in that gay metropolis, the vicious and reckless course which he pursued was in exact keeping with his own inclinations, his associates, and the place.

At length, having finished his education, fearing to await the arrival of his father, he presented a draft of several hundred dollars on his father's banker, and receiving the sum he took passage privately to Canada.

From here he obtained a situation as surgeon and physician in a government vessel bound for the Pacific, and at California left her secretly, for what reason we are unable to say, but we infer from some grievous offence, as his mother wrote him some years afterwards thus:

"Mr. —— was exceeding anxious about his son, as he had learned that he left the vessel in company with you, and that the officers pursued you for two days and nights, intending to shoot you if they had overtaken you."

In California he sojourned some time, giving himself up almost exclusively to the indulgence of vitiated habits. *Once* a gentleman who had observed his skill in surgery offered him a lucrative situation, but was again influenced to withhold it by the reports of Ewing Young of Oregon against his character.[1]

We pause here to say, of all the evils to which society is subject we consider that of meddlesome gossip to be the deadliest. How many persons has this very evil ruined! who, but for it, would oftentimes have retraced the erroneous path they had pursued, and rose to usefulness, respectability and eminence—but *by* it have become discouraged and returned again to their wallowing in the mire, till they were lost to the world and perchance to hope!

Dr. Binney then betook himself to trapping beaver in the mountain, and eventually started with a small party for Oregon overland, when the party was defeated by the Indians, all the number being killed but five and the beaver and horses all taken from the remainder. Two of these died in the Umpqua, and three, Dr. Binney and two others, arrived in the Willamette settlement about the year one thousand eight hundred and thirty five.

Dr. Binney was badly wounded by the blow of a tomahawk upon his chin, yet was obliged with the others to pursue his way to Oregon on foot.[2] He arrived at the Methodist Mission at Willamette in a most distressed and forlorn condition. The wound on his face was most severe, he had been compelled to use his shirt to bandage; his shoes were worn out; his whole clothing was lost but his pantaloons and vest, which was all that covered him when he reached the mission.

Messrs. Lee and Shepherd were at home when Dr. Binney reached their house. Rev. Messrs. Lees soon after took their horses and went away to hold meetings in the settlement. Mr. Shepherd offered him one of the Indian boys' shirts, and when he had tarried about two hours without any farther attention being paid to him, Mr. Turner, one of the three who had arrived the evening before, came to the house and urged him to go to a Frenchman's with him, "for," said he, with curses, "I came here yesterday, and not a bite of anything would they give me." They went to a Frenchman's and received every attention which it was possible to bestow.

Mr. J. Lee afterwards finding he was censured for neglecting to succor these suffering persons, said he thought they would be there when he returned from meeting, and then he intended to attend to their wants.

We have been informed that Dr. Binney was not sparing in his reproaches on what he considered the censurable neglect of men professing piety, and, moreover, whose avowed purpose in coming to the country was to benefit their fellow men.

This misunderstanding between Rev. Mr. Lee and Dr. Binney was probably the reason why the latter was not employed at some mission on the return of the former from the States, as he and Ruth Rover were led to expect at the time of their marriage, and but for this encouragement, given by two influential members of the mission, Ruth would not, we have heard her say, have left the mission to marry, however great were her trials there.

Dr. Binney, having recovered from his wounds, went to California with a party of the settlers and Mr. Edwards of the Methodist Mission, for a band of cattle, and returned to the settlement in 1837, and took board with Dr. W——— of the mission. He, at this time, in speaking of himself, said his course had been vicious through his whole life, but he wished to reform and try to rise in the world. He readily found friends to assist him. Dr. White very generously trusted him for board, and endeavored to encourage him in a course of sobriety and industry.

Some time after he commenced the practice of medicine in the settlement, and established himself at Champoeg.

In February, 1839, he was among the number of those who professed to have met with a change of heart, during the revival at the mission. He connected himself with the methodist church, and for a time was called "brother Binney" and favored with all the honors of the sanctified. Pity some of those encouragements could not be given when waywardness begins to appear.

Mr. Edwards having brought very unfavorable reports of Dr. Binney's character while travelling with him,[3] Rev. Mr. Leland remarked that it was "the best evidence he possessed that the work was of God, that *Dr. Binney, a man who had been the very off-scouring of the earth,* was brought into the church."

There was another evidence, if he could only have thought of it, viz: that of *Wiley* being so suddenly forgiven for the "crime" he had committed, and received into such peculiar favor with the Almighty that "the reformation was more indebted to him than to any other for its life." This certainly was *"depths of mercy!"*

After this preparatory qualification, Dr. Binney offered himself in marriage to Ruth Rover. She at first objected to leave the mission, but being told by the superintendent, Dr. W———, that there was no doubt at all but on Mr. Lee's return Dr. Binney would be requested to accept an appointment as physician at some one of the mission stations, and that meantime she would have a very extensive opportunity of doing good among the sick in the settlement, she consented. The unhappy dispute between her and Mr. Wiley was revealed to him in the way her enemies pleased, and neither Ruth nor her husband knew how either had been deceived till some time after.

Dr. Binney said the information he had received did not at all lessen the esteem he entertained for Miss Rover, and some time after their marriage requested Wiley to give him a written apology for the injurious report he had caused to be circulated about his wife. Mr. Wiley said he would take the paper home and consider it. But Dr. Binney insisting it should be done immediately, fell to cursing him, when Wiley put spurs to his horse and made off in affright.

But let us to the wedding. It must be considered that Oregon was not in those days as now. There were not at hand those magazines of goods which can now be found in many towns in Oregon, where a bride may array herself "in style." Or if there had been, we know not if Ruth would have availed herself of any of these temptations, for she did not even dress as well as her limited wardrobe would have enabled her to do, for we see her standing at the altar in a *green merino*[4] dress and a black and green handkerchief about her neck.

The only witness to the ceremony, besides the parson's family, declared he thought he was at a funeral.

Some of the Frenchmen and Indians who had been married by the missionaries, had had wedding parties made for them—but at Ruth's wedding not even an Irish wake was offered her.

Ruth was herself very sad. A few minutes before the ceremony was to be performed, one of the mission family—the same officious person who had wished her, when she first arrived, "to marry,"—had said to her, "not one of this mission family approves of your union with Dr. Binney."

"For what reason?" she asked.

"Why they say that you'll not live together long—they know his character and temper, and think that *you* are too independent to bear with him—and that your separation will be a disgrace to the mission."

"But why could I not have been informed of this before now? I have ever been encouraged to accept his addresses."

"Why, they liked it very well when they considered that you'd have a home of your own, and be much happier away than here—but *now* they think your dispositions are so different that you can't agree."

"Well," said Ruth, "I'll not disappoint the man now, at this late moment, even if I sacrifice myself to fulfill my engagement."

Immediately upon this she went to the altar. All the old womens' bad omens she had ever heard she thought fulfilled at that time. The day was rainy—pigs and chickens ran across her path—the ceremony was performed with the parties standing the wrong way of the floor—the dogs barked on her entering and leaving;—and what affected her more than all this, she had accidentally read in scripture that morning: "Thou shalt be ashamed of Egypt as thou hast been of Assyria—yea thou shalt go forth from him and thy hands upon thy head."

But, *did she love him?* that's the question. We think not particularly. She had asked a lady where he had boarded: "If you were single would you marry Dr. Binney, provided he asked for you?"

The lady replied, with astonishment: "What! marry a mad dog! no indeed, I'd live and die an old maid before I'd do that!"

Ruth remembered the expression, and several others she had heard, but concluded that if her affections were not very great for him then, she could not *live with a husband* and not love him, especially as he was a *christian*. She anticipated great pleasure in religious exercises with him, as he was a "young convert," and 'tis always supposed that such are very devotional.[5]

They left the mission house soon after the dinner bell had rung—neither one having been invited to eat although they had fifteen miles to ride in the rain. Mr. and Mrs. Shepherd and Mr. Whitcomb were at the head of the house, and we are not sure there was any thing "to spare."

'Twas an interesting sight, that wedding party, that day, as Ruth Rover plodded her way through the mud and rain, sometimes a quarter of a mile behind her husband, who occasionally would halt and tell her to "come along!" And Ruth went along behind her lord till they had arrived within a mile of their home, when the husband requested her to "go ahead" and he'd go into a neighbor's and see if his *table* was made. He overtook her, however, before they reached the house, and very politely said to her, as he assisted her from the saddle, "this is our home."

"I'm very glad to reach it," she replied, "for I'm very tired."

The doctor soon made some tea in a tin kettle—fried some bacon and eggs—had some good bread, made by an Indian woman—set the whole, with some white sugar, on the shelf beneath his few vials of medicine, which, as his table had not come, served them very well. Ruth enjoyed the meal very much, as she had not eaten since morning, and we presume the doctor did also, for he amused her afterwards till half past nine with reading aloud in an old English magazine, and laughing heartily at the jokes. But we had forgotten he was religious! He did not, however, commence family prayers till morning.

The bridal bed, as prepared by him, we had better describe somewhat, as 'twill show what bachelors had to bear in those days. The bedstead, made with high posts and board floor, by a farmer, was really stylish for Oregon. The doctor had borrowed a straw bed and one pillow, the latter covered with deer skin, and the former covered in part with borrowed blankets. This was very well, however, for a bachelor, inasmuch as he had evidently provided the best he could.

Ruth began in the morning to look about the premises, and to apply herself to whatever required to be done in her new home. The doctor read a chapter in the bible and prayed "in his family," and the next morning did the same, which was the last of this exercise—he telling his wife he *could not pray.*

He had taken a claim and erected a log house for which, with the chimney, he was to pay one hundred dollars; he had two horses, a few articles of clothing, a few dishes, two chairs, two blankets, and a kettle and frying pan for cooking, which were all the possessions he could boast.

He told Ruth one day he thought he had done very well since he came into the country two years before entirely destitute, for he had maintained himself, accumulated a little property and only owed a few dollars at the fort and seventy to Dr. White of the mission, which were due mostly for board. When Ruth learned this she requested him to take what was due her there, being fifty-nine dollars, towards paying it, and gave an order to that effect. In this world's goods they certainly both were very poor—but what matters it? they were industrious and willing to work.

Dr. Binney was an excellent surgeon and physician and was already very popular with the French settlers, and there being no physician in the settlement but himself and Dr. White of the mission, he soon had enough to do. But wages were very low, and we have heard some persons complain because he charged one dollar a day for himself and horse when travelling. He liked the practice of his profession and to be out among the people, while Ruth, wishing nothing to be neglected which would tend to improve their circumstances, built the first pen for a pig, and laid the first rails for a garden. She had an object in view in thus giving her assistance to whatever required to be done, which she wished much to be able to accomplish, which was to assist her husband in obtaining a sufficiency to enable her to refund to the education society of Boston a hundred dollars which they had expended for her at Wilbraham academy. She considered this would be just and honorable inasmuch as she had left the service of the mission before the time had expired for which she was engaged.

She consequently indited a letter to Rev. D. S. King of Boston, acquainting him with her purpose, and received the following reply:

"BOSTON, ———, '40.

"DEAR SISTER: Your letter to me was duly received, making enquiries, stating purposes, &c.

I am sorry for our sakes you have left the mission, but hope you have bettered your personal condition. So far as refunding to the education and missionary society is concerned I will say it is probably your duty to do so, but, far away as you are, we shall be obliged to leave that matter to your discretion and conscience. Wherein you have not, in services, rendered an equivalent for the assistance you have received on the promise of being a missionary, you will, I am happy to think, try to make up the deficiency in another way. * * *

Affectionately,

D.S.K."

When Dr. Binney and herself were in Boston, in 1843, they had not means to spare, and when there in 1851 Ruth called several times at his office for this purpose but was ever unable to find him. She however presented the church in Saugus with one hundred dollars and received a receipt to this effect:

"Received of Mrs. Ruth Binney the sum of one hundred dollars for the M. E. church in Saugus, to be disposed of as they shall see fit, it being in part a donation and the remainder, twenty-six dollars, the sum received by her as an outfit for the Oregon mission in 1837.

D. K. BANNISTER

"Saugus, June 17, 1851."

But we must hasten along with all the rapidity possible over the materials before us, in order to arrive, in *this* number, to something like a general result or conclusion, for we fear we shall not be able to continue these numbers to the extent at first intended, at least not till a considerable number shall have been sold, in consequence of the great expense of printing and the smallness of our means to meet that expense.

Let us say then at once, and rather abruptly, that Dr. Binney and his wife were not very happy together after the third day of their marriage—but we find not in all Ruth's journals and letters the least reference to the subject, except that she sometimes expresses unhappiness but does not give the cause. Dr. Binney's impetuosity of temper and rashness of expression often occasioned her great grief, and as she does not refer to *him* as being the cause, *we* will not, at least not at present—but we will tell the story of their lives very nearly as we find it in the manuscript before us.

Of this, however, we are certain, Dr. Binney loved his wife ardently, and we fully believe that but for the bad habits he latterly indulged overruling him as they did, mostly through the influence of bad associates, that but for these he might have been to this day living with and *happy* with his wife.

CHAPTER XVI

❦

A few scraps from Ruth's letters and diary will denote the circumstances surrounding her, to some extent:

"MY DEAR MOTHER:

"'Tis Sabbath evening, and I feel just disposed to dictate a letter to you. I have just been gazing at your portrait, and yet cannot reveal all I have felt of regret that I possibly may see your face no more.
* * *
"You probably have before this learned that I am married. In what way my life is to be spent I cannot determine, but the lesson learned the hermit will do for me, 'what you can't unriddle learn to trust,' and I hope I shall quietly await the indications of Providence, believing that as He has made all things, so He will overrule all for the best good.

"We live in a squared log house of two rooms on the ground floor, one fire-place, four windows, one piazza, one flight of stairs and a garret. We have a little patch of garden with onions, turnips, cucumbers, cabbage and corn, all growing heterogeniously together in as much confusion as if they had blown from the skies in a gale of wind. This has been occasioned by my inserting a new plant or seed where the chickens had picked up the first.

"The last spring there arrived here from Canada two catholic priests.[1] One of them has a church in this settlement, the other itinerates from one place to another, teaching the people and Indians the catechism. The French catholics here have had Maria Monk's book, and lately expressed their fears of its truth to the Rev. Mr. B—, the same probably of whom she speaks, when he told them the story had been forged at the instigation of a methodist minister who had seduced her![2] Romanism is coming in like a simoon.

"To let you know how destitute we sometimes are, and how hard we find it to get our wants supplied, I will tell you that for some time back there could not be bought nor borrowed a sheet of paper in the whole settlement, and in the house not even a piece of waste paper large enough to wrap a vial, or a piece of cloth for a bandage. Husband keeps the house stripped of every thing he can use for the sick and afflicted, for 'tis in vain to look for anything in the form of comfort or convenience in a Frenchman's house. I had not even a towel to use, not a pair of shoes, and they could not be obtained in the country. I resolved to bear it quietly, if such were my lot, when there came to hand a box of goods from a friend at Oahu—then your box, in which was also every needed article. So I believe our wants will be all supplied.

"O! how grateful to my feelings is your christian counsel! I laid my head upon my pillow last night with uncommonly comforted and serene feelings, and even now I find my heart warm with placid and resigned emotions. What, of a terrestrial nature, can be compared to the hope of the gospel for producing in the human breast joys that decay not, though the heart be distracted and riven with earthly sorrow?

"James thinks we have not much to eat. I can tell him better than that. Last eve we had for our meal some hasty pudding, a small bit of butter, some molasses and a cup of tea. This evening some more pudding, remains of a pea soup, some fried cakes, with blue berries, tea, &c. Our staple dishes have been, this summer, salt pork and coarse wheat bread, also tea when desired, and occasionally a cup of coffee. Poor as you may think this living is, we never repine for better, as with this we can satisfy hunger, and from it obtain strength to do our work. 'Tis often a matter of surprise to me that my husband never complains of this kind of fare. But he has for many years been accustomed to deprivations which would be hard to bear in your place, and here he seems to expect nothing different. 'Tis one satisfaction that he obtains for our use the best that can be obtained.

"Have had the pleasure for a few days of benefitting an Indian and his wife and child who are sick, by providing food, medicine and attendance. When they left this morning, after being well paid for consenting to be benefitted, I offered the man pieces of flannel, thread and needles to mend his clothes, when he said 'twas better to give him *new* clothes, and went away offended because he did not receive them.

"Visited by Dr. and Mrs. White of the mission, accompanied by two gentlemen lately from the States.[3] Husband and self rode about half way home with them, it being a fine moonlight night, and enjoyed the pleasure much.

"Been reading 'Manning's Shortest way of Ending Disputes about Religion,' in which he declares the 'Romish church to be the only true church—herself and doctrines infallible, and *all* not within her pale, heathen and heretics, are doomed to endless misery.' He declares farther, that 'she being infallible, can never err in any matter of faith—that Martin Luther was a vile impostor—and that the conversion of the Duchess of York from Episcopalianism to Romanism was a powerful evidence that in the church of Rome exists the holy awakening spirit of the Apostles.'"[4]

Nov. 21st. "Rora, the Hawaiian, a faithful servant of the mission, died in full assurance of a home in heaven. During the revival of religion last winter he said to me, on referring to the happiness of the converted Indian boys, by-and-bye all do like that up there, pointing to the skies and smiling as he spoke. Pleasing reflection that Rora, the brown Islander, is now praising God in heaven with as favorable acceptance as the delicate European.

January 1st, 1840. "Mr. Shepherd of the mission died from abscess in the knee. During his sickness he gave abundant evidence of a mind at peace with God—attachment to his Master's cause—and happiness in the expectation of dissolution. Mr. Shepherd has without doubt been principally instrumental in gathering together the children of the mission school and taking the care of them—never shrinking from any employment, however debasing it might appear, which would promote *their* or the mission's good—at once washing, baking, scouring, mending, making, or teaching, as occasion might require. He had many infirmities or failings, without doubt increased or wholly brought upon him by his many cares and great labors.

"Yesterday took a *circuitous* ride of twenty-four miles (the bridges having been carried away) to the mission, to attend the Lord's Supper, and although much fatigued in consequence, was well repaid by the delightful impressions I received in its observance. There is no duty in the church which I perform with so much pleasure or advantage as that of receiving the symbols of the Saviour's death. To feel forcibly impressed upon the mind the conviction that His blood washes us white from sin, and covers with a spotless robe these vile hearts of ours—'tis holy and heavenly delight.

"Doctor and myself been on a visit to the mission and took tea with several members of the late reinforcement;[5] was sorry to perceive that Dr. White had succeeded in very much prejudicing this company against Rev. J. Lee. Dr. White and Mr. Lee have lately had a serious contention in which, 'tis reported, they gave each other the lie! and it has resulted in Dr. White's saying he will go to the States and have Mr. Lee deposed from being any longer the superintendent of this mission, and he is now making preparations to leave in the brig Maryland.[6] A strife lately occurred between two members of this family, both preachers, in which a neighbor says they called each other liars, and used such language as was scandalous. An infidel remarks, 'tis pleasant to see brethren dwell together in such unity!'—doubtless 'twill result in great good, and many converts be made!''

"Miss ———, a mission teacher, has been appointed to Nisqually, the station of Mr. Wiley, with a hope that she will consent to become his wife.[7] 'Tis said she very much dislikes him and refuses to marry him.

"Dr. W——— has been tried by the mission church and declared guilty of the several charges preferred against him, one of which was that of embezzling the mission money, and was in consequence expelled from the church. Dr. W——— is probably as guilty as has been represented, but these faults of his have been the subject of remark for some two or three years and have been passed lightly over, but now, when he is going to New York, as he says, 'to expose Mr. Lee,' he is expelled the church to prevent his influence!— thus leaving the inference as unavoidable, that *not* for the offence was this done, but for the benefit of the injury done the man.''

There is, in Ruth's journals, much written in regard to the disputes and disagreements of the missionaries, which we shall omit, as they are not important to our purpose.

"This morning Dr. Binney takes a subscription list to the settlers for means to erect a hospital in this settlement, such a building being very much needed for the settlers and Indians. He subscribes twenty dollars and proffers his services, while I engage myself to perform every possible labor for the sick, and make gratuitously all the bedding, &c., which shall be needed in the institution.

"Mr. S——, an infidel, has been for some time at our house for medical aid. It being very uncertain whether he might recover, I forwarded a note to Mr. Lee, informing him of his danger, and saying that possibly he might *now* submit to listen to religious instruction, but he paid no attention to the request.

"A half-breed woman wishing much to obtain two silk dresses of mine, for which I have not much use, offered me a *cow* for them, and insists on my taking her.

"A young man from the mountains says that once 'being encamped with fifteen men, a party of Indians came among them whom they shot, *and every man in the camp secured the skin of an arm to cover his razor strop!*'

"Dr. ——, of V——, made us a short visit, and says, 'I intended to have become a missionary, but having seen the missions in this country, have lost all idea of it.'

"A gentleman in England has sent husband a present of a box of surgical instruments and a box of medicine without cost."

The correspondence which ensued between Rev. Mr. Beaver and Dr. Hodgkin of England, and Dr. Binney, we would like to present, but are obliged to forego the pleasure.

"An old woman telling me she had lost all her children and lived alone, I asked her 'where is your husband?' She burst into a laugh and exclaimed, 'when did you ever see a man live with an *old* woman?'

"The funds of the benevolent society being exhausted, a woman begged me very hard for a dress—said she would always be my friend if I would give her one. Having but two calico dresses for my own winter's use I was obliged to deny her.

"Been reading the 'Methodist Preacher'[8] for the years 1832-3, and while I have admired the sermons, I have been led to exclaim in the language quoted by brother Lindsay, 'O! the depths of the riches, both of the wisdom and the knowledge of God! How unsearchable are His judgments, and His ways past finding out.' At whatever time I read texts from the word of God my mind is enlightened by them, and wherever I place the accent of the sentence I perceive a labyrinth of ideas which overwhelm me, and I can only exclaim, *'how unsearchable and past finding out!* O! the depths of the riches!'

January, 1841. "Time flies and 'tis but little good I do in the world. Have been for some months mostly confined to my room by ill health, when my husband has been my only attendant, and then only what little he can wait on me in the morning and late at evening, when returned from the sick. Poor man! he has a hard task riding in the rain and mud, cooking for himself when at home, and waiting on me. He fastens the doors when he leaves, to prevent any one from coming in, and thus I spend the day, alone upon my bed, till late at night, when he frequently says he is afraid to speak when he returns for fear he'll find me dead. And we have to bear it, for help cannot be obtained, and I prefer he should go to the sick to staying here with me.

"A French neighbor says he will never bend his back to a hoe while he keeps so many womans! My mind is pained for the want of christian society. Infidelity, blasphemy, worldly business, and all manner of ungodliness are the principal ornaments of conversation in those about me. O! for the society of some of my former friends, who having the germs of friendship and kindness in themselves, know how to appreciate its presence in others.

May. "The first general meeting of the methodist mission closed on Friday evening. I have felt considerable hope that we should be employed at some mission station, but have received no intimation of such being the intention. J. Lee does not like Dr. Binney I am well aware and perhaps this keeps him from giving him the desired situation."

> I have no joy—how strange the tale—
> Though fed and housed in lovely dale;
> Tho' clothed, and blessed with husband true,
> And earthly wants remain but few.
>
> "The birds, nor flowers, nor lovely sky;
> Nor grass, nor grounds, nor stars on high;
> Nor sin, nor saints, me ease can give
> While such a *useless* life I live.

"Miss ———, of Nisqually, has consented to marry Mr. Wiley, giving as a reason for the change of sentiments towards him, that she thought it her *'duty!'*

Sabbath. "Went to the mission to attend the sacrament of the Lord's Supper, and was so ill while travelling as to be obliged to lie down twice upon the ground to recover strength, and was after all disappointed, the meeting having been postponed on account of Rev. J. Lee's absence. Was greatly disappointed as I have not for fifteen months enjoyed that privilege.

"Received into our house a little French girl who has suffered such ill treatment from her aunt, that there is scarcely hope that she will recover. Her collar bone is broken, there is a dreadful contusion on her head and forehead, her finger and toe nails are nearly all torn off—her flesh is covered with wounds, and her hair has been entirely cut from her head, to remove vermin! She is indeed an object of pity." The history of this child by Ruth Rover is interesting, but we must omit it in this number."

"An Indian woman, wife of a neighbor, buried to day—her corpse being carried to the grave on a cart, and followed by six men on horseback.[9] When passing the wheat field, two of the men left the procession to look at the wheat! an evidence of what is the ruling passion.

Wishing to go to the mission, husband tries to borrow or hire a cart. Our neighbor told him that one wheel was his and the other his partner's, and if he was willing, he could have the cart.

We perceive in looking over R. R.'s manuscripts that she wrote much in rhyme—indeed we heard her say that at one time she could scarcely think or speak but in rhyme; and this tendency she considered an affliction, inasmuch as it diverted her mind from subjects on which it should have been placed; and we have thus far omitted all of this kind of writing that has not been illustrative of her feelings or situation. To the following we think we may give space:

To my nieces, M. E. and H. M., of Gloucester:

DEAR MARY E. AND HELEN MAR:

What are you now, away so far,
Children, or grown to womanhood?
Your aunt enquires in thoughtful mood.
    In by-gone days your sprightly lays
    And nimble step did so beget
        In me an ardent fondness
    For you, my dears, that many years
        Have never turned to coldness.

How blithesome was your merry smile,
Which oftentimes did so beguile
The moments 'blest with your embrace—
How much I wish I'd now such place!
    That I might see your love for me,
    And hear you tell with joy how well
        You prized each favor given
    By parents here, and friends most dear,
        To raise you up to heaven.

Methinks you now would like to hear
About your aunt at distance here—
In woods, and ravenous beasts among,
And savage tribes of barbarous tongue;
  And hear me say how, every way
  The tide doth run, I'm helped to shun
    The whirlpools of dejection—
  God gives me hope to keep me up,
    And proffers His protection.

And more than this, I always share
Favors which neither trifling are;
Raiment and food I always have,
More than I ask, and some to give
  To such as need—a friend indeed—
  But seldom find, in human kind,
    One blest with generous feeling,
  To ope the door to save the poor,
    Though they may seek it kneeling.

Those moments, too, are rich to me,
When I my Maker's works can see,
And lessons take from bounding deer,
Panthers, and wolves, and glossy bear;
  And tiger cat, and big muskrat,
  And mouse, and mole, in stealthy hole,
    Which gnaw my eating treasure,
  And tiny thing upon the wing—
    All these afford me pleasure.

Fine birds are here of various hue,
And others of one color too;
They swarm the place when chum's away.
They seem to understand, I say,
  That in this land I've held the hand
  That would them kill, then quickly fill
    His pouch with food most dainty;
  But, thanks, to me they seem to gie
    In notes not harsh or scanty.

But most I love the blackbird's song
So blithe and free, nor spare nor long;
While every twig of monstrous pine
With them is black and made to shine.
  So charming are, in morning air,
  Their million notes, that he who pouts,
    Because they pick his grain up,
  Is only fit to smoke, and sit,
    And eat, and drain his tea cup.

Others there are of wondrous wing,
Who only coarsest notes do sing;
They mostly dwell on hidden tree,
Nor seem to wish mankind to see;
    While shiny crows, in crooked rows,
    On fence and post, will seem to boast
        They are the world's enamor's,
        But if a shot be heard in grot
        They'll rend the air with clamors.

But you would tire if I should tell
What creatures live in mount and dell,
In *bed* and *house,* you'd think it strange
Aught should be suffered there to range.
    Not a flea, hateful to me,
    Or red bed bug is found to lug
        Away my blood or body;
        But houses here deserted are,
        How to conquer none can study.

The climate, too, unhealthy is,
For those who've felt New England breeze,
For health once gone 'tis all in vain
To try to get it back again!
    But bitters greet the sugar's sweet,
    And often your aunt in vain doth pant
        To take another sea cruise;
        So here I lie with weeping eye,
        To *wish* I find is no use.

For when another warm shall come
I flatter self I'll start for home,
And then I'll see my darling girls,
And kiss their brows among the curls
    That dangle there in finest hair;
    O! how that hope doth cheer me up;
        But ah! I'm still in Oregon.
        But so strange the blows, sometimes, who
            knows
        What change for me may come upon?

''Comus'' I'm now, perhaps you'll say,
To read my verse, so strange the way
I take to send my thoughts to you,
But then I hope you'll make it do.
    I tell no lies, for butterflies,
    And bleating herds, and humming birds,
        I have become a lover,
    And, too, I'm lame, so now my name
        I'll tell, it is
                                    RUTH ROVER.

"Some Indians have brought for sale some berries they have just been picking. They appear not to know the difference in the days of the week; and this is strange, as they have been living for three years in the parish of the catholic priest. I bade them leave their berries and come to-morrow and trade. We are living in about the centre of the catholic village, and my infirmities keeping me mostly at home on the Sabbath, I have been able to observe how the settlers employ their time on this holy day. I have known them to cart and pack their wheat to mill, go for their flour, trade cattle and horses, gamble, run races, &c., on the Sabbath. This people are mostly profane and intemperate, yet, for all this they do not lose their standing in the church! No wonder 'tis called the '*Universal* Church,' while she will retain within her borders any and every kind of character the earth maintains.

"A severe cold, taken last winter, in addition to the former weak state of my lungs, make me apprehensive of a pulmonary consumption, and I fear to spend another winter in Oregon. Husband also thinks that the only chance for my recovery is to effect a change of climate, and being induced to the step by sundry other considerations, he has resolved to take passage with me to the United States, intending, possibly, to return. Yet, I do not want to go—my heart is knit to this people, although I have done so little for them, and how gladly would I spend a long life to bring them to God!

"An interesting party of converted Indians from the Dalles, with Seletsee at their head, have come here for the purpose of trading horses for cows. We have offered Seletsee and his family a house to remain in over the Sabbath, while the others encamp under the trees. He invited me in to join them in their evening devotions, in which he took the lead. Speaking in Chenook I was able to understand him.''

SELETSEE'S PRAYER

"Thou great and good God who dwellest in the skies above us, and who seest all we do—Thou hast been with us in our journey, night and day; and Thou hast preserved our health, and we are here in safety. We have every day had enough to eat and drink; and though, like the birds of the air, we have been for many days without house or home, yet Thou hast given us a home here in this house among good people, where we can rest through the Sabbath and find comfort.

"I thank Thee for such a good day as the Sabbath day, when we can leave all our other thoughts, and think only of Thee.

"Long ago my people spent the Sabbath like all other days, but now they know the difference. May my people who have come here with me, all stay in their tent tomorrow and worship Thee.

"I don't know what has become of my father and friends who died before this good news came among them.

"Let Thy Holy Spirit wash the hearts again of those of my people who loved Thee at first but now have forgotten Thee.

"Give to my wife and me an angel's heart, that we may always love Thee more and more."

We would like to conclude the narrative of Seletsee, but we have not space. We will only add:

"I really felt myself the only sinner among them. O! that God would give me to this people, and permit me to live and die in the service of instructing and enlightening them, to the honor of His Holy name."

The following being somewhat descriptive, we will admit it:

TO MY BROTHER, S. R., 1842:

Receive the affections of a heart,
Which not possessing poet's art,
Yet grieves to be from you apart,
    Dear brother.

As oft upon this burdened bed,
In tears and grief I lay my head,
For you I tears of friendship shed,
    Dear brother.

But tell I cannot what the pain,
Or what the ill, or what the bane,
Which scarcely lets me hope again,
    Dear brother.

That God will raise me from the dust,
And His rich grace to me will trust,
That I may baffle satan's thrust,
    Dear brother.

For, as I deemed five years ago,
I've passed through many scenes of woe,
Which to death's door have brought me low,
    Dear brother.

And I've been kept through sorrow's reign,
Till I scarce hope to rise again,
My *lungs* being now the seat of pain,
    Dear brother.

Labor and grief have done their part
To fix thus here this death like smart,
And thoughts of death do *rend* my heart!
    Dear brother.

For though I know 'twere well to die,
If I like martyred Paul could cry,
"I have obtained the victory!"
    Dear brother.

But not like this, when just begun
To run my course, *to die at noon!*
Or, earlier yet, *at dawn of sun!*
    Dear brother.

I'd rather live that I may bring
Long years of love to God my King;
How pleasant *then* to fall and sing—
    Dear brother—

"I've kept the faith—I've fought the fight—
Now take me, Lord, to realms of light—
Of perfect day without a night."
    Dear brother.

O! that the Lord would once more grant
To give to me what much I want,
For which I every hour do pant,
    Dear brother.

Good health and strength, and length of days,
A heart made pure to give Him praise—
Grace, Him to serve in all my ways,
    Dear brother.

For only this I wish to live—
Without this, life is but to grieve—
For what, all else can never give.
    Dear brother.

But lo! I think I'm doing wrong,
To sing of self through all my song—
The rest doth sure to you belong,
    Dear brother.

My love for you words cannot show;
Nor midnight stars nor heaven's bow,
Nor morning sky doth brighter glow,
    Dear brother.

And oft I've wished we had you here,
To live with us and always cheer
Our hearts with smiles or friendship's tear,
    Dear brother.

But mother old, and sisters true,
And loving friends, they want you too,
So to that hope I bid adieu,
    Dear brother.

Now paper much to you I've sent,
With little sense within it pent,
Say, are my pains for *nothing* spent,
    Dear brother?

Or will you send me, once a year,
A sheet half filled, the rest white clear—
Or send a *score well filled,* my dear,
    Dear brother?

And now I'll close, my hand it aches,
And head it "swims," and heart it breaks,
To say adieu for our own sakes.
    Dear brother."

A few extracts from letters may not be out of place here.
To her sister, Ruth says:

"You wish to know just when I expect to return to the States. I will tell you fully and frankly my wish with regard to my return. I have not a desire to see a civilized country till I have served the mission for the term of six years; but whether I may again enter upon that service I cannot tell, but will say I should not have married out of the mission but for the encouragement given me that such would be the case. However, make up your mind to see me before many years, for I have become satisfied that I cannot enjoy health here, at least I cannot *regain* my health without a change of air.

"I am very lonely here; have been married one year and five months, and have not once been to a social meeting in that time. But we have occasionally preaching in our house. I seldom see a civilized person but when they come to meeting, and Indians, (I would they thronged my path,) they only come here when sent for medicine.

"How different is my state from what I thought it would be when I left home—but I can do nothing better than to submit. If there are those in the country who have wronged me and misjudged my nature, let the Lord recompense them. There is a day coming when the hypocrite will be brought to shame, and they who have oppressed the poor and ignorant will receive their just desert.''

"I will now tell you, brother I——, something about my success in horticulture. People here begin to make gardens in February, and as we *two* were made *one* in March, I was quite late at that business. So, without waiting for a fence, or for husband to feel disposed to help, I commenced turning the sod, and without mellowing or rooting, I introduced the seeds, as thick as grains of flour in happy porridge. The seeds were those I brought from home, and were many of them two or three years old, so that I did not expect them to germinate, but they came up like a host and could not grow for fighting. So Master Frost thought he would remedy the matter, and passing over the beds one night, I found in the morning the potatoes, and corn, and beans, and vines, all black with wrath, and I did not much care for such quarrelsome things, if they were dead. The beans thought to subdue him with love, and offered their *hearts* to him, but it only made his work of destruction more sure. The corn consented to become pleasant again if I would remove their black looks; and the potatoes said they didn't care for him, for they were *well grounded* in hope.

"This is my *first* attempt at gardening—maybe next time I'll do better.

"Be very dutiful, my little brother, to your surviving parent, and render her last hours smooth and happy by your filial attendance. Remember, too, that you number *one* in the family of mankind, and endeavor to have that *one* as good as any other.''

CHAPTER XVII

❦

August, 1842, Dr. Binney and his wife took passage to the United States with Capt. Couch, Brig Chenamus.[1]

We are obliged to pass over nearly every note of this passage, and will just say there were on board, besides themselves, Rev. Dr. Richmond and family,[2] Rev. Mr. Leslie and daughters,[3] and Mr. and Mrs. Whitcomb.[4]

In relation to the passengers, Ruth says, when out a few days:

"Three sly, slandering, venom-tipped tongues on board, with which I as much dread to come in contact as with the poison of asps. With the character of two I have been acquainted in former days, and another soon discovered itself to be of the same woof, by stinging in my presence the fair reputation of some with whom I happened to be acquainted."

Dr. Binney seemed much dissatisfied with the thought of leaving Oregon, and his wife would at any step have been glad to have returned with him, had he determined to do so.

At Oahu finding the passengers disagreeable, and an opportunity to go home in another vessel presenting itself, he took passage with Capt. Price, in the Java.

They passed some islands in the passage to Tahiti, and from some of which obtained specimens of coral and shells, and also tropical fruits.

At Tahiti they were obliged to wait for the vessel to repair, and meantime enjoyed life very much in the society of residents and missionaries there.

Dr. Binney, however, in an evil moment, when under the influence of wine and the beguiling arts of false friends, decided on settling at Tahiti, and expended nearly all the money he had in his possession, in purchasing medicines which proved to be *no* medicines, but mostly empty bottles. Expressing great dissatisfaction, those who had encouraged him to the purchase recommended him to have the case decided by arbitration. Still trusting those who were so free to *treat* him, he submitted to their opinion—suffered them to choose arbiters for him, and found on their decision, that he must pay nearly three hundred dollars more.

He commenced practice but disliked the place and people, and at last resolved, as the Brig Chenamus had arrived on her way home, to have his wife make a visit to her friends in the States, while he would sell his little property there and return to Oregon. She consequently went on board, leaving him with great regret, in a very dejected state of mind.

We make some extracts from letters she wrote him during the voyage:

"MY DEAR HUSBAND: Although we have been separated but two days, yet I would rather see you this evening than any other person of whom I think. I am quite unhappy when I remember how unpleasantly you are situated. Could I but know you were on your way to Oregon I should consider you were in the way to prosperity and safety. But, as you are, I know not with what new trials you may have to contend, or what other enemies may unite together to ruin you.

"We are favored with a fair breeze, and although many persons are about me I take no pleasure but in anticipation of speedily doing my errand in the States and returning to you."

"Much as before, lonely and unhappy. How much I wish that time, for once at least, would hurry along. It seems in prospect a long *long* time that is to pass before I can hear from you. I do indeed almost wish I had remained in Tahiti where this anxious suspense about your destiny would have been spared me.

"My *dear husband*—how unspeakably gratifying is the remembrance that amidst so many enemies there is one in the world I can call *such*—how I wish I could see you, and, instead of *writing, tell* you what I would express. Would you believe that this vile enemy of mine, Mrs. W——, (formerly Mrs. Shepherd) has spread the bane of her hatred so far that Mrs. H——, the half breed wife of Captain H——, will not sit near me when she can avoid it, and has twice moved her chair when I have been helped to a seat near her. Mrs. R——'s friendship I do not wish and cannot accept, knowing as I do that she is a back-biter. I perform acts of kindness for her and shall continue so to do during her illness, but not with a motive to obtain her favor. How exceedingly do I find I have been injured by my enemies! and what shall I do? Shall I still bear on and let their reports take the desired effect, or shall I expose their plans against me and endeavor to regain that respect which through them I have lost? I may indeed endeavor so to do, but I am again alone! Yet I enjoy the pleasing reflection that when the secrets of all hearts shall be revealed, it then will be known of me that I have been accused of and made to confess faults of which I was never guilty, and all because I could not help myself, and because the honor of my enemies could not subsist unless *mine were destroyed!*

"'Tis Sabbath below but not on deck—and Monday with you.*

"You'll be tired, I'm sure, 'of my saying I wish to see you, and although we may sometimes have thought each other deficient in mutual affection, yet I am satisfied that were *mine* much increased these dull breezes would greatly accuse me of impatience and ingratitude. I believe it best to be resigned to all the changes of life which are uncontrollable, and therefore, though I would most satisfactorily spend this evening, at least, in your society; yet, as I cannot, I would improve the moments in considering how I may best perform the task allotted to me, that when I shall have returned to your friendship and home I may not have been absent in vain. Similar occurrences transpire every day, which renders the voyage monotonous, and I spend much of my time in the retirement of my state-room.

"*Dear* W. J., may God bless you, and restore to you the joys of His salvation, for *then* you will be as happy as you can never be *without* that great inheritance.

"Providence has greatly favored us with fair and strong winds, so that the captain says he hopes to be at home in two months and a half. I improve the time by reading till my eyes ache, writing till my hand aches, sewing till my side aches, and being alone till my *heart* aches. My beloved husband how happy should I be to have you step in occasionally and help to pass the time away.

"We are in latitude forty-four, and find the weather so cool that cloaks, hoods, furs, &c., are very comfortable. Ministers and missionaries are much of the time engaged in taking, tormenting, killing, and skinning albatros, but I envy not the pleasure nor the

---

*The people of the Society Islands observe Saturday for the Sabbath, in consequence of the first missionaries from England having sailed East to go there, by which they gained a day in their reckoning.

prize. To *them* be the plunder and the guilt—and to *me* the loss and the *innocence.* The *latter* affords me infinite satisfaction while I shut myself up in my little room attending to my studies, works, &c. But the employment, I dare say, affords them a kind of gratification which springs neither from virtue nor the fear of God, and will end in no increase of wealth or spirituality.

"It begins to hail and greatly darkens my sky-light, so good-night;—I must again go lonely to bed, when I should be so happy to sleep in your arms. God bless you my dear, *dear* husband! If any person breaks the seal of this letter who has no right so to do, let him or her consider it is written from a wife to her husband, and therefore all expressions therein contained are lawful.''

"A few moments since I involuntarily exclaimed, O! I wish I could see my dear Doctor! and the wish induced me again to commence writing to you.

"Although we have had a very good passage thus far, time passes slowly, and the remaining two months which must elapse before we reach Boston seems like a long time in anticipation.

"Yesterday, in a gale and very, *very* high sea, the captain was obliged to furl all sails and let the ship 'lay to' during the night and day. The cold was very severe, and the appearance of the sea very sublime.

"We have generally very cheerful times on board. Capt. H—— and his wife are the life of the company; and I shall always have reason to respect Capt. Couch for his attentions to me. At the present moment Capt. H—— is drumming on the piano, and singing a sailor's song; Mr. C—— is dancing, and steward and others are listening and laughing. You may by this imagine how time passes with us, who are in this little vessel alone upon the mighty ocean— God all around us, and nature within!

"I have to-day been weeping, and grieving much at the thought of living so long at a distance from you, and feared I had done wrong in leaving you; but may the Lord permit us to be again united in love and prosperity. One has said,

> "Love, with man, is a thing apart—
> 'Tis woman's whole existence.''

And I think I prove something of the force of the remark, for if I had not a being, an *earthly* being to love, how lonely at the present moment would be my lot.

"I hope to be able during my absence from you, to improve every moment to the best advantage, having your wishes concerning me, and yourself constantly in mind. Permit me to say you are ever in my thoughts, and occupy in my affections the highest place next my God. I bear you on the altar of my heart in my devotions praying God to bless you and make you happy. Man and wife have a right to be blest in each other's affections, and may be, if they will suffer daily trifles to pass unnoticed.

"I am permitted the honor of instructing Mrs. H——— in grammar, letter-writing and reading; find her an interesting scholar.

"The two captains have been bringing me whale's teeth on which to sketch designs to be etched with the pen-knife. I have thus prepared nine, which I hope will be the last, for I find my eyes very weak, and I fancy my right hand has too much exercise, and I cannot give it rest until all my work is done.

"I think that going to sea alone must produce a bad effect upon the memory—perhaps *good* I should say—as I have forgotten all the causes of disquietude which ever existed between us, and I can only think of your kindness and love—which recollections afford me much pleasure.

"The lovely S——— continues to monopolize the favors of the gentlemen by making cakes and pies, and adorning her person, and although you have reason to suppose me equally capable of such arts, yet I despise favor procured in this way. If *merit* will not secure for me the regard of my acquaintance, let me be without it, for favor purchased in this way is of little worth. Do not fancy I am not noticed by the gents here, on the contrary, they seem to be greatly my friends, but in my situation it is not proper I should make intimates of them. I am more content alone in remembering him whom none can condemn me for loving.

"I am most constantly brooding over the unwelcome thought that some unforseen event will prevent us from meeting again in Oregon, and am most anxious to reach home that I may hear from you by the Java."

We think these extracts are sufficient to denote the affection Ruth Rover entertained for her husband; and yet it was *affection* rather than *love*, but was sufficient to have kept her blest and happy, had it been encouraged and rewarded.

There is a difference between affection and love; *that* depends too much on earth to be very enduring—*this*, (we do not speak of that gross excitement which has only sensuality for its object), pure as the fount from which came the breath of life, and eternal as the Throne of God, looks to the future for its consummation.

Ruth reached home in safety, and having passed six weeks very agreeably among her friends, was anxiously awaiting letters from her husband, when she was agreeably surprised at his arrival in New York—he having concluded, after she had left Tahiti, to take passage to the States rather than to return to Oregon without her. They left again in the same vessel, in 1843, for Oregon.

We must also pass over much which occurred during the voyage, and which might be interesting to the reader, as enabling him to obtain some idea of life at sea, and confine ourself to such items only as will illustrate and assist us in our object.

In the "diary" Ruth says:

"This morning, to the great joy of the whole house, Dr. Binney arrived. His mother was particularly delighted, for she had felt great disappointment by his not coming with me, as she feared she would never see him again. Dr. Binney thinks it best to return to Oregon as soon as may be, and the object for which I came (to improve my health) being accomplished, I am myself anxious to return, as I consider that Oregon is my home."

CHAPTER XVIII

🍎

Ruth Rover was subjected, during this visit, to be grieved by the waywardness of her husband, and which we will not explain here, as we have to
review this ground again; but this trial with him led her sometimes to ponder
on the hope of the realization some day of happiness with those she loved, and
of whose goodness of heart she felt assured.

Thus we find her saying, when leaving Boston,[1] of

"TRUE LOVE."

"Long years have past and gone,
Since we in heart were one—
Changes have gone to come,
    My dearest dear.

Yet still I feel thee mine—
My heart doth round thee twine,
Nor can it yet repine,
    Thy love to share.

Another hath my band—
Perchance an equal hand
Doth now thy thoughts command—
    So let it be!

I would not these should part,
But still my wayward heart
Will not be ruled by art;
    It loves but thee!

Afflictions have been thrown
Round me, and sorrow strown,
But thoughts have never flown
    Of thee my love.

Though in this world I may
In grief but pass away,
There comes a better day
    In heaven above.

'Tis *there,* when we shall meet,
I hope thy love to greet,
Though hopes fate may defeat
    Of meeting here.

Believe this one word true:
I love but only you—
A fond, a long adieu,
    My only dear!''

Of Ruth's anticipations in returning to Oregon we have some indications, in a letter to her mother, when she says:

''DEAR MOTHER: I have awaked as out of a dream and find myself actually on the ocean destined to Oregon! I can, at this moment, hardly realize that I have been in the United States—can hardly believe that I have seen my mother, brothers and sisters, and again bade them farewell. It seems to me some narcotic power must have pervaded my senses, or I could not have done this so willingly—so forgetfully of the weariness of my life when separated from them. But now, alas! I realize the dream has fled. To me again appears a long, heavy, dreary course in this world, without a relation or friend to animate, to bless my footsteps. *Now,* indeed, I go, I know not whither or wherefore—the future is all uncertainty and joylessness—and of this I am assured, I must face the current—·oppose the dangers—war with my own feelings, and endure on till my change come. And what then? What shall I have accomplished? Why, done that which I could not help, and have gone to sleep singing ''Victory!'' How glorious such an exit!

''But, mother, don't suppose me wild. You have known my wish about my life, and that now my hopes appear utterly blighted; and you know I can no longer direct my own course—perhaps best I should not—for if an Almighty hand shall condescend to control my fate, all will indeed be well. But I am not assured of the watchful care of the Most High—and yet a secret, pleasant, comforter within whispers ''Trust.'' I do so, and resign my future walks to His guidance who alone is capable of directing me. Do not be uneasy about me, I shall labor to do good and to be good, that at last I may die in peace.

"Life on the ocean is very dull indeed, and the prospect of seven months such living is painful. How much we wish *you* here to talk and keep us lively. Doctor finds society in the men, but I, ah! I must stay below and be dull all by myself. I have work, O yes, a plenty, but I cannot always work—and books, the cabin is half filled with them—the table, too, is so frequently spread that one is quite tired of the rattling of knives and forks—and anon the lamp is lighted, and darkness dawns, and dreams follow; then the body becomes weary of lying—the mind experiences a sensation of horror at daylight, that what was done the last day must be repeated the coming day—and so the scene is, and will be repeated, till the heavy anchor shall drop in Baker's bay."

From the journal of this voyage we make a few extracts:

"We are delightfully hastened on, as far as wind and waves are concerned. Yet oh! how much I feel the need of a friend, a confidential friend, with whom I may converse, and who would sympathise with all my feelings. But I consider myself utterly alone in the world. Separated from every relation, I have, perhaps, to finish my course in loneliness and intense deep seated grief. Hitherto I had not one true friend in Oregon—many there were who loved to be thought friends—loving to possess my confidence but only to betray it, and expose my sorrows. On board the vessel I seldom speak, and conversation I never partake! My thoughts, for need of expression, are become like a stagnant pool, and my soul is overcharged with earthly matter, which it needs unalloyed friendship to remove."

The reader will wonder at expressions like these, after reading the extracts made from Ruth's letters to her husband on the passage home, when considering that he was on board with her. But the cause is found in the great dissimilarity of their dispositions, their wishes and pursuits.

"Just spent a profitable half hour at the window, in looking at the birds, admiring them, and adoring their Creator. Here are the magnificent albatros, the booby, the cape pigeon, cape dove, and Mother Carey's Chickens, all of them beautiful divers and entirely fearless of wind and storm.

"Just now was reading with deep feeling 'Scenes in a Court of Justice,' when my husband brought me to read, and over which he had been for some time greatly amused, *'An Irish Hulaballoo!'* So different are our pursuits!

❦

"More books brought to me to day. How are these trifling considerations calculated to beget and expand esteem for those who bestow them! While I would desecrate forever the narrow-minded man who would keep his books nailed up during a seven months voyage, I would admire, for the same length of time, that person who would circulate his library through the ship, that time, with every one, might pass pleasantly.

"I am sometimes so overwhelmed with the remembrance of my sorrows that I almost fear life will depart. Such has been the case for a few days last past. I have been so dreadfully burdened in mind that I have found it next to impossible to smile or speak. Truly, I find

"NOTHING BUT SORROW.

Toiled, strove, have I, for what, through life?
    Nothing but sorrow!
With what is every moment rife?
    Nothing but sorrow!
On what my thoughts during the light?
    Nothing but sorrow!
Creates my dreams throughout the night?
    Nothing but sorrow!
What brings these tear drops from my eyes?
    Nothing but sorrow!
What the result of "Gossip's" lies?
    Nothing but sorrow!
On what reclines my weary head?
    Nothing but sorrow!
Companion, too, of my lone bed?
    Nothing but sorrow!
What chills me when I think of home?
    Nothing but sorrow!
What sweet remembrance brings a groan?
    Nothing but sorrow!
With inexperienced youth comes what?
    Nothing but sorrow!
With trusting foes of bitter hate?
    Nothing but sorrow!
What in my countenance may be read?
    Nothing but sorrow!
Of my whole aspect may be said—
    Nothing but sorrow!
What gnaws my spirit like a worm?
    Nothing but sorrow!

Makes me in safety fear alarm?
        Nothing but sorrow!
In future life what can I see?
        Nothing but sorrow!
No joy—no hope—no peace for me—
        Nothing but sorrow!
But what in heaven shall I find?
        Contrast of sorrow!
Reward what? if to fate resigned?
        Glory to-morrow!

"After many days of intense mental anguish, I was last eve enabled to realize a blessing from God which yielded peace, faith and consolation to my wounded spirit. I do not remember to have ever realized the Saviour of sinners so near me. The same Son of David who walked about Gallilee, Nazareth and Bethlehem, granting the requests of lepers, the blind, the palsied, and the wretched of every class—the same Lamb of God who conversed freely with the women of Canaan and Samaria, and many who were suffering the reproaches of their enemies—seemed to be present in my little stateroom, and to say, 'What wilt thou have me do?' My answer was, Lord deliver my life from reproaches—my heart from sin, and come thyself and abide with me. I experienced an almost overwhelming sense of His glorious presence and willingness to accomplish for me all I asked—yet felt I must wait for different events to transpire before they could all be attained. 'Hitherto ye have asked nothing,' dwelt very forcibly upon my mind.

Aye *nothing* to what Thou hast to give,
        Poor mourners;
Help us to ask that Thou mayst save,
        Sojourners;
Thou bidst us ask that we may have
        Thy favor;
And yet we doubt we shall receive,
        Dear Saviour!

The stores are open night and day,
        To seekers;
And yet we empty stay away.
        Poor creatures!
Ask what we will, Thou givest free
        As nothing;
Give what Thou will, 'tis not missed by Thee;
        'Tis nothing!

So are thy mercies running o'er—
　　Expending—
Does not decrease, Thou still art more,
　　Extending;
Like bread and fish when thousands ate
　　Believing;
There more remained than when they sat
　　Receiving.

Lord! I have asked, and it was far
　　From *nothing.*
I asked *Thyself! bright Morning Star,*
　　Thou art something!
So full of bliss that I can ne'er
　　Express Thee!
So past my powers! I sometimes fear
　　To bless thee!

And yet I love Thee! O! Thy love
　　Is giving
Such thirst for more, I cannot live,
　　Not having.
And I will seek, while life shall last,
　　Before Thee,
Thy holy love, and, saved at last,
　　Adore Thee!

"How peaceful is the state of my mind to-day. As the disciples on going to Emaus, my heart burns within me because my Redeemer accompanies me.

"The delightful emotions swelling the bosom of a person when first he sees land, after a long sea voyage, can only be experienced and appreciated by those who have been thus situated.

"Yesterday we passed two of the Sandwich Islands, while proceeding to Oahu. Their majestic forms, reared in the midst of the ocean, impressed me with an all-pervading sense of the magnificence of the Deity in their construction and preservation. Here, too, are souls, immortal souls, as much under the care of the Almighty as any in Europe or America—and to them has been manifested as great tokens of His power in their redemption. Missionary zeal, in all its strength, was awakened in my bosom when I contemplated that on those solitary shores are numerous persons engaged in the evangelization of the heathen. Blessed work! how do I long to be engaged in it—but I am prevented. Perhaps I am not worthy of so distinguished an honor, and it becomes me to submit, though I must do so with intense mental disappointment.

"Arrived at Oahu, Dr. Babcock, of the Oregon Mission, invites us to become his guests for a few days, at his boarding house.[2]

"Visited at the house of Mrs. ———. The conversation happened to turn on poets, and I made the remark, 'I never read Byron without experiencing a degree of sadness on my mind afterwards.'

"'Byron!' she exclaimed, 'do you ever read Byron?'

"'O! yes; I have read all his works, I believe.'

"'And did you ever read his *Don Juan?*'

"'I believe so. But I remember nothing in particular in relation to it.'

"'You don't? Why I could hardly get through with it, 'tis so bad!'

"'Then *you* have read it?' I asked.

She replied, blushing, 'yes; but I would never read it again. Such a dissolute man! Such a wretched life he led!'

"'He undoubtedly committed many errors,' I replied, 'and he seemed to be sensible of them, and in some measure at least to deplore them, when he said, 'The thorns which I have reaped are of the tree *I* planted; *they* have torn me and I bleed; I should have known what fruit would spring from *such* a seed.' But he possessed a towering genius and the fine ideas scattered throughout his writings I have wished to glean, and moreover I have been so much afflicted myself I have learned to commiserate the sufferings of others.'

"'And so have I been afflicted,' she said, 'but my afflictions were never of a character to lead me to compassionate the lewd!'

"'Neither were *mine,* Mrs. ———, but I pity the sorrowing, wherever they are found, or from whatever cause they are sorrowed. Be they in prisons or palaces—rich or poor—suffering from their own errors, or those of others—'tis the same to me, I feel for their distresses.'

"This lady's course through life has been as gentle as that of a feather borne by a zephyr over the surface of a polished stream or verdant lawn, alighting only on earth to replenish her means of support. To *her* sorrow is a thing apart—a strange, unearthly sensation, pervading only the lower walks of men.

"Passed the day with Mrs. Jones, the lady of the former American consul,[3] her daughter and her son, Mr. R. G. Davis and his wife. Was most agreeably entertained, and at eight in the evening was on the point of leaving when our vessel was reported to be on fire. The report produced great panic as there was said to be much powder on board; and she lying in the midst of many vessels, 'twas thought advisable to scuttle her and let her sink, the water at the wharf not being very deep. This was accomplished, and she went down with all her cargo.''

This was a very unpleasant occurrence to Dr. Binney and his wife, inasmuch as all their furniture and wardrobe was on board. The kind Mrs.

Jones, although a Hawaiian woman, insisted on their remaining in her house during their stay.

Next day the vessel was raised and the goods taken out. The furniture was mostly ruined, and but a small part of their wardrobe could be restored. After a detention of about three weeks they were again on board the Chenamus, bound to the Columbia River. Dr. Babcock, and Rev. Mr. H———, and Mr. Cushing,[4] and some others in company.

We must pass over, also, the notes of this voyage, as well as of the time spent at Oahu, and simply say in relation to Ruth, that, although she could seldom please her husband, and this was apparent to every one about her, she sometimes met those who would offer her a word of encouragement in the way of praise.

At Oahu, in conversation with Mr. G———, the mate of the vessel, in referring to the hatred of her enemies, and their slanders against her, she said:

"Well, I can't help it. I do as well as I can, and must submit the event."

"And so you do, Mrs. Binney," he replied. "By George! I never saw a woman do better than you do. You have been in our vessel nearly a year, and I never knew you to do anything wrong yet. By George! if I had a wife who did as well as you do, I should think she was worth keeping; and I'm not the only one who thinks so, either."

"Passing the reef, on the first view of the billows as they dashed over it, I was favored with a delightful sensation of pleasure at the thought of the grandeur and purity of the works of God, compared with those of men.

"Leaving the dissipated and unpleasurable town of Honolulu, I greeted with delight the sublime ocean, which is capable at all times of subduing my mind to a calm as tranquil and reflecting as its own, or raising it in tumultuous breakings towards the Throne of God."

Of this voyage the captain remarked, it was the pleasantest he ever made, both as regarded the weather and the company.

During the voyage to the Columbia river, Ruth amused herself, as usual, mostly in her stateroom alone—writing rhyme,—journalizing,—paraphrasing psalms, &c.

As an evidence that she could, at one time, scarcely think "straight," as she termed it, we will admit the following, which was conjured to her mind while waiting for the people to come to the table, and as giving some idea of life at sea.

SATURDAY'S DINNER AT SEA

(112 Days From Home.)

Come, stewart, come, I pray you'll run,
    The dinner it is colding;
And I feel drear, while sitting here,
    The food not ate beholding.

That salted fish that's on the dish,
    My olfactories are regaling;
I long to taste, I pray you'll haste,
    While we're so smoothly sailing.

Those onions, too, how kind in you,
    Our tastes so much regarding;
Potatoes fine, at this late time,
    We'll not be found discarding.

Hot coffee here? bless me how clear!
    In cup without a saucer;
All sweetened, too! I guess 'tis true,
    Ne'er such found Caspar Hauser.[5]

And then fried cakes, piled up in flakes,
    And butter and molasses;
No thirsty lad e'er felt so glad,
    For water drank from glasses.

Quick, ring the bell, which will all tell,
    That dinner's on the table;
Captain and "Bill," and Henry "Quill,"
    And Doctor—all are able.

We'll eat away, till close of day,
    The dinner so inviting;
A happy group, without the soup,
    Which English so delight in.

Again, when preparing to retire, we find what she terms—

❧

EVENING NODS

To bed, to bed, I go,
  Kind place for secret woe;
And here I weep, and sometimes sleep,
Till morn doth peep up o'er the deep;
And ope my eyes to view the skies,
While o'er them hies such beauteous dyes
  As charms my soul within me;
Then sleep must go, and whining too,
  And sorrows which do sting me.

Life speed, life speed away;
  And come, thou perfect day,
When shall begin life free from sin,
And all within my God shall win—
And all I do be offered through
His love most true who died for you
  And I—who reads believes me;
O! glorious hour bring near thy power—
  Lord let me cease to grieve thee.

Draw near, draw near, thou day,
  When I from earth away,
In glory bright in realms of light,
In God's own sight shall claim my right,
By Jesus bought, when me he sought,
And early taught, though good for naught,
  To join in giving glory
To heaven's King, and then I'll sing
  Redemption's wondrous story!

How blest, how blest, when there,
  With no more cause for fear
Of lying tongue, which hate hath rung,
Or devil sung, because it stung;
A christian name or fairer fame,
Than some who came wild hearts to tame,
  But found their own the wildest;
O! much I deem, fair as they seem,
  Their own hopes are the blindest.

Lord wash, Lord wash me clean
  From every sinful stain;
My heart inspire with holy fire,
Of true desire to mount me higher,
In hallowed love come from above,
That I may move just like the dove—
  Offence to none giving;
And saved at last—troubles all past—
  May dwell with Thee in heaven.

CHAPTER XIX

JOURNAL

❦

May, 1844. "Arrived at the falls. Very pleasing associations arise in my mind as I realize I am again in the Oregon and among the people of my choice, viz: The Indians. Rev. Mr. H—— told me on the passage here that once being requested to preach to the Clackamas Indians, they consented to have him provided he would talk *good* talk, and when he commenced by telling them their hearts were bad, they said they had heard enough, and commenced going out.

"An Indian woman tells me to-day that the reason why the Indians will not hear the missionaries is because they have heard that the people of the United States have sent them clothing, and they not having received it, they say their own hearts are as good as the white people's hearts.

"Situated again on our former place, for which Dr. Binney has paid seven hundred dollars, although when we left two years ago he sold it for three hundred.

"The people have organized a form of government and laws corresponding with those of the Territory of Iowa. Dr. Binney, on his return, was elected one of the three governors, styled the executive committee.[1] A light tax of twelve and a half cents on a hundred dollars has been levied on the people for the support of the government. A law framed by missionaries prohibiting all settlers, *except missionaries,* from holding a land claim on which was a mill privilege, or water power sufficient for mechanical operations, has been repealed; and a law passed for the expulsion of negroes from the country, and preventing their entrance.

"A man who has lately bought about four thousand dollars worth of property says he thinks he will sell out and go to the States, for his wife wants to see her folks—she has been four years absent from them, and thinks it a long time! How much does that woman respect her husband's interest?

"Mr. Cushing, one of our passengers from the States, and brother to Hon. C. Cushing, has passed a few hours here in pleasant conversation. How I do admire a sensible person who can converse on other subjects than the faults of others.

"An Indian woman died here this morning. Her husband brought her from the Clackatack country, having heard of Dr. Binney's skill, but he could not save her. She said she did not want to go where God was, for she knew nothing about him. She wanted to "go to sleep."

"A gentleman remarked her to-day, on referring to a preacher who had taken advantage in trade, "ministers of the gospel are getting around sinners." Mourn for Zion, for the shepherds feed themselves and the flocks are scattered.

"Two orphan children given me to raise.

"For some time held a school on the Sabbath for my neighbors' children.

"The Indians remark of the skirmish lately had between the Indians and whites at the plains, that the reason the Indians did not die as quickly as the whites is because of their peculiar strength.

"A Frenchman who is to break some ground for Dr. Binney this week has sent his plough this (Sabbath) morning! He is a member of the catholic church.

"At a 'hullaballoo' of white men at the falls, when about twenty were intoxicated, a cup of beer was offered some Indians outside which they refused, saying, 'No! we don't want anything that will make us act like those Bostons!'

"I have a neighbor whom I have heard a young clerk call a 'hag.' She is a great business character, and takes the lead, in preference to her husband, in buying and selling, collecting debts, going to mill, &c. She has been pleased, in passing about the country, to accept of our hospitality, in preference to staying at houses where Indian women are at the head. She is remarkably sensible and well informed, and her conversation is very interesting. Whether she merits the name of *hag* I know not, nor is it my place to inquire. I have seen no reason to treat her otherwise than as one of the children of the family of Adam, and as I would wish to be treated.

"She says she was once travelling near Salem, and stopped at a blacksmith's shop and inquired the way. 'Take the dug path,' said the blacksmith, and continued striking the anvil as if to drown her voice.

"'But where is the dug path?' she inquired.

"'Oh, I guess you can find it,' he replied.

This same man is one of the supporters of a school for the education of youth, and his conduct in this respect led the woman to say, 'I have an adopted son whom I thought to put to that school, but as much as I think of learning, he shall go down to his grave in ignorance before he shall go there!'

This reminds me of an acquaintance I made at the Sandwich Islands. The lady, when I first met her, was the widow of the first mate of a brig. Some years afterwards her daughter married a fashionable gentleman. At this time the wife of a ship's carpenter lay sick near her—a stranger in a strange land.

" 'Have you been to see Mrs. S———?' enquired a lady.

" 'No! do you think I would call on a *carpenter's* wife?' was her indignant reply.

"It is popular to affect to despise the poor and unpretending, but by such alone, as I consider, whose character and circumstances need repairs.

"The father of the orphan girls in my care for over a year, has gone to the falls with the expectation of going to the States, and taken them with him. He says if he should not go he will bring them back to me, for he would not take them from me to give to any person in the country. He says he is perfectly satisfied with my treatment of them, and is very grateful.

"Harvest ended last night. Two hundred and forty bushels of wheat threshed by horses and run through the fanning mill—for want of help, assisted husband myself at the fanning mill.

"Doctor called to a Frenchman, who in a drunken frolic, set out to run a race with one foot in the stirrup and no bridle on his horse; he has been thrown from his horse and nearly killed. On the way met a man coming for him to visit an Indian woman who had been shot by a white man—having mistook her for a bear.

"Indian woman carried by in a cart, for burial. Her husband and another sitting upon the coffin.

Sabbath. "And nothing to read but Bible and 'Rise and Progress of Religion.'[2] Greatly dejected; weep till my head aches severely. When I consider my great loneliness for want of good society—my being never able to attend church—loss of all religious privileges—and the little prospect there is of a change for the better, I am quite discouraged and broken spirited. Attend to my work about the house and weep meantime.

"Dreamed of pious friends and awake greatly refreshed. Gathering peaches early, the birds sang most charmingly in the trees around me, which made me but the more sensible of my loneliness.

"Doctor turned out the calves to-day, twenty-one in number, the mothers of which I have milked mostly alone through the summer. No more luxury of milk this year. Grass being scarce, and the cows poor, it is important the calves have all the milk by this time to prepare them for winter. They ran away in every direction, throwing their heels in the air, bleating and chasing each other. Our band of cattle number at this time eighty-six head, horses thirty.

October 1. ''Only two days of rain since spring; the weather is as fine as summer; flies numerous and annoying. Sent peaches to friends in Oregon City; given many to neighbors—preserved many, and still have many left.

''Dr. McLaughlin sent a request for Dr. Binney to visit his son; sick with the consumption.[3] The bearer of the message says Mr. McLaughlin requested his father to visit him, for he could not live long, and the old gentleman exclaimed: 'send for me! send for me! tut, tut, 'tis all nonsense—so much business; tut, tut, 'tis all nonsense—can't do it—can't do it—tut, tut, can't do it, tut; send for Dr. Binney!'

''La de Roote says he always speaks well of me to every one—says he came to my house great many times—see always tidy—every thing in place—very clean myself—very pretty —(O! what a mistake!)—and work hard, *very* hard—my work all same as man. Also he was 'here fifteen days sick, and I treated him all same like sister!' This will do very well for a simple but kind hearted Frenchman.

''Abundantly blessed with all the necessaries and some of the luxuries of life. Our Heavenly and Good Parent be praised. Husband gathered to-day the winter apples. One tree has yielded about six bushels, and we have probably gathered this fall six bushels of peaches. Dr. Binney's practice has always been extensive. No physician coming into the country has been able to compete with him. The French doctor complains that not only do the people refuse to pay him their bills but they give him bad talk when he asks them. A man returns a book he had borrowed, enveloped in a number of the 'Christian Advocate and Journal.' This is the first number I have seen since I left the States. Eating cake and pie to-night and anticipating reading the 'Christian Advocate' to-morrow, almost fancy I am in the land of the living.

''Angelica, formerly of the mission, visited me. She is married and has two children. She is frightfully deformed, her right shoulder growing very large and the left shoulder growing not at all, while she is bent nearly double. She says this was occasioned by her carrying about Mrs. S———'s children when she was small and not well, and I remember to have seen indications of it while she was living with her. She says she has great trouble to take care of her children, and she sometimes has a mind to send for Mrs. S——— to nurse them for her, as she used to be called 'sister,' when in the mission, and 'tis but right that among sisters there should be a 'turn about' sometimes.

Sabbath. ''Doctor reads Waverly novels[4] and I read over and over again my number of the 'Christian Advocate,' afterwards 'History of the Bible.'[5] Grieve for friends at home. When will the time come—will it *ever* come—of my release from present afflictions? Notwithstanding I somewhat indulge the hope of better days, I sometimes cannot avoid weeping freely. While indulging this weakness this morning the sheriff of this county and a lady came in, I could not hide my swollen eyes though I could wipe away the tears. I am thus frequently surprised by strangers, and I know not what they think or say.

"This morning the blackbirds, (to my fancy the sweetest and the prettiest birds of Oregon,) alighted in great numbers in the yard, and the chickens, probably jealous of their intentions, tried to drive them out by running them through the fence, but to little purpose, for they would quickly return again.

"A heavy shower yesterday and summer to-day. A few very frosty nights of late. The forest trees are changing their summer green dresses for colors more suitable to the season—orange, brown, grey and darker green. Reading and pondering in the woods which are pleasant now. The leaves from the underbrush have fallen sufficiently to enable one to look about and feel safe from wolves, bears and panthers, and the majestic, full-foliaged, forest trees protect one from the rain and wind. In groves of my own choosing I have passed many an hour in meditation, prayer and praise, and the reflection afforded me that in them I was quite alone with nature, and with God, was an irresistible charm.

"A half-breed young woman whom I much love came here this morning with her husband. He was much intoxicated, and 'tis the first time I have ever seen him thus. His amiable wife tried to hide his shame, and when he attempted to light his pipe she passed him a coal of fire, having blown it to make it light; he still finding difficulty, she lighted it for him—while I admired her for it. She says her husband never was intoxicated till he went to the infamous John Hord's at Champoeg.[6]

November. "It appears the winter rains have at last set in. The oak trees over our house are full of young leaves and buds—the earth is covered with fine short grass, which has grown since the first showers in the fall—little birds swarm the bushes and sing all about me, while my heart knows no pleasure.

"Doctor absent two days. Of two hundred and fifty dollars he tried to collect he received twenty-five cents. Husband borrowed books of a young man, who also made him a present of six numbers of the 'Cascanet' mostly poetry. So selfish am I, I could not help saying, 'did this man consider that here in the woods lives a woman who would like to read books like these?' if so, long life and blessings to him. In looking them over my eyes caught Mrs. Southey's 'My Evenings,' which has already made me love her; and her verses on 'Ranger,' when he says, 'Mistress mine, all's right—all's well—thou art there, and here am I.'[7] How delightfully expressive of what a faithful dog is supposed to say.

"Much wheat in the country—people's barns full. The Hudson Bay Company refuse to take any more; their granaries are full and bursting from the wet weather.[8] Husband has eleven hundred bushels in the fort—sold them for sixty cents per bushel.

"An old blind Indian to beg; says he'll work for *sugar;* that all his friends are dead; his wife and children all gone, and he has no pleasure left now but in eating *sugar;* says he lies awake oftentimes at night to eat it all the time, and feel it going down his throat, and all he wants more in this world is *sugar.* I furnished him with everything I thought could be of benefit to him in the way of provisions, and gave him pantaloons and a shirt, and needles and patches to mend those he had on, when he told me 'twould be better for me to mend them myself, and pulled them off for the purpose, sitting naked while I did so. He then said he should not work any more till his sugar was all gone.

"Miss C——— to stay with me while doctor shall be absent to legislative assembly at the falls.[9] Accompanied him to Champoeg to bring back his horse, he going down in a canoe. Returning, got very wet in a heavy shower. Take care of my horses and dry my clothes, and enjoy the company of Miss C——— for the balance of the day.

December 31st. "The winter thus far has been dreadfully severe. Snow covered the ground for nine days. Pigs, chickens and cattle have frozen to death; and in one instance a child, on being out with its parents, was so severely injured with the cold that it died in a few days.

"An acquaintance, who has been on his farm about one year harvested last fall two thousand bushels of wheat, and has seventy acres sown again. His brother and partner went to California last fall, and has, he writes him, obtained fifteen hundred dollars in gold! So much for perseverance and prudence. Another, formerly a neighbor, for some time in California, has plenty of gold sometimes, yet spends it as fast as he gets it, and goes about in rags, drinking and gambling.

"Some time last summer my better half would buy a pair of sheep in opposition to my wish—for somehow he wanted to do as others did. Well, he gave ten dollars for two; they jumped the fence and got away, and the male got a limb broken in being caught again, when I nursed him three weeks in the hospital, feeding him daily with water and grass. Next the mother of the lamb was killed—then the lamb, and last of all died the other. Does a man gain anything by acting in opposition to his wife?

"Doctor gone all day. Man leaves ten dollars if he will visit his wife when he returns to night. Sets out at dark to ride fourteen miles in rain and snow. No fire wood all day but two rails with ends resting on a chair. I cannot myself cut oak, and the snow prevents me from going to the woods to get any other. A gentleman called, and laughing at my fire, said the Indians differ from bears only in the fact that Indians can build a fire and bears cannot. Wonder if he thought me a bear because I had no better fire? I did not tell him what I thought of him for not offering to cut me some wood.

"The weather is still very cold. 'Tis very painful to see animals, especially work oxen, feeding only on withered leaves and tops of dried brush;—and starving birds, as thick as flies in summer, almost under your feet when walking. Never was a winter in Oregon as dreadful as this.

"An Indian woman says of a hoosier woman who is married to a Frenchman, '*I* am an Indian; I don't pretend to be any thing else, and yet I am not as bad as that white woman. Her children are dirty—her house is dirty—her hogs root up her garden—she never washes her bedding—and I, if I am an Indian, know better than that!'

"Assist my husband to load rails on a sled in the woods to build around my rose bushes and honey suckles, which the cow sometimes manages to crop.

"The picayune clerk at Champoeg, who offered eight dollars in goods for gold dust per ounce, says that what annoys him the most is, 'to see mean, dirty fellows—ignorant and low-lived—return from California with pockets full of gold, feeling as big as Billy ———!'

"Another says that 'many men who were formerly so poor that they were glad to work for their board, come here now independently rich and call on their former masters to work for them!'

"Money is merit here, and 'tis pleasant to see the poor have an opportunity to enjoy the good things of life as well as their task masters.

"A great carousal at John Hard's to-night—a plan to get money from those lately from California.

"Two members of the legislature from this county have come to accompany the doctor to the falls. They have sat all the time in the parlor with their hats on, and the hearth and rug are covered with whittlings—I conclude they are yankees.

February. "Husband gone; my company Miss C———. Trim trees in the garden; mere guess work with me; with Dr. Binney no better.

"A curious old visitor from the upper country brought a letter from a patient descriptive of her sufferings, symptoms, &c. Dr. Binney being away he wished me to answer it, and said he had hoped he would have found him at home that he might have got on the right side of him and persuaded him to have given Mrs. N——— a good hackling, 'for,' he says, 'her sickness is mostly feigned; her children are suffering, and she will not exert herself at all, though her husband has to leave his work to wait upon her.'

"I commenced to answer her note when he exclaimed, 'be sure to give her a good hackling, and tell her to mind her own business.'

❦

"Taking no returns for the old man's accommodation or his horse, which, poor animal, appeared glad enough to get a feed of oats, he went away with a 'God bless you ma'am—not every woman will do as you have done.'

"Dr. ———, from Oregon City, wishes to tarry all night, on his way to Salem. I could not refuse as he is an acquaintance of my husband.

"Dr. ——— left this morning, after breakfast, without a 'thank ye,' although I had made no charge for his accommodations or his horse's feed. On going into the stable to see if all was right there for husband's return, I found about eight bundles of oats partly eaten and trampled under his horse's feet. For this I shall be blamed for suffering him to help himself. Like many others, I presume Dr. ——— left his manners at home, thinking they would not be appreciated by us country people. We often have such visitors from Oregon City. Our place being half way to Salem, and twenty-five miles from either, 'tis a very convenient resting place for man and beast, especially as there never yet was anything charged for the accommodation—for we always receive our pay in a very gracious invitation to visit them when in Oregon City—but when we happen to be in their town we are never recognized, and 'tis not known that we have been about them till we are gone.

"A man calls to see our place; says he heard it was for sale. I told him husband offered it for six thousand dollars—the cattle and household furniture being included; he is to consider.

"During Miss C———'s stay here we have set out two hundred and forty-six scions of apple and peach trees in my garden, for her mother, when they shall have settled on a farm.

"Doctor returns, having been absent two weeks, he having been elected a member of the legislature. He has paid sixteen dollars in cash for his board—four for his passage—was absent a week to the same last December—lost all his practice meantime, and received for his pay thirty-eight dollars in Oregon scrip' Costly honor! Previously to sitting of the legislature this year, great exertions were made to elect members who would vote to change the Organic law sufficient to insert *prohibit* instead of *regulate* into that clause relative to ardent spirits, but several who promised their constituents that they would vote for the change have opposed it, and the law reads as formerly. The majority of the members of this session are unprincipled men, at least if we may judge by their works. They have also, on the petition of J. Brooks, divorced his wife.[10] Only three of this body voted against this barbarous decree, and thus prove they have no sympathy with woman kind. This business has been accomplished mostly by a lawyer who has not much to do, and is the same person who recommended Mrs. Brooks, formerly, to apply to court to obtain a bill from her first husband. Mr. Brooks is to furnish her five hundred dollars. She boards in the country, and Dr. Binney attends her.

"For a week or more a sick woman in the house to attend upon; under Dr. Binney's care. She says she has great compassion for me in the lonely life I lead; thinks it would kill her to live thus.

"Mrs. L—— left and Mrs. N—— comes, with two children, to remain several days, for medical treatment. Then an Indian woman with her child wishes to stay. Surely, I have not much peace in my own premises.

"A man comes who is willing to give six thousand dollars for our property, but has not the sum; says he will give three thousand dollars for the place alone, but Dr. Binney wishes to sell all together.

"Husband requests me to receive Mrs. Brooks to board, as no one about will receive her, it being popular to despise her, especially by those who are none too good themselves.

"Mrs. Brooks comes. She cannot read, and requests me to teach her. Dr. gone for his cattle; a little girl and myself plant half an acre of potatoes; transplant rose bushes and honey suckles; sweep part of our spacious yard, and act as polite as possible to two gentlemen callers from Catholic Mission.

"Mrs. Brooks in the house and Mrs. N—— in the hospital to wait upon; gives me a plenty of house work; my heart ever aches; I find pleasure in none of these things.

"Teaching Mrs. Brooks to read—she beginning at ba, be, &c. O! had I at this time of life, got to commence reading there! Poor, poor woman! She has led a gay and fashionable life—attending all the balls and parties, and no one in Oregon City, 'tis said, was equally accomplished in dancing. But these accomplishments are more easily learned than the spelling book and moreover are more attractive to some classes of persons.

"Dr. Binney has been again for his cattle, and finds twenty-two head missing. We have been told that half-breeds and whites frequently kill them for beef. They have a good opportunity, as they range in winter about twenty-five miles away and no one takes care of them.

"Two English ladies make a call; one asks me, 'How long is it since you came from England, ma'am?'

"I told her I was not from England, but from the state of Massachusetts—I was a yankee.

"'O,' said she, 'I am almost a yankee, for I have lived several years in the State of *Indiana!* How far is Massachusetts from Boston?' she enquired.

Being unable to inform her, I was glad to change the subject.

Sabbath. "Much pleased with 'Dick's Works'—they have yielded me much information and delightful contemplation.[11] Walked to Putnam's Grove; both cats followed me in a frolic.[12] The rose bush we planted is budding beautifully, but an ugly thistle by its side grows faster than it. A fine day since

❦

yesterday's rain; grasses, flowers and birds combine to render the spring delightful.

"Last eve rode out with doctor to the band of cattle to look for young calves; find two. Try to separate them from the herd with the cows; find great trouble, my horse rearing upon his hind feet whenever he approached them, and nearly throwing me from the saddle. It getting late, gave up the chase, and returning found a young calf but a few hours old; try to drive it, but find it too weak to walk. Doctor then took it in his arms, when the cow flew at him; he then took it upon his saddle, when she ran off to the woods to look for it. Getting her upon the road again, I tried my skill, raising the calf in my arms and walking backwards that the cow might see it. This was troublesome, too, for every time I raised it from the ground the cow would fly at me and compel me to drop it again; but by persevering I succeeded in progressing homeward a few feet at a time, though backwards, till the cow became fatigued and stopped. I then carried the calf in my arms, the doctor leading my horse, till we reached home, when my arms were so much wearied I could not use them for some time afterwards—but, notwithstanding, I had to get supper for a stranger who wished to tarry all night.

"Heard that all the Frenchmen who went to the fort last week have got black eyes! Church members! Partakers of the *real* flesh and blood of Jesus Christ, you must do penance for that!

"John Creepeasy brings rails with oxen, and *I* lay them, being anxious to divide a field before the cattle and hogs can go into injure the oats. Some persons pass and see me thus engaged, but I work on not seeming to perceive them. Don't be alarmed, reader, let me show you an extract:

"'A Mohamet Bey had promised a Bey of Algiers to discover to him the secret by which he had acquired his great wealth, and sent him spades, hoes, and other implements of agriculture, informing him that *these* were the instruments of real magic which could convert everything into gold.'

"I am not a lazy person, and should never wish to have to say, 'All things are busy only I, neither bring honey with the bees, nor flowers to make that, nor the husbandry to water there.'

"Again at fence; sun shines very warm, but a breeze from the north helped me to endure till noon, when I was completely tired. At four had my fence across, five rails high.

"Mr. N——— calls for Dr. Binney, and seeing me in the field comes to me and says: 'You work too hard, Mrs. Binney, this is no work for a lady.'

I told him my reasons for being thus engaged, and continued my work.

May 1st. "Fine day. In the morning trim one hundred and eleven young trees, all of which I set out last year, mostly alone; all doing well. Flowers are abundant, various and rich—birds washing at the pump trough, scarcely move for my presence—wrens building in three corners of the house, and warbling their anticipated pleasures—sparrows drinking drops of dew from grass in the yard—martins darting about from houses to trees, preferring the houses for building, but thinking certain little, black, glossy, looking animals they see about are rather too fair in appearance to suit them.

"How beautiful is nature! I thought, this evening, as I leaned over the yard fence. The sun had descended midway the trees before me—the ground was sprinkled with late rain—the oak trees at either end of the house and in and out of the yard are full of flowers, hanging in tresses with young green leaves—three turtle doves in the open yard before me are walking about picking whatever they can find, and talking the sweetest language ever heard by mortal—my cats, two on the fence on either side of me, brushing my arms with their furs and asking me to notice them, while the other on the ground waiting a chance to jump up beside me—young pigs running about in a frolic—horses and young colts eating salt—cows coming up to their calves to be milked, while the calves, twenty-three in number, were racing from the opposite side of the pasture to the kraal, to their mothers, each one trying which would get their first. Yes, how beautiful is nature! The weather, too, is fine.

> Not a cloud in the skies appears to my eyes—
> The rain it is gone;
> The azure I see is delightful to me—
> Beyond is Immanuel's throne.
>
> Nothing else to my mind, exquisite I find,
> When God in creation I see;
> Let worldlings pursue worldly pleasures and few,
> But nature—O! nature for me.

Sabbath. "Alone. Dr. Binney's two horses having but poor feed in the pasture, think I'll take them into the garden where is better grass, and sit under the trees and read meantime—believing 'it is lawful to do good on the Sabbath day.' Soon find them running about over the young trees and beds, &c.; try to turn them out, but no! they liked the place too well, and began to make it a play ground—thinking, perhaps, it is lawful for *horses* to play on the Sabbath. Have at last to call for help to subdue their fun and return them to barren pasture. For once I think satan has been transformed into an angel of light in making me think it was lawful to do *such* kind of good on the Sabbath. I think the horses will be hungry before my sympathies will let them into the garden again.

"Rose soon after daylight to let my cows go. The woods echoed with the notes of mourning doves and birds singing charmingly their morning songs. Being unable to milk twenty-three cows alone twice a day, I milk them at evening and leave them with the calves all night, turning them out early and the calves to their pasture.

"Dr. Binney is nearly ready for the California trip. Turning his prepared coffee into a bag find it all running out at the bottom, which I had neglected to sew. Think it ominous of the way his money will go.

"Dr. Binney is at last ready for his tour to California. He leaves me on the place alone, except with Mrs. Brooks, who is miserable company, and who would not stay only that she desires me to instruct her in reading, and I dare not refuse, and I know of no place in the country where she could find accommodations.

"Dr. Binney leaves two thousand dollars in my care, and when bidding me farewell told how he wished I would dispose of it in the case of his death.

"I asked him, if the case should be the other way, and *I* should die, will you give the Missionary Education Society one hundred dollars for me?

"He replied that 'they don't deserve anything,' but finally said he would.

"He is well fitted out; has seven horses—four with packs—a servant man—good clothing, good health, and a good prospect. My desires towards him are that he may do well, keep in good company, meet with no accident, and return in safety and happiness.

"I am here alone with this weak-minded woman, and no one can tell the dearth of mind at the prospect of no society but her.

May 31st. "Several frosty nights—potatoe vines and young oak leaves are entirely black with rage. The sun is scorching hot and the earth is excessively dry. Grasses crumble under my feet—garden seeds do not put forth, and my pretty house-yard is a desert of dust and dying green, except a few tufts of iris which seem resolved to live at any rate.

"Trouble, too, among the birds. I expect Misses Puss are the cause. Building and singing have ceased, except one wren singing plaintively alone, and another saying only chirp, chirp, on the same twig, most of the day.

An evil never has been known for which a remedy's not given, nor without evil any good for mortal man this side of heaven.

"A French neighbor calling says he is going to church next Sabbath, for his daughter is going to begin to eat Jesus Christ next Sunday!

"Go to my favorite bower, and reclining my head on a moss covered root of an enormous fir tree, as I gazed upwards and caught a glimpse of the sky through the tops of the trees, I found my mind at peace with God—at peace with nature—and at peace with itself. Only a few of mankind caused me bitter reflection. My faithful dog Caesar kept running about on the scout for wolves and, as the hoosiers say, for 'varmints,' so that I reposed securely. My lonely bird was there over my head, its only note chirp, chirp. Thought of husband's remark last Sabbath, 'next Sabbath I shall be somewhere, and where?' Is he fortunate? Is he travelling, and where?

"Where are the augurers?—the dog howls—hens crow—doves coo— scissors stand upright when falling, and birds mourn their mates—what would they say is about to happen?

"I have by me a flower which I cannot class by my small work on botany, which I think much more resembles the Passion Scene of the Crucifixion than the real Passion flower.[13] It is about the form of a cup, of the size of half an egg. In the centre stands the pericarp, which ends at the top in three points in the form of a cross. Close around are six stamens—three large and three small—which may represent the immediate favorite disciples of the Lord, male and female. Around the bottom of the pericarp, and cross is a smooth space on the white petals, thickly spotted with fine purple spots, which may be considered blood and the shade of the surrounding multitude. There are three petals thickly studded on the inside with small white points—the people assembled; those nearest the cross are tinged with purple, the mourners in grief—and the others being white denote carelessness. Three leaves, the covering of the calx, close the opening between petals and resemble a guard, and the three long slender leaves on the stalk remind one of the long continued blessings of the sacrifice and the union of the Godhead. The flower is very beautiful, and whatever others may call it *I* shall name it the Oregon Passion Flower.

"A fine shower of rain last night. Each faded shoot, and withered root, and shallow brook, and sunburnt nook, must receive it gladly. Lupins, iris, larkspuns, culendines, wild rose and honeysuckle now in bloom. Wrens incubating again in the house and trees over it.

"An ugly spider on the window sucks the life of a poor fly; vain his feasting, 'twont be lasting, for this moment he shall die.

* * * Having killed my spider with boiling water, I now again resume my pen; but all my singing's not worth penning while I listen to that wren.

"The sheriff from Oregon City and a gentleman in pursuit of a murderer called for some refreshments, when I proposed making them some coffee. They said they preferred *baughnaughclaughbaugh* or *buttermilk* to anything else.

"At eve had milked eighteen of my cows when I looking out I perceived a train of pack horses coming to the house, which I recognized as Dr. Binney's.

"When I met him at the gate I asked, 'What has brought you back?'

"He replied: 'I came back to see *you*—what do you think?'

"He informed me that being uneasy about me from the way he left me alone with Mrs. Brooks, and having lost his flour, he resolved to return and take me with him next time.

"A visit from Madame Lucien, a Chenook Indian woman. She says the wives of the French say of me that I am the only one of the Boston missionary women whom they like, for I am always the same, kind, pleasant, and social, and never too proud to speak to them. A very good compliment, if true.

We regret that we cannot give the history of Mrs. Brooks, and her sickness and death, as found in Ruth's journals. We have only space to quote:

"I closed her eyes—washed her person—brushed her beautiful hair— dressed her in clean linen—put a nightgown on her, and wrapped her in a sheet; supported her head upon a pillow, and her hands upon her breast. In all this I was quite alone; yet the terrors of death were not there, and I only felt that I was placing a friend comfortably to sleep. Peace to her afflicted and erring mind.

"Her body was carried to the grave by Dr. Binney and C. W———, the coffin supported by ropes on a pole. The only followers were myself and our dog Caesar.

"I have never done anything for her comfort without feeling happy in the thought that I had made her comfortable and decent, and 'tis pleasant *now* to reflect that she lies in a sweet and clean grave, released from all her worldly sorrows. She leaves about four hundred dollars in money and clothing.

"A bad neighbor is being too neighborly, so the cows say who have lost their calves.

"Corn in the garden putting forth spindles only five inches above the ground.

"O! how exceedingly does my soul pine for the society of dear friends in the States! I can never express the loss I feel of their presence, and the blessed means of grace I there enjoyed. For six years I have been to but one meeting, and not in all that time have I been once to the Lord's table! Of what use is life spent in this manner?

"Rising at day light to turn the cows from the kraal, I saw sweet Venus in great glory at the westward of the sun—the first time I have seen it for several months, when it was the evening star—and so beautiful! Her disc appeared about the size of a silver dollar. The moon also was near the sun, and the planet Mars and another planet whose name I could not determine, were more distant. Seven fixed stars were also visible.

"O! how I love those heavenly bodies; and how I have wished, when tired of earth, to go and dwell among them!

"The planet *Earth,* too, is lovely, as I am just now reminded by some double roses in a vase before me, and which seem looking up to me for me to love them, and *I am* among the stars and clouds even here, and perhaps as near the Throne of God as those I have named; but sin and sorrow blind the eyes to any good which is near us; and exciting discontent with present scenes leads us to indulge in longings for those which are far distant.

"When I returned to the house, Dr. Binney was still sleeping and had lost the exquisite sight of this part of nature's works.

"Visited the graves. Over Putnam's blooms the double rose we transplanted there; but around Mrs. Brooks' the bushes are twisted in a most singular manner. Two young pines are broken quite off—the sod is torn up—the loose dirt of the grave is scattered about, and the place really looks as if certain imps had been having a fandango there.

"Husband and I ride out in search of berries; find not many but plenty of spear-mint growing wildly in all its fragrance. Several kinds of mint are found here in a wild state.

"An old man who has twice been here for grafts from our apple trees, has been again for more. When he had received all he wished without charge, and got the promise of some rose bushes in the winter, he said: 'I have some pear trees I would like to sell you—I ask fifty cents a piece.'

"Wasn't he generous!

"Dr. Binney is obliged to gather his oats himself as help cannot be obtained. He was at work bright and early this morning, then was called to visit a sick neighbor; returning, read and prescribed till the sun had declined somewhat and then went to work again; then was called eight miles away, whither he is still absent.

"For myself I have to-day baked pies, cake and bread; sewed and read some. This eve milked my cows, fed my hogs and taken care of my calves and hens and turkeys and ducks; closed the doors at dark, lighted my hoosier lamp, and read in the Ladies' Magazine the story of Caroline Grahame.[14] The story is extremely well written and profitable.

"One dog has gone with doctor, and the other chained in the yard, will not bark at any intrusion. My two cats have been hunting and brought a mouse or bird for their kittens, who are asleep snug and warm, knowing neither care or fear.

"Through a broken pane of glass the wind is raising the curtain, and I am ever fancying an Indian may be outside ready to shoot me. 'Tis eleven o' clock. And I wish the doctor would come for I am lonely.

"An Indian woman says the Chenooks will soon be extinct, for they have no children, and she can remember when they were as numerous as bushes.

"A neighbor Indian woman has been to buy hogs to turn into her wheat field to fatten. She says 'tis all the way she can get any good of the crop, for her husband and all her neighbors are gone to the mines. She says in the winter they will have to eat their gold, for they'll have no wheat.

❦

"War among neighbors. Back-biting, slandering, tale-bearing, and disputing, the business of the day—for once I find pleasure in solitude. I some time since set my immediate neighbors down for just what they prove to be. All slanderers love to fan the fire to burn their neighbor's face.

Worms love to grovel in the fire, for 'tis their native place.

"A sick hoosier under Dr. Binney's care whistles between pauses of conversation.[15] He might as well be a yankee and *whittle* away the time.

"An urgent call for Dr. Binney. The man goes in pursuit of him—meets him, and tells him he has fifty dollars in his pocket, and was told to bring him at any price.

"Returning in the night lost his way, and as he could not find it he threw his saddle upon the ground, rested his head upon it, and waited for morning.

"Returned this morning, tired and sleepy, when he was obliged to go again.

"Hired man came with his team to cart oats to the stable, and was myself obliged to assist in unloading, it being necessary for one person to throw it into the door, while another, on the inside, put it away. Strange work for a governor's lady! but it being doctor's request when he went away, I could not refuse, and I was more willing as the man is a pious good neighbor, and his wife an amiable friend of mine.

"Two gentlemen called for medicine, when I told them these are *golden* times when every one must be his own servant. Seeing another load coming, they waited and assisted, thus saving me the trouble.

"At evening doctor returns, when he and I pack away the remainder of the oats. Having finished, another call was made for him, fee in hand, and I am thus to be alone another night.

"Sitting down to write, my mind dwells on the cruelties practised against Lord Byron by his lady, having been reading his 'Fare Thee Well' to his wife. One verse, particularly, will occupy my thoughts, viz:

> "'Though my many faults deface me,
> Could no other arm be found,
> Than the one which once embraced me,
> To inflict a deathless wound?'

"Poor, suffering, Byron! Sensitive tenderness like thine, could not have come from a heart altogether depraved.

"'Tis a strange fashion among western people of visiting on the Sabbath. 'Tis in vain I try to discountenance the practice by staying home myself and speaking against it; they will come—and I must spend the day in labors instead of *rest,* as it should be spent.

"A settlement on Pudding river is called the 'City of Babylon,' from the confusion arising from too much exercising of that evil member, the tongue.

"Our hoosier friend who whistles so much about the house has gone home. He reminds me of what Dryden says:

"' He whistled as he went, for *want of thought.* '

"Last eve a delightful breeze had cleared away the smoke—the moon was shining brilliantly, and the leaves on the oaks at either end of the house were constantly on the bound, seemingly to show thereby their sense of the beauty of the evening, and I almost resolved that with them I would shake off sleep for the night, that I might enjoy the beauties of nature.

"Some Indian women to visit me. One says she was brought from the Shasta country and sold to a Frenchman for a musket, tin kettle, and seven blankets.

"An editor says of Mrs. Sigourney: 'She was one of the first, if not the *very* first to successfully prove that American women can be intellectual without leaving the proper sphere of their sex.'[16] Was there any doubt before that American women could not do this as well as English women or those of any other nation?

"Since writing thirteen quails have alighted in the yard, and walked about the door picking what they might find—chattering about what they saw—drank at the trough, and went away quietly and unharmed.

"Smaller birds have a fine time here every day, dusting in the fine dirt and then washing in the trough—making me happy to see them so. This is pleasant, but a neighbor killing calves and pigs for us is not pleasant.

"A gentleman was here this morning who some time ago lived near this people, and he says he *knows* they killed his animals. He has found his calves heads at their doors—has killed two cows that had bullets in their shoulders—and of twenty-two calves he turned out last fall with the cows, in three months there were but seven left. These families are never known to buy meat, and none in the settlement set better tables.

"The French are returning from California, mostly in poor health. They say they have made but little—lost their summer's work—lost their horses and cattle, and have got no crops, &c. Such is the result of an undue love for gold.

"Rev. Bishop Blanchard called and invited me very kindly to visit him at the falls, and spend a week with his niece.[17]

"Whatever the catholic religion may be this people have ever treated me with great kindness.

"Rev. Mr. B—— lent husband a bundle of English papers. What a holiday we shall have in reading them. The fashions appear in them. Alas!

how would we look in the Oregon backwoods dressed in the style of the English and Parisian ladies!

"A gentleman from Oregon City once told me there had some fine dress silks been received there, and I should go down and purchase. Oh! me, what could I have done with it unless worn it to milk my cows.

"Flocks of grouse and quails in the garden and yard, feeding with the chickens and nearly as tame.

"Mrs. H———, of Oregon City, says she never 'knew the Fourth of July to be celebrated in Canada,' and wonders why!

"C. R——— wishes Dr. Binney, when he goes to the States again, to bring a bonnet for his wife, and a barrel of Jamakka for himself.

"A western woman seeing me sweep with a floor brush, exclaimed: 'Well, that is the last thing I would have thought of fixing to sweep with!'

"A hoosier woman said to Dr. Binney to-day, when he had called on a young man with fever, 'Did you ever see a case like that before, doctor? The doctors in Missouri have a kind of truck to break the fever at once. Did you ever see any of it?' The young man being on the recovery he left but one powder, expecting to see him next day. 'O!' said she, ''tis not worth while to ride so far just to leave such a mighty little truck as that!'

"Another says: 'The first truck you gave did no good at all; the second did right smart good; and the third did a might heap of good; and he has slept a heap!'

"A hoosier family to visit me, and certainly I am glad they are gone. The lady exercised herself by walking to and fro upon the carpet, schuffling her feet at each step, probably the better to enjoy its softness. The gentleman sat most of the time tipped back in his chair, with his pipe, and showed his good manners in not spitting upon the carpet, by spitting between it and the wall as nearly as he could. The children amused themselves, some by looking at their faces in the furniture, and making marks for their eyes, nose and mouth; others by thrusting their fingers through the holes in the flag button chairs, and observing, by their difficulty in getting them out again, that some fingers were larger than others; and the remainder got into a contention about who could rock farthest back in the rocking chair, till they turned it over and broke it. Such are some of the best from Western America, and our improved state of society.

"Another says the word *plunder,* as used by hoosiers, viz: to represent all kinds of property, is soon to be introduced into our dictionaries! Alas for our dear English language, when hoosiers shall dictate its vocabulary. Then I fancy we shall read:

Honesty. Intention to steal all we can.

Slander. Meat and drink.

Modesty. Looseness in conversation and conduct.

Neighbors. Those I mean to hurt all I can.

Gossip. Performance of duty.

Back-Biting. Going about doing good.

January, 1850. "Monday eve. A sweet influence has pervaded the space around me today, and affected my mind powerfully this evening, and I have felt certain I was remembered somewhere with affection. I was not able to understand these impressions till I remembered it was the time of the monthly concert of prayer in the United States. Perhaps some one was remembering unworthy me at the Throne of Grace, and I was receiving the benefit.

"Dr. Binney has resolved to go again to the States. He is tired of his practice and of the people, especially of this neighborhood. He is much annoyed by the people killing his cattle, hogs, &c., and lately, after having lost some fine colts, he finds a mare on the prairie with her neck broken, which could never have been occasioned but by some individual.

"Dr. Binney gone away for two days; self alone on the place except an old Indian, who wraps himself in his blanket and goes to sleep at an early hour. Reflecting on my position thus alone with an Indian I have no fears—the dogs give no alarm—all the animals on the place are well housed and full fed—the rain patters on the roof—I have good lodgings, and peace and pleasure in my heart—and thus I close my eyes for the night, thanks and praise to a blessed God who doeth all things well and never slumbers or sleeps.

"A Frenchman coming for medicine for his wife, says: 'My gal sick—much sick; I sorry for my gal; I can't leave my house with nobody to look after my gal; I go to get one Frenchman's gal to look after my woman—pauvre woman! Suppose you go see Doctor—me very glad.'

"Next time he came, he asked the doctor: 'How is your gal this morning? Very well? Suppose my gal is all the same, me very glad.'

March. "Again commence at gardening, though the prospect is we shall leave this year.

"An old Spaniard, who is very polite, but does not know a word of English, wishing to be able to thank me when grateful for any assistance, asked Dr. Binney, in Spanish, what was *"Thank you,"* in English. The Doctor, being busy at the moment, and not wishing to be annoyed, told him to 'Go to h-ll.' Assisting him in the garden, I told him I had sown all the seed he had given me, when he raised his hand to his mouth and with a polite bow replied, 'Go to h-ll, Senora.' I could not comprehend his meaning till I obtained the explanation from my husband.

"Doctor sold his band of mares and colts at twenty-five dollars per head, and this spring's colts given in; the sum amounting to five hundred dollars. About twelve or fourteen of them were my own.

"This is a great relief to me of the anxiety I have felt when they have suffered without food in winter, and from the envy of neighbors.

"He has also sold the band of cattle at twenty-five dollars per head, excepting this spring's calves, amounting to two thousand and four hundred dollars—one hundred being thrown off for the risk of some which may not be found.

"These animals have all come from three cows, being all that were ever purchased of the stock. The balance I have taken care of when calves, milking the cows and attending to the calves, so that the whole band are as tame as any ever seen in the United States.

"This is also a great relief, as what we lose by men and wolves is about equal to the increase; and Dr. Binney is unable to look after them, and he is constantly saying they are more trouble than they are worth.

"Commence keeping a purse of my own separate from my husband's. Begin with the silver dollar, my fortune from my father, four dollars given me for a bonnet, and thirteen particles of gold dust picked from the table after the doctor had been weighing some. Hitherto all I earned or received for any article belonging to myself, has been given to him.

Sabbath. "The floods and tempests overwhelm me, but I am supported by the conscious integrity of my own heart.

"About forty-three head of our cattle which were sold this spring and driven some distance towards the Rogue river, have swam the rivers and returned to our place. One cow came away with her young calf to the gate of the kraal, and would not go away till it was taken inside. It has since been put out to her, but she will not go away with it. Mooley insists on it remaining in my care.

"Another cow actually succeeded in getting her calf into the corral, but how we cannot tell, we only know we found it there.

"'Tis gratifying that dumb animals at least can believe there is goodness in me.

"Some French neighbors have bought barouches—undoubtedly their Indian wives will now *out-shine* the white ladies.[18]

"With what increasing delight do I contemplate the ways of God to man; our destiny—immortality—the delights of religion and the prospect of an eternal increase of knowledge and joy in God. 'O! how love I Thy law—it is my meditation day and night!' I often feel disposed as now to break out in songs of praise and gladness, but the shadow of coming distressing events forbids the utterance of my secret joys and hopes in God.

"Some prospect of soon leaving for the United States, at which prospect my heart bounds within me.

"Since I have been in this country, 'the snares and pains of hell,' as the psalmist says, 'have had hold upon me,' but should God deliver me, as I shall think he does when I am permitted to leave Oregon, my life henceforth is to be the Lord's. Whatever opposition, persecution and deprivation I may meet, my constant purpose shall be to serve God and His cause in every possible way.

"I have felt much this morning of the consecrating influences of the Holy Spirit, instigating, accepting and sanctifying this resolution made from these considerations. This life is of but little use but to prepare for the next. After this life is ended I have to live forever in happiness or woe. My bliss hereafter will be proportioned to my capacity for enjoyment, or, in other words, to the amount of favor I shall receive of God for the way in which I have served him here. And this life being passed and lost can never be recovered and spent again.

"Walking alone in my garden can't help exclaiming:

> O! how I wish I had a friend
>   To love with me these things I see,
> One who knew how to comprehend
>   The pleasing, unsolved mystery—
>   The light, the love, the power divine,
>   Of Flora's lovely, sacred, shrine.
>
> I walk these paths each day and pause
>   To view the changes in each vine,
> And plant and flower, and trace the cause
>   Of all the wealth which I call mine;
>   Not worth in me, 'tis understood
>   God loves the evil and the good.
>
> 'Tis said some flowers immortal bloom,
>   But they're not Flora's these decay—
> Beyond the confines of the tomb
>   They flourish in perpetual day;
>   Where I perchance some time may be,
>   And dwell with God eternally.
>
> O! how I love these lovely things,
>   These roses, poppies, princes' feathers,
> And humming birds with buzzing wings,
>   And morning-glories, all together;
>   And marigolds, and pinks not least—
>   I love them all, no one the best.

"The prettiest flower in my garden is a solitary white poppy. No bride, in all the perfection of youth and innocence, was ever half as beautiful.

July. "Occasional showers through the summer thus far, and vegetation growing rapidly.

"At twilight, in a gentle shower of rain, my slate caught the following:

> Blessed clouds, O, how I love ye,
>   Dropping down your gentle rain;
> Lovely clouds, not far above me,
>   Here ye have returned again.
>
> In the region where ye travel
>   God is seen, and everywhere;
> Sinners here, how great the marvel!
>   Still receive His sovereign care.
>
> Sitting here I gaze around me,
>   Loving earth, and skies, and life,
> Grateful thoughts are found within me,
>   Thoughts with joy and praises rife.
>
> Birds asleep and insects waking
>   Tell the bliss of twilight's hour;
> Wandering herds repose are taking;
>   Flowers on air their fragrance pour.
>
> Here I trace my little ditty,
>   Scarcely light enough to see;
> Whether what I write is witty,
>   Poor or good, 'tis the same to me.
>
> Lovely sky and lovely tresses,
>   Lovely earth, and all I see,
> When my heart my God possesses,
>   All is light and love to me.

CHAPTER XX

FAULT-FINDING

The reader having accompanied us in our rapid examination of Ruth Rover's journal, during a term of six years, in which we have quoted only such items as would illustrate her employment and the tenor of her mind, we shall ask his indulgence now, when we contemplate a different subject, viz: the improper course of Dr. Binney—a subject as painful to the compiler to record as it must have been painful to Ruth to witness; and for the feelings which inspire the compiler, in view of this part of her task, she must refer her reader to the first part of the ''Introduction'' at the commencement of this number.

We believe we have stated somewhere that Dr. Binney's greatest error was a want of principle, and his greatest weakness a too ready yielding to impressions.

We have no antipathy toward Dr. Binney as an individual; we respect him for his good qualities—pity him for his errors—and most sincerely lament that state of mind into which he has fallen, by which he cannot maintain a good purpose nor avoid the ruin which he perceives so glaringly before him.

Without the aids which the love and fear of God produces, he has no strength to enable him to keep a good resolution but the regrets of a past error while fresh in his mind—and these are rendered powerless from the effects of evil associates and intoxicating drinks, which are ever resorted to to assuage the pangs of an outraged conscience.

On Dr. Binney's associates will fall the heaviest punishment for his ruin—on those who, to obtain his gold, or services, or property, or influence, or from jealousy, have been the most active in alluring him again to scenes and habits of dissolution, from which he had endeavored to escape. And in this chapter we shall fearlessly refer to such, and as far as our influence extends, shall expose their names to obloquy and contempt.

Could *writing* send such persons sooner to the oblivion which they deserve, and which is before them, *our* feeble efforts should not be wanting—but the earth *is* and *ever will be* cursed with their foul presence. Shame and exposure but makes them more intent on their purpose, for then they are goaded by revenge, as we have met many instances in our contemplation of the evils to which Ruth Rover has been subject from this class of individuals—and our only hope is in the justice of that decision which will hereafter be made against them.

Dr. Binney's religion lasted during two seasons of prayer with his wife. He then told her he *could not* pray; and shortly after told her, when she was entreating him most fervently to continue his efforts to be religious, that he did not mean to pray, and furthermore he did not intend to remain a member of the church, and she might make herself easy.

The third morning after their marriage he told her she was a *pest,* in consequences of her having made an enquiry relative to a friend of his, but which she had no suspicion he would be unwilling to answer.

In a week he was cursing his horse, notwithstanding the profession of religion; and, as an evidence of the precipitancy of his temper, in *three weeks* after marriage he attempted to strangle his wife, by seizing her by the back of the neck, and for which she was entirely off guard, not having yet learned his disposition.

When he retired at night, he asked her what she thought of his conduct that day. She replied she did not know what to think of it! He told her he wished her to think no more about it, for he could not tell what ailed him sometimes to make him act as he did.

But 'tis needless to attempt to delineate every circumstance of this kind which occurred. We only wish to notice such as will denote Dr. Binney's disposition and general course, and explain some occurrences which are imperfectly understood.

The impetuosity of his temper was equally apparent in shooting his horses and hogs—in breaking his furniture—in destroying his clothing—as in mistreating his wife; with this difference, however, that while an animal could die, or furniture be repaired, or clothing be restored, his wife had to endure her griefs uncomplainingly, or breathe them only to herself with the oft-repeated exclamation:

"What have I married?"

At this time Ruth indulged hope that it would not always be thus with him. Perhaps she thought 'twas the loss of religion, and in all her prayers to heaven she besought God to influence him by His good spirit and save him. Perhaps she thought, too, 'twas poverty which irritated him, and she bent all her energies to assist him to become in easy circumstances, by denying herself every article she could do without—by laboring with her own hands to save expenses in hiring, and in earning all she could by needle-work which was always given to her husband; but these were of no avail—if she labored, it was, he said because she had been always used to it, and 'twas a sign of her low origin—if she worked at needle-work it was, he said, to obtain favor of other men, and not to please him—and if she bore his reproaches without reply, it was, he said, because she was a d—d coward, and knew she was in the fault.

Ruth had flattered herself that he was cured of intemperance, but she was destined to be disappointed here, for having a good pretext for obtaining liquor from the fort, viz: "for medical purposes," she discovered his wish to indulge to excess, and many times subjected herself to his violence from her wish to save him by removing the cause of danger.

During the period of her ill health, when she was unable to wait on herself, he sometimes was exceedingly kind and attentive to her, and bore his own privations and labors with great patience; and at other times in his rashness he would dash the remedies he had prescribed away and leave her with curses and destitute of assistance.

In this way six years had passed, and Ruth saw no remedy for the restoration of her husband but to remove him, if possible, away from *evil* influence, and place him where that of the moral and religious would predominate. With this hope, and the wish to benefit her health, or to remain with her friends, Ruth encouraged him to go to the United States in 1842.

The doctor, by industry and perseverance, had obtained a handsome sum, and Ruth also, by industry, prudence and economy, had greatly assisted him in acquiring and saving it, and this was sufficient to have borne their expenses home and to have enabled them to return, but for his foolish expenditure at the Society Islands, by which he lost about seven hundred dollars, and which caused him, on his return, to be greatly straightened in pecuniary affairs.

During this visit to the States, R. was greatly desirous that the good impressions Dr. B.'s family had received of his reformation should not be interrupted, but his hasty spirit soon manifested itself, in occasioning offence to the members of the household, and resulted in his mother and sisters telling him he was no longer welcome there. He left them and passed the remainder of his time mostly with Ruth's mother, a period of several weeks. While there and visiting among her friends, they discovered, to R.'s great mortification, that Dr. Binney was a man of intemperate habits, and rash and dangerous in his temper. In a sudden passion, he abandoned his wife at her mother's, taking his clothing, and affirming she should never see his face again, he left to take the cars, but being too late, he returned, asked her forgiveness, and next morning was equally anxious for her to prepare to return to Oregon with him.

Being returned to his old place and practice, the temptations and besetments which had before allured him to the committal of error, were greatly increased. He could scarcely ride for a day without encountering some who made or sold liquor; and, ever as ready to drink as to pay his own and others expenses, he was a very agreeable addition to the numbers of those who sought these remote hovels for the commission of iniquity—for gambling and inebriation. But an unnecessary expenditure of money, and absence from home was not the worst feature of this course. Ruth had, during his absence, been compelled to attend to all the business on the place; whether the care of cows, horses, swine, poultry, or garden, or housework—she was the sole manager, and almost always the sole laborer on the place. And when she had spent days and nights in loneliness and toil for his benefit, the most cruel part of his course was ingratitude on his return. Many times has she been first apprised of his approach by hearing most profane curses heaped upon her before he reached the house, at the supposition of something which he thought had been neglected. And, on entering the house, it was not with any affectionate salutation, which would have rewarded her for all her toils, but with sullenness, or reproaches, or accusations of some evil of which she had never thought, or the repeatal of some slander her enemies had furnished him with. If his meals were not in readiness, which was impossible oftentimes, from the irregularity of his hours, all the dishes he could find would be broken—if he could see nothing but tea or coffee in readiness, he would kick it into the fire, or dash it across the room. If everything was on the table, and he were invited to eat—if his wife had not cried herself into a merry mood in the course of the day, after his abuse in the morning, the whole affair of victuals and dishes would be swept into the fire, and herself ordered out of the house for her "d—d sullenness." Extremely wearing and prostrating was it to soul and body to live thus, and oftentimes Ruth's powers of endurance being entirely exhausted, she would go to a neighbor's house to pass a few days, to regain an equilibrity of feeling, by which she might again pursue her labors, or retire for a few hours or a day to the grove, and endeavor by relaxation, to forget the keenness of her sorrows; but although they might be overcome for that time— yet the cause being not removed—she had to realize their renewal, and each time find herself driven nearer and nearer to despair.

Oregon was then, not as now, when facilities for travelling are so greatly multiplied, and what would appear *now* a very rash undertaking, could be contemplated *then* with some hope of success, especially if *necessity* should seem to warrant the attempt.

Ruth Rover, before Dr. Binney had determined to once more return to the United States, had many times contemplated the subject of leaving him and endeavoring to return to her friends. She was satisfied her life was being wasted—she was being of no service to her husband only to enable him to acquire money to waste—hopes of his reformation she did not in the least indulge while he lived in Oregon; and as he had been home once and was not contented to remain, she thought it of little use to encourage him to go again unless he was willing to remain; and as his practice was extensive, he had abundance for his support in his farm and stock. Ruth often thought that she could relinquish every right which she held to the property, if she could again regain her friends and be permitted to live in peace and quietness among them.

But how could she get there? Dr. Binney would never furnish her the means, and she could never attempt such a long voyage at sea alone, even if she could have gone on the credit of her friends East. In these perplexities, and driven to extremes, she sometimes thought she could travel all the distance by land; or, if she could reach Walla Walla, she could remain till an opportunity presented itself for her to go home.

But impracticable, of course, were all these schemes, and her only course was to *endure*—and *she* thought to endure on till death should end her sorrows.

Persons there were in the neighborhood who loved to lead Dr. Binney into intoxication for the certainty, as they thought, of the disturbance which would ensure between him and his wife, when he, at variance with her, would accept of friendship from any one, and would be in the best humor to lend money, or give away property, or sell it at an under price, for the sake of friends to uphold him in his conduct to her.

John Hord of Champoeg, was of this class. Being of the same country as Dr. Binney, viz: an Irishman, his invitations to "come in and drink" were never disregarded, and when once there he seldom left till he had been all the rounds of sin, and *weariness* induced him to seek his own home for repose.

Another of this class was Robert Newhall, and to manifest his duplicity we shall cite one case out of many.[1]

R. Newhall had been a member of the legislature, and on Dr. Binney's return to Oregon in 1843, the French settlers, ever great friends to *him*, nominated and supported him in the office of governor, or one of the three persons in the executive committee. After this they elected him to the legislature greatly to the annoyance of R. N. During this, Mr. Newhall visited at Dr. Binney's and pretended great friendship, while he was always received by Mrs. Binney with kindness and treated with attention. At a caucus meeting in the settlement, previous to the struggle of the people to introduce the word *prohibit* instead of *regulate* into the organic law as relating to liquors, Dr. Binney and Mr. Newhall were both nominated as candidates for the legislature, on the promise that they would vote for *"prohibit."*

On retiring, Mr. Newhell invited Dr. Binney to come to Champoeg that evening. He went to Mr. Newhell's house, and was invited to go to "John's," and when there was urged to drink, and having done this once, needed no more urging, but continued, with the occasional example of Mr. Newhall, to drink until he forgot all danger, and with him remained, drinking and gambling till daylight on Sabbath morning, when he returned home and took his bed.

Ruth rose as usual and attended to her cows and duties about house, and having promised two half-breed girls she had living with her that they should go to meeting that day at a neighbor's, she prepared them to go.[2] Dr. Binney, somewhat recovered from a state of inebriation, said they should not go. Ruth ascertained that his only objection was that he hated the man at whose house the meeting was to be held, and as she had, in compliance with his wish in this respect, never attempted to go there herself, and the children being deprived of all indulgence of this kind which they enjoyed at home, and as she had faithfully promised them that they should go that day, replied to Dr. Binney that his wish to keep her and the children from indulging in recreation of that kind could not be always indulged—that she stayed away herself to gratify him, but the children could do no harm by going, and it was her intention to have them go to meeting sometimes when there was opportunity.

He became enraged, and thrust them and her out of the door, telling her to go with them, and never enter his house again.

The children went to church, and found, on their return, they were not permitted to enter the house. Mrs. Binney had gone from the sun, and from the gaze of strangers, to the hospital, an unfinished log house on the place.

Some time after, the children were told to go into the house, and Dr. B. going to the house where his wife was, told her to leave it and the place, or he would burn it down over her head. She remained all night without bedding or covering, having attended to her cows and calves as usual. In the morning Dr. Binney called at her door, and told her if she wanted her clothing to go for it, for he was going away and wished to shut up the house. She went, and took a few articles, which were taken from her again as he went out of the door—her husband saying, "No, I'll be d—d if you'll come that game over me." When he had gone away, she secured some clothing and some bedding and concluded to remain where she was if the children would bring her food; and attend her garden, and milk her cows, make the butter, &c., all of which she could do without going into the house where Dr. Binney was, and if these things were neglected, she was well aware there must be great waste. At evening, after having milked the cows, and being about to carry the milk to the dairy, she saw Dr. Binney leaving her house with the clothing and bedding she had carried there, and her bundle of manuscripts and journals which she feared he would destroy. She wept for those, and he refused to give them up. He told her again she should leave the place—or he would take straw and burn the house over her head—that "not a d—d article of her clothing should she have"—and that the girls should bring her "no more food, for if he caught them at it he would break their heads." Ruth passed another uncomfortable night—having eaten nothing since dinner but some strawberries; and pondering on the course which appeared most proper for her to pursue, she could not think it right for her to remain there, for certainly she could not subsist without food; although she would willingly have submitted to deprivation for the sake of attending to her cows, it being the early part of summer, when the milk was so abundant the calves could not drink it, and the cows were liable to injury by not being milked. She told Dr. Binney, that notwithstanding his ill treatment on Sabbath morn, she had resolved to remain for this purpose; and if she could not live with him—to live by herself where he would not be troubled with her presence; but he told her he had engaged a person to take care of the cows, and he didn't want her on the place, and she should not stay on it at any rate. Early in the morning she walked on foot through the dew to an acquaintance's house in Champoeg, and from thence found her way to the Falls. After she had gone, Dr. Binney went to Champoeg and posted upon the blacksmith's shop there, a notice for no one to harbor or trust his wife on his account for he should pay no debts of her contracting, which notice the young man tore down the moment he was away.

At the falls Ruth took board with Mrs. Hood. It was soon noised abroad that Dr. Binney and his wife had separated again, and Robert Newhall was quickly on the spot. He recommended that some person should wait upon Mrs. Binney and enquire into the cause of her leaving home—to ascertain if it were the intemperance of Dr. Binney, for if so, he ought to be prevented from holding a seat in the legislature.

Ruth, not understanding the design, related frankly the circumstances of his inebriation on Saturday evening—when Mr. Newhall declared that, he having already broken his pledge to the people that he would use his endeavors for the suppression of ardent spirits in the Territory, that he ought not to be allowed to vote on the subject! What did he think of his conduct in remaining in a groggery till Sabbath morning, gambling and drinking, if not to great intoxication, to at least *excess,* and to the injury of a man who would have been glad to have been peacefully and soberly at home?

Robert Newhall having been the cause of the trouble thus far, let us see how he conducted himself through it.

Ruth, while at Oregon City, having not even a change of apparel, addressed a note to Dr. Binney, of which this is a copy:

"OREGON CITY ———.

"DR. BINNEY: I have determined to give you an opportunity to give up my clothing in a peaceable manner, if it be your choice to do so.

"If there be neither love, friendship, nor humanity in your heart, is there at least no *shame* that your wife, who has served you so slavishly for years, and of whom you have, in your rational moments, avowed you had no fault to find—have you no shame that she should be cast out upon the world with but an old faded dress with which to cover herself? I request you to send me my clothing and bundle of papers, and direct them to the care of A. Hood, Esq.

"You have treated me as you have, and your own conscience must testify to you whether it be right or wrong—I have only this to say: I advise you to act as will enhance your own reputation and promote your happiness.

"I am your friend, although I have so little reason to be so.

RUTH BINNEY."

In about three weeks Dr. Binney came to Oregon City, without bringing her any article, and sent her the following note. As it will, in connection with other papers, denote the fluctuating mind of the man, we give it entire:

"MRS. BINNEY: I received your letter, Saturday evening, stating you had come to the determination to see whether I would give up your clothing in a *peaceable* manner or not.

"I have only to say that my character, reputation, honor, &c., have suffered so much from your scandalous misrepresentations respecting me, and from the fact that the whole affair has now become a matter of public notoriety; and that you left your *house* and *home* without any just cause; it was your own voluntary act in going away in the manner you have done—and if you are in a distressed situation you must blame yourself for it.

"I am sorry to think you are suffering for the want of clothing, but the affair has gone such a length that I consider it a duty I owe to myself not to attend to your request, except it be made through the medium of a third person.

"I am now in town, on my way to Fort Vancouver, and if you feel so disposed you can send Andrew Hood, Esq. 'to Moss' where he will meet me and through him I will communicate freely on the matter, and do what I suppose is right, both in justice to you and myself. I will wait two hours for that purpose.

"Your injured husband,

W. J. BINNEY."

Ruth Binney felt no desire to "communicate" further on the subject as he proposed, and seeing no prospect of obtaining clothing, concluded to try to obtain something on Dr. B.'s credit from the dry goods stores where he had money, and sent to McKinlay's for two calico dresses, and a few cheap articles—but was denied, although Dr. B. had several hundred dollars in the Fort, and was in the practice of taking goods from this place on that consideration. She sent also to Pettygrove's, and was denied—and to Kilbourn & Lawton's, but could obtain nothing—they having heard of the "notice," put upon the blacksmith's shop at Champoeg. Ruth attempted to work, and presented a notice of "Millinery and Dress Making by Mrs. Binney," to the editor of the *Free Press* who would not insert it, for a few weeks, when it was too late to be of service. This was all done from *fear of the man.*

Dr. Binney finding his wife silent in relation to his letter, sent Mr. T'Vault to inform her that "if she would confess herself to be in the fault, she might return again to his house." She informed Mr. T'V. that she had nothing to confess, if she had, she would refuse to do so; and as to her returning to his house, she did not feel particularly in a hurry to do so. Dr. Binney passed on to the fort, and several persons recommended Mrs. B. to improve the opportunity of his absence, and go home and get her clothing. It was now about ten o'clock, and having resolved to go, she walked up the Bluff to Mrs. Holmes, and having communicated to her her plan, which she approved, she assisted her in obtaining a horse and saddle, and at twelve o'clock she was on her way—having twenty-five miles to ride alone, on an unfrequented road. Having a miserable saddle, she stopped at a house and borrowed a small quilt to cover it. On she hurried through sun and dust—up hill and down—fording two rivers, and traversing woods, not daring to consider whether she was afraid of panthers and bears, until she reached the creek within a mile of her house about sunset. The banks to this stream being steep she alighted and drove the horse across, walking herself upon a log—but when upon the other side she could not again catch the animal, which turned about, re-crossed the creek, and returned to the road towards home, dropping the quilt into the midst of the water. Ruth perceived it would be useless to pursue the horse or to get the quilt from the stream, as it was then saturated with water, and it being late she thought it best to go directly home.

When she reached there Mr. Newbanks was sitting on the piazza, who rose and accosted Mrs. Binney very friendly; shook hands with her, desired her to walk in, and requested his wife to get her some tea. Ruth informed Mr. Newbanks of her errand home, and of the horse escaping from her.

Mr. Newbanks told her that Dr. Binney had left all things in his care, with the command to suffer nothing to be taken out of the house.

Ruth thinking she was to have trouble from his opposition, told him resolutely that she wanted nothing but her clothing, and *that* she was resolved to have, and 'twould be useless for him to oppose her.

Mr. Newbanks had always been greatly Ruth's friend—had been to her house a great many times when in poor health, as had also his Indian wife. He ever manifested grateful and kind feelings towards her; and although he liked to take a glass with Dr. Binney, yet he upheld Mrs. Binney in her course, and told her in reply that he was willing she should have her clothing, and he would assist her in taking it away; he only wanted her to have a witness to the fact of *her* taking them, that Dr. Binney might give him no trouble about them.

This being readily agreed to, Mr. Newbanks told his boy to drive up the horses, while Ruth prepared the articles she wished to take with her. All that she cared about were in one chest, this was locked up and the key could not be found. This chest had been made and given her by her kind brother, when first leaving home—he making it with his own hands to be sure of its goodness. Finding no other way to do she broke it open, where she found what she wanted of her clothing, and her papers, and about five hundred dollars in cash. She took her clothes and books, and hesitated about the money, but concluded as she left all the property to which she had a right, the five hundred dollars was a small compensation for what she left, and concluded to take it.

Mr. Newbanks and his boy caught two horses for her—one of them being of the increase of the animal she had bought with her salary, due her from the mission at the time of her marriage—and put them into the stable; and in the morning brought them out to the yard, loaned her his pack-saddle to carry her things, and offered to saddle her horses for her. She preferred he should not do this, as it would place him in a position to be blamed by Dr. Binney, and she went with her things to the hospital where was living Mr. and Mrs. Morris, whom Dr. Binney had put upon the place to take care of the cows, &c.

They secured the two bags of clothing upon the horse as securely as they were able, and Ruth having desired Mr. Newbank's boy to accompany her to the creek to get the quilt from the water, set out to return to the falls. She found great trouble with the pack-horse, in consequence of the insecure manner in which the packs were prepared, and at the creek, with the assistance of the boy, endeavored again to arrange them so that the motion of the animal would not make them liable to loss, but found it impracticable, and at last concluded to call at a Frenchman's, near by, and get him to accompany her.

As she was leaving the creek, and the boy was turning to go back, a man on foot, from Champoeg, made his appearance, and saluted her very civilly. Ruth asked how far he was walking, and if he would be so kind as to lead her pack-horse to Mr. Obishaw's.

He replied that he was going about half way to the falls—to the other side of the two rivers which were in her way.

Ruth thought at once it would be a good opportunity to get assistance, and enquired if he were willing to assist her that far.

With the utmost readiness he proffered his services.

When in view of Mr. Obishaw's house he tried to adjust the packs securely, and Ruth observed he took especial care of that in which was the money—liking to cause it to sound by striking it with his hands, &c. She became suspicious and resolved she would not go with him, and told him that as she perceived she would have much trouble, she had concluded not to go that day, and would stop at Mr. Obishaw's until she could obtain some one to accompany her all the way to the falls.

He went on reluctantly, having told her he would render her every assistance possible, and even go all the way with her if she desired it.

Mr. Obishaw, with the greatest readiness and kindness, consented to accompany her, and having been detained about an hour for him to get a horse and prepare himself, they set out and soon overtook the man on foot, who had proceeded but about a mile, evidently having been waiting to see if Ruth would follow.

When crossing Pudding river, three young men passed them in a race, shouting at the top of their voices, in great glee, and proceeding as if they were in good service and sure of a good reward.

By three o'clock Ruth, having called and paid for the lost quilt, reached Mrs. Holmes'. She put the money into Mr. Holmes' hands for safe keeping, and her clothing and papers she entrusted with Mrs. Holmes, and in the morning returned to Oregon City and engaged boarding with Mrs. Jeffries.

At noon, she felt impelled, from some unknown but powerful influence, to go at once to Mrs. Holmes and get her money and papers. She could not reason the impression away. 'Twas mid-day in the last of June—the heat was intense,—the dust was suffocating, and the road was tedious—yet *go she must,* was an inward impulse which she could not resist. She went, and having obtained the money and papers, returned to Mrs. Jeffries'.

She was surprised, on coming in view of the house, to see it surrounded by men—lawyers, private citizens, and the sheriff were outside and in. She passed to the kitchen window and delivered to Mrs. Jeffries her bundle. On going in she was accosted by Dr. Binney, and seeing many she did not know she passed into the kitchen to Mrs. Jeffries and told her she wished to entrust the contents of her bundle to her keeping, and if Dr. Binney should ask for the money to let him have it, but not to give up the papers, for he could have no claims to them as they were strictly her own.

Dr. Binney soon signified to Ruth that he wished to speak to her, when he made a reference to a *letter* he had received.

Ruth requested to see the letter, and was denied. She told him, 'twas useless to speak with her on any subject till she had learned the contents of that letter, whatever it might be, and with great reluctance it was at last handed her, the sheriff standing by her side while she read it to prevent her, it appeared, from destroying it, as he thought she might do from the astonishing disclosures which it contained. The following is a copy verbatim:

Champoeg June 21t 1848

Dear Sir

    I have just arrived from M Newmans across Pudding River on my way home I called at your place and was informed by Mrs. Morris that Mrs Binney arrived there last evening a little before sunset and remained until this morning it appears she made herself altogether at home or rather acted like one from home. My information is to this effect. Mrs. Binney arrived entered the house with an axe, notwithstanding forbedden by M Newbanks, broke open chests trunks and took of their contents what she wished also two horres packed them and left this morning. I have taken upon myself to give you this information that you know when you arrive at the falls what has ben done that you may manage accordingly.

    I have engayed Young Hall to carry the letter.

    Mrs. Binney it appears did not come alone but accompanyed by one man who stoped at the creek between your horse and Faciors, who he is we will find out.

    Would it not be better for you to say nothing about it until you come here and get the pariticulars that you may provide accordengly After leaveing your house I met Newbanks who had ben in search of Ms Bs trail and to find out who was with her but saw nor herd any thing., M Newbanks tells me that he forbid her taking any thing from the house or entering it, She said it was her house, but said M N. you have left it, she observed not for good, and also told Newbanks that she had taken legal advice and that it was only taking her own property &c&c—

I am in hopes you will get this when you arrive at the city it is my only reason for sending it Mrs B. told Mrs Morris that you left for the Fort about 10 ollock and she left at 12 so you see some one was in with her waching you.

I hope you will conclude to come up before you decide on any course and hear the particulars. it is certainly a high handed step of the madams.

Respeclfully yours
Robert Newell

W. J. BINNEY

This result had been occasioned by the boy who had gone with Mrs. Binney to the creek, going home and saying a man met her there, and had gone on with her. "Young Hall," was the express man who passed her at Pudding river, shouting—having the letter for Dr. Binney, and which cost him eight dollars for its conveyance to Oregon City, and Mr. Newhall, *was the man* (?) who after being the cause of this difficulty with Dr. Binney and his wife for political motives; did now turn about, and injure his wife to regain *his* favor.

When Mrs. Binney read the letter, and perceived the injustice, as well as want of truth it contained, she was overcome by astonishment, and grief, and could not for some moments suppress her feelings sufficiently to make an explanation of the occurrences connected with her ride home; but in broken sentences and many tears asserted that the letter was entirely false—no person had accompanied her or returned with her but Mr. Obishaw, &c., &c.

Her grief at this new form of persecution was most intense and exciting. It aroused the remembrance of the accusations she had endured at the mission—and on no subject was her mind so susceptible of impression as on that which referred to her truth to her husband. The cause of the grief which affected Ruth was misunderstood by Mr. Jeffries, who said afterwards that he could perceive that Mrs. Binney was a "violent tempered woman."

But what *is* temper? Is it mere sensitiveness—or is it a disposition to take revenge when injured? If it be the latter then Ruth Rover has *no* temper—if it be the former, then she has it to a great degree—alas! for her happiness.

Mr. Holmes had informed Dr. Binney that Ruth had entrusted clothing, money and papers to his wife's and his care, and if he would go home with him he could have them. Having reached Mr. Holmes' he learned that what he most wished to obtain, viz: money and papers, was *not there!*

In the morning he asked Mrs. Jeffries if his wife had entrusted a sum of money to her care, and received it of her. He then asked for the papers, but was answered evasively, and did not obtain them.

Dr. Binney, by this time, began to relent towards his wife, having discovered the atrocity of Mr. Newhall's character, and wished her to accompany him home. Not being able to prevail with her, he engaged two friends he had with him, H. Cosgrove and B. Kennedy, to endeavor to encourage her to return. H. Cosgrove made every effort to affect the object Dr. Binney desired, but B. Kennedy recommended him to apply for a bill of divorce, as she would not return to his home. This he perceived he could not do as he could not accuse his wife of a single fault, and he at last returned home without her.

This was Ruth's first acquaintance with the above named persons, and we will have to refer to them again as they have both done their share, perhaps, in accomplishing the misfortunes of Dr. Binney. They are both Irishmen and of intemperate habits, and possess great influence over the impressible mind of Ruth's former husband.

In ten days Dr. Binney went again for his wife—and informed her that he had become acquainted with the rascality of R. Newhall and some others—told her he could *not live* without she would consent to return—that he was willing to acknowledge the cause of the difficulty was in himself—that he was resolved to use no more spiritous drinks, for he knew it would soon kill him, and as an evidence of his sincerity he told her he had that morning turned half a keg of brandy upon the ground, to save himself from the temptation of drinking it, (another evidence that he would gladly have reformed.) and was ready to settle upon her any amount of his property she might wish for her security in case of her return. This course was strongly recommended by Mr. and Mrs. Jeffrys, and Ruth seeing repentance in her husband, was ready to forgive him, and receiving the following note from him, she accompanied him home.

"TO MRS. BINNEY:—My dear wife. I wish you to return to me and your home, and if you will do so I will tell you what I pledge myself to do. In the first place I will certainly drink no more liquor for at least one year, hoping that if I can refrain that long, I may be able to refrain forever. I acknowledge I have treated you with undeserved severity, and if ever it should come to pass that I should put you from home again, I promise to let you have half my property for your support. This I promise faithfully to do if you will never give me occasion to ill treat you"—(referring to the circumstance of her having insisted on the children going to meeting without his consent.'')

''I also promise to request those storekeepers, who refused to trust you on my credit—to let you have anything you want while my credit is good. I also promise to give no more business to W. T'Vault without your approval; nor will I request Robert Newhall to visit our house without you are willing. Newhall's letter about your visit here I found was a misrepresentation, and I will correct the false impression it has made as far as I am able.

Your affectionate husband,

W. J. BINNEY''

If the reader will compare this writing with the letter from Dr. Binney on page 248-249, he will perceive the change which has been effected in his mind.

Peace reigned in the dwelling of Dr. Binney for a few days. Ruth, encouraged and hoping, exerted herself to the utmost to have it enduring, but he was in the midst of the same influences and they again prevailed.

We must relate the particulars of another disturbance between this couple, inasmuch as it greatly affected the ultimate decision of the court in relation to the amount of alimony granted Ruth when she obtained her bill of divorce. The suspicion which she had long had that Dr. Binney's vicious indulgences when at J. Hord's and other places of dissipation, were not confined to drinking and gambling alone, were one day confirmed by her meeting him with an Indian woman in the bushes near her house. The doctor did not attempt to deny the fact, but told Ruth it was ''the d—d liquor that drove him astray.'' And on her proposing to apply *then* for a bill of divorce, he agreed to give her one-half the money then on hand, viz: $5,000, if she would forgive him and let it pass, and said it was unnecessary for the sum to be taken from the rest as she had the keys of the chest and could take it at any time.*

James Binney, a brother of Dr. Binney, having deserted from the U. S. Navy at California, was shortly after a visitor at Dr. Binney's house. He was excessively addicted to inebriation, and had been since childhood. He soon discovered that there were frequent causes of dissatisfaction existing between his brother and his wife, and that he had a large sum of money on hand, and recommended him to leave her and take his money and go to the mines.

This conversation being overheard by Ruth, and, perceiving that her husband had determined to deposit his money at Fort Vancouver, get an outfit and leave her alone with the farm for her dependence, resolved to take

*Of the half of the property referred to before she received nothing but the paper promising it.

the part of the sum which he had promised her on her consenting to live with him again after the committal of the error in which she had detected him. She took about four thousand dollars, leaving about six thousand. The result was barbarous treatment, on his part—and the taking up of her abode at the Butte, on her part.[3]

The officers of the ship James Binney had deserted pursued him to Oregon, offered a reward of one hundred dollars for his apprehension, and he was obliged to secrete himself to escape punishment. This was well for Dr. Binney, as he sooner recovered his proper feelings, and he then addressed the following letters to his wife.

The reader will not and *cannot* fail to commiserate the condition of an enlightened mind, so deplorably subjected to the domineering power of evil influences.

"DEAR RUTH:—This I now write you may not be received. With the good intention that compels me to send it but I venture to let it go, hoping that it will be destroyed as soon as read.

"What has been the matter with me? why! drink is the sole cause and I know it. Of course I cannot think of ever showing myself again to you for the purpose of a reconciliation—but I would be happy in letting you have all your things that are here, and would be glad to know where to send them, as I purpose to leave to-morrow to try if I can bring my shattered mind from dropping into deep melancholy, by the aid of some society more congenial than is to be found in this detestable place. I feel I want to get out of this soul destroying place—and I believe were I again among my kindred and friends at home, that I could enjoy that happiness in God that I desire. I am most undoubtedly laboring under partial derangement of mind, and if there is any happiness for me I pray the Lord will direct me to find it. Strong drink never will I touch again, and I pray that God will sustain me in so doing. I am going, if God willing, by the next steamer to the United States, and I would be willing to leave the greater part of my effects for you to take care of. The place I will abandon and leave, for it seems worse than torments to dwell upon it. I will go and see brother Simeon if the Lord spares me to reach him.

"What shall I do with your things, for from this place I must go or my soul is lost.

"The following passage I opened upon this morning, and I believe forcibly tells me to follow it:

'And the Lord saith unto Jacob, return unto the land of thy fathers and to thy kindred and I will be with thee.'

Fear no more trouble or molestation from me, but write me—if it is only three lines—what I request of you.

W. J. BINNEY.''

''I am going to deposit what money I have in the old Doctor's hands, but would as leave it be in yours.

''I actually cannot bring my mind to write what I wish, for I cannot place it one moment on a steady way of thinking, for I am become like a bottle in the smoke. Would Mr. G——— keep my things for me if I should send them there? Please ask him. Will you be willing to give me an interview at San Francisco? I would now venture to ask you to write your feelings towards me, for bad, for good; let me know it all. Shall I send you anything as a remembrance. I would wish to do it if acceptable.''

''DEAR RUTH: I feel grateful that you answered me; and as far as liquor is concerned I mean, with God's help, never again to touch it; and I hope my resolution is firm, and that the Almighty will sustain me in it. I firmly believe what you say regarding those Champoeg friends, but I firmly purpose that a dollar of my money will never go that way again. Newell, if he told Mr. G——— what you say, must be an infamous man, and I am sorry that Mr. G——— was prevented from asking my advice by such a slander. I believe there were some persons about the house last night, which caused me to get very little sleep. The things must be taken from here and deposited in safety. I wish things were so fixed that I could at once go about settling my business. I wish you would come up immediately and fix all the things and take them in your charge to the Butte. You can return again immediately after doing so. I likewise wish to see you to tell you of a message that was sent me yesterday, which I think not prudent to mention in writing. If you come I assure you I will not offer to detain you a moment longer than you wish. Yours, &c.

W. J. BINNEY.''

Ruth returned and tried again, Dr. B. introducing her when she reached home as his *fifth* wife, in view of the many times she had separated from and returned to him. Ruth added, ''not your fifth but your one hundredth wife.'' Peace and honeymoon again for a few days, when, after forgetting the pain of her absence, he one day, in a fury about something, called her a d—d w—e! This was the first outspoken accusation of the kind she had ever heard from him. Many times he had tried to insinuate that he had suspicions of that nature, and many, many times had cursed her in language which none but Satan could frame, and with every base epithet found between A. and Z. of the Satan's vocabulary, but never applied this dreadful word to her. Ruth waited till his anger had subsided, and asked his reasons for the accusation. He told her he had none, and wished her to forgive him—that he was in a passion, and she should not mind what he said when he was mad, &c., and to satisfy her still further, wrote the following acknowledgement to her:

"DEAR RUTH: The doubts I expressed of your chastity towards me are *altogether unfounded.*

W. J. BINNEY.

To Mrs. Binney.—April 5, 1850.''

Dr. Binney made no further objections to Ruth's keeping the money she had taken, and for a time made active preparations to go home to the States. To ascertain what were Ruth's views on the subject of going again to the United States, we will refer to a letter written to her mother about this time. She says—

"I perceive my husband remembers you with gratitude, and I wish most certainly he could be prevailed on to go and live in the vicinity of his and my relatives, and try to enjoy a little of life ere life is all gone. His practice at present is profitable, and yields ready pay; hence he says when I have a little more and a little more, then I will go and live among my friends. Let me, he says, but get enough to buy a neat cottage and to furnish it, a carriage, a horse, and have some money to live on, then I'll leave Oregon.

At other times he is so impatient to be away he can hardly wait to close his business. His health is, I think, less good than formerly, and my own is poor; indeed, I am a constant sufferer; and but for some unseen power that upholds me I know not from whence comes the powers of endurance. I would I could be employed more to my wish, but as it is I can only hope, and wait, and trust, which, in itself, yields rich delight and renders delay supportable. Of this, however, I am assured; if Dr. Binney does not soon decide to leave this country, I shall leave without him, for this reason; my life is utterly wasting. I am by no means engaged as I expected to be when I came to Oregon. I cannot live my time over again and hence what I would do must be done quickly or not at all. And can I waste all my time on trifles for trifles sake; or shall I rather—from respect to the recompense of reward—burst all these shackles and do what I have to do ere time with me is no more? I wait to be instructed and led by the unerring

spirit of Truth ere I take any decisive steps. Only of this one thing I
am certain; that little more of my time is to be suffered to go as much,
too much has already gone without my making an effort, a
determined effort to be what I wish to be. Live longer, my dear
mother, if Providence will permit; I do most earnestly hope I may be
permitted to see you again and administer, in some way, consolation
to your last moments.''

Dr. Binney's mind being ever vacillating between temptation and seduc-
tive influences on one hand, and a secret prompting to break away from all
and be good, respected and happy, he was very tardy in closing his business;
and Ruth, would he have reformed, would have been content to have lived in
Oregon with him; and she tried another plan which was to have him live at a
further distance from Champoeg, hoping thus the inducements to lead him
astray would be lessened.

With this object in view she encouraged him to hire a house on the
French prairie, about ten to twelve miles from Champoeg, and move to it. He
did so, but it was of little use. He could easily ride to his favorite haunts, and,
moreover, similar houses to J. Hord's were found in every direction.

In a few weeks they returned home again, and here his abuse of his wife
became so intolerable, and his conduct so entirely beyond what it is proper for
any one to bear, that Ruth came to the resolution that she would leave him,
and if she could not get home to her friends, she could at least, she thought,
maintain herself by her own industry.

Having thus determined, she prepared the following note for her husband,
and went away to the Butte:[4]

   ''DR. BINNEY: The last moment of my time is expended which I
can give to you till I do something to increase my own happiness and
renew my strength.

   ''The sufferings which I have endured, for the last nine months
particularly, in body and mind, are evidently undermining my health
and rendering my mind totally unfit for cares which must necessarily
be upon it.

   ''I can do no more for you—I can bear no more from you, and
suffer all the deprivations which have been my lot ever since I became
your wife.

   ''Since my return from the Butte I have tried every possible way
to please, serve, and live in peace with you, but all in vain. You have
broken every promise you made to induce me to return—have every
day for a month poured every kind of abuse upon me at every
interview—have refused to do anything for your own or my

good—and have bade me leave the place to yourself, for I was, you have said, hanging about it with the intention of robbing it and filching your property—all of which I cannot bear in addition to what I have already borne and suffered from you. I therefore utterly refuse to live any longer alone with you in Oregon.

"I will never again recommend you go to the United States or elsewhere to gratify me, or for your own benefit, for every time I have done so you have poured abuses and curses on me, and sworn I was trying in every possible way to urge you to ruin. I therefore leave you to yourself to act as you shall choose, and the consequences, if evil, must rest only upon your own head.

"You said some time since you were sensible of the evil which intemperance was doing you, and were resolved to drink no more, but have again returned steadily to the practice, which has blasted the last ray of hope I indulged of your being yet prosperous and happy, or of myself living with any kind of harmony with you.

"'Tis all in vain for me to entirely destroy myself for your good, which yet will do you no good—for you will accept of no advice nor be benefited by any thing I can do for you.

"I therefore leave you, resolved to live with you, alone, no more till I shall be satisfied you are a reformed man.

"Besides the above I am aware that you are nearly every day —— —— Indian women. And, after all this, to bear the horrid abuses and curses of such a profligate man as yourself, and at the same time perform every drudgery for him, I am certain that neither man nor *God* requires it of me.

Your suffering wife."

At the Butte Ruth hired a room, taught school for her board, and did some sewing as she had opportunity.

Dr. Binney soon found himself wishing her good services about the place, and again endeavored to induce her to return. But this she would not consent to do. He then told her he was determined to leave Oregon as soon as possible, and wished her to permit him to board with her at the Butte, while he arranged matters to leave. She consented, and lent him every possible assistance in her power to get ready.

Two or three weeks went pleasantly by, during which time he had persuaded her to put the money in her possession into his chest with the balance, for he said they were now going home, and the money having been earned by them both he wished that both should enjoy the use of it, and it was more secure together, &c. Ruth, ever confiding when he seemed to be doing right, placed the money in his chest according to his request.

Presently some business took him to Oregon City, where he met some persons who were great friends to him while he had a heavy and well filled purse. They enticed him to drink and to the usual accompaniments, gambling, &c., and after a full indulgence and a heavy expense he returned to his wife. His conduct towards her was then entirely changed. The usual curses and accusations followed, and finally he privately ordered a Frenchman to come with his cart to the door, when he lashed and bound his chest containing the money, put it into the cart and went away, leaving his wife without one dime to help herself.

One would think that this had been sufficient to have blasted the last glimmerings of interest which Ruth Rover could have felt for her husband, but she forgave again—knowing that he was in an error and believing that he could yet be saved.

Dr. Binney attempted to leave the country alone, taking his property with him, but he learned that there were persons who were watching him and intending to prevent him from going till he had provided for his wife's maintenance.

Dr. Binney at this time had in cash about sixteen thousand dollars, including the five thousand dollars he had of his wife's. Those persons who were knowing to the hard services she had performed for her husband, both on the farm and for sick persons, of whom there had been many boarding at his house, were outraged at this act of his, and affirmed, some that she should have no less than one-half of the money then in his hands, others that two-thirds was fully her due—for, they said, they had known Dr. Binney for years, and that he had nothing when he married and never would have had anything but for his wife, and that if she left him he soon would be a poor man again; and some who made these remarks were his most intimate friends. Nevertheless, he kept the money and soon again proposed to Ruth to accompany him home to the States.

The farm as yet was not sold, and, according to the law of the land, Ruth had an undoubted right to one-half of this, viz: three hundred and twenty acres.[5] She wished Dr. Binney to leave it in some person's care till it could be sold at a proper price. He was opposed to this, and affirmed he would sell it if he got but ten cents for it. It was advertised and sold at auction for twelve hundred and seventy-five dollars, although Dr. Binney had been offered three thousand for it but a few months previously. There being but one person to bid besides the one he had employed as an out-bidder, Dr. Binney's recklessness was the cause of this loss.

Dr. Binney and his wife at last were in readiness to leave for home, and there we will accompany them.

CHAPTER XXI

We must omit nearly every particular of this voyage, but will, by way of change, give a hoosier's first view of California—an old man who, with his wife and daughter, was travelling to the mines, and were passengers with Ruth and her husband from Oregon.

All the passengers were gone but the old man with a family. Being well in liquor he concluded to visit the shore and pass the night with a friend.

Next morning returning to the boat he related to his wife what he had seen and heard the evening before in the far-famed city of San Francisco—famed for its wealth and vices. Said he:

"I declare, it beats everything I ever heard of or saw. There was one place I went into where there was a woman sitting at a table—and a well-dressed thing she was, too! (Don't be jealous, old woman.) Well, by gosh! if she wasn't sitting there with more money before her, I believe, than our two mules could haul! I declare, I never saw so much in my life!

"Well, she was sitting there, and the room full of men; and there was a kind of a thing with a ball which went round—O, I can't tell you how. I declare, 'twould take me all day to tell all about it. Some men would bet two or three hundred dollars on the way that are ball went! By gosh! I wanted to overhaul them—them are fellers. I never saw the like in my life!

"And besides this," said he, "I came plaguey nigh getting into a scrape, too, myself. There was that are *Long* there, and I'll be hanged if they didn't get every cent from him that he had, and I broke on them thar—well I did. I told them 'twould never do to cheat a man that way where I was. Yes! I told them that I was a *dimocrat,* and I would have none of them are tricks there! By gosh! I believe I was pretty near a scrape, and should have had one if they hadn't pulled me away!

"Come, old woman, I've got a notion to send you on in the launch to Benicia,[1] and I'll stay here to-day: 'tis a going to be a terrible great day!* and I want to see it. What say you, will I stay?"

At this the old sharer of his fortunes said:

"No! no! 'tis all nonsense for you to stop."

But he would not believe it, and told her:

"I think I must stay to-day; 'twill be but one day—and oh! I forgot to tell you; if I didn't see some of the prettiest women there, then 'tis no matter. Dressed!—I never saw women dressed so fine! I'll be hanged if 'twouldn't take something to keep one of them! Oh, I must stay to-day—I must, old woman. Daughter, what do you think of it?"

The daughter thought 'twas best for him to proceed to Benicia, and the old woman declared.

"If you go to that are place to-day, I'll follow you every step of the way!"

At which the old man jumped up and called for water to shave, for he was going on shore to see the pretty women. He soon, however, was in the launch, and went off singing about democrats and whigs.

Dr. Binney and his wife, after a few days very uncomfortably spent at San Francisco, from the frequent occurrence of accidents and disasters, were well pleased when they were able to go on board their vessel, the California packet, Capt. Hunt, of New York. Ruth says—

"Soon at the vessel and introduced to the captain, quite a young man, of gentlemanly deportment, who showed me my room which was made very comfortable with new mattresses, new blankets, and white Marsailles quilts, and the luxury of an arm chair. The steward—the second person whom I saw on board—was a mulatto, tall, graceful, with a highly intellectual head; dressed in black pants and white, yes, *white* shirt, and a red silk sash around his waist—not a *new* one just for that occasion—but one that had been worn and well used. I felt immediate respect for him, and have never had occasion to feel otherwise. Nothing can exceed the politeness and kindness with which he treats the captain and passengers, his excellent cooking, or the order and quiet with which he performs his task. For several days I have been quite ill with dysentery, and this kind steward will often force my mind to revert to the time when I tried so hard in '37 to induce the steward of the Peru to forsake the ways of sin and follow those of righteousness, and to the promise that if we cast our bread upon the waters we shall find it after many days; and if this be

---

*The *jubilee* in consequence of the admission of California as a State into the Union.

its fulfillment in my case 'tis *many* days indeed, but the *bread* of kindness needed and acceptable.''

The tediousness of a sea voyage is often rendered less irksome by a sight of the varieties of fish and birds inhabiting the waters and floating in the sky above. The contemplation of these is very interesting and profitable. As our travellers approached Panama, being, however, nine hundred miles from land, they were surprised at the appearance of a butterfly on board. How it had lived to be carried thus far at sea, is very surprising. Of it Ruth says—

> ''Poor weary wanderer o'er the trackless deep,
> Your fragile form is far too light for sporting
> With ocean winds; see where they've brought you now to sleep,
> While you in vain have been their mercy courting.
>
> ''Perchance you now remember well the dear
> And rich delights you left within your bowers;
> You tasted, fed and filled yourself with dainty cheer
> Which none can know that live not 'mong the flowers.
>
> Go quickly back to Panama's broad bay,
> And tell each living, winged thing I'm coming;
> Prepare! your perfumed courts to feast me there some day,
> And sing your songs to me when there I'm roaming.
>
> Go quick! go quick! away from angry storms
> And hands which long to have you in their power;
> Go quick! they're watching now on air your lightsome forms;
> Your lives at best are but a summer's hour.
>
> This is the luck of all who trust their strength
> In sailing down life's dangerous current;
> They're overmatched, and find it hard at length
> To turn about and face the whelming torrents.''

In the packet in which Dr. Binney and his wife went to Panama there were about eighteen gentlemen in the upper cabin, and probably one hundred in the second cabin below. Their pastime during a voyage of eight weeks had been mostly gambling and games of chance. At length they took to discussion, and Ruth being obliged to hear all that was said, for there was no retreat, says of their debates:

''There is a great disposition among the passengers to contend and dispute, while almost every subject within creation's bound has been agitated, but with little good, however, other than to betray the weakness of the agitator. I was indignant yesterday to hear 'the weakness of woman's intellect' named as a subject for discussion. Nothing was proved, of course, by our lords, but that woman is dependent on man, and, as one said, that 'she can make herself happy by pleasing him.' But I had my own thoughts, which were: Should she be educated to the same extent as men, and have the same call for the exercise of her talents I am persuaded this stigma of her weakness would be removed. Instances have been known when she has been found capable of the same intellectual training as man, and she has thus shone with equal splendor—except that her light has resembled the modest light of the moon, while *his,* who can go out upon creation's face unabashed, has resembled the more dazzling rays of the sun. And instances have occurred (the Lord forbid they should be many) when woman has conducted public business—has met the bluffs of and the rebuts of the world—been familiar with scenes of vice—and has, in all, proven that her mind is not *weak,* but as capable of endurance and perseverance, and I believe *more* capable of passing the ordeal and maintaining its own strength and purity, than man's.

"I often ponder on the probable results if women instead of men had gone to the mines of California, with characters for morality and religion as good as men have borne. Would the result have been as great a sinking into vice as it has been with men? I am constrained to reply to myself that in nearly every instance they would have returned unscathed, and exalted and strengthened in virtue.

"I long my sex should be emancipated from the thralldom of erroneous public opinion—her worth appear in its true light—her injuries be redressed, and herself occupy that position in society which she is capable of adorning. I wish not to see her a mere bauble—a doll—to dress fine and lay by in a drawer—suitable to be seen and used only as a pastime—but disrobed of the imputation of weakness and unchastity, and adorned with the confidence and estimation of the opposite sex, which she deserves.

"Were all these passengers women instead of men, would they pass day and night in dissipation and contention? Verily, I believe not. Work and books would at least engage their attention."

"Last Sabbath a young gentleman brought me to read the 'Christian Keepsake for 1849,' and as I studied the illustrations my spirit melted within me. My heart had been ready to burst with sorrow for nearly the whole voyage, and in contemplating the representations of Faith and Hope it found language to vent itself.

"I was also affected by the kindness of the young man who was willing to impart of the good he himself possessed for the pleasure of another.

"And I have been often taken by surprise, during the voyage, when I have thoughtlessly expressed a wish, by the captain immediately gratifying me if it was in his power to do so. I have been so long accustomed to have my wishes disregarded, that I would not have spoken if I had supposed he would trouble himself to gratify me.

"'Tis now the twenty-fifth of December, and our passage seems a tedious one. Light winds, squalls, head winds, and calms constantly assail us; and our good sailors, I should think, can but seldom have on dry clothing. I observed yesterday the man at the wheel standing in a rain for two hours, looked entirely chilled, while his hands and face appeared, as we say, par-boiled. He was bare footed, and from every part of his clothing the water was dripping. But this is but a small part of their labors: the worse the weather, the greater their trials and exposures.

"Our kind captain, who moves about the ship respected by every one, giving his orders calmly, without cursing or noise, referred feelingly to his home to-day. He said it being Christmas Eve he knew exactly what his wife and children were doing. I wonder that any sea captain will go to sea without his wife, and that any woman will suffer her husband to go to sea without her—for where there is mutual love existing, as there must be in this case, what a great satisfaction it must be to each party to be with the other, and be saved the suspense and uncertainty connected with absences prolonged sometimes to years.

"Have suffered from chronic dysentery for the whole voyage; find my strength rapidly failing, and can stand but a few moments without fainting fits attacking me. Death is not appalling, and the "River" once passed, I contemplate with delight the employments of eternity. Free from suffering, and enraptured in adoration of God, the future life is very desirable, and I can never tell how much I wish my work here was *finished* and I entered upon it.

"Dolphin every day by some of the passengers. The captain always requests a piece for me, even when it all belongs to the men below. A brother's kindness could not exceed this!''

After a tedious passage the California at last anchored at Taboga, an island in the bay of Panama. This place we would like to describe, but have not space.

During this passage Ruth had been very ill, yet had received not much attention or kindness from her husband. The passengers were mostly *gentlemen,* and were very kind and pleasant to her, and no one could exceed Captain Hunt in his considerations of her disagreeable situation, or the steward in rendering her every possible service and attention.

Arrived at Taboga they were obliged to cross the bay in a small boat, rowed by the men, in which Ruth was for about eight hours exposed to the intense heat of the sun; and found herself, when at Panama, in addition to her former illness, suffering from a high fever.

Captain Hunt had kindly engaged for Dr. Binney and his wife rooms at the American Hotel, where she was glad to rest after such exposure and weariness, but dreadful were the sufferings of the night she passed there. Dr. Binney was soon intoxicated and paid his wife no attention at all. One of the passengers sent into her room, when she arrived, a glass of lemonade, which was the first refreshment she had taken for the day. The hotel was dreadfully filthy; emmets were running about the beds, and mice over the floors; the house was thronged with men indulging in every dissipation; no air could be let into the room because of the people about before the door and window. There was no respectable female in the house, and no one to render her a service only as she could call a servant.

Late in the evening Dr. Binney was assisted to his room in a state of perfect inebriation, and Ruth had to pass the night in watchfulness and suffering alone, hearing what she could not avoid hearing in all the rooms above and around her.

The passengers of the Packet had, all but five, gone to the other side of the Isthmus. These were to leave next day, and they were all the persons in the place with whom Dr. Binney and his wife were acquainted, and with whom she thought it would be prudent to trust themselves and their money in passing so dangerous a place. Seeing the course her husband was going to take in the dissipated town of Panama, Ruth wished much to prevail on him to accompany those five gentlemen that day to Cruces, and in the morning, long before light, she rose while he was yet sleeping, and prepared every article for leaving, that there might be no delay nor excuse, for the reason they were not ready.

But he refused to go, and 'twas in vain she urged that they might not have an opportunity of travelling with friends for a great time to come—or of the expense of remaining there—or of her ill health, which made her wish to reach home and be with her friends—he only became enraged and rewarded her with curses. She then tried to convince him that she would go without him, and the mate of the Packet having called at the door to enquire if they were going in their company, she asked him to bring horses for them, for she thought she could prevail on Dr. Binney to go, and if not, she would go without him.

But this was of no use; he forbid the man to bring animals there, and cursed his wife before them all; calling her vile names, and swearing she had made an agreement with one of the men to murder him on the route, and rob him, and marry the man when she reached home.

Ruth had to submit, but she resolved she would stay no longer in the hotel, after being so much abused by her husband before the boarders; and in consequence of finding herself suffering for want of better accommodations, and thinking there must be American or English families in the suburbs, if not in the city, resolved to walk out and endeavor to find them.

She could scarcely travel from illness. Nevertheless, she found trees, and shade, and air, and for some time rested herself outside the walls. Walking on as she was able, enquiring for Americana, she found none, but at last met a young man who said he was from Philadelphia, who told her there was no English or American families in the place, only some traders—and perceiving she was very ill recommended her to go into an American's store and rest, and he would endeavor to find a room for her where she could receive attention.

The store-keeper recommended her to a new house where resided a Frenchman and his wife, and to this she went and was soon comfortably reposing in a pleasant, airy chamber. She applied to an American physician who informed her she had the prevailing fever, and had better go to the house of his partner where she could have an English nurse and every attention required.

Dr. Binney, immediately on her leaving the hotel, had her clothing sent across the bay to the Packet, and himself engaged a passage in her to go to Valparaiso. Captain Hunt informing the American Consul of her situation in thus being left destitute and sick, it was insisted that Dr. Binney should provide for her wants before leaving the harbor. He would not resign to her the five thousand dollars and half the price of the land claim, which she thought was strictly her own, but consented to let her have two thousand dollars on her arrival at New York, and which he told her he would never try to get from her.

Ruth's illness increasing rather than decreasing, her physician informed her that to save her life she must, if possible, endeavor to reach a colder climate. Dr. Binney had ere this again regained the proper state of his mind, and was also anxious to go home.

In Ruth's description of Panama, Gorgona, Cruces, and intervening places, appears some interesting information which we wo'd like to quote but cannot do so here.

Her physician had recommended, in consequence of the great prostration of her strength, that she be carried over the Isthmus in a hammock, by natives; but she feared the unpleasantness of being put upon the ground every time they wished to rest, and was also aware that such a plan would cause great fatigue to those employed, she therefore determined to try to ride upon a mule, as no carriages could be obtained and horses were not considered as safe as mules.[2]

She found great difficulty in maintaining her seat upon the saddle, fancying each time she nearly fell on either side, through weakness, that the girth was loose, and had it tightened till the poor animal could scarcely walk.

Of the road she says:

"The sun was high enough to cause considerable heat, which was modified by the shrubbery on either side, and by our frequently descending into low passes between the mountains where was generally a stream of water.

"Sometimes we came to a few acres of plain land where would be seen large herds of cattle grazing.

"The road was of every possible variety which can be imagined; up hill and down hill—rough and smooth—through gulches and over precipices—through water and over parched earth—broad and narrow—level and uneven—around and across—shady and exposed to the scorching sun—slippery and firm—lonesome and congregated— beautiful and frightful—tame and wild—rocky and clayey—wooded and barren—crooked and straight—colored and colorless—flowered and unadorned—through and over—under and above—by and with alternately every possible hue depicted on the verdure and soil. Frequently we came to passes just wide enough for a mule and his pack to get along, with the banks some feet above them, and in these there could be no turning, hence, as some persons might enter at the other end, which was generally some rods off, the guide would halloa when he came to them, and if there came no answer he would enter and keep up the same noise till he was out again.

"The road was very much worn as could be seen, particularly on ascending and descending a hill, in the deep steps which had been made by the feet of the animals, and from which they would slide to the next in descending and leap to the one in advance in ascending, and which movement many times nearly placed me under their feet in front, or at their heels after them. In either case I should have rolled into a stream below.

"Mules are the best for travelling these dreadful places—indeed, I believe no *horse could* travel this road without accident—but the former are so accustomed to it that they seem to know every step they should take, and the exact course which is best, and 'tis in vain you may try to rein him where you fancy he will do better: you may pull the bridle as though you would raise an oak—his head is unmoveable, and you find him just as "obstinate as a mule." He will go where he pleases, and you can't prevent him.

"Many a hard word did the one in advance of me receive for this same reason, but at the last the rider acknowledged he was an excellent beast and had taken him through safely, which was beyond his expectations."

'Tis unnecessary and unpleasant to relate, particularly, the course pursued by Dr. Binney during this visit to the States. Some particulars must be shown in the petition afterwards presented by Ruth to the court praying for a bill of divorce, and we will only hastily refer to his general course.

Mrs. Binney could not have lived probably two days longer at sea when she reached New York, yet she found the severe cold of the season, it being the month of February, immediately effective in restoring her to health.

She tarried with her husband's friends till she was able to travel, and then proceeded to Massachusetts. Her husband accompanied her, but returned again to New York next day, being anxious, as he said, to go to the mint in Philadelphia to get his gold dust coined, and had promised to meet her again in Massachusetts, in three weeks.

Seven weeks passed, and she had not heard from him. She feeling very uncomfortable at his long absence and silence, in view of the astonishment of her friends. At length he wrote her, giving as the reason of his silence that he had been ill of *influenza,* and was intending to visit her in a few days; adding that he entertained for her the same affection as ever. This relieved Ruth's mind considerably, but two weeks more elapsed without seeing him, and she supposing him again ill, went to New York and found him not ill but robust and hearty, and apparently enjoying himself fully. She perceived by his appearance and the remarks of his friends that he was pursuing a round of dissipation and pleasure not at all calculated to encourage him in a moral and upright course, or to destroy that tendency to evil which had beset him through life, and so many times occasioned to him great suffering if not actual danger.

Hitherto Ruth had indulged confidence in his friends, that they would try to exert an influence over him which would have a tendency different from this, but she now perceived that New York was not the place to reform him, nor his friends the persons to encourage it.

A son and brother who was *rich* and able to pay all expenses to balls, theatres, parties of pleasure, &c., was too great a desideratum for the extravagant and far-fetched gaiety of the Binney's, and what did *they* care about his wife or her rights, so long as *they* were benefited by this godsend of money.

Dr. Binney was exactly suited with the encouragement given by them, and as it would take some time to run through sixteen thousand dollars, he felt no fears for the future, and was bent only on the full enjoyment of the present.

Besides this evil influence on the part of his mother and sisters, he was constantly enticed into vice and extravagance by a younger brother, then about twenty-eight years of age. He had been born since his father's failure and death, and being the pet he was a great favorite in the family.

The sisters, seven in number, had, after they became reduced, given their attention to dress making, and by this means had raised and educated Thomas, which should certainly redound much to their praise. By his education he was qualified to act as clerk, but he had never, in consequence of his disposition for gaiety, been able to be otherwise than dependent on them for assistance in obtaining a livelihood, and it was a most lucky occurrence that a brother of such generous disposition, and love for the tinsel of life had come among them with such abundant means to ''show out.''

Dr. Binney related to him the troubles he had passed with his wife, and found the readiest sympathy, which operated like a charm in unloosing his pursestrings for every want of such a considerate and feeling brother.

Dr. Binney was for a time enraptured with the winning society of ''Tom,'' and all the warnings Ruth could suggest were not sufficient to open his eyes to the real intents of the family towards him.

He however consented to accompany Ruth home, where he for some time visited among her friends, but at last said he did not like to be living on others, and wished to go again to New York.

She then, the better to please him, and always fearing he would become dissatisfied and return to Oregon, hired rooms and commenced housekeeping till he should have determined on some place to settle which would please him. But this was not effectual—he was away again to New York. Shortly after he offended his mother by leading Thomas, as she said, into intoxication, and he came to Ruth again in Massachusetts.

When Ruth, to entice him still more to remain in the States, engaged the half of her mother's house, including the garden and orchard, at her own expense, and commenced house keeping there; but this did not suit him. He would not, he said, be dependent on any of her friends, while he had money enough to keep himself. She then took rooms entirely *away* among strangers, in Salem, Mass., where he for a few days remained with her, she bearing every expense for their living, except that occasionally he would purchase some trifling article, such as a lobster, to regale his own appetite.

He had many times said to her that he meant to have the two thousand dollars back again, which he had given her at Panama; and which he told her his mother and sisters had said was a most unheard of occurrence for a woman to be permitted to hold that amount of money independantly of her husband.

As he could not obtain it of her, he seemed resolved that he would obtain all he could of it in a way of making her bear her own expenses, and his too if possible. But Ruth did not regard the money;—her husband had a deeper hold upon her affections than mines of gold could have had, and she was intent only on saving him. From there Dr. Binney went to the mint for his coin, and returned with it to Salem.

The gold dust he took home amounted when coined to nearly nine thousand dollars—and this he had with him. He had selected the largest pieces, when in New York, and distributed them in the shape of rings, buttons and keepsakes to every member of his family—and Ruth, who had contributed so largely towards obtaining it, and preserving it, was not remembered in this distribution—she received not the smallest particle from her husband by way of reward, nor as a remembrance, and had not a specimen only the four particles picked from the table in Oregon, to show to her friends in Massachusetts, who had never seen "gold dust."

Small acts generally speak a plainer language than great deeds; and Ruth understood this act of her husband to be an evidence either that he was totally ungrateful for all the services she rendered him; or that he was entirely overruled by his friends. Both these ideas were supported by circumstances—for he must have been *ungrateful* to have cast her so many times out upon the world without the means to help herself; and many occurrences had convinced her that his friends preferred that all the funds should be in *his* hands, rather than that she should be possessed of any of them.

Dr. Binney in two days after his return from the mint, found it very desirable to get angry enough, though without any known cause, to take his money and go to New York. He took up his abode in a hotel in the first place, being too angry with his mother to go to her house; but she learned through "Tom" that he was in the city with his money, and all feuds were at once forgiven, and he was urged to return to them. He told them that the reason of his returning to the city was trouble again with his wife, and he intended to leave her, and return at once to Oregon. He was pitied, and condoled, and encouraged in the plan he had suggested, and moreover informed that as she had two thousand dollars which she would not give up—it was enough to support her—and if she should happen to come short she could work like themselves, and 'twould hurt her worse—and besides this, if he would take "Tom" with him, he could assist him, and be company for him, and they two could do a handsome business of some kind, especially if the "watchful and saving Ruth" were not along. This plan seemed advisable to Dr. Binney, who acquiesced in it immediately; and thought as "Tom" was a good clerk he could tend store—and himself having at this time about eleven thousand dollars remaining, he could take out a quantity of goods which would sell well in Oregon, and in a few years they both would be rich, and then farewell to want or care! Meantime Ruth knew nothing of the whereabouts of her husband; but ventured to write to New York enquiring for him. She had become satisfied that he would go into no business in the States, and his money was being rapidly expended, and the influence of friends she had hoped would be *good* over him, she found was even worse than that to which he had been subjected in Oregon; and she now felt that she cared not where they might live, if he would only settle himself in a home of his own—be industrious, and suffer her to live with him in peace and happiness.

With these feelings she wrote him thus:

"DEAR HUSBAND,—In haste I would like to enquire whither you have flown? and if I may be informed if you are in the land of the living? or shall I suppose you have met with some accident and are among the missing? You may perhaps be pleased to learn that I have made up my mind to accompany you wherever you may wish to go out of the country, providing you will come here and wait a little for me, and providing *you go alone,* ———. Do at least write me and let me know where you are, for all are surprised at your absence, and I know not what to say. You had better live with your wife than any other way—'tis more respectable, and desirable for both. In haste, yours,

RUTH ROVER,"

Ruth soon received the following:

"MY DEAR WIFE,—I am still happy to hear from you, and I certainly feel pleased that you are now willing to accompany me wherever I wish to go. That place is Oregon—but as to your wish of me going alone, that is now out of the question, as I have entered into partnership with Thomas for five years, and have at this time a quantity of goods shipped and still purchasing, which will prevent me from going to Salem to see you, for the vessel sails in the course of ten or twelve days. Thomas is a pretty good business man, and I am in hopes we will do well. It is impossible to state to you clearly by letter our projects, prospects, &c., but if you should feel interested enough in our affairs to come to New York, of which I would feel happy, then we will be able to understand each other, as it is and always has been my wish to live and die with my wife. If you come you had better come quick as possible, in case you should want to get anything ready to ship, for you see the vessel sails in a few days. Give my respects to all, and believe me

Yours, affectionately,

W. J. BINNEY."

"P. S.—Please let me hear from you as soon as possible."

Having learned that Thomas Binney was very much given to intemperance, she felt great fears that her husband, in case of his returning to Oregon, would take him with him, and knowing that in this case they must bear every expense, and that he was very extravagant, and remembering what she had suffered in her domestic relations by having James Binney come into her family in Oregon, she felt a great aversion to his accompanying them.

Had Thomas Binney been a moral young man, and not liable to lead her husband astray, Ruth would have done anything in her power to assist him in rising in the world; but she had seen enough of his impertinence already to convince her that she could have no good influence over him. Hence her wish that her husband should "go alone."

She thus answered Doctor Binney's letter:

"MY DEAR HUSBAND: I have just with much pleasure received your letter, and though very happy to hear from you, regret exceedingly the precipitancy with which you have lately proceeded.

"I am satisfied you have acted unwisely from what I have known in times past, and from what I every day discover of people's disposition to commit error, and of the indications of Providence to deter us from what is wrong.

"What text do you think accidentally met my eye the day you left here? It was this:

" And these two kings shall set their heads together to do mischief; and they shall tell lies over one table; *but they shall not prosper.* '

"By which I then gained an intimation of what you have since done.

"And this morning when praying most earnestly for God to preserve you and keep you from every evil, I also accidentally met these texts in scripture:

"'And I will scatter him, and the wealth I have given him, to the four winds; and because he would not have Me to reign over him he shall wander destitute and forlorn, and famine and want shall be his portion.'

"You say 'Tom' is something of a business man. He may be. But what is his intention in encouraging you to do as you have done? It is this, and nothing else, viz: to build himself up at your expense! And what is the object of those who are backing him? *This.* To get your money in a road which will bring it to them! This is evident from eight years' observation. And where would your money go in case of your death in Oregon? You can readily perceive. And what is the prospect before me should I go with you? *This.* Slavery to an enemy, viz: Thomas Binney, and destitution should you die.

"You will readily remember that I, some years ago, discovered the disposition of your relatives towards me, and since my return this time that feeling has been fully carried out. Notice the concealing of the gold you gave them that I might not know its value. They knew they had no right to it without my knowledge, hence their caution.

"No, my husband, you know how arduously I have labored to help earn and save the property God has been pleased to bless us with since our marriage; and when you enter into schemes to expend that property on others and leave me you will never prosper or be happy. I can never approve of your partnership with Thomas, nor consent to his enriching himself at your and my expense.

"Remember this: If you thus do without my consent and approbation, you do wrong, and certain calamity will befall you! Think of Mr. Leslie's remark to us when he married us: *'Neither one can ever act, in matters of any importance, independently of, or in opposition to the wishes of the other, without incurring the risk of the anger of God!'*

"This is not trifling. 'Tis a fact that we are 'man and wife,' and what we have got of money has been gotten by both—neither one had much to start with—hence, what there is belongs to both and none other.

"Remember, also, what I suffered by receiving James into our house in Oregon, and I can never again trust to the chance of putting myself in the power of your relatives. They have injured me, and are still injuring me; and they would not care if I were a beggar in the streets if they had your money. *Why* this favor to you now? When you were poor in '43 they could send you from their house, but now how differently do they treat you? I cannot go to New York, but would like to see you here exceedingly. I have in view the purchase of a beautiful place near by with two pretty houses. One has been built *nine* years, the other *one*. The whole, with land well improved, has been offered me for three thousand dollars. I expect to get it for two thousand five hundred; fifteen hundred to be paid in cash; the rest to remain on interest till I can earn it, unless you will give it to me. I have made engagements for the printing and publication of my books; they will be out as soon as I can re-write them. I have bought a piano and am taking lessons; succeed very well. I have also bought a pair of canary birds, male and female, which will not sing a note till you come!

"You see by my engagements that I cannot be ready to go with you at the time you name, neither would such haste be best.

"*Do,* my husband, gratify me enough to come and see me immediately! I want your opinion of the place in view; 'tis very pleasant and cheap; three persons have already applied to rent one of the houses, but I cannot pay for it till I have your approval. *Dear*

Doctor, your interest lies nearer my heart than that of any other person's living; and while I now write, with tears dropping profusely, God is my witness that I desire your happiness more than my own life. *Do* take my advice ere it is too late; if not, preserve this letter and see if I am right in predicting for you greater wretchedness than you have ever yet known, and irreparable sorrow. I do not wish to scare you, but if you do not wish to believe me, try it, and may God sustain me when I remember that the man whom of all others has the best seat in my affections is lonely and unhappy in the extreme in consequence of the ill advice of his enemies, and cannot retrace his steps. I have wept till my head aches violently. Do let me at least see you once more, for if you go off in this manner I shall not long sustain the shock, nor do I wish to. Farewell.

RUTH."

Dr. Binney having informed her that it was impossible for him to leave then to visit her, she went to New York, and found active preparations making for him and his brother Thomas to go to Oregon.

The contract made by the brothers was that W. J. Binney should find the capital for a quantity of goods they were to take to Oregon—should pay T. Binney's passage and expenses—advance some money for his outfit and to pay some debts and was to receive his pay in services rendered by T. Binney in selling this merchandise. Long before they sailed he became satisfied that he had acted unwisely, and would gladly have retraced his steps sufficiently to have been released from his agreement with his brother, and at different times hinted proposals of this kind; but he was bound in writing and the agreement was too advantageous to Thomas to be broken; and the latter could only at these times curse Ruth for being, as he said, the cause of this dissatisfaction, and by every suggestion in his power endeavored to induce his brother to leave her in the States. This Dr. B. was not inclined to do; and the female members of the family desiring "Tom's" advancement more than anything else, endeavored to induce her to stay by telling her she was a fool for going back with him to Oregon, for they did not see how anybody could live with him; and they advised her to remain at home, as W. J. would be obliged to maintain her—having first said among themselves that she had enough money already for her support, and they should not encourage him to give her any more.

Ruth would have liked to have remained in the States would her husband have tarried with her, but being more anxious for him than for her own happiness and prosperity, concluded that she would be better satisfied with herself in the future if she were with him and sharing all his trials and knowing what they were, rather than to be living so remote from him, unacquainted with his wants and unable to relieve them, merely to obtain ease and comfort for herself, and resolved to go. And moreover the fact of Thomas Binney being with him—whom she knew to be of dissipated and reckless habits— excited her more fully to a sense of her duty to her husband, which she thought was nothing less than an entire devotion to him while life should last.

Our limited space will not permit us to copy but a few lines from the notes on this return voyage. We find Ruth saying of a passenger who figured largely afterwards at California: "Another passenger, a Doctor Lee, a young man of intemperate habits, going to California, will soon be used up by vices of that place." And again: "Another young man raised in New York (T. Binney) and entirely tainted with the opinion that no other place will bear any comparison with it. He has to speak, act, and try to behave just as New Yorkers do; while I often pity him for his limited knowledge of the world, and of society in general. He is heavily in debt, yet his fingers are loaded with gold rings, (the gold given by W. J. Binney,) and his wristbands shrink with the weight of gold buttons and pins. The truth is, to *appear* a gentleman he has had recourse to beggary and the credit of all who would trust him. If a word be spoken about a watering place within the limits of the United States, he at once makes it known that he has been there. *Irish* New Yorkers are undoubt- edly rightly called 'Shamrock.' But I am at the last line of the page, so good-bye Sham.

"Our New Yorker last Sabbath proposed a game of cards as a pastime; the Catholic priest said 'twould be no harm, as it was not God's day any how! The fear of the captain detained them.

"Our captain seems to be in fear of the steward, who does pretty much as he pleases with him. One day he had reserved no dessert for his master, and told him when he came to the table he was going to make a bridge of his nose. The captain quietly went without, although, when the second mate ate his dinner, he had some dessert for him. This morning the captain told him he ought to have had some fish for breakfast, as Mr. S. did not eat meat on Friday, who said 'There is a plenty *else* on the table, sir!'

"The captain says this steward was his smuggler in Spain—carrying his silver ashore in his market basket. No wonder he is now in the ascendancy.

"Two boys being set to scrape the deck in a very hot sun, one of them exclaimed: 'Is there nothing better to be got by going to sea, than this? 'tis worth while to sell the farm to go to sea for this!'

"The captain permits me to go to his library, and there I saw to-day several bibles given by the New York Bible Society, for seamen, safely stowed away where they will not be read or hurt. Better far they were in the forecastle, for then they would be prized, and read, and perhaps *stolen;* but if so, the Word might be to the thief like fire shut up in his bones, which at some time might burst forth and consume his sins. The bible could not be in a better place than in the chest, or hands, or hammock of a rascal!' 'Tis good seed, carry it where we may.

"Last evening the sailors shaved the lads in the ship who had not "crossed the line," and introduced them to Neptune as his sons.

"This was done by blackening one of the old sailors, putting an uncouth dress on him and setting him upon a barrel ready to receive his newly adopted children. The boys were then stripped to the waist one by one, their faces daubed with tar and scraped with an iron hoop, then a bucket of salt water was thrown over them, and they were brought to his Seaship and introduced as his sons. He of course received them very graciously.

"Accidentally passing the catholic priest when not expected, an oath was just slipping from his lips, although he is so careful to abstain from meats on certain days! *'Of what use are your fasts to Me? saith the Lord.*

"For some time have wondered at the petulance of my female canary bird. She has seemed unwilling her mate should come near her or sit on the same perch. I do not now wonder at her ill humor, for I perceive that when he wants a feather to bite for amusement *he pulls it from her back!*''

We trust we shall not be accused of too great partiality for our friend Ruth Rover, if we copy the following item found in her journal. When they had been nearly four months out she says:

"The steward surprised me this morning by saying to me in the presence of Dr. Binney: 'I have a nice little box, Mrs. Binney, that I mean to give to you before we go on shore. It was my poor wife's, and I mean to give it to you because I don't think any one can see you for any length of time and not like you! and the captain, too, says he never saw a pleasanter woman!'

"Indeed! thought I, this is quite a feather in my cap, for at sea, if anywhere, if there be evil in the heart it will show itself. I have made no extra efforts, and indeed have been sometimes *careless* of pleasing. I have merely taken things as they have come and made the best of them. And this is perhaps the reason, I know no other, why I am thus complimented by the steward."

Of the *social* pleasures Ruth enjoyed during this voyage we can give some idea from the following:

"Our New Yorker and the Connecticut pill-maker, (Dr. Lee,) are the most notorious blackguards I ever met! Their constant pastime is to make fun of others. At the table and elsewhere they mimic and make faces, and talk much in a deprecating tone of 'low origins,' low births, servants, &c.

"What a pity the young could not have the experience of after years, or would not take the advice of older persons—their middle age and old age would not then be the source of so much regret for wasted privilege and debasing influences.

"The Connecticut pill-maker is a very disagreeable person to one of my disposition. Whenever he can offend me he does it, and at table and elsewhere tries to insult me by mimicking my downcast look. This is done in company with the New York coxcomb, who encourages him and does the same himself.

"Poor wicked souls! did they but know it, I would gladly assist them to obtain that wisdom from above which would enlarge their hearts and so fill them with blessedness that they would not need to have recourse to such low-lived and scandalous employments for pleasure.

"I have accomplished considerable sewing during the voyage, but have been very lonely most of the time. I have not found a social kindred spirit during the passage! I have, however, enjoyed good and blessed seasons in religious devotions, for which I bless the God of Heaven.

"Writing, sewing and reading alternately engage my attention, while at the same time 'My mind to me a treasure is,' and affords me sweet repast by day and night. I have less of social enjoyment here than any other on board, for there is here no spirit congenial with my own with whom I may have fellowship."

Dr. Binney had found amusement suited to his taste, in company of Dr. Lee and his brother, and was seldom in his wife's company. During the severe weather off Cape Horn they were all three most of the time intoxicated, drinking, as they said, to keep off the cold. And getting together in Dr. Lee's room, would make merry by laughing and cursing the violent plunging and rolling of the vessel, and indulge in all other demoniacal ravings which none can understand who have not witnessed such outrages.

We have before us a letter written by Ruth to her husband at the latter part of the voyage, and which evidently had been excited by the treatment of her husband and brother-in-law during the voyage. We cannot make it public on account of the allusions to Dr. Binney's conduct in New York and elsewhere being made in such plain terms as would shock the reader. A paragraph or two will give some idea of its purport.

"And is it for this I am to live with you in slavery and degradation all my days? It is too common a thing to talk of the threats I have received to be murdered by you, and the constantly ignominious names I am called, but my character must be brought down to a level with yours as an excuse for your misconduct! I have labored like a slave to save money, and denied myself of every comfort to gain enough for you to live away from scenes of vice, and to pay the debts contracted by my leaving the Mission to marry you, and have seen it all squandered on ———. If strength is left me and God permits us ever to set foot on shore again, I mean to leave you if I die of hunger! You wisely kept your abuse restrained a little before we started but I am awake now, and all my past sufferings come freshly into my mind. * * * If I were breathing my last breath I could breathe it in prayers that you might meet the punishment which is your due. I believe you will if God is just, and I know that he is, and he has seen and known all the sufferings and exposures I have met from you.

"I can hardly close, so great is the indignation I feel toward you! To think, in addition to every other abuse I have suffered for twelve years, that a mean beggar of an upstart must be employed by my *husband* to proclaim to strangers that I am a w—e, and have received presents from *Kanakas* to that effect! Yes, a *husband* to employ such a one in such a business, to get his wife abhorred and despised that his own sins may not show out!''

'Tis said there is a time when forbearance ceases to be a virtue, and sometimes Ruth seemed to have come to it, but it was only to surrender again and suffer some more.

In the course of the voyage Ruth had thought that, for the sake of a little rest, she would remain in California for the winter, it being November when they arrived; and on making this proposal to Dr. Binney, and he having consulted his brother who was highly pleased with the project, Dr. B. engaged board for her at Rev. Mr. Wheeler's, and accompanied her to shore, taking a part of her clothing and promising to send her the rest and call again and bring her money to pay her expenses.[3] The time arrived for the departure of the steamer, and no more word has been received from him. Mr. W. advised her to ride with him to the wharf and ascertain the cause, when they found the boat about starting; and Dr. Binney being in liquor—and also his brother— told her he did not intend to give her any money nor to let her have her things, Mr. Wheeler advised her to take passage in the boat and go to Oregon with him, and himself made arrangements with the captain to that effect. Dr. Binney and his wife occupied separate rooms and did not appear to recognize each other. In two days the steamer put back for better coal, when, as Mrs. Binney was now going to Oregon, Dr. Binney was advised by "Tom" and the infamous Dr. Lee and b'hoy they had met in the person of Mr. Spencer, to tarry *himself* in California and let his wife go where she pleased. Meantime

Thos. Binney received charge of the goods, which were in a vessel bound to Columbia River, and was entrusted with three thousand dollars in cash, all that now remained of the sixteen thousand Dr. B. had when leaving Oregon. Mrs. B. tried to expostulate with her husband, but, being in liquor and urged by his brother, she could make no impression upon his mind, and he only told her he "did not know her; she was only his mistress anyhow, and what right had she to stop him!" He went on shore, and the steamer left again, and the winds and waves seemed combined to make it necessary that they should not throw a Jonah overboard, but return to San Francisco and get one left there.

In two days the engine had broken and they were obliged to turn about once more, and when arrived at the harbor Dr. Binney was almost the first on board and in his wife's state-room asking forgiveness, and permission to go with her to Oregon.

Dr. Lee had succeeded in borrowing a sum of money of Dr. Binney, having been "kicked out" of his hotel for not paying his board, and had gone off no one knew where; and Thomas, thinking his brother had gone to the mines, went on shore, and before he met Dr. Binney had expended forty dollars of the money entrusted to his care.

There now occurred a turn about: Dr. Binney became enraged at his brother, and on their arrival in Oregon was greatly inclined not to suffer him to have any dealings with the merchandise belonging to him, and well would it have been for him if he had not.

At Portland Ruth Rover was subjected to a very unpleasant occurrence, and as it very clearly reveals the suspicious character of her husband, we shall enter somewhat into details.

The second day at her boarding-house, having no employment, she asked a Miss Wood, who was sewing, if she should not assist her. Miss W. replied, "I would be very glad if you would; and if you please you may make these collars which I'm to have finished before Christmas." Ruth busied herself, and by evening had made two, and was working on the third; the two that were finished lying upon the table before her when her husband came in. He stopped before the table a moment, looking first at Ruth and then at the collars, and finally, taking them in his hands, he said:

"Who are these for—are they for me?"

"No," replied Ruth, "they are for *Miss Wood.*"

His scarlet face became crimson; his small deep eyes brightened and contracted at the corners, as if to say, *Now I've caught you!* He threw them upon the table, but said nothing, as there were three of the gentlemen boarders present, and went quickly to his room. Ruth, soon after, finding herself alone with the gentlemen, and having finished her work, went into the dining-room, and taking a book sat down by the fire.

Presently Dr. Binney entered, and giving her a tap on the shoulder, said: "Here! go into your room."

She rose, and as her only course then was to "obey," she walked on before him.

When they were inside the room, Dr. Binney locked the door and put the key into his pocket.

"Now sit down *there* and read," said he, "or else go to your bed."

"What is the matter with you?" asked Ruth.

"I'll let you know presently, d—n you," he answered.

Ruth read some time, while he sat and looked at her, his eyes sparkling and contracting, and his breathing becoming laborious, as if meditating something of importance.

The evening being very chilly, Ruth told him she wished to go out to the fire.

"No," said he, "you will not leave this room again to-night."

"Why, what ails you?"

"Don't speak to me, you d—n w—e of h-ll," said he.

Ruth saw it was useless, and retired to her bed. In the morning, when she thought he might be in a better temper, she asked him what the cause of his ill feelings towards her, when he, in great anger, replied—

"G-d d—n you, shut up, or by G-d I'll kill you!" at the same time raising a stick of wood from the hearth over her head in a threatening attitude.

Ruth retired to her room, grieved, but thinking time would bring an explanation. At evening, it being the Sabbath, the lady of the boarding house invited them to go to church. Dr. Binney objected to going, as he said he had business in town to attend to. He went out and soon returned, when Ruth asked him again, but he said he was going to bed. He went to his room and got into bed with his clothes on. Ruth asked him again if he would not go, as it would be a pleasure to her, having been so long at sea; but he refused, when Mrs. M. said—

"Perhaps he'll be willing you should go without him. Mr. C. is going with me, and I would like your company too."

Ruth asked if she should go without him, and he told her to "Go, go, if you want to."

When at the church and waiting for the conclusion of prayer, Dr. Binney entered in haste, and passing by Ruth, who tried to stop him, he hurried on to the body of the church. Returning, he kept some distance behind her but did not speak.

Retiring to her room, Dr. B. locked her in as before, and she having retired he sat by the candle and was for some time very busy in examining her papers, journals, &c., laying by themselves such as he pleased, and finally commenced to burn them, lighting them by the candle.

This Ruth could not consent to, and catching the papers from his hand she blew out the light. Dr. Binney immediately commenced making some movement about the head of the bed, which Ruth thought might be an effort to obtain his pistols. She arose, and having an opportunity she endeavored to ascertain if he had taken them, and in so doing her hand came upon his gold watch lying between them and in danger of being injured by them, or of falling upon the floor. She took it, and put it by with her papers.

Dr. Binney soon after went quietly to rest, and the night being past he arose early and while dressing, with many reproaches and curses, told his wife he was going to leave her that day—that he was glad the steamer was not gone—that he thanked God he was now satisfied of the fact he had long suspected—and that she might look to him no more for assistance or a living, for he was fully determined to abandon her to those she loved better than himself, &c., &c. All of which Ruth did not understand and she could get no explanation from him. But it being similar conduct to what she had many times witnessed, it did not give her particular uneasiness, only that she feared that the steamer of which he spoke might be about departing and that through his precipitancy he might take some rash step which could not be easily remedied.

He went out saying she would never see his face again—taking no clothing, but saying he should send for them—and did not, apparently, think of his watch.

Ruth concluded that, whether he went away or not, it was a better and cheaper way to hire rooms and keep house than to pay a high price for board, and as Dr. Binney had, in the first place, tried to obtain a small house, she now, having heard of one to rent, engaged it at her own expense, and prepared to move into it.

Dr. Binney's trunks she did not like to leave in the boarding house, and he having much linen to be washed, after the voyage, she prepared them to take with her, desiring Mrs. M———, if he should return, to tell him that she had taken his trunks for the purpose of washing his linen, and he could have them by coming to her house, it being but a few steps distance.

The draymen had them on his cart with hers and was leaving the house when Dr. Binney returned and ordered them to be taken into the house.

Ruth desired the man to take *her* trunks to her house, but Dr. Binney ordered him to return them all to the house where he took them from. Ruth saw no alternative but to go without them. She had thought to remain at the boarding house but her husband told her to go away, as she had started to do, and not attempt to stop at a house where he was.

She bought a baker's loaf for her subsistence through the day, and at night slept upon the floor before the fire, with two dirty saddle blankets she had found in the house for her bedding.

Early in the morning she went to Dr. Binney's room, he being yet in bed, and commenced folding a dress she had left hanging on the wall, when he jumped up and told her: "No! d—n your soul! you don't get a d—n thing here! Go out of this!—d—n you, be off!" and pushed her out of the room.

She returned again and attempted to take her things, saying that all she wanted was her clothing.

He refused, and they contended, and finally he seized her firmly by the throat and attempted to put her altogether from the house. Coming near the front door, she cleared herself from him, and seeing her advantage, she sprang back into her bed room, and in her turn turned the key on her husband.

He immediately sending for "Tom," commenced storming at the door, threatening to burst it and take her life if she did not open it, and when he once got hold of her again she should not leave his hands alive!

Ruth feared his violence if he should succeed in forcing the door, and seeing the money on the bed, all that he had, she took it in her hand, and making her escape by the window, entered the kitchen door.

"Tom" had arrived, and Dr. Binney had told him to go and stand by the window of her room, for what purpose we do not know, lest she should escape that way. He, however, did not attempt to stop her, but gave information to his brother of her having gone into the other part of the house, where she was followed immediately.

Dr. Binney approaching her she told him to put his hands upon her if he dared. There being several persons present in the dining room, Ruth went into it, thereby to feel the more secure.

He replied to her calmly he was not going to harm her, he only wanted the *money* she had got.

Many altercations ensued, Ruth giving as the reasons of her conduct, that she had only attempted to take her clothing, which she could not do without as she had no money to buy more—that he refused to let her have it—that there being now but a little more than two thousand dollars remaining of all they had taken home—that she had a right to some of it—that he was permitting Thomas Binney to expend, in every luxury and dissipation, the money which belonged to them—and that she could not get her clothes, she thought she had a right to some, especially as the goods he had brought from New York he had put out of his hands at San Francisco to prevent her from obtaining anything in case she should sue him for her support.

He then told her he wanted his *money,* and if she did not give it to him he would tear her clothes off her there, in presence of them all, and take it.

She having put it all into her pocket, she told him if he put his hands on her for that purpose she would hurt him if she could.

"But you can't do that, you've nothing to defend yourself with," said he, tauntingly, approaching still nearer. "O, yes," he continued, "there is a bell on the shelf—and there is a *flat-iron* by your chair; better take that."

"Very well," said Ruth, "if you say so I'll take it," and she raised it to her lap.

"But," said he, "where is my watch?"

Ruth feeling angry and not much like indulging him, answered: "I have not got your watch."

He told her he knew she had, when she said: "Your watch is safe, and you can have it and your money too, whenever you resign my clothing, *that* is all I want—and you know that both are safe in my possession."

He would come to no agreement and Ruth went home.

At noon she went there again, and sitting in the dining room a young, illy dressed man entered and accosted her very familiarly, telling her he was an "officer" on board the Chenamus on a former passage with her. She could not recall him at all to mind.

Dr. Binney not coming to dinner, she went to his room, and finding the door shut and hearing two voices, she listened a moment and perceived she was the subject of conversation. She felt impelled to return immediately to her house, and having passed about half way she looked back and perceived Dr. Binney and this same young man standing upon the piazza looking after her. She hurried on, and soon found herself safe in her own house.

Not long after, Dr. Binney's anger having passed the meridian, he surrendered himself to her wishes, and went to live with her, acknowledging the fault was entirely his own, the affair of the *collars* having caused it all—he thinking she was making them for some lover and trying to conceal the fact by saying they were for *Miss Wood*—adding:

"I have got a h-ll of a temper, and I don't know what ails me."

"But who," said Ruth, "was the little man who spoke to me and said he was an officer on the Chenamus?"

"Why, that was the marshall of Portland!"

"The *marshall of Portland!* and what was he doing there?"

"He was going to *strip you* and get the money!"

"Why, who was he—I never saw him on the Chenamus as I remember?"

"Don't you remember that little fellow who used to go about the deck hammering the iron rings, &c.?"

"Yes; and he used to 'slush' the masts!"

"Yes, yes, that's the very fellow!"

"And *he's the marshall of Portland?*"

"Yes, *he's the marshall of Portland!*"

"And he was going to *strip me?*"

"Yes."

"Well, 't is well he did not attempt it, for he would have found *himself* stripped about as soon!"

While living in this house of Ruth's hiring, she found all the provisions, yet, however she got discouraged by his destroying frequently the food she provided, saying it was "not fit for a dog to eat" and one Saturday evening, she having boiled a leg of pork to eat cold on the Sabbath that she might be able to attend church, he threw the contents of his supper and it, with the dishes, into the fire, where she let them remain till consumed, the dishes being all broken. She then told him he might maintain himself, for she would expend no more to be wasted in that manner.

After various other troubles, which we cannot recapitulate here, we find them living at Butteville, Dr. Binney having purchased a house and four lots for one thousand dollars. He had taken a part of his goods to Butteville and opened a store there, but liquors constituting a large part of his stock, he was, while here, most all of the time intoxicated.

It will be impossible, in this number of our work, to detail the particulars of the disagreement of Dr. Binney and his wife, while here, but we will do so elsewhere if we have an opportunity. Suffice it now to say that such was his reckless course and the power of Thomas Binney over him, that Ruth resolved that before everything was gone she would apply for a bill of divorce, and endeavor to obtain something of the property. Thomas Binney had surrendered the papers which had placed the goods at his disposal when at San Francisco; and Dr. Binney, suspecting that his wife intended to leave him, sent to Portland for his brother, and while his wife was on a visit to a friend's, sold whatever was at Butteville at a great discount, and commenced arrangements for securing the balance at Portland, so that, as he said, she could "not touch it."

Ruth, becoming aware of this, hastened to Linn City for advice and to endeavor to prevent the consummation of this plan. Finding a lawyer[4] she made application to the Hon. Judge Pratt for a "bill," and to have some part of Dr. Binney's property secured to her.[5]

We need not present her complaints in this petition, as Dr. Binney's answer—which we shall give—will make them apparent. We shall, however, notice the doings of the *Judge* on this occasion, in order to show the difference of feeling between him and the one who ultimately had the decision of the case, viz: between the honorable judges, O. C. Pratt and George H. Williams.[6]

From the petition we copy:

> ''T‍ᴇʀʀɪᴛᴏʀʏ ᴏꜰ Oʀᴇɢᴏɴ,
> Washington County.

''On this 15th day of May, before the undersigned personally appeared 'Ruth Binney,' complainant in the above bill, and being by me duly sworn, says that the facts stated in the above bill are true, according to the best knowledge and belief of complainant; and that the above complaint is not made by collusion between complainant and defendant, nor through fear, restraint, nor out of levity, for the mere purpose of being separated from each other; but in sincerity and truth, for the reasons mentioned in said bill.

> R‍ᴜᴛʜ B‍ɪɴɴᴇʏ.

Subscribed and sworn to, &c.''

> ''T‍ᴇʀʀɪᴛᴏʀʏ ᴏꜰ Oʀᴇɢᴏɴ,
> Washington County.

On the filing of the foregoing petition with the clerk of the Marion County District Court, let a temporary injunction issue, enjoining and commanding the said defendant to instantly desist from cruelly treating or beating the complainant; that he allow her to take from his mansion-house her wearing apparel and other proper personal effects; that he desist from transferring or encumbering his real property at all, or his personal property, except at a fair market value, and for cash; and not to waste or squander the proceeds during the pendency of this suit. And further, that he, without delay, pay over to the clerk of the Marion Count District Court the sum of $600, or cause the same to be paid in monthly installments of $50 each, to the satisfaction of said clerk, for the maintenance and proper expense of the said complainant whilst this suit is pending, and until further orders.

> O. C. P‍ʀᴀᴛᴛ,
> Judge 2d Judicial Dist., Oregon Ter'y.
> Dated ——.''

Here follows Dr. Binney's answer, on oath—omitting preliminary re-marks as unnecessary. Those parts marked with figures, and denied by Dr. Binney, were afterwards proven in court by the testimony of witnesses; and those parts which are in brackets are untrue, but no testimony was sought to prove so:

"U. S. DISTRICT COURT, SECOND JUDICIAL DISTRICT, TERRITORY OF OREGON, COUNTY OF MARION: IN CHANCERY.

"THE ANSWER OF WILLIAM J. BINNEY TO
THE BILL OF COMPLAINT OF RUTH BINNEY,
COMPLAINANT

"This defendant reserving to himself all the right of exemption to the said bill of complaint, for answer thereunto, saith:

* * * "That true it is that some time before said marriage defendant became impressed with the importance of religion, but that such impressions were afterwards materially, as the defendant believes, impaired by perceiving that the walk and conversation of complainant, a professor of religion, so far from being in accordance with her professions, were, and continued to be, and still are, as hereinafter set forth.

"That it is true that prior to said marriage, defendant had been robbed by Indians, and had lost much property by them; but it is not true that defendant then was, or in the then circumstances of the country was, considered to be very poor.

"That he had taken and then resided upon a good and valuable land claim at Champoeg, in said Territory, with complainant. That he was possessed of horses, [cattle] and other property; but not of much money, of which there was then but little in this Territory; and that defendant and complainant enjoyed all the usual outward comforts of life which the country afforded.

"That from a time shortly after the said marriage to the time of their first departure for the States, in the year 1842, defendant was greatly grieved and disappointed in the conduct of complainant; that while she fully possessed and occasionally exercised all the qualifications calculated to make a home comfortable, she was frequently sulky and morose—at other times irritable, often striving by her [taunts and insulting language and conduct, to annoy defendant and provoke defendant into retaliatory expressions.]

"That true it is defendant and complainant returned from New York to Oregon Territory about April, 1844, when they again lived on same land claim, which defendant had previously sold for $300 and re-purchased at $750, and continued to reside there till about April, 1850, at which time defendant possessed stock, property of various kinds; was in all respects comfortably situated, and, as defendant believes, in independent circumstances; yet the afore-described conduct of complainant increased in virulence and bitterness. She became dissatisfied with the country, and desirous of returning, though not on a visit, wrongfully implied in said bill, but to reside permanently in the States. That although contrary to defendant's own views, yet with the desire to gratify complainant, [and in hopes that thereby her temper and conduct to defendant might become improved,] he consented to return, and [on her account thus sacrificed what to them, and still believes to have been, permanent prospects of success in life, and again left Oregon about April 1, 1850, for the States.] That the conduct of complainant did not improve during said last-named absence, and defendant again returned with complainant to Oregon about the month of December, 1851. That defendant and complainant remained in Portland, as stated in said bill, a few weeks, and then defendant went to Butteville, in said Marion County, where he purchased a house and four lots of land, which he still owns, and where defendant resides.

"That true it is when leaving Oregon in April, 1850, defendant sold cows and horses, and other things, to about the sum of $2,700; but it is not true that said stock was raised by the personal labor and attention of complainant, nor that [five or six of the horses as sold were the produce of a mare purchased at the time of defendant's marriage, with funds of complainant;] that a portion of said stock sold was purchased by defendant—other portions were received by him on account of professional services as a physician—[some were loaned on shares, and had been kept at other places than the homestead of defendant, and their increase never even seen by complainant.] That the mare named in said bill was a small Indian poney purchased for fifteen dollars, [and which died some years after; and to the best of defendant's recollection and belief, but one of the horses sold was her produce.]

"That true it is complainant was capable and generally did aid and assist defendant in his affairs; but that defendant bought and sold and [raised stock] and attended to his said other professional business, peaceably and industriously, and [thereby] accumulated the means which he possessed at the time aforesaid.

"That true it is the defendant did, for the purpose above in this answer stated, sell his said land claim at auction and received therefor the sum of twelve hundred and seventy-five dollars.

"That true it is defendant is possessed at this time of goods, or their proceeds, which cost in New York about seven thousand dollars, and of property consisting of houses and lots, as in said bill stated.

"¹That defendant distinctly denies that he has ever, since his marriage, treated complainant, continuously or otherwise, cruelly or injuriously, or in any wise either endangered her life or given her any just cause to believe that he ever intended so to do. ²That defendant has not even offered indignities intolerable, or otherwise, to the person of complainant. That [defendant denies that he has been, since the summer of 1839 to the present time, or at any time, or that he now is, addicted to habitual intemperance.] That true it is defendant is not of that cold and phlegmatic temperament that can submit with indifference to the [irritating, galling, insulting and abusive language which complainant has often, from time to time, poured forth upon him for the purpose, as defendant then and still believes, of goading him into anger,] and defendant may not always, under such continued and wholly [unjustifiable provocation,] have exhibited perfect equanimity of temper; but he does deny that even such strong provocation has ever driven defendant to the conduct stated in said bill.

"That complainant appeared to be laboring under constant suspicion of defendant's fidelity to her, and very frequently accused him of improper intercourse with other females; [that all such charges, so made by complainant, are and have always been utterly groundless and false.] That complainant, from the frequency with which she repeated these charges, the number and [respectability] of the persons with whom she accused defndt. of such improper intercourse, and the strong language and [violent manner] with which she urged such charges [appeared to be either constantly seeking a cause of quarrel with defendant,] or to be laboring under something approaching an imagination [morbid] in this particular.

"³That it is wholly untrue that defendant, in 1844, or at any other time, at table or otherwise, struck complainant a violent blow with his fist, or otherwise, thereby causing permanent or any other injury.

"'⁴That it is not true that in 1842, or at any other time, defendant struck complainant several, or any, violent blows upon her naked arms, with a whip, in the presence of any third person; ⁵nor did defendant then, or any other time, drive complainant out of the house.

"'⁶That it is not true, as stated in said bill, that some time in the year 1846, or at any time, that defendant, when drunk, ordered complainant to come to bed, and in consequence of her refusal, or otherwise, rushed towards or attempted to take a musket, or other deadly weapon, for the purpose as stated in said bill, or other purpose; but true it is about the time in that behalf in said bill stated, [complainant became, as then frequently happened, morose and obstinate,] and refused to come to defendant's bed, and on defendant enjoining her so to do complainant left the room and went to sleep in the same room with an Indian woman; that defendant admits that he was thereupon angry at this improper conduct of complainant, ⁷but denies using any violence towards her, or putting her in fear. That true it is that the [sulkiness and obstinacy of complainant still continuing,] she went the next day to the Willamette falls, where she remained until brought back by the defendant, [but not, as wrongfully stated in said bill,] on defendant's ⁸promise to conduct himself towards complainant otherwise, but, [as defendant believes, because the complainant had then, for the time at least, regretted her own conduct.]

"'That it is not true that in the spring of 1850, or at any other time, [complainant heard defendant and his brother, James Binney, making arrangements to take what money there then was in the house and go to the gold mines, and abandon complainant,] without the means of subsistence, [or any other conversation to that effect;] nor did the defendant express such intention, except under the circumstances and in the manner following. That it is not true that defendant ran complainant out of the house; that it is not true that [defendant caught complainant by the hair and dragged her into the house, and abused her brutally, or otherwise; that it is not true that defendant injured complainant's hip, or otherwise, as stated] in said bill. But it is true that at the time in that behalf specified, defendant had in the house about ten thousand dollars in gold, and considered it too large an amount to be there kept with safety, and was anxious to find a more secure place of deposit, for safe keeping [only] and remarked to complainant that he thought he had better deposit with Dr. J. McLaughlin, or some other good man, for safety, to which [complainant violently objected with much obstinacy;] that soon after, defendant wishing to go to the Willamette falls, requested his said brother to get a horse for him; that complainant suspecting defendant meant to take the said money with him for the purpose aforesaid, took between [five and six thousand dollars] from its usual place of deposit, and concealed it from defendant; that on defendant discovering that the money was gone, he called his said brother and showed him the trunk from which it had been taken, and irritated by this interferences with his affairs, and this further addition to the previous annoying conduct of complainant, used expressions to his brother to this effect: "I have a good mind to let her take this money and go to the devil—I can go to the mines, and by hard work again do something for myself." That complainant took [said money] so abstracted, and carried it away to the Buttes, where defendant, some few weeks subsequently, after much difficulty, succeeded in again obtaining possession of it.

"That it is not true, as stated in said bill, that [defendant, at Panama, in 1850, or at any time, whilst complainant was ill, abandoned complainant among strangers, and spent his time in drunkenness;] but true it is that complainant was unwell on the said passage to Panama, but had in part recovered on arrival there. That true it is on the occasion of a dinner given by the passengers to Captain Hunt, for his kindness and gentlemanly conduct on the passage, defendant, with other gentlemen present, may have exceeded the bounds of strict sobriety, [but in no way to the detriment] or injury of complainant, [or at other times more than the said occasion;] but it is also true that defendant had at that time with him a large sum of money, and from indications feared to cross the Isthmus at that time, and intended to remain at Panama a day or two and then to cross to the other side, and notified complainant of such his intention; [that defendant, notwithstanding, forthwith] proceeded to pack up all of complainant and defendant's trunks and other things, [including the money,] and expressed her intention to go at once. That defendant again objected, whereupon [she, complainant, called the mate of the vessel] on which they did come to Panama, into the room and in defendant's hearing requested him, the said mate, to take charge of her, said complainant, and her effects, across the Isthmus; that defendant [ordered the mate out of the room and forbade his interference in his, defendant's family affairs;] that defendant then left the house for a short time and on his return found that complainant had left the house; that after enquiring for some time for complainant and being unable to obtain any information respecting her, defendant determined to go to Valparaiso; but did not leave Panama at that time; that [complainant had then with her from three hundred to five hundred dollars.]

"That soon after, with the aid of the captain, Hunt, defendant found complainant, and they afterwards crossed together and proceeded to New York.

"That true it is while at New York in 1851, complainant visited her mother in Massachusetts; but it is also true that on that occasion defendant accompanied complainant and conducted her to her mother's from New York, and then returned to New York. That it is entirely untrue [that defendant squandered in dissipation and licentiousness about $3000, or any other sum] as stated in said bill. And this defendant states, [that any assertion that he then contracted the venereal disease to be an unmitigated falsehood, and fully believes that the statement and testimony of complainant's belief that such was the case to be utterly and absolutely false.]

"That before crossing the Isthmus on the said last-named occasion of returning to New York, defendant gave complainant a draft for the sum of $2000, which sum complainant received of said defendant in New York, and placed at interest in Massachusetts, and as defendant [fully believes still has the sum] free from all control of this defendant, [who has allowed] and still allows and intends to allow her to have and use it as her own.

"That it is untrue that [defendant by promises induced complainant to return to him]; that complainant returned willingly and of her own accord to defendant, and to Oregon, where defendant considered it best for his business prospects he should return. That the statement of [defendant attempting to abandon complainant at San Francisco in the month of October, 1851, or at any time; and also the statement that defendant called complainant his mistress and used other abusive language to complainant is all absolutely untrue;] that complainant had at this time about $500 in her hand; that the statement in said bill that [defendant at Portland (or anywhere) in 1852, (or any time) drew a stick of wood over complainant's head, and used the expression in that behalf in said bill stated, or any such language is wholly untrue.]

"That during their stay in Portland this defendant treated complainant with his usual courtesy and kindness, while she conducted herself with her customary [violence] of language and conduct, [and on one occasion, while there, raised a smoothing-iron to strike defendant.] That defendant absolutely denies that [he took, or was detected by complainant in 1852, or at any other time, in taking indecent liberties with any female, or that he made proposals of connubial intercourse with any one, or that he struck or in any wise abused complainant for speaking of such subjects.

"That true it is that defendant frequently, in the course of his professional practice, received visits from ladies for the purpose of medical advice and assistance for themselves or their children; and that the *morbid* spirit of jealousy which [seemed constantly to possess complainant and govern her conduct,] frequently led her to [practice a system of espionage upon the defendant and his patients] most annoying to him, both as a physician and as a husband. That on one occasion, and long after defendant had tried all fair and reasonable means in view to disabuse the mind of complainant of this her prevailing [false idea, defendant detected complainant personally watching him at his own house] while attending a little child there seriously ill, in its mother's arms, and requiring and receiving care and attention both of defendant and its mother; that to the moment defendant's [sole attention had been devoted to relieve the child;] that it was neither [a time nor place,] nor were the [circumstances or the character of the persons such] as even—if (which he positively denies) [he ever entertained so base a wish] as stated in said bill—[to have led the most depraved to expect to be able to realize so degrading an intention.] That, smarting under the irritation of [detecting complainant] under such circumstances [in such an employment,] defendant, in a spirit of retaliation, and [in that spirit and for that object alone,] did make use of a single expression [expressly intended to excite the jealousy of complainant;] and on no other occasion did he ever condescend to such mode of retaliation. That while the defendant does not, in strict propriety, justify this expression, and regrets having used it, he respectfully submits the whole circumstances attending it to this honorable court.

"That defendant denies the whole statement in said bill contained of [9]presenting a pistol at complainant, or threatening to lay her flat on the floor. That defendant denies both the commencement and [continuation] either of [drunkenness on his part, or brutality towards complainant,] or that he, about the 12th of May, 1852, or at any time, [declared that he would proceed to Portland and convert his merchandise into money and leave the country and abandon complainant,] as in said bill stated. That defendant [neither expressed nor had any such intention, for such a purpose;] but true it is that defendant, about the time above last stated, did express an intention to sell off his goods and close his business in Portland, for other and different reasons, relating solely to his said business prospects. That the fear alledged by complainant of defendant's intention to abandon complainant, [proceeds, as defendant believes, from the knowledge which complainant has that her conduct to defendant has been such as to render it impossible for defendant— with any regard to his own peace and happiness—longer to continue to live with her as man and wife.]

"That true it is that complainant, about the 13th of May last, did leave the house of defendant against his, to her, expressed wish, and acting in the [spirit of arrogance which has so long marked her conduct;] that defendant expressly denies that complainant was [induced to do so either by cruel treatment or threats of personal violence on his part.] That so far from complainant having used her best endeavors to live with defendant, as his wife in peace and quietness, she has been jealous and suspicious [without cause,] sulky and irritating [without provocation,] harsh and ungovernable in temper and deportment, without attempting to restrain her [bursts of passion,] and on very many occasions, as defendant [believes, for the purpose of irritating defendant.]

"That in the year 1847 complainant, [without cause,] left the house of defendant at Champoeg and went down to Oregon City, and remained there about two weeks. That during the absence of defendant from the house at that time, complainant returned to his house and broke open a trunk and took therefrom about $500 in gold and silver, and also some other things, and took also two horses of defendant and returned to Oregon City therewith. That defendant, after about a fortnight, succeeded in obtaining back the silver, in part, but that [about 2 to $300 in gold have not yet been received by defendant.]

"That defendant has proceeded, and is still proceeding in the usual course of business, and not otherwise, and not for the reasons set out in said bill, to dispose of his merchandise and other personal property from time to time as he can do so to advantage."

Usual conclusion, praying dissolution of injunction, that bill be not granted, and against alimony and expenses.

We shall make but few comments on the foregoing "Answer," as we intend to review it fully, if practicable. The reader will perceive that through-out there is no accusation against the conduct of Ruth Rover otherwise than as she is said to be "sulky, morose and irritating in her language," and, as defendant believes, for the "purpose of irritating him to anger." This is said to have been "without cause." We wonder, if such were the case, what would have been Ruth's object in exciting to anger an innocent, harmless and inoffensive man. Was it because she so much liked troubles of that kind? It must have been.

Again, the money left in Mr. Holmes' hands, of which he says there were from two to three hundred dollars missing when he received it again of Mrs. Jeffrey's. When Ruth Rover received the money of Mrs. Holmes it was counted and found to be the exact amount delivered to Mr. Holmes the day before. It can be proven by the boy who carried it for her to Oregon City, that Ruth did not open it on the way, and by Mrs. J. that she saw it not again, after she delivered it to her, till Dr. Binney counted it before her in Mrs. J.'s house. When he did so he remarked to Mr. Kanady that he believed some of the gold was gone, as there was not as much gold as he thought there should be. There was the full amount of money, viz, $500, or near it, and Ruth understood him to mean that the proportion of gold to the silver was not as great as he had supposed it to be; and the conclusion is, if any of the money is missing, it must have occurred while in Mrs. J.'s hands, which thought cannot for a moment be indulged.

Further; Dr. Binney states that the mare, of which his wife speaks, died in a few years after their marriage. The Rev. Mr. Boldue gave information that he saw her dead on the prairie in the year '50, a little before his sale of his band of horses early in that year, and after he had spent some time in looking for her in view of that sale. This was *eleven* years after she had been purchased, and she having a colt every year—several of which were also females—was there but one animal he obtained from that mare?

Again, he speaks of cattle of his having been loaned to others, by him, on shares. We are sure that Ruth never heard of such a circumstance, and we believe that Mr. Durbin, who bought the band, will not assert that he received any in that way. When Dr. Binney went to the United States in '42, he entrusted his cows to the keeping of R. Williams, who was to receive a part of the increase for his reward. When Dr. Binney returned, four only of the increase was due Mr. W., which Dr. B. kept in exchange for property given to Mr. W.; and again, if, as he states that *"the conduct of complainant has been such as to render it impossible for defendant, with any regard to his own peace and happiness, longer to continue to live with her as man and wife,"* why did he pray that the *bill* might not be granted—and in *what* capacity did he want her to live with him?

While Ruth lived in Linn City awaiting the action of the court, Dr. Binney spent much of his time in Portland; and while she, as she wrote him, had not and could not obtain even *straw* to sleep upon, desiring him to permit her to have her feather bed she had brought from the States, he was boarding at the best hotels, walking the streets with an Indian boy behind him to carry his valise, and doing, in all things, exactly as *such gentlemen* do. He joined the Free Masons and Sons of Temperance,[7] and at last requested Ruth to withdraw her petition and live with him again, promising her to forever abstain from liquors—to treat her kindly—to pay all expenses as yet incurred by her application to court, and to give her in cash the first one thousand dollars he should earn by his practice. The Judge having informed her of his expected absence to the States, and of the probability that a hearing of her case could not be had for some time, in consequence of the fact that there would be no judge to attend to it when *he* should be away, she, considering that the prospect before her of her husband's temperance was better than ever it had been, because of his having publicly taken the "pledge," consented, and went with him to Champoeg.

We have before us some curious extracts taken by W. J. Binney from letters received by Thomas Binney, while in Portland, from his sisters, which, as they denote the kind of minds which may sometimes be enclosed within silks, jewelry, cotton, wool and whalebone, we insert them in the "Grains:"

> *"February* 7, 1852. "I want to know if she has put anything in the store, or has opened it on her own account. The latter I should prefer for your own happiness."

> *"February* 23, 1852. "Before the steamer brought the letter you may be sure mother imagined fifty things were wrong. She went so far as to say she had killed you, which will appear very ludicrous to you I know.
>
> "We are sorry to think your prospects are so unfavorable.
>
> "We are not at all surprised to hear of their behavior; [troubles in Portland,] it must have been mortifying to you. I am glad you kept your resolution by not stopping in the house with him. Watch well what you are about, for you have a d—l to eye you in sheep's clothing.
>
> "Tell us, when you write, if W. J. has been kind to you as he promised."

> *March* 8, 1852. "I would like to know how the beauty, gets along, as you say. I think she is a smart hussy. I can imagine I can see her, the long, tall, banshee—particularly when she is eating. I think you must abhor the very sight of her."

March 28, 1852. *   *   *   "Another thing. It must be pleasanter for you to have W. J. and his dear creature such a respectful distance from you. You must be happy in your little back room, eating, drinking, &c.

"Have you ever been to W. J.'s place? What kind of place has he? Does he have much practice? and how is he liked?

"We think W. J. very mean in wanting every cent from you in the way he has done. You will feel more independent however."

April 23, 1852. "W. J. gave ma two hundred dollars before he left. She thought you knew it. After you left that morning he gave it. He had borrowed five from ma, and there was a dollar to pay for him soleing a pair of boots to come out of that—this makes it six less, anyhow.

"You had better be cautious with *her,* for I think if she can she will injure you. Keep a bright look out, too for *him.* I think it such a strange idea of him opening another store! I suppose *she* is to be the sole mistress of it. She will no doubt have her aticles for sale—cloaks, and vests, &c. She is a donkey, anyway you will fix it.

"I hope that *"gold vein"* will prove to be a rich one for your sake. I hope there is good luck in store for you, after going."

CHAPTER XXII

❧

What is my life? Death in a night gown!

[Ruth Rover.

On settling at Champoeg, Ruth for the first day felt hope flickering around her heart, like a flame around a substance which had been dipped in alcohol, and which, like it, departed as soon, leaving nothing but a scathed impression. The *second* day there her husband returned to his cups.

Many disagreeable occurrences transpired which we cannot stop to delineate—we have only space to denote the most important.

On the occasion of the death of a friend, Dr. Shiels, Ruth went to Oregon City to purchase mourning apparel for the widow, she being a cripple, and Ruth's sympathies being much excited for her, (notwithstanding which she has received but a poor return.)[1] She bore her own expenses, and returning the next day found her husband would not permit her to enter the house, accusing her of having been away for vile purposes.

Ruth was obliged to find accommodations elsewhere, and the result was that Dr. Binney sought her again and requested her to return, and to induce her to do so presented her the following testimony of his feelings towards her:

> "*Know all men by These Presents,* that I, W. J. Binney, have set off and assigned, and by these presents do set off and assign unto my wife, Ruth Binney, one dwelling house and four building lots, in the town of Butteville, Marion County—to have and to hold the same with all the tenements and appurtenances thereto, during her natural life.

"In witness whereof I hereunto set my hand and seal this 19th
day of February, 1853.

Champoeg, Marion County,
February 19th, 1853.

"Witnessed by
HUGH COSGROVE.''

Ruth returned *again,* and after a time found it necessary to seek the
protection of the law, as her husband had now given full bias to his evil
disposition in the way of threats with pistols, knives, and clubs. In a time of
great abuse and danger she sent for the Justice of the Peace living near; he
came, and although Ruth was weeping under the smart of Dr. B.'s blows and
ill-usage, he joked and laughed with Dr. B., who was endeavoring in this way
to do away the impression that there had been any violence attempted. The
magistrate returned, saying he would see if he could do any thing for her.
Next day came, and she saw no indications that he intended to endeavor to
assist her, and her husband's abuse continuing, she wrote him the following:

"MR. DURRETTE—Sir: I wish you to inform me if you refuse to
grant me the assistance for which I applied to you yesterday. I am
not asking for your sympathy or friendship, or any assistance
unconnected with your duty as Justice of the Peace, and this you are
bound to render me. I cannot endure my husband's abuse! My
health is daily sinking under it, and I ask the protection of the law,
and a home, and support. You cannot urge in this application as you
did in another I made, that you are unwilling to offend Dr. Binney. I
now have made a complaint to you, and applied for assistance, and
am ready to give my affidavit that my life is daily and almost hourly
threatened by my husband; and I am much of the time disabled by
his abuse, while I am as frequently ordered to leave the house I now
occupy. I wish you to inform me by the bearer, in writing, if you
refuse to afford me the assistance which is in your power.

"Respectfully,
RUTH BINNEY.''

"I told my girl yesterday to tell you I wished you to come over in
your official capacity as a magistrate. She says she told you I wanted
you to come over and *sacrifice the office!* I do not now wonder that you
were so much inclined to laughter when here. R. B.''

This resulted in Dr. Binney's submitting to heavy bonds that he would
keep the peace with his wife. And the three weeks following was, we have
heard Ruth say, the pleasantest period she ever passed with her husband.

She endeavored, in every possible way, by attentions, endearments, kindnesses, praises and encouragements, to induce him to *continue* in the good way he had again commenced.

At evening, when he had returned from his professional tours, he would show the fee he had received to her, exclaiming:

"I can retrieve all my lost fortune yet, if I can only let the d—d liquor alone."

"Yes, she would reply, that is all that is wanting to enable you to become respectable, successful and wealthy—and you *will* let liquor alone *won't* you? I'm *sure* you have suffered enough from its use!"

The spoiler came this time in the person of Barney Kanady. He had called on the Sabbath and requested the doctor's presence at his house to visit a sick woman, and when leaving went to the grocery and bought liquor to carry home with him.

Dr. Binney did not return till several hours after the time when he might have been at home from going so short a distance; but when he did come, he came—alas! how fallen! How our heart bleeds while recurring to this part of our story! Alas! alas! how fallen! The fresh pleasant countenance he bore away with him, was now downcast and crimsoned with shame and guilt. He could not look his wife in the face when he staggered into the house, trying with smiles to remove the conviction that she might have received, while he said:

"I'm quite a ladies' man! You see the ladies love me, Ruth, and they won't let me alone."

"And I think you love the ladies," she replied, "if I am to judge by the appearance of your coat," which being white linen, denoted very plainly some such finger-marks as we think might be made by the hands of some dirty Indian woman.

He looked at his shoulders and, in spite of his inebriation, manifested confusion at the revelations they made.

'Twas over now! Hope had presented her last bait, and Ruth discarded it as a phantasm not to be relied upon, and made up her mind to meet the realities of her life, which seemed to be only bitterness and sorrow, with all the fortitude God should give her.

She had, about a year before, set a day when she would leave her husband finally, if there should appear no better prospect for her happiness with him, or usefulness to him. She had told him of this, and many times *reminded* him of this, her firm determination. But he seemed not to fear, and now, as the time was approaching, he would tell her, tauntingly, to "get ready, the time is near, and you have got to go then, any how."

She made preparations slowly and sure. She packed her clothing and effects, but had the mortification to have them frequently thrown out of her trunk, to see, as her husband told her, if she had anything belonging to him.

The talked of morning at last came. Dr. Binney apprized her of it, and said he wanted her now "to go, as she had so long talked about it, and to hurry and be off, but not a d—d article was he going to permit her to take with her, not even an old stocking; and if any person came to the house to assist her to take any thing away from it, he would shoot them dead at the door!"

Ruth told him that he had expressed a wish for her to go, and she intended so to do, but she wanted a change of apparel, and could not be comfortable without it.

He said she might "take *one* trunk of clothes, and that was every d—d thing she should have."

She went away resignedly, believing the court would allow her to obtain them.

She had purchased, when in New York about three hundred dollars worth of millinery articles, with her own funds. The most of these she left. And about three months before leaving her house she had bought, also with her own money, ninety-four dollars worth of household furniture, which was also remaining.

In a few days Dr. Binney wrote her to this effect:

"MY DEAR RUTH: I have suffered yesterday from fire![2] Both houses are burnt to the ground, and very little of anything saved.

"I think of leaving the country, and would be glad if you would come up and get what is left.

"I am likewise unwell and would be glad to see you. I wish to do towards you what is right, and if you feel any reluctance in coming, please let me know by note, and oblige,

"Yours,

W. J. BINNEY."

Ruth *did* feel reluctance in going, and so informed him, and also said if there was anything saved which he felt disposed to allow her to receive, he could place it in a person's hands whom she designated—but no such act did he perform.

By this fire Ruth lost, according to an estimate before us, to the amount of about nine hundred and twenty dollars, entirely of her own purchasing and the gifts of friends—without any reference to her share of the other property thus destroyed.

She awaited the term of the court which was to be held in Salem in the month of October following.

❦

Dr. Binney many times endeavored to induce her to return, but to no effect. He made another effort to be free from the ruinous consequences of intemperance, resolving, as he thought *firmly,* that he would drink no more; and he said he wished people would not ask him to drink, for he believed if they would not he could keep clear.

O! ye enticers to evil! we wish the punishment due your errors might fall upon you now, and restrain you hereafter from spreading any more snares for the feet of the unwary.

As soon as Dr. Binney returned to Champoeg he was enticed to drink at Mr. Steven's tavern, and many a dollar did he spend at his bar before he again obtained resolution to free himself from the company he met there.

Ruth's second petition to court was similar to the first, with the additional mention of some indignities she had suffered from her husband at Champoeg, and was prepared by A. Holbrook, Esq., of Oregon City,[3] in a very able, clear and feeling manner. She awaited its action during the week, her case being in chancery and the last on the docket.

Mr. Holbrook, her attorney, did not attend court, which greatly excited her regrets; but through two other excellent gentlemen, who seemed to possess authority to attend his business in his absence, she endeavored, if her case could not be attended to at that term of court, that there might be some provision made for her support during the period she was waiting its decision.

The law had allowed but one week for this term of court, and Saturday noon came and Ruth's petition had not been considered.

It was in vain she suggested, through the gentlemen referred to, that her wardrobe had been almost totally destroyed by fire, and that her health was poor, and that winter approaching she needed clothing and means to pay her board—she could get no hearing or action on the subject.

And herein we may see the difference between the two Judges. She asked if she might receive an order to obtain her piano and a trunk of a few articles of hers which Dr. Binney still had in his possession, and was informed that those she could do without till the next term of court, and as there had been no decision made in her case neither these articles nor money could be obtained.

The Judge afterwards informed her that having but one half day not required for other business, if her petition for a bill had required only a mere form of proceeding she could have been heard, but perceiving that her application would be contested there was not time to attend to it.

This was undoubtedly right. We confess we are ignorant of law in such cases, but we wonder, if Judge Pratt could make the provision he did for Ruth's support, aside from the immediate action of the court, why another Judge could not have done the same thing under the same circumstances.

Ruth waited till April following, and obtained a bill of divorce in the following terms:

"RUTH BINNEY

     vs.   *Bill for Divorce*

"W. J. BINNEY

"This cause coming on to be heard, upon the pleadings and evidence of the parties, the court finds that the allegations of adultery and gross and habitual drunkenness, made in plaintiff's petition against defendant, are not supported by evidence, but that the charge of harsh and cruel treatment is to some extent sustained, and that the welfare of the parties require separation.

"It is therefore ordered and adjudged that the bonds of matrimony now existing between the said Ruth and William J., be and are hereafter held for naught.

"It is further ordered that the said Ruth have the exclusive property in, and possession to all monies, evidence of indebtedness, and personal effects, of every description, now in her hands, or which have been deposited by her, or for her use, or of which she has heretofore had the sole control.

"That she have the piano and clothing now in the possession of the said W. J., as her own property, to be delivered to her by the said William J.

"That the said W. J. pay the said Ruth the sum of one hundred dollars, and also the costs of this suit, and that execution issue therefor.

"It is further ordered that the said William J. have all the residue of his property, of every kind and description, free from any charge or claim of the said Ruth, or to which she might be entitled in law if this divorce had not been granted."

At this trial not one allegation was presented against Ruth. One or two witnesses said they had heard her speak angrily, as would have been *severely,* if she had received no provocation. Aside from this, with all her husband's cruel accusations and reproaches, her conduct as a wife had been irreproachable.

As to the remark that the "allegations of adultery and gross and habitual drunkenness not being supported by evidence," we will say that Ruth had asked her attorney how *little* of the accusations against her husband it would be necessary to prove in order to obtain a bill, as *it* was all her object—she having no wish to present any proof against him which was unnecessary, it being not her object to do him injury but to benefit her own situation.

She was told that any one of the allegations being sustained by proof, was sufficient to enable her to obtain a bill, and her instructions on the subject of testimony required ran to this effect:

1st. "Testimony to show habitual and gross drunkenness.

2d. "Harsh and cruel treatment and personal indignities, rendering life burdensome."

In seeking testimony Ruth made *not one* attempt to prove licentiousness, and at the time of the trial she suggested a question to her attorney which would have referred to the subject, but he declined putting it to the witness, saying: "The court would not like to hear it."

On the subject of drunkenness, she had only sought *one* witness, as she happened to be in her vicinity, but she being unable to attend she made no further attempt to obtain testimony on this subject.

At the close of the trial Dr. Binney remarked that he was "glad he had got off without his character being injured!"

On the subject of alimony the law reads thus:

"In granting a divorce the court shall also make such disposition of the property of the parties as shall appear just and equitable, having regard to the respective merits of the parties, and to the condition which they will be left by such divorce, and to the party through whom the property was acquired and to the burdens imposed upon it for the benefit of children, and all property and pecuniary rights and interests * * * not otherwise disposed of or regulated by the order of the court, shall by said divorce be divested out of the guilty party at whose instance the divorce was granted."

Ruth's petition on this subject ran thus:

"And also that your honor will enquire as to the amount of his property, and how it has been acquired and preserved, and make such order as alimony, and her support, and legal expenses during the progress of this cause, as may be just and equitable. And that your honor will grant such other and further relief as may seem fit and proper."

We believe not one question was put to any witness by the court as to what extent Mrs. Binney had been influential in acquiring and preserving the property of Dr. Binney. Some questions as to the amount he then had in his possession, were put, and evasively and unjustly answered in nearly every case by his witnesses. Testimony abundant on these subjects could have been obtained and would have been procured, if any suspicion had been entertained that the decision of the Judge would have been what it was—but Ruth never having been at court before, and knowing nothing of its manner of proceeding, trusted that justice would be awarded her, and this was all she wished. At the time of this decree Dr. Binney possessed a dwelling house and eight lots at Champoeg—one dwelling house and four lots at Buteville which were not confirmed to Ruth—four fine horses, fourteen cows and calves, (he had told Mrs. M—— a few days before court that he had that number engaged and was to receive them in a few days,) a stock of goods in Allan & McKinlay's store, at Oregon City, and about three thousand dollars or upwards in the hands of Dr. McLaughlin at Oregon City, (this Ruth knew him to have there when she left home, and there had not been any withdrawn to her knowledge,) probably three or four thousand in debts and his household furniture, medicines, cash on hand, and besides a good profession which was a fortune in itself, and health and strength.

It had been shown in court that Ruth had on interest in the States one thousand dollars. She had borne her own expenses since her separation from her husband, much of the time paying seven and eight dollars per week for her board.

On leaving the States the last time, Dr. Binney had, to induce her to come with him, made a will entirely in her own favor, and in many other ways denoted his wish toward her relative to property. There are some of the facts in the case; *all* of which however were not made apparent in court.

Considering these things, was there any justice in the decision which decreed that she should retain what was in her possession, and receive *one hundred dollars to pay her counsel?* If this be justice, what is wrong?

We were told that the reason of the Judge in making this decision was because he perceived that Dr. Binney had more friends in court than Mrs. Binney, and that he was in ill humor. Ruth had not known that *friends* would produce an influence in a court of equity. Had she known this she could have produced some more—but there would have been a difficulty here which Dr. Binney did not meet. *Her* friends were mostly females, and in several instances, wives of Dr. Binney's witnesses who did Ruth the greatest injury by presenting false testimony;—for instance one of her greatest friends was Mrs. Cosgrove, wife of Hugh Cosgrove, and another was Mrs. Demick, wife of Mr. Demick. The husbands of these being opposed to Mrs. Binney, would not have suffered them to appear as her friends; and women cannot travel about the country as readily as men.

We have a few more remarks to make on the testimony of witnesses.

Mr. Cosgrove testified on oath that he did not know whether Dr. Binney owned a cow or not, which we are certain was false—for 'tis impossible that he had forgotten that Dr. Binney and his wife had at different times inquired of him relative to stray cows and calves, and also he has seen cows in the yard, and Mrs. Binney milking them, and has expressed his opinions of their good qualities, and cost &c.

He also stated that he never saw Dr. Binney intoxicated! Did he never *make* him so, when he has gone to his grocery a sober man, and left it with scarcely ability to get home? Was he not in that state when he passed the night in revellings with him at McKoy's mill; and when in that condition took the gift of a valuable horse, which he afterwards sold for one hundred dollars. But 'tis said, "the fly that feeds on d—g is colored thereby." 'Tis probable that being so much that way himself, he could not distinguish the difference between sobriety and drunkenness.

We think it not strange that when giving testimony he stood all the time with his hand over his mouth, to prevent his confusion from becoming apparent. Robert Newell also testified that he could not say that he ever saw Dr. Binney intoxicated. The same reason blinded his eyes as in the case of Cosgrove, especially at the time he enticed him to drink at J. Hord's, and remained drinking with him till Sabbath morning. He also testified that he would not be willing to give twenty-five hundred dollars for all Dr. Binney possessed. This he might have said conscientiously—for likely he did not wish to buy. George Aplin also said he could not say he ever saw Dr. Binney intoxicated. What ailed him when having gone to his house to see his wife, and he had sent to Champoeg for liquor—he being unable to return, tarried all night, and caused him to say to Mr. Gearing—"Dr. Binney did not do anything for my wife—he was in such a state he was not capable of attending to his business!"

This latter person had been much of this time at Dr. Binney's house in poor health, and had been waited upon by Mrs. Binney in the best manner she was able. He afterwards rewarded her by bringing liquor privately to her husband, and thus exciting disturbances in her house.

When Mrs. Binney arrived at the Butte from the States the second time, she related to Mrs. Demick the reasons which had induced her to return to Oregon, and among others, said that Dr. Binney had left her suddenly in Massachusetts, and before she had learned where he was he had expended about seven thousand dollars in goods in New York to come to Oregon. This statement she also made in a letter to a lady in Butteville.

Mr. Demick testified on oath that being at Butteville at the time referred to—and in another room, in conversation with another person—he heard Mrs. Binney say that when she left to come to Oregon, she had *about seven thousand dollars in a bank in New York*. This was entirely a misunderstanding, and Mr. Demick's unwillingness to be convinced arose most probably from the fact of his being a Universalist, and having no fear of perjury, and from the start he felt in losing a valuable cow after having broken his contract with

Mrs. Binney in taking her from her, the consequence of which was the loss to him of eighty or ninety dollars.

Before the time of court Mrs. Binney went with Mrs. Stanton of the Marion Hotel, Salem, to call on Mrs. Pentor of Salem, and Mrs. Binney asked in Mrs. Stanton's presence if she remembered the circumstance of Dr. Binney having struck his wife in the face.

"O, yes, perfectly."

"Did you see him give the blow?"

"Yes."

"Did you notice the conversation?"

"I heard you talking, but I could not tell you what you said—I was very sick at the time."

"Did you hear Mrs. Binney say anything out of the way? I want you to try and think, and don't be afraid to say so if you did."

"Well, I *didn't* hear her say anything that was ugly at all—but I know I thought at the time that Dr. Binney was mighty provoking in the way he acted."

This person afterwards at court, testified that at the period named she heard Mrs. Binney speak *harshly* to Dr. Binney. We are unwilling to suppose that Mrs. Pentor would take a false oath if she understood the responsibility— but we have reason to suppose that she might have been influenced to testify thus by her husband who was always irritated against Mrs. Binney because she would not receive his children into her house when his sick wife came there under her care.

Dr. Binney's counsel were quite tame on the subject of the divorce—but on that of *alimony* they were deeply interested. We were not surprised at this as in one case there were two old maids and a fortune in the scales, and in the other case, *"money! money!!"* seemed to be the only subject on which the man could muster any ideas. They both tried to make it appear that the five thousand dollars spoken of had not been received again by Dr. Binney.

The reader will perceive that Dr. Binney in his answer says:—"and of which I afterwards with much difficulty obtained possession."

When Ruth returned home after learning the decision of the court—she opened her bible to refresh her mind, and was much surprised to find the first passage read as follows:—*"Thou hast drunken the dregs of the cup of trembling and wrung them out."*

THE MONSTER

But *two* have responded to our challenge, viz: "Quintus" and "Squills," both in the *Oregonian.*

The first we leave to wallow on in the mire of his choice. *"Il ne faut jamais defier un fou."*

The second we will notice. Having forwarded a copy of the "Grains" to the editor, he acknowledged the receipt in the following language:

    * * * "We seldom read books of feminine production, believing *their* (the females) province to be darning stockings, pap and gruel, children, cook-stoves, and the sundry little affairs that makes life comfortable and makes them what Providence designed them to be *Helpmeets*." "It is bad enough to have unjust laws, &c., without this last visitation of Providence—an authoress." "In the words of Homer (or his translator) we say, 'and may this first invasion be the last.'"

From these remarks it appears this editor wants a helpmeet in the affairs named above—and we conclude if a young lady who died in Portland, a few years ago, had lived, he would have found one.

Again. Does he consider the first number of the "Grains" to be a "visitation of Providence?" If so, no wonder he wishes no more such.

We did not compile the "Grains" for the special information of "Squills," and we advise him to lay the book aside and read "Homer" till he shall be able to perceive the difference between him and his translator.

And now then Mr. Monster Evil stand forth! but not on the boggy ground of the *Spectator,* nor on the slimy soil of the *Oregonian,* but on the fair ground, and let the world be witnesses. Harness on your scales of scurrility, and in your right hand take the spear of a corrupted press, and prepare for combat; and, if you must take a stomachic, don't take squills, for they are very nauseating in their effect, if given in large doses. Come on to combat, and, with the help of Omnipotence, we defy you!

For the benefit of our readers who may think to subscribe for the *Oregonian,* we will say that we have seen *one* clean number of that periodical. It made its appearance in the month of August, 1854, when the editor was on top of Mount Hood, and we think if he would always stay there the *Oregonian* would take a respectable position among its contemporaries.

OUR REASONS FOR THIS PUBLICATION.—We think our readers have perceived them, but we will only conclude that we consider the expenditure of *millions,* if necessary, none too much to remove the foul aspersions cast upon a helpless female by her enemies.

OUR NEXT NUMBER, if published, will contain "Passages in the life of Ruth Rover," continued, and "Pictures of Oregon," illustrative of life and the state of society in Oregon since 1837 till the present day.

HYMN TO THE DEITY.

Father of mercies, let me be
A faithful worshipper of Thee.
Though clouds of grief around me lower,
And angry demons on me pour
Malignant curses, trusting Thee
What harm can e'er befall to me?

Though in this lonely land alone
I spend my months and years unknown,
Save where that Hatred doth proclaim
My injured yet unworthy name;
Yet Thee in nature's works I see,
And like as they *I'll* trust to Thee.

I bless Thee—Thou art every where,
Dost know Thy people's every care;
What pains oppress, what ills betide,
Canst by Thy faithful spirit guide
And bring to mansions of the blest,
And give Thy weary pilgrims rest.

Father of mercies! let me be
A constant worshipper of Thee—
Where'er my lot, what e'er my case,
Supported by sufficient grace,
I'll joy my only joy is Thee,
Thou ever-present Deity.

THE SAVIOR

"All night in prayer!" O! sacred, blest condition,
　To close the eyes on earth and view the sky;
To contemplate alone thy holy high commission,
　And commune with thy Father God on high.

"All night in prayer!" vile men for rest retiring,
　Thou goest forth alone to weep and pray—
To bathe thy soul with love thou art so much desiring,
　For man, and prayest till the glow of day.

"All night in prayer!" and Thy disciples sleeping—
　They for whose peace Thou groan'st in agony—
They for whose sake Thou art such anxious vigils keeping,
　Too unconcerned to watch one night with Thee!

"All night in prayer:" Hell's legions cease their revels,
　And quail their terrors in such notes as these:
"Darkness, nor flesh, nor all our labyrinth of devils,
　Can drive that son of Jesse from his knees."

"All night in prayer!" O! did no good inspire thee,
　Thou Intercessor, but mean Jesse's blood?
We'd fear thee not, Jehovah's holy essence fires thee:
　For *this* we fear—thou hated Son of God.

" All night in prayer!' and thus are we rewarded;
　For thousand years we've labored hard in vain,
And toiled with all the skill and wit these walls have hoarded,
　To counteract God's mighty love to man.

" All night in prayer!' Heaven's gracious King can never
　Resist such cries from His own darling Son;
Let war be waged by us with Heaven and earth forever—
　His prayer has now prevailed—man's bliss is won!

"All night in prayer." The stars in contemplation,
　Now view the scene in morning's glowing light—
Thour't reconciled to death, and death secures salvation—
　Earth glows with love, and heaven with glory bright.

Notes

Introduction

1. Parenthetical references identify citations and specific sources used in the introduction. For longer discussions of Oregon history in the pioneer period, see Dodds (1977:3-114), Johansen (1957:112-246), and Pomeroy (1973:22-63).

2. Duncan (1973) refers in her article to many sources that she used to substantiate the truth of Bailey's claims. See, for example, Carey (1922c), Clark (1927), Gay (1936), Gatke (1935), Hussey (1967).

3. In William L. Adams's *Treason, Strategems, and Spoils, a Melodrame in Five Acts by Breakspear,* William H. Wilson is the pseudonymous Grub. The play, a political satire, in which Adams pokes fun at leading Democrats of territorial Oregon, was first published in installments in the Portland *Oregonian* in 1852 (Bingham 1983:152-157).

Chapter I

1. Simeon Smith, Margaret's father, was listed as a wheelwright in his death record (New England Geneological Society, Beverly 2:557).

Chapter II

1. M.E.: Methodist Episcopalian.

Chapter III

1. Lady Maxwell D'Arcy (?1742-1810) was a Scots Methodist. A book based on her journals was published in 1826 by John Lancaster; it was printed in many editions in England and the United States *(Encyclopedia of World Methodism* 1538-1539).

2. Saugus is located in Essex County, Massachusetts, about eight miles northeast of Boston.

3. There was a cholera epidemic in the United States, starting in 1832 on the East Coast, which spread up and down the coast, and then west where it was especially fatal. In 1832 there about 6,000 cases in New York City, half of them fatal (Riegel 1949, 1973:307).

Chapter IV

1. *Daily Food for Christians; being a promise and another scriptural portion for every day in the year, together with the verse of a hymn.* Available in many editions.

2. Mrs. Fletcher is probably Mary Bosanquet Fletcher (1739-1815), a British philanthropist, preacher, and diarist *(Encyclopedia of World Methodism* 852-853).

3. Wilbraham Academy, the oldest institution (1815) of the Methodist church, is located near Wilbraham, Massachusetts. Many students went from there to the various missions of the church (*Encyclopedia of World Methodism* 2561).

4. After Margaret's brother, Simeon Smith, married Sarah Stocker of Saugus, September, 1818, they moved to Illinois. Sarah and a child died there in 1835, at which time Simeon moved back to Massachusetts with his two daughters (New England Geneological Society, Lynn 2:351).

Chapter V

1. Miner Raymond (1811-1897) "...occupied a prominent place in the councils of the church, and was frequently called upon to represent the church on special occasions. It was as a theologian, however, that he was most widely known and exerted his greatest influence. As a teacher in a theological school he profoundly impressed a whole generation of ministers and missionaries in all parts of the world. The three volumes of his *Systematic Theology,* published in 1877, attracted wide attention. . ." (Johnson et al. 1944-1981; 8:413-414).

Chapter VI

1. Rev. Thomas C. Pierce was the pastor of the Methodist Episcopal church in Saugus, Massachusetts. His wife, Jemina (Klinne) Pierce was the sister of Mary Amelia (Klinne) Leslie. This connection helps to explain why Margaret was thought of to join the mission party on such short notice (Perley 1915:330).

2. Mr. and Mrs. Leland are the names given in *The Grains* to David and Mary Leslie. Sometimes their real names are used, usually in connection with official documents or actions.

3. In a letter from Leslie to Nathan Bangs, Secretary of the Methodist Mission Society, January 12, 1837, we read: "You have been consulted on the subject of a female going out with my family. I understand by Br. King that you will be at the expense of the passage and board etc until we shall arrive at the mission. There is a female in Lynn who will go. She is well recommended as a suitable person to be employed as a teacher under the direction of the board when it shall be thought that her services are needed and it is with this expectation she will go out. Yourself and the board will probably be addressed on that subject by those who can furnish certificates of her character & qualifications in due time,—the lady's name is Margaret Smith" (Leslie, Oregon Methodist Papers).

4. Henry Kirk White Perkins was born in Penobscott, Maine, November 21, 1812. He went to Oregon with the Leslies and Margaret Smith. Perkins and Elvira Johnson were married November 21, 1837. Most of their work in Oregon was done at the mission at The Dalles with Daniel Lee. The Perkins returned to the States in 1844 (Vaughan 1975:151-180).

5. The voyage to Oregon followed the then usual route to the West Coast. The ship sailed south along the coast of North and South America, around Cape Horn, north along the coast of South America, then to Hawaii. Hawaii was the center of all Pacific Ocean commerce, and it was there that the last leg to Oregon would be arranged.

6. Utilitarianism is the doctrine that the principle of greatest utility should be the criterion in ethical matters, and that the criterion is to be applied to the consequences flowing from ethical decisions. The principle is often expressed as the greatest happiness or the greatest good for the greatest number (Reese 1980:601).

Chapter VII

1. Cherrymoi is probably cherimoyer, the pulpy fruit of *Annoma cherimola,* a tree of Peru. The fruit is heart-shaped with a scaly exterior and numerous seeds.

2. Edwin Oscar Hall (1810-1883), a member of the Hawaiian mission of the Presbyterian church, was stationed at Honolulu (Smith 1956:342).

3. Cyrus Shepard (1799-1840) was born in Phillipston, Massachusetts. He went west with Jason and Daniel Lee in 1834 and was the teacher of the Indian school at the mission. He and Susan Downing were married in July 1837 (Corning 1956:221-222).

4. Donald McTavish (1772-1814) was a fur trader with the Northwest Company. He came to Oregon in April, 1814, as chief trader, accompanied by Jane Barnes. On May 22, 1814, McTavish and four others drowned while crossing the Columbia River (Carey 1971:217-218).

5. Dr. John McLoughlin (1784-1857) was the Chief Factor of the Hudson's Bay Company, Columbia District, from 1825-1846 (Johnson 1944-1981, 6:134-35).

6. Crash pants are pants made from a coarse linen called crash.

7. Dr. William Fraser Tolmie (1812-1886) was the physician at Fort Vancouver from 1836-1841 (Scott 1924, 5:226).

8. Rev. Daniel Lee (1806-1895) was the nephew of Jason Lee and accompanied him to Oregon in 1834. He married Maria Ware in 1840. Much of his work in Oregon was done at The Dalles. In 1843 he and his family returned to the States because of his wife's ill health (Corning 1956:144; Gatke 1935:74-75).

Chapter VIII

1. *Children of the Abbey,* a luridly sentimental novel, written by the Irish novelist Regina Maria Roche in 1798, was immensely popular for many years.

2. Rev. Hiram Bingham (1789-1869) was the head of the Presbyterian mission at Hàwaii at this time (Smith 1956:346).

3. Jean Baptiste McKay came to Oregon with the Astoria expedition in 1814. He stayed in Oregon after the breakup of that company. About 1830 he settled at French Prairie and became a prosperous farmer (Munnick 1960).

4. The women in the mission at this time were Anna Maria Pittman Lee, Susan Downing Shepard, Elvira Johnson, Rachel Beers, Sarepeta White, Mary Leslie, and Margaret Smith. In speaking of the working arrangements before the arrival of the second reinforcement, Anna Maria had written: "We all have our work to do, the present arrangement is, Mrs. White and I at the head of domestic affairs Mr. Shepard and his intended assist us in the care of the children Miss Johnson is in the school" (Gay 1936:157).

5. James Birnie (1800-1864) from Aberdeen, Scotland, spent many years in charge of Fort George for the Hudson's Bay Company (Corning 1956:28).

6. Dr. Elijah White (1806-1879) came to Oregon in May, 1837, with his wife and two children. He left the mission and returned to the States in 1840. He was commissioned Indian Agent in Washington, D.C. and returned to Oregon in 1842 (Corning 1956:263; Gatke 1935:75).

7. William Holden Willson (1801-1856) was born in New Hampshire. He worked at a variety of jobs before joining the Oregon Mission as a carpenter in May 1837. In *The Grains* he is called 'Wiley' (Dobbs 1932:56-59).

8. Philip L. Edwards was a native of Kentucky. In 1834 at age twenty-two he joined the Lee mission party to Oregon as a lay helper. He taught school in Champoeg in 1835, and in 1836 went to California with the other settlers in the area to obtain cattle for the mission. In March, 1838, he returned to the States with Jason Lee (Edwards 1932:Intro.; Corning 1956:79).

9. The difficulty to which Jason Lee referred was Alanson Beers' charges against Elijah White. Beers (1800-1853) was born in Connecticut. He came to the Oregon Mission in May 1837 as a blacksmith (Dobbs 1932:63-65). He accused Elijah White of being uncharitable on board ship coming to Oregon. Jason Lee had the two meet in trial three times before finally dismissing all charges (Loewenberg 1972).

10. Joseph L. Whitcomb came to Oregon in May, 1837. He was employed by the mission as farm superintendent. In 1841 he married Susan Downing Shepard, the widow of Cyrus Shepard. In September, 1842 they returned to Lynn, Massachusetts, and he died soon after (Gatke 1935:164-168).

11. This was written after the arrival of the large reinforcement to the Mission on the *Lausanne*.

Chapter IX

1. The Indians of the area were the Calapooyas.

2. In a letter home Margaret provided a sample of a short sermon she preached to the Indians: "Mican tum-tum cloosh? (Your heart good?) Mican tum-tum wake cloosh. (Your heart no good.) Alaka mican ma-ma lose. (By-and bye you die.) Mican tum-tum cloosh mican clatamay Sakalatie. (Your heart good you go to God.) Mican tum-tum wake cloosh mican wake clatamay Sakalatie. (Your heart no good you no go to God.) Mican clatalmay sayyah; hiyas wake cloosh Schochen. (Go ye great way off; very bad devil.) Sakalatie mamoke tum-tum cloosh. (God make heart good.) Wah-wah Sakalatie. (Speak to God.) Sakalatie mamoke hiyas cloosh mican tum-tum. (God make very good your heart.) Hiyack wah-wah Sakalatie. (Quick speak to God.)" (*Oregonian and Indian's Advocate,* Nov. 1838: 60).

3. Wah-wah means talk.

4. Timnah Tufts was the second wife of Simeon Smith. They were married May 28, 1837, in Lynn, Massachusetts. They had two children; Merritt (September 4, 1839-September 19, 1839) and Sarah Timnah (July 28, 1843-December 6, 1844). Timnah Smith died February 12, 1844, age thirty-four (New England Geneological Society, Lynn 1:374; 2:351, 592-593).

5. Sir James Douglass (1803-1877) was educated in Scotland. He came to Fort Vancouver in 1830 and was second in command for many years (Sage 1926).

6. Eloisa McLoughlin Rae was the daughter of John McLoughlin. She was married to William Glen Rae (1809-1845), an employee of the Hudson's Bay Company, in February, 1838. McLoughlin went to London in 1838 and returned in 1840 (Holman 1907:24-25).

7. Rev. Herbert Beaver was the chaplain at Fort Vancouver from 1836 to 1838 (Beaver 1959).

8. Mrs. Spalding and Mrs. Whitman stayed at Fort Vancouver while their husbands selected and began preparation of their mission sites.

Chapter X

1. Abigail Willis Tenny Smith, wife of Lowell Smith, missionary at Honolulu, 1833-1891 (Smith 1956:345).

2. Wailatpu was the name of the Whitman Mission. It is mispelled here.

3. Sarah Gilbert White Smith, wife of Asa Smith, of the mission of the American Board of Foreign Missions. The Whites arrived in Oregon in 1838 and returned to the States three years later because of Sarah's ill health (Drury 1: 273-280; 3: 25-125).

Chapter XI

1. See, for example, letter from Pierce to Leslie, August 16, 1837: "The mission committee have appointed Sister Smith a teacher in the Oregon Mission when she may be wanted by the Superintendent of that mission with a sallary I think of $200 her outfit and half year is considerd paid in what she rec'd from us who engaged her I believe we have redeemed our pledge she is now one of the mission family" (Pierce, Mss 1216).

2. For a fuller account see the *Mission Board Report on the Oregon Mission:* "There is, perhaps, no one of the missionary fields under the supervision of this Society respecting which public opinion has been so fluctuating. At one time, it has been the most popular of all our missions; at another, it has been set down as a perfect failure. In some instances, the Church's expectations concerning it have been entirely too sanguine; and in others she has shown herself but too ready to yield to despondency. Had it been practicable for her to have taken a sober and enlightened view of this Oregon enterprise, in all of its various circumstances and aspects, she could not have been so easily elevated or depressed by counter representations from the country. But the extreme distance of the mission from the seat of the Society's operations, the long intervals between our dispatches, and sometimes the conflicting statements of the missionaries, rendered it next to impossible, even for the Board, to judge correctly the facts in the case" (Carey 1922a:340-341).

3. Angelique Carpentier (1828-1859). The daughters of Charles Carpentier, Angelique and her sister Sophie, were placed in the Methodist Mission School near Salem for a few years when left motherless. After leaving the mission, Angelique seems to have had a number of lovers. At the time of her murder, at the hand of her current husband, Charles Roe, the *Oregonian* reported that "She had previously lived with a Negro and a Kanaka and had children by both" (Munnick 1979, 1:A-14).

4. Anna Maria Pittman Lee (1803-1838) came to Oregon in May 1837. She married Jason Lee in July 16, 1837 and died June 26, 1838, after the birth of their child. The child, too, died soon after birth (Gay 1936).

Chapter XII

1. Daniel Lee, W. H. Willson, and Joseph Whitcomb were bachelors at the mission.

2. Binney is the name given in *The Grains* to Doctor William John Bailey.

Chapter XIII

1. Michael Sellers was convicted in Marion County Circuit Court of breaking into the store of Schlussel and Cohn and taking $5,000 in gold dust and coin. He escaped from jail just before his trial, was captured and sentenced to five years in the penitentiary (*Oregon Statesman* July 19, 1853: 2; October 18, 1853: 2; November 1, 1853: 2; *Spectator* October 20, 1853: 3).

2. Letter from Leslie to Bangs, March 5, 1839: "It is [propper?] to let you know that Margaret J. Smith is married, to a gentleman in this country not connected with the Mission;—This I suppose disolves her connection with the mission; We have [rec'd?] no official notice of [her?] appointment and know not what salary she was entitled to receive" (Leslie, Oregon Methodist Papers).

Chapter XIV

1. The Oregon Provisional Migration Society was formed in Lynn, Massachusetts in 1838 with the object of furthering the settlement of Oregon and continuing the work of converting the Indians. It proposed to send out a company of settlers in 1840, and efforts were made to secure funds and recruits for the project; it failed, however, to send anyone. The society published a newspaper, *The Oregonian and Indian's Advocate* (Lavender 1958:197-199).

2. David Brainerd (1718-1747) was a missionary to the Indians in western Massachusetts, New York, and New Jersey. He was the author of a journal published in 1746 and 1749, which was very popular (Johnson 1944-1981, 1:591-92).

3. Rev. Samuel Parker (1779-1866) was a Congregational clergyman. He and Marcus Whitman came west in 1835, looking for a mission site among the Indians. Marcus Whitman returned East to organize the mission and Mr. Parker continued to explore. He spent the winter of 1835-36 at Fort Vancouver. In 1838 he published *Journal of an Exploring Tour Beyond the Rocky Mountains* (Johnson 1944-1981, 7:237-238).

4. Caleb Cushing (1800-1879) was a U.S. Congressman from Salisbury, Massachusetts. As Chairman of the House Foreign Relations Committee he compiled a report on Oregon which was presented to Congress in January, 1839. He was also a member of the J. P. Cushing firm which made a fortune in the China trade. The firm explored trade possibilities in Oregon and started a store there in 1842 (Johnson 1944-1981, 2:623-630; Throckmorton 1961:29-30).

5. The Whitman Massacre occurred on November 29, 1847. Indians raided the mission, killing Marcus and Narcissa Whitman and twelve others. Fifty-three women and children were captured by the Indians and held hostage until rescued by the Hudson's Bay Company (Drury 1963-1966, 1:161-70).

Chapter XV

1. Ewing Young (ca. 1810-1841) was born in Tennessee. In May, 1834, he met the Oregon promoter, Hall Jackson Kelley, in southern California and the two, with twelve others, arrived at Fort Vancouver in October, 1834. In 1837 he organized the Willamette Valley Cattle Company to bring cattle from California. In this venture he and ten other settlers were successful, returning with 600 head. After this he became a leader in Oregon (Johnson 1944-1981, 10: 627).

2. John K. Townsend, the naturalist, was at Fort Vancouver when Bailey arrived. Townsend describes Bailey in his journal: "This is certainly by far the most horrible looking wound I ever saw, rendered so, however, by injudicious treatment and entire want of care in the proper apposition of the sundered parts; he simply bound it up as well as he could with his handkerchief and his extreme anguish caused him to forget the necessity of accuracy in this respect. The consequence is, one side being considerably lower than the other" (Thwaites 1904-1907, 21: 331).

3. Philip Edwards in his diary of the cattle trip recounts the events this way: "Gay and the Indian were sitting within ten feet of each other, when the former shot. The Indian sprang up to run when Bailey also shot at him. The Indian ran about 20 paces and fell dead, down the hill....I sprang up, calling it a mean, base, dastardly act, and that such men were not to be depended upon in danger!...Turner, Gay and Bailey were three of four survivors of a party of eight men who had been defeated at the next river, and several of the survivors were much mangled...This they allege as their justification. But the murder was committed four days before reaching the place of their defeat, and the Indians may have been of another tribe. Nor could any consideration of private revenge, allowing its legality in itself, authorize endangering the property of others" (Edwards 1932:42-43).

4. Merino fabric is a soft woolen material like fine French cashmere.

5. In a letter home Susan Shepard expressed her feelings about Margaret, her marriage, and some of her difficulties: "I hope I shall not be as sadley disappointed as I was in M Smith who is the *beatum* of all the persons that ever I was acquainted with she has now married Dr. Bailey an Englishman who has ben til within a year or so the vilest wretch in the country he has made a profession of religion and appears to be trying to do well now I think when people are educated and sent out for missionaries they aught to have something more than piety to recommend them to be sure this is indispensable grace may subdue the most stubborn willful disposition and the most devoted christian may backslide and if they were not amiable and qualified to be useful and happy in all most every station at home I would not advise them to be missionaries for missionaries have many sacrafises to make besides leaving home and dear friends but I did not mean to say all this you will begin to say come home and make room for others that can be more useful" (Shepard, Mss 1219).

Chapter XVI

1. The two Catholic priests from Canada were Modeste Demers and Francis Norbet Blanchet. They arrived at Fort Vancouver in late 1838 (Lyons 1974:18-20).

2. Maria Monk's *Awful Disclosures of the Hotel Dieu Nunnery of Montreal,* New York, 1836, was an anti-Catholic book widely known in the period.

3. One of the visitors may have been Thomas Farnham who visited the Baileys not long after their marriage and noted them in his official report: "Leaving M'Kay's mill, we traveled along a circuitous track through a heavy forest of fir and pine, and emerged into a beautiful little prairie, at the side of which stood the doctor's neat hewn log cabin, sending its cheerful smoke among the lofty pine tops in its rear. We soon sat by a blazing fire, and the storm that had pelted us all the way, lost its unpleasantness in the delightful society of my worthy host and his amiable wife. I passed the night with them. The doctor is a Scotchman, his wife a Yankee. The former had seen many adventures in California and Oregon and had his face very much slashed in a contest with the Shasty Indians near the Southern border of Oregon. The latter had come from the States, a member of the Methodist Episcopal Mission, and had consented to share the bliss and ills of life with the adventurous Gael; and a happy little family they were" (Thwaites 1904-1907, 29:18-19).

In 1841 another visitor to the Baileys was Charles Wilkes. His impressions of his visit to the Baileys' farm were also reported officially: "After passing the ridge, we again entered on fine prairies, part of the farm of Dr. Bailey. This was one of the most comfortable I had yet seen, and certainly in the neatest order. Dr. Bailey had married one of the girls who came out with the missionaries, and the mistress of the establishment was as pleasing as it was well conducted. Dr. Bailey desiring to accompany us to the falls, I gladly concluded to await their dinner, and before it was served had an opportunity of looking about the premises. The locality resembles the prairies I have so often spoken of, but there was something in the arrangements of the farm that seemed advanced beyond the other settlements of the country. The garden was, in particular, exceedingly well kept, and had in it all the best vegetables of our own country. This was entirely the work of Mrs. Bailey, whose activity could not rest content until it was accomplished. She had followed the mission as a teacher, until she found there was no field for labour. She had been in hope that the great missionary field to the north, of which I have before spoke, would be occupied; but this being neglected, she had left them" (Wilkes 1844, 4:361-362).

4. Manning's Shortest Way of Ending Disputes about Religion was probably a sermon written by Henry Edward Manning (1808-1892), a popular religious writer.

5. This was called the Great Reinforcement, arriving in Oregon in 1840 on the *Lausanne.* In the party were seven preachers, one physician, four mechanics, two farmers, one steward, one stewardess, and four lady teachers (Brosnan 1932:146-156).

6. There was much ill feeling between Dr. White and Jason Lee. This ended in a trial (September 12, 1840) of White on the charges of disobedience to the order of the church, dishonesty, and imprudent conduct. White left Oregon on September 15, 1840, determined to have Lee removed as head of the mission. The mission board in New York did not agree with him (Loewenberg 1972; Lyons 1974:81-85).

❦

7. Chloe Clark came with the missionary party on the *Lausanne* in 1840. She was assigned as teacher in Nisqually, Washington, where Willson was assigned as a carpenter. They were married in Washington (Gatke 1943, 1:95-97).

8. *Methodist Preacher: or, Monthly Sermons from Living Ministers* was published by J. Putnam of Boston, starting with volume 1 in January, 1830.

9. "The Indian woman was Marie Tchalis, 'wife of the widower Quesnal, buried in the old cemetery at St. Paul, aged 30 years'" (Munnick 1957:10).

Chapter XVII

1. Captain John Couch was a representative of the Cushing family in Massachusetts. "Couch was the first American tradesman, except for Abernethy, whose business career, first at Oregon City and later at Portland, was identified with the early development of the region. He established a store at Willamette Falls, soon to be called Oregon City" (Throckmorton 1961:29-30).

2. Rev. Dr. Richmond had come with the 1840 reinforcement to the Oregon Mission and was returning to the States.

3. Leslie was taking two of his daughters to Hawaii for education after the death of his wife Mary.

4. Mrs. Whitcomb was the former Susan Downing Shepard, now married to the mission farmer Joseph Whitcomb. They were going back to the States because of his ill health.

Chapter XVIII

1. "The *Chenamus* sailed, Sept. 16, 1843. Dr. Wm. Bailey and his wife, Mr. Cushing and Henry Johnson came as passengers....They reached the Sandwich Islands near the end of February, the next year, and lying by until April, finished the voyage to the Columbia in twenty days" (Oregon Pioneer Association 1886:62).

2. Dr. Ira Leonard Babcock (ca. 1808-1888) was a physician, judge, and executive in Oregon. He arrived in Oregon with the 1840 reinforcement to the mission. Following Ewing Young's death intestate he was made Supreme Judge with probate powers, a position he held for two years. In 1843 he spent a year with his family in the Sandwich Islands. Upon his return he was again elected Supreme Judge, holding that office till he left Oregon in November, 1844 (Dobbs 1932:74-80).

3. John C. Jones was the U. S. Commercial Agent at Hawaii for many years. He was anti-missionary. He had two Hawaiian women as common-law wives whom he left behind when he went to California in 1837 (Smith 1956:134-135; 212).

4. Brother of Caleb Cushing, he was in Oregon to examine the commercial possibilities for J. P. Cushing and Company of Newburyport, Massachusetts.

5. Kaspar Hauser (1812?-1833), the subject of the novel *Caspar Hauser* (1908), by Jakob Wassermann, was a German foundling who at about age 16 wandered into Nuremberg.

Chapter XIX

1. Dr. Bailey was elected one of the three members of the Executive Committee of the Provisional Government in 1844-1845 (Turnbull 1959:9).

2. *Rise and Progress of Religion in the Soul: Illustrated in a course of serious and practical addresses, suited to persons of every character and circumstance, with a devout meditation or prayer added to each chapter,* written about 1744 by Phillip Doddridge, and available in many editions.

3. Joseph McLoughlin (1809-1848), oldest son of John McLoughlin and his first wife, settled as a farmer near Champoeg, and was on the committee to draft a code of laws for the provisional government. He died from the effects of a fall over a cliff in the Umpqua region (Corning 1956:162).

4. A series of thirty novels written by Sir Walter Scott.

5. *History of the Bible* was a miniature book published by various publishers in several editions. The first edition was probably about 1814.

6. John Howard (Hord) came up from California with Ewing Young in 1834. He was a farmer, carpenter, and tavern keeper at Champoeg (Munnick 1979, 2:A-51).

7. Caroline Anne Bowles Southey (1786-1854) was a writer of poetry and prose; she was noted for the pathos of her stories.

8. Hudson's Bay Company bought the wheat of the farmers in the Willamette Valley for export to the Russians in Alaska.

9. Bailey was elected to the legislature from Champoeg district three times.

10. The petition for divorce of the Brooks "states that his said wife at this time is labouring under a secondary symptom of the veneral disease which has come to the knowledge of your said petitioner within a few days past and further states that your said petitioner has become perfectly satisfied from medical tests that his said wife has been laboring under the effects of said disease for a long time past and that the [condition?] of the said Mary Ann is such that it [is impossible?] for your said petitioner to bear longer with his said wife…" (*Oregon Papers* 660).

11. *The Works of Thomas Dick* were written by Thomas Dick (1774-1857), a Scottish secession writer and minister.

12. Bailey signed an obituary for N. J. Putnam on June 10, 1847. A letter to Mrs. T'Vault from Margaret Bailey states: "He had said when trying to rise, 'I think I'm going to faint' and died without a struggle, probably the exertion caused a rupture in his diseased heart.…I have reason to think that my services were acceptable to him, for the Sabbath morning on which he died, he said to his brother, 'Is not Mrs. Bailey a kind woman' 'I dont think I could have gone to another house in Oregon and found a lady who would have treated me so kindly.' This I say not boasting, but because it assures me that what I did for him, pleased him." (Bailey, Mss 191).

❦

13. Possibly the Mariposa Lily *(Lillaceae Calochortus)*. "Branched or simple herbs with coated corms; leaves narrowly linear; flowers large, showy, peduncled; perianth-segments separate, spreading, whitish, purplish or variegated, the three outer sepal-like, narrow, the three inner petal-like, gland-bearing, and bearded or spotted within; stamens 6, hypogynous; ovary 3-celled; ovules numerous" (Piper 1915:96).

14. Ladies Magazine is probably *American Ladies Magazine;* containing original tales, essays, literary and historical sketches, poetry, criticism, music, and a variety of matter connected with many other subjects. It later merged into *Godey's Ladies Book.*

15. Hoosier appears to be used by Margaret in the sense of denoting an ignorant person.

16. Lydia Howard Sigourney (1791-1865), a poet and writer from Connecticut, wrote sixty-seven books and was very popular in her time.

17. Blanchard is Bishop Blanchet.

18. A barouche is a four wheeled carriage, having a seat in front for the driver and seats for two couples inside where they sit facing each other.

Chapter XX

1. Robert Newell (1807-1869), one of the leading citizens of Champoeg, had been a free trapper or 'mountain man' in the Rocky Mountains before coming to Oregon with his brother-in-law, Joseph Meek, in 1840 (Johnson 1944-1981, 7: 458).

2. Sarah and Eliza Flett lived with the Baileys between 1845-1847 and testified for Margaret at the divorce trial.

3. In her petition for divorce Margaret describes this event in more detail: "Caught complainant by the hair of the head and dragged her into the house, and abused her brutally. Defendant injured complainants hip at this time so that complainant was for a long time unable to walk upon it, and to this time has not wholly recovered from the effects of said treatment" (Marion County No. 180).

4. Butteville is on the East Bank of the Willamette River in the northern part of Marion County. It was named for a hill about a mile to the southwest. This hill was called by the early settlers La Butte. Butteville was laid out prior to 1850 by Abernethy and Beers (McArthur 1974:101).

5. An act of Congress providing donation to settlers of public land in Oregon Territory, passed in 1850, under which a citizen of the U.S., or one who had declared intentions before Dec. 1, 1850, and who had resided upon and cultivated the land for four consecutive years was granted, if single, 320 acres; if married or marrying within one year, 640 acres, half to be held by his wife (Clark 1927, 1: 406).

Chapter XXI

1. Benicia was the capital of California 1853-1854. The city was founded in 1848.

2. In 1846 the U. S. made a treaty with Columbia guaranteeing the neutrality of the Isthmus of Panama in return for the promise of free transit across the Isthmus by any mode of communication which might be constructed. The Panama Railroad was completed in 1855, but until that time the trail described in *The Grains* was used to get across, saving the long trip around the Horn (Andrews, 1962:707).

3. O. C. Wheeler was a missionary sent by the American Baptist Home Missionary Society to California in 1849 (Goodykoontz 1971:284-285).

4. Margaret's lawyer was Mathew Deady, prominent in Oregon from 1849 to 1893. In a letter to him in June, 1852 she voices her fears: ''I am compelled to trouble you again, to my regret. Dr. Bailey passed here yesterday on his way to Buteville. He has closed his business at Portland, & is on his way to the Mines with his brother. I am satisfied that it is his intention to avoid the Court, & giving means of support, allowing me to have the remainder of my effects at Buteville. You will best know if there is any remedy, if there be—it must be found immediately, or it 'twill be of no avail. I presume you will without my urging you, do what you can, at once'' (Johnson 1944-1981, 3:167-68; Bailey, Mss 48).

5. Judge O. C. Pratt (1819-1891) arrived in Oregon in December, 1848, the first of the Territorial officers to reach Oregon. He was Supreme Court Judge in Oregon from April, 1849 to December, 1853 (*History of the Bench & Bar in Oregon* 273-274).

6. Judge George H. Williams (1823-1910). In 1852 Williams was appointed Chief Justice of the Supreme Court of the Oregon territory. He arrived in Salem in 1853 and served as judge until 1859. He was Oregon's U. S. Senator from 1865-1871 and U. S. Attorney General 1873 to 1877. He served two terms as Mayor of Portland, 1902-1905 (Johnson 1944-1981, 10:262-63).

7. An interdenominational organization comprised of total abstainers, Sons of Temperance was founded in 1842.

Chapter XXII

1. James Shiel (1829-1853) was one of the first practicing physicians at French Prairie (Munnick 1979, 2: A-89).

2. In the *Oregon Statesman,* September 13, 1853, there was an item about this fire: ''The dwelling of Dr. Bailey, Champoeg, a new and valuable one, was destroyed by fire on Tuesday morning last, with all the furniture, &c. The Doctor's stock of medicines only were taken out, and they were soon afterwards completely destroyed by a runaway horse, which found his way into the yard where they were lying upon the ground. The house is supposed to have taken fire from a cigar.''

On October 18, 1853, there appeared another article about Bailey containing information that might have had some bearing on the divorce proceedings:: ''Territory vs. Wm. K. Beale—assault with intent to kill—indictment found at March term. McCabe and Barnum for defendant moved to quash indictment. Overruled. Dr. Bailey, the person assaulted, testified that Beale and himself had been drinking wine during the evening at the house of the doctor at Champoeg, and that some words occurred in the house, and he requested Beale to leave, which he did. Afterwards hearing some noise in front of his house, he went out in the dark and received a heavy blow on the head with a club, which was followed by a stab with a knife near the shoulder, from someone he could not see; that the wound was a dangerous one; that Beale was intoxicated; that he shot a pistol at Beale after the stabbing.

Wm. Reese testified that Beale came to his house in the night and told him that he had had a fracas with Dr. Bailey; that Bailey had fired a pistol at him, and that he had stabbed Bailey; that Beale was intoxicated, and that Dr. Bailey was excited with liquor. Acquitted.'' *(Oregon Statesman)*

3. Amory Holbrook (1820-1866) was a lawyer and politician. He was appointed U. S. Attorney General for Oregon and arrived in May of 1850. He was mayor of Oregon City from 1856-1859 and an Oregon state legislator in 1859 (Corning 1956:116).

Selected Bibliography

Works by Margaret Bailey

Letter. *Zion's Herald*, 11 April 1838:2.

Letter. *Oregonian and Indian's Advocate*, November 1838:59-60; 63-64.

Letter. *Zion's Herald*, 5 December 1838:3.

Letter. *Oregonian and Indian's Advocate*, May 1839:249-250.

Letter. *Oregonian and Indian's Advocate*, July 1839:309.

"Sally Soule" [story]. In Mudge (1848).

"Love" [poem]. *Oregon Spectator*, 5 February 1846:3.

"Affliction" [poem]. *Oregon Spectator*, 4 March 1846:3.

"May Morning in Oregon" [poem]. *Oregon Spectator*, 28 May 1846:1.

"New Columbia" [poem]. *Oregon Spectator*, 26 November 1846:3.

"It Charms Me that I Hope to Live" [poem]. *Oregon Spectator*, 22 July 1847:4.

"Slander" [essay]. *Oregon Spectator*, 19 August 1847:2.

"Ladies Department" [column, including poems and short stories by R. R.]. *Oregon Spectator*, 12 May through 16 June 1854:3.

Advertisement for *The Grains*. *Oregon Statesman*, each week 8 August through 7 November 1854:3.

Advertisement for *The Grains*. *Oregonian*, each week 8 June through 5 August 1854:3.

"Advertisement." *Oregon Weekly Times*, 16 September 1854:3.

The Grains: Or, Passages in the Life of Ruth Rover, with Occasional Pictures of Oregon, Natural and Moral. 2 vols. Portland, OR.: Carter and Austin, 1854.

Letter to Mathew Deady. Mss 48. 16 June 1852. Oregon Historical Society Library. Portland, OR.

Miscellaneous papers. Mss 126. Oregon Historical Society Library. Portland, OR.

Letter to Mrs. T'Vault. Ms 1191. (n.d.) Oregon Historical Society Library. Portland, OR.

Other Materials

Adams, William L. 1968. *A Melodrame Entitled "Treason, Strategems, and Spoils."* Edited by George N. Belknap. Hamden, CT: Archon Books.

Ahlstrom, Sydney E. 1972. *A Religious History of the American People.* New Haven, CT: Yale University Press.

Allen, A. J. (compiler). 1850. *Ten Years in Oregon: Travels and Adventures of Dr. E. White and Lady, West of the Rocky Mountains;...* Ithaca, NY: Press of Audrus, Gauntlett, & Co.

Andrews, Wayne (editor). 1962. *Concise Dictionary of American History.* New York, NY: Scribner.

Atwood, Rev. A. 1907. *The Conquerors: Historical Sketches of the American Settlement of the Oregon Country Embracing Facts in the Life and Work of Rev. Jason Lee.* Tacoma, WA: A. Atwood.

Baker, Abner Sylvester III. 1968. "The Oregon Pioneer Tradition in the Nineteenth Century: A Study of Recollection and Self-definition." Ph.D. dissertation, University of Oregon.

Bancroft, Hubert H. 1883-1890. *The Works of Hubert Howe Bancroft.* Vols. 27-28, *History of the Northwest Coast,* and vols. 29-30, *History of Oregon.* San Francisco, CA: The History Company.

Barclay, Wade Crawford. 1949-1950. *History of Methodist Missions.* Vol. 1, *Early American Methodism, 1769-1844,* and vol. 2, *To Reform the Nation.* New York, NY: Board of Missions and Church Extension of the Methodist Church.

Baym, Nina. 1978. *Woman's Fiction: A Guide to Novels by and about Women in America, 1820-1870.* Ithaca, NY: Cornell University Press.

Beaver, Herbert. 1959. *Reports and Letters of Herbert Beaver, 1836-1838, Chaplain to the Hudson's Bay Company and Missionary to the Indians at Fort Vancouver.* Edited by Thomas E. Jessett. Portland, OR: Champoeg Press.

Beaver, R. Pierce. 1980. *American Protestant Women in World Mission: History of the First Feminist Movement in North America.* Grand Rapids, MI: W. B. Eerdman Publishing Co. First edition published under title: *All Loves Excelling.*

Belknap, George N. 1968. *Oregon Imprints 1845-1870.* Eugene, OR: University of Oregon Books.

Bingham, Edwin R. 1983. "Pacific Northwest Writing: Reaching for Regional Identity." Pages 151-174 in *Regionalism and the Pacific Northwest.* Edited by William G. Robbins, Robert Frank, and Richard Ross. Corvallis, OR: Oregon State University Press.

Bode, Carl. 1959. *The Anatomy of American Popular Culture 1840-1861.* Berkeley and Los Angeles, CA: University of California Press.

Bowen, William A. 1978. *The Willamette Valley: Migration and Settlement on the Oregon Frontier.* Seattle, WA: University of Washington Press.

Brier, Warren Judson. 1957. "A History of Newspapers in the Pacific Northwest, 1846-1896." Ph.D. dissertation, State University of Iowa.

Brosnan, Cornelius J. 1932. *Jason Lee: Prophet of the New Oregon*. New York, NY: Macmillan.

Brown, J. Henry. 1892. *Brown's Political History of Oregon*. Vol. 1, *Provisional Government*. Portland, OR: Wiley B. Allen.

Burrell, Orin K. 1967. *Gold in the Woodpile: An Informal History of Banking in Oregon*. Eugene, OR: University of Oregon Books.

Canse, John M. 1930. *Pilgrim and Pioneer: Dawn in the Northwest*. New York, NY: Abingdon Press.

Cantwell, Robert. 1972. *The Hidden Northwest*. Philadelphia, PA: J. B. Lippincott Co.

Capital Journal, Salem, OR. 13 January 1947: 9.

Carey, Charles H. (editor). 1922a. "Excerpts from Methodist Annual Reports Relating to the Willamette Mission 1834-1848." *Oregon Historical Quarterly* 23:303-364.

Carey, Charles H. 1922b. *History of Oregon*. 3 vols. Chicago, IL: The Pioneer Historical Publishing Co.

Carey, Charles H. (editor). 1922c. "Mission Record Book of the Methodist Episcopal Church, Willamette Station, Oregon Territory, Commenced 1834." *Oregon Historical Quarterly* 23:230-266.

Carey, Charles H. 1971. *General History of Oregon Through Early Statehood*. Portland, OR: Binford & Mort.

Clark, Robert Carlton. 1927. *History of the Willamette Valley, Oregon*. Chicago, IL: The S. J. Clarke Publishing Co.

Cook, S. F. 1955. "The Epidemic of 1830-1833 in California and Oregon." *University of California Publications in American Archaeology and Ethnology* 43:303-326.

Corning, Howard. 1947. *Willamette Landings: Ghost Towns of the River*. Portland, OR: Binford & Mort.

Corning, Howard. 1956. *Dictionary of Oregon History*. Portland, OR: Binford & Mort.

Decker, Robert James. 1961. "Jason Lee, Missionary to Oregon. A Re-evaluation." Ph.D. dissertation, Indiana University.

Degler, Carl N. 1980. *At Odds: Women and the Family in America from the Revolution to the Present*. New York, NY: Oxford University Press.

Dobbs, Caroline. 1932. *Men of Champoeg: A Record of the Lives of the Pioneers Who Founded the Oregon Government*. Portland, OR: Metropolitan Press.

Dodds, Gordon. 1977. *Oregon: A Bicentennial History*. New York, NY: Norton.

Douglas, Ann. 1977. *The Feminization of American Culture*. New York, NY: Alfred A. Knopf.

Drury, Clifford M. 1963-1966. *First White Women over the Rockies: Diaries, Letters, and Biographical Sketches of the Six Women of the Oregon Mission Who Made the Overland Journey in 1836 and 1838.* 3 vols. Glendale, CA: The Arthur H. Clark Co.

Dryden, Cecil P. 1968. *Give all to Oregon! Missionary Pioneers of the Far West.* New York, NY: Hastings House.

Duncan, Janice K. 1973. "'Ruth Rover'—Vindictive Falsehood or Historical Truth." *Journal of the West* 12 (April): 240-253.

Edwards, Philip Leget. 1932. *The Diary of Philip Leget Edwards: The Great Cattle Drive from California to Oregon in 1837.* San Francisco, CA: Grabhorn Press.

Eells, Myron. 1882. *History of the Indian Missions on the Pacific Coast: Oregon, Washington and Idaho.* Philadelphia, PA: American Sunday-School Union.

Encyclopedia of World Methodism. c.1974. 2 vols. Nashville, TN: United Methodist Publishing House.

Faragher, Johnny, and Stansell, Christine. 1975. "Women and Their Families on the Overland Trail to California and Oregon, 1842-1867." *Feminist Studies* 2:150-166.

Ferguson, Charles W. 1971. *Organizing to Beat the Devil: Methodists and the Making of America.* Garden City, NY: Doubleday Co., Inc.

Foster, Ellen. 1977. "Margaret Bailey's Book Scandalous: For Its Day, It was That—But Her Story Reflected the Period as Well." *Oregon Territory* in *Oregon Statesman,* Salem, OR, December 11:10.

Frost, O. W. 1959. "Margaret J. Bailey: Oregon Pioneer Author." *Marion County History* 5:64-70.

Galbraith, John S. 1957. *The Hudson's Bay Company as an Imperial Factor 1821-1869.* Berkeley and Los Angeles, CA: University of California Press.

Gaston, Joseph. 1912. *The Centennial History of Oregon, 1811-1912.* 4 vols. Chicago, IL: The S. J. Clarke Publishing Co.

Gatke, Robert Moulton (editor). 1935. "A Document of Mission History 1833-43." *Oregon Historical Quarterly* 36: 71-94; 163-181.

Gatke, Robert Moulton. 1943. *Chronicles of Willamette: The Pioneer University of the West.* 2 vols. Portland, OR: Binford & Mort.

Gay, Theressa. 1936. *Life and Letters of Mrs. Jason Lee: First Wife of Rev. Jason Lee of the Oregon Mission.* Portland, OR: Metropolitan Press.

Geneaological Forum of Portland, Oregon. 1957-1975. *Genealogical Material in Oregon Donation Land Claims Abstracted from Applications.* 5 vols. Portland, OR.

Goodykoontz, Colin Brummitt. 1939. *Home Missions on the American Frontier: With Particular Reference to the American Home Missionary Society.* The Caxton Printers Ltd. Reprint, New York, NY: Octagon Books, 1971.

Gill, John. 1933. *Gill's Dictionary of the Chinook Jargon.* 17th ed. Portland, OR: J. K. Gill Co.

Gray, William H. 1870. *A History of Oregon 1792-1849, Drawn from Personal Observation and Authentic Information.* Published by the author for subscribers. Portland, OR: Harris & Holman.

Grimshaw, Patricia. 1983. "Christian Woman, Pious Wife, Faithful Mother, Devoted Missionary: Conflicts in Roles of American Missionary Women in Nineteenth Century Hawaii." *Feminist Studies* 9 (Fall): 489-521.

Hartman, Mary S. and Banner, Lois. 1974. *Clio's Consciousness Raised: New Perspectives on the History of Women.* New York, NY: Octagon Books.

Hines, Gustavus. 1851. *Oregon: Its History, Condition, and Prospects: Containing a Description of the Geography, Climate and Productions, with Personal Adventures among the Indians during a Residence of the Author on the Plains Bordering the Pacific while Connected with the Oregon Mission: Embracing Extended Notes on a Voyage around the World.* Buffalo, NY: Geo. H. Derby & Co.

History of the Bench and Bar in Oregon. 1893. Portland, OR: Historical Publishing Co.

Holman, Frederick V. 1907. *Dr. John McLoughlin, the Father of Oregon.* Cleveland, OH: The Arthur H. Clark Co.

Horner, John B. 1902. *Oregon Literature.* 2nd ed. Portland, OR: J. K. Gill Co.

Howison, Neil M. 1848. *Oregon, a Report.* Washington, D.C.: Tippin & Streper printers. Facsimile reprint, Fairfield, WA: Ye Galleon Press, 1967.

Hussey, John A. 1962. *Champoeg State Park, Oregon: A Summary Report of Its History and a Proposed Plan for Its Development.* Prepared by Western Region, National Park Service for Oregon State Highway Commission, State Park Division, San Francisco, CA.

Hussey, John A. 1967. *Champoeg: Place of Transition, a Disputed History.* Portland, OR: Oregon Historical Society.

James, Janet Wilson. 1978. *Women in American Religion.* Philadelphia, PA: University of Pennsylvania Press.

Jelinek, Estelle C. 1980. *Women's Autobiography: Essays in Criticism.* Bloomington, IN: Indiana University Press.

Johansen, Dorothy O. 1957. *Empire of the Columbia: A History of the Pacific Northwest.* New York, NY: Harper.

Johnson, Allen, et al. (editors). 1944-1981. *Dictionary of American Biography.* 15 vols. New York, NY: Charles Scribner's Sons.

Judson, Lewis. 1971. *Reflections on the Jason Lee Mission and the Opening of Civilization in the Oregon Country.* Salem, OR: Wynkoop-Blair Printing Service.

Lamar, Howard R. (editor). 1977. *The Reader's Encyclopedia of the American West.* New York, NY: Thomas Y. Crowell.

Larsell, Olaf. 1947. *The Doctor in Oregon: A Medical History.* Portland, OR: Binford & Mort.

Lavender, David. 1958. *Land of Giants: The Drive to the Pacific Northwest 1750-1950.* Garden City, NY: Doubleday.

Lee, Daniel, and Frost, Joseph H. 1844. *Ten Years in Oregon.* New York, NY: Published for the authors by J. Collord, printer.

Lee, Jason. 20 April 1834 to 7 August 1838. "Diary of Reminiscences of Jason Lee." *Oregon Historical Quarterly* 17(1916): 116-146; 240-266; 397-430.

Lee, L. L., and Merrill, Lewis. 1980. *Women, Women Writers, and the West.* Troy, NY: The Whitston Publishing Co.

Leslie, David. 5 March 1839. Letter to Dr. Bangs. Oregon Methodist Mission Papers. University of Puget Sound, Tacoma, WA.

Loewenberg, Robert J. 1972. "Elijah White vs. Jason Lee: A Tale of Hard Times." *Journal of the West* 11:636-662.

Loewenberg, Robert J. 1976. *Equality on the Oregon Frontier: Jason Lee and the Methodist Mission 1834-43.* Seattle, WA: University of Washington Press.

Loewenberg, Robert J. 1977. "Creating a Provisional Government in Oregon: A Revision." *Pacific Northwest Quarterly* 68 (January): 13-24.

Loewenberg, Robert J. 1978. "New Evidence, Old Categories: Jason Lee as Zealot." *Pacific Historical Review* 47:432-468.

Lyons, Letitia Mary (Sister). 1940. *Francis Norbert Blanchet and the Founding of the Oregon Missions (1838-1848).* Studies in American Church History, vol. 31. Washington, DC: The Catholic University of America. Reprint, New York, NY: AMS Press, 1974.

Marion County. *Deed Books.* Salem, OR.

Marion County Circuit Court. No. 180 Book 1. Bailey vs. Bailey. Marion County Circuit Court. No. 744: Register of Actions Book 2: 269. Waddle vs. Waddle.

Mattson, Sylvia. 1978. *Missionary Foot Paths: the Story of Anna Maria Pittman (Mrs. Jason Lee).* Salem, OR: Mission Mill Museum Association.

McArthur, Lewis A. 1974. *Oregon Geographic Names.* 4th ed. Portland, OR: Oregon Historical Society.

Merk, Frederick. 1967. *The Oregon Question: Essays in Anglo-American Diplomacy and Politics.* Cambridge, MA: The Belknap Press of Harvard University Press.

Mudge, Z. A. 1848. *The Missionary Teacher: A Memoir of Cyrus Shepard, embracing a brief sketch of the early history of the Oregon Mission.* New York, NY: Carlton & Porter.

Munnick, Harriet D. 1957. "Oregon's First Farmer." *Marion County History* 3:8-13.

Munnick, Harriet D. 1958. "The Transition Decades on French Prairie 1830-1850." *Marion County History* 4:35-42.

Munnick, Harriet D. 1960. "'Dupatti' (Jean Baptiste Desportes McKay)." *Marion Country History* 6:27-32.

Munnick, Harriet D. (compiler) in collaboration with Mikell Deloros Warner. 1979. *Catholic Church Records of the Pacific Northwest: St. Paul, Oregon 1839-1898.* 3 vols. Portland, OR: Binford & Mort.

Nelson, Herbert B. 1944. "First True Confession Story Pictures Oregon 'Moral'." *Oregon Historical Quarterly* 45(June): 168-176.

Nelson, Herbert B. 1948. *The Literary Impulse in Pioneer Oregon.* Studies in Literature and Language, no. 1. Corvallis, OR: The Oregon State College Press.

Nelson, Herbert B. 1950. "Treasure Lurks in Your Attic: Diaries, Journals, Early Newspapers—All May Be Upstairs." *Oregonian Magazine.* September 17:14.

Nelson, Herbert B. 1959. "Ruth Rover's Cup of Sorrow." *Pacific Northwest Quarterly* 50(July): 91-98.

New England Geneological Society. 1901-1945. 216 vols. *Vital Records of the Towns of Massachusetts to the Year 1850.* Boston, MA.

Oregon. 1841-1859. *Papers of the Provisional and Territorial Government of Oregon, 1841-1859.* 660; 8675-8676.

Oregon Pioneer Association. 1881. "Copy of a Document Found among the Private Papers of the Late Dr. John McLoughlin." *Transactions of the 8th Annual Re-Union for 1880:*46-55.

Oregon Pioneer Association. 1886. "John H. Couch." *Transactions* 59-65.

Oregon Spectator, Oregon City, OR. 5 February 1846:3; 4 March 1846:3; 16 April 1846:4; 28 May 1846:1; 26 November 1846:4; 22 July 1847:4; 19 August 1847:2; 12, 19 May 1854: both 3; 26 May 1854:2, 3; 2, 9, 16, 23 June 1854:all 3; 26 August 1854:2; 16 September 1854:2; 9 December 1854:2; 3 February 1855:1.

Oregon State Library. 1945. *Biennial Report of the State Library.*

Oregon Statesman. Salem, OR. 19 July, 1853:2; 13 September 1853:4; 18 October 1853:2; 6 June 1854:4; 8 September 1855: 3; 10 November 1855:3; 10, 17 February 1857:both 3; 14, 21 April 1857:both 3; 17 September 1869:3; 6 February 1872:3; 7 August 1929:4; 1 January 1935:4; 7, 8, 10, 11, 12 March 1936:all 4; 21, 22 November 1941:both 4; 5 July 1944:4; 28 August 1964:4.

Oregon Weekly Times. Portland, OR. 5 August 1854:3; 2 September 1854:2; 9 September 1854:2-3; 16 September 1854: 3.

Oregonian. Portland, OR. 8 July 1854:2; 5 August 1854:2; 9 September 1854:2; 12 February 1876:1; 24 August 1958:52; 11 August 1963:37.

Oregonian and Indian's Advocate. Boston, MA. November 1838:59-60; 63-64; January 1839:125-128; April 1839:216-219; May 1839:249-250; June 1839:283-285; July 1839:309.

Parker, Samuel. 1840. *Journal of an Exploring Tour beyond the Rocky Mountains, under the Direction of the American Board of Commissions for Foreign Missions Performed in the Years 1835, '36, and '37; Containing a Description of the Geography, Geology, Climate, and Productions; and the Number, Manners, and Customs of the Natives. With a map of Oregon Territory.* 2nd ed. Ithaca, NY: The Author.

Parsons, John. 1924. *Beside the Beautiful Willamette.* Portland, OR: Metropolitan Press.

Perley, M. V. B. 1915. "James Leslie of Topsfield, Mass. and Some of His Descendents: David Lesslie." *Essex Institute* 51:255-256; 329-337.

Pierce, T. 16 August 1837. Letter to David Leslie. Mss 1216. Oregon Historical Society Library, Portland, OR.

Piper, Charles. 1915. *Flora of the Northwest Coast.* Lancaster, PA: Press of the New Era Printing Co.

Polk County. *Deed Books.* Dallas, OR.

Polk County District Court, 1st Judicial District. April term 1858. Waddle vs. Waddle.

Pomeroy, Earl Spencer. 1973. *The Pacific Slope; a History of California, Oregon, Washington, Idaho, Utah, and Nevada.* Seattle, WA: University of Washington Press.

Portrait and Biographical Record of the Willamette Valley, Oregon; Containing Original Sketches of Many Well Known Citizens of the Past and Present. 1903. Chicago, IL: Chapman Publishing Co.

Powers, Alfred. 1935. *History of Oregon Literature.* Portland, OR: Metropolitan Press.

Puget Sound Weekly Courier. Seattle, WA. 19 May 1882:4.

Reese, William. 1980. *Dictionary of Philosophy and Religion: Eastern and Western Thought.* Atlantic Highlands, NJ: Humanities Press.

Richards, Kent D. 1970. "The Methodists and the Formation of the Oregon Provisional Government." *Pacific Northwest Quarterly* 61(April): 87-93.

Riegel, Robert E. 1949. *Young America 1830-1840.* Norman, OK: University of Oklahoma Press. Reprint, Westport, CT: Greenwood Press, 1973.

Robbins, William G., Robert Frank, and Richard Ross (editors). 1983. *Regionalism and the Pacific Northwest.* Corvallis, OR: Oregon State University Press.

Sage, W. N. 1926. "James Douglas on the Columbia, 1830-1849." *Oregon Historical Quarterly* 27:365-380.

Schaefer, Ruth. 1929. "The Influence of Methodism in Early Oregon History." Master's Thesis, University of Oregon.

Schlissel, Lillian. 1977. "Women's Diaries on the Western Frontier." *American Studies* (Spring): 87-98.

Scott, Harvey Whitefield. 1924. *History of the Oregon Country.* Compiled by Leslie M. Scott. 6 vols. Cambridge, MA: Riverside Press.

Scott, Leslie M. 1928. "Indian Diseases as Aids to Pacific Northwest Settlement." *Oregon Historical Quarterly* 29:144-161.

Scott, Leslie M. 1931. "Modern Fallacies of Champoeg." *Oregon Historical Quarterly* 32:213-216.

❦

Shepard, Susan. 15 September 1839. Letter to Mrs. Joseph Lloyd. Mss 1219. Oregon Historical Society Library, Portland, OR.

Smith, Bradford. 1956. *Yankees in Paradise: the New England Impact on Hawaii.* New York, NY: J. B. Lippincott Co.

Stage, H. H. and Gjullin, C. M. 1935. "Anophelines and Malaria in the Pacific Northwest." *Northwest Science* 9(September): 5-11.

Stewart, Earle. 1938. "Some Aspects of the So-called Wilson Land Dispute and Willamette University." Master's Thesis, Willamette University.

Taylor, Herbert C. and Hoaglin, Lester. 1978. "The 'Intermittent Fever' Epidemic on the Lower Columbia River." *Ethnohistory* 9 (Spring):160-178.

Throckmorton, Arthur L. 1961. *Oregon Argonauts: Merchant Adventurers on the Western Frontier.* Portland, OR: Oregon Historical Society.

Thwaites, Reuben Gold (editor). 1904-1907. *Early Western Travels: 1748-1846.* Vol. 21: *Narrative of a Journey across the Rocky Mountains to the Columbia River,* by John K. Townsend, and vol. 29: *Travels in the Great Western Prairies, the Anahuac and Rocky Mountains and in Oregon Territory,* by Thomas J. Farnham. Cleveland, OH: Arthur H. Clark Co.

Ticknor, Caroline. 1969. *Hawthorne and His Publisher.* Port Washington, WA: Kennikat Press.

Tolmie, William Fraser. 9 May 1882, 6 August 1882. Letters to Minto, Mss 752. Oregon Historical Society Library. Portland, OR.

Turnbull, George S. 1931. *History of Oregon Newspapers.* Portland, OR: Binford & Mort.

Turnbull, George S. 1959. *Governors of Oregon.* Portland, OR: Binford & Mort.

U.S. Department of Commerce, Bureau of the Census. 1869, 1870. *United States Census of Population.*

Vaughan, Thomas (editor). 1975. *The Western Shore: Oregon Country Essays Honoring the American Revolution.* Portland, OR: Oregon Historical Society.

Victor, Francis Fuller. 1876. "Literature of Oregon." *West Shore* (January): 2-3.

Walker, Cheryl. 1982. *The Nightingale's Burden: Women Poets and American Culture before 1900.* Bloomington, IN: Indiana University Press.

Warren, Sidney. 1949. *Farthest Frontier: The Pacific Northwest.* New York, NY: The Macmillan Co.

Wilbur, James Harvey. 1975. *Travels of J. H. Wilbur: Journal Written from September 27, 1846 to January 25, 1848 from New York around Cape Horn to the Oregon Institute and the Onset of his Methodist Mission Work in Oregon Territory.* Edited by Gertrude Wiencke Johnson. Salem, OR: Willamette University.

Wilkes, Charles. 1844. *Narrative of the United States Exploring Expedition during the years 1838, 1839, 1840, 1841, 1842.* 5 vols. Philadelphia, PA: Lea & Blanchard.

Yarnes, Thomas D. 1957. *A History of Oregon Methodism.* Edited by Harney E. Tobie. Printed by the Parthenon Press for the Oregon Methodist Conference Historical Society.

Zion's Herald, Boston, MA. 18 January 1837:2; 25 January 1837:3; 11 April 1838:2; 5 December 1838:3; 29 November 1843:4.